D1446811

To Jean,

David Griffin

THE MYSTERIOUS COLLAPSE OF WORLD TRADE CENTER 7

Why the Final Official Report about 9/11 is Unscientific and False

by David Ray Griffin

OLIVE
BRANCH
PRESS

An imprint of Interlink Publishing Group, Inc.
www.interlinkbooks.com

First published in 2010 by

OLIVE BRANCH PRESS
An imprint of Interlink Publishing Group, Inc.
46 Crosby Street, Northampton, Massachusetts 01060
www.interlinkbooks.com

Copyright © David Ray Griffin, 2010

Library of Congress Cataloging-in-Publication Data
Griffin, David Ray, 1939–
The mysterious collapse of World Trade Center 7 : why the final official report about 9/11 is unscientific and false / by David Ray Griffin.
p. cm.
Includes bibliographical references and index.
ISBN 978-1-56656-786-2 (pbk.)
1. September 11 Terrorist Attacks, 2001. 2. World Trade Center (New York, N.Y.) 3. National Commission on Terrorist Attacks upon the United States. 9/11 Commission report. I. Title.
HV6432.7.G76 2009
974.7'1044--dc22
2009026294

Book design by Juliana Spear

Printed and bound in the United States of America

To request our complete 48-page full-color catalog, please call us toll free at 1-800-238-LINK,
visit our website at www.interlinkbooks.com or write to:
Interlink Publishing
46 Crosby Street, Northampton, MA 01060
e-mail: info@interlinkbooks.com

It is difficult to get a man to understand something when his salary depends upon his not understanding it.
—Sinclair Lewis, 1935

To Niels Harrit, Steven Jones, and Kevin Ryan,
three scientists who have done so much to help us understand
what happened in New York City on September 11, 2001.

And to the memory of Barry Jennings, whose truth-telling
may have cost him his life.

Table of Contents

Acknowledgments

In writing this book, I received an enormous amount of help from many people.

The most help was received from Elizabeth Woodworth, who has become my volunteer assistant. Besides making countless suggestions for improving each chapter, she checked and in many case provided the information in the notes.

I also received much help from my two other regular sources of assistance, Tod Fletcher and Matthew Everett, each of whom improved both the text and the notes for the entire manuscript with suggestions and discoveries of various sorts. I also received help of this nature from Daniel Athearn and attorney James Gourley, whose critiques of several chapters enabled me to improve them significantly.

With regard to scientific issues, I received much help from David Chandler, Niels Harrit, Steven Jones, Kevin Ryan, and John Wyndham. Special thanks are due to Frank Greening, who assisted my efforts in spite of not agreeing with this book's conclusions (except for its negative conclusion that the NIST report on WTC 7 is false).

I also gratefully acknowledge assistance of various types from Dylan Avery, Ron Brookman, Richard Gage, Crockett Grabbe, Colman Jones, Graeme MacQueen, Alan Miller, Aidan Monaghan, Susan Peabody, Edward Rynearson, and Chris Sarns.

Finally, I wish to thank publisher Michel Moushabeck, editor Pamela Thompson, and all the others at Olive Branch Press (of Interlink Books), which has played a major role in making public the truth about 9/11. Special thanks are due to Hilary Plum, who handled the editing for this book.

Frequently Cited Works

Interim Report on WTC 7, NIST, June 2004 (wtc.nist.gov/progress_report/june04/appendixl.pdf).

NIST NCSTAR 1-8, *The Emergency Response Operations,* by J. Randall Lawson and Robert L. Vettori, September 2005 (wtc.nist.gov/NCSTAR1/PDF/NCSTAR%201-8.pdf).

NIST NCSTAR 1A, *Final Report of the Collapse of World Trade Center Building 7,* Draft for Public Comment, August 2008. (wtc.nist.gov/media/NIST_NCSTAR_1A_for_public_comment.pdf). This is the brief version of NIST's Draft Report, being 77 pages long.

NIST NCSTAR 1A, *Final Report on the Collapse of World Trade Center Building 7,* Final Report, November 2008 (wtc.nist.gov/NCSTAR1/PDF/NCSTAR%201A.pdf). This is the brief version of NIST's Final Report, being 87 pages long.

NIST NCSTAR 1-9, *Structural Fire Response and Probable Collapse Sequence of World Trade Center Building 7,* Draft for Public Comment, August 2008. This is the long version of NIST's Draft, consisting of two volumes. Volume 1 (wtc.nist.gov/media/NIST_NCSTAR_1-9_Vol1_for_public_comment.pdf) contains pages 1–360; Volume 2 (wtc.nist.gov/media/NIST_NCSTAR_19_vol2_for_public_comment.pdf) contains pages 361–719. (Because the pagination is continuous, the citations give only page numbers without distinguishing between volumes.)

NIST NCSTAR 1-9, *Structural Fire Response and Probable Collapse Sequence of World Trade Center Building 7,* November 2008. This is the long version of NIST's Final Report on WTC 7, consisting of two volumes. Volume 1 (wtc.nist.gov/NCSTAR1/PDF/NCSTAR%201-9%20Vol%201.pdf) contains pages 1–360; Volume 2 (wtc.nist.gov/NCSTAR1/PDF/NCSTAR%201-9%20Vol%202.pdf) contains pages 361–729. (Because the pagination is continuous, the citations give only page numbers without distinguishing between volumes.)

Shyam Sunder, "Opening Statement," NIST Press Briefing, August 21, 2008 (wtc.nist.gov/media/opening_remarks_082108.html).

"WTC 7 Technical Briefing," NIST, August 26, 2008 (event.on24.com/eventRegistration/EventLobbyServlet?target=lobby.jsp&eventid=1181 45).

INTRODUCTION:
THE BACKGROUND TO NIST'S
WTC 7 REPORT

There are two main theories as to who was responsible for the 9/11 attacks. According to the theory put forth by the Bush–Cheney administration (and it *is* merely a theory, because no proof has ever been provided[1]), the attacks were planned and carried out solely by al-Qaeda terrorists under the authorization of Osama bin Laden. The alternative theory, espoused by members of what has come to be known as "the 9/11 truth movement," holds that the attacks were orchestrated by officials of the Bush–Cheney administration itself.

According to members of the 9/11 truth movement, the attacks were a "false-flag" operation, in which evidence is planted to implicate the groups or countries the actual perpetrators wish to attack. In this particular case, the Bush–Cheney administration had already decided, months before 9/11, to attack Muslim countries in the Middle East, most immediately Afghanistan and Iraq.[2] In planning and carrying out the 9/11 attacks, the perpetrators planted evidence to implicate Middle Eastern Muslims—evidence that, when examined, can easily be seen to have been fabricated.[3]

The 9/11 truth movement holds that, when the official account of the attacks is subjected to critical scrutiny, it can be shown to be false. Many members in the movement believe this falsity to be most obvious in relation to the collapse of Building 7 of the World Trade Center, usually called "WTC 7." This collapse is, accordingly, often referred to as the official account's "Achilles' heel" or "smoking gun."[4]

WTC 7: The Official Account's Achilles' Heel & Central Mystery

According to the official account of 9/11, the Twin Towers—WTC 1 and 2—came down because of the impacts of the airplanes and the ensuing jet-fuel fires. Even if that account makes no sense to increasing numbers of scientists, architects, and engineers,[5] it has had enough apparent plausibility to be convincing to a majority of the US population.

But WTC 7 also collapsed that day, and it was not hit by a plane. It seemed, therefore, that it had been brought down by fire alone—a fact that would have made its collapse an unprecedented occurrence. As *New York Times* writer James Glanz wrote a couple of months after 9/11: "[E]xperts said no building like it, a modern, steel-reinforced high-rise, had ever collapsed because of an uncontrolled fire." Glanz also quoted a structural engineer as saying: "[W]ithin the structural engineering community, [WTC 7] is considered to be much more important to understand [than the Twin Towers]," because engineers had no answer to the question, "why did 7 come down?"[6]

This question did, to be sure, have a possible answer: that WTC 7 was brought down with pre-placed explosives in the procedure known as "controlled demolition." This is the only way in which steel-framed high-rise buildings had previously been caused to collapse. From a purely scientific perspective, therefore, the most likely explanation for the collapse of WTC 7 would have been that it, too, had been brought down by explosives.[7]

Public discussion of the destruction of the World Trade Center, however, occurred in a political—not a scientific—context. America had just been attacked, it was almost universally believed, by foreign terrorists who had hijacked planes and flown them into the Twin Towers and the Pentagon. Publicly interpreting this as an act of war, the Bush administration had launched a "war on terror," purportedly in response to the attacks. Because the idea that one of the WTC buildings had been brought down by explosives would have implied that the attacks were not a surprise, this idea could not be entertained by many minds in private, let alone in public. Even less could it be suggested in the mass media (at least after the day of 9/11 itself, on which a few reporters did suggest that the buildings had been brought down with explosives[8]).

And so the collapse of WTC 7 was classified as a "mystery"—to the extent that it entered into the public consciousness at all. But this was not much. Although WTC 7 was a 47-story building and hence in most places would have been the tallest building in the city or even the state, it was dwarfed by the 110-story Twin Towers. It was also dwarfed by them in the ensuing media coverage. And so, James Glanz wrote, the collapse of WTC 7 was "a mystery that... would probably have captured the attention of the city and the world," *if* the Twin Towers had not also come down.[9] As it was, however, there was little discussion of this mystery.

Indeed, it almost seemed as if the authorities did not want the public to think about WTC 7. Although television viewers repeatedly saw the Twin Towers being hit by planes and then coming down, footage of the collapse of WTC 7 was seldom if ever seen on mainstream television after 9/11 itself. And when *The 9/11 Commission Report* appeared in 2004, it did not, amazingly enough, even mention the fact that this third building had collapsed. Although the 9/11 truth movement, in response, increased its efforts to publicize the collapse of WTC 7, a Zogby poll in May 2006 found that 43 percent of the American people were still unaware that WTC 7 had collapsed.[10]

If the authorities did deliberately try to keep the public from thinking about WTC 7 by focusing its attention on the Twin Towers, there would have been good reason for this. Besides the fact that WTC 7 had not been hit by a plane and did not have large fires spread by jet fuel, its collapse as seen on videos looks, compared with that of the Twin Towers, much more like the kind of controlled demolition known as *implosion*, in which the collapse starts from the bottom and then the building comes down into its own footprint, ending up as a rather compact pile of debris. The videos also show that WTC 7 came down in virtual free fall—which would normally be possible only if all of its support columns had been removed by explosives.

Accordingly, when people who know something about these matters see a video of the collapse of WTC 7, they almost immediately conclude that it must have been brought down by explosives. For example, Daniel Hofnung, an engineer in Paris, wrote:

> In the years after 9/11 events, I thought that all I read in professional reviews and French newspapers was true. The first time I understood that it was impossible was when I saw a film about the collapse of WTC 7.[11]

Likewise, Chester Gearhart, who before his retirement was a civil engineer for Kansas City, Missouri, said:

> I have watched the construction of many large buildings and also have personally witnessed 5 controlled demolitions in Kansas City. When I saw the towers fall on 9/11, I knew something was wrong and my first instinct was that it was impossible. When I saw building 7 fall, I knew it was a CD [controlled demolition].[12]

Another example is provided by chemist Niels Harrit of the University of Copenhagen, whose paper on nanothermite in the World Trade

Center dust will be discussed in Chapter 4. When he was asked how he became involved with these issues, he replied:

> It all started when I saw the collapse of Building 7, the third skyscraper. It collapsed seven hours after the Twin Towers. And there were only two airplanes. When you see a 47-storey building, 186 meters tall, collapse in 6.5 seconds, and you are a scientist, you think "What?" I had to watch it again... and again. I hit the button ten times, and my jaw dropped lower and lower. Firstly, I had never heard of that building before. And there was no visible reason why it should collapse in that way, straight down, in 6.5 seconds. I have had no rest since that day.[13]

Still another example is provided by Danny Jowenko, the owner of a controlled demolition company in the Netherlands, who also had not known that WTC 7 had collapsed. Upon being asked in 2006 to comment on a video of this collapse without being told what it was, he immediately said that it was obviously a controlled demolition.[14] When asked later, after he had had time to study the matter, whether he stood by his initial response, he replied: "Absolutely."[15]

When Jowenko and others declare that WTC 7 was obviously brought down with explosives, they base this conclusion not merely on the fact that, prior to 9/11, no steel-framed high-rise had ever collapsed from any cause other than controlled demolition. They also base it on the fact that, as mentioned above, the collapse of WTC 7 has many features in common with collapses produced by the type of controlled demolition known as implosion.

To enumerate seven of the most obvious features of this similarity: (1) The collapse of WTC 7 started from the bottom; (2) the onset of the collapse was sudden (not gradual, as it would have been if—impossibly—it had been brought on by fire heating the steel);[16] (3) the building came down totally, leaving none of its steel columns erect and intact; (4) it came straight down, symmetrically; (5) it came down in free fall, or very close to it (suggesting that the steel columns supporting the building had been removed); (6) much of the building's concrete was pulverized into tiny particles, resulting in a huge dust cloud; and (7) most of the debris ended up in a relatively small, compact pile. (These similarities are emphasized in a video called "This is an Orange."[17])

For most people who know anything about steel-framed buildings, the idea that WTC 7 could have come down in this manner without the aid of explosives is completely implausible. Accordingly, if they are not already skeptical of the official account of 9/11, they become so when they become aware of the collapse of this building—as illustrated by the above-quoted statements by Daniel Hofnung, Chester Gearhart, Niels Harrit, and Danny Jowenko. This is why the 9/11 truth movement has thought of WTC 7 as the official account's Achilles' heel.

A positive correlation between 9/11 skepticism and WTC 7 aware-ness was suggested by the aforementioned Zogby poll, which showed that the number of Americans who were unaware of the collapse of WTC 7 (43 percent) was roughly the same as those who believed that a new investigation of the 9/11 attacks was unnecessary (47 percent). In thinking of the collapse of WTC 7 as the Achilles' heel of the official account, therefore, the 9/11 truth movement has believed that, as the facts about this collapse become more widespread, so will skepticism about the official position, according to which no explosives were used.

The difficulty of providing an explanation of WTC 7's collapse without mentioning explosives was illustrated by the first official report on the destruction of the World Trade Center, which was put out in 2002 by the Federal Emergency Management Agency (FEMA). As a federal agency and hence an agency of the Bush–Cheney administration, FEMA had to provide an explanation that did not involve the use of explosives. It was unable, however, to find a plausible explanation of this type.

The solution settled on by the authors of the FEMA report was to provide a possible explanation and then to distance themselves from it. That is, they first provided an imaginative scenario, in which burning debris from the collapse of WTC 1 (the North Tower) might have produced—by igniting the "diesel fuel on the premises," which "contained massive potential energy"—a raging inferno in WTC 7 that, after burning for seven hours, brought the building down. But these authors then quickly added a caveat, saying that this scenario—which was their "best hypothesis" as to why the building collapsed—had "only a low probability of occurrence."[18]

This admission of defeat increased the conviction within the 9/11 truth movement that the collapse of WTC 7 was indeed the official story's Achilles' heel—the part of the official story that, by being most vulnerable to critique, could be used to bring down the whole body of lies.

NIST Takes on the Mystery

By the time the FEMA report appeared, in any case, the assignment of coming up with the definitive explanation of the collapse of the Twin Towers and WTC 7 had been given to the National Institute of Standards and Technology—which will henceforth be referred to simply as NIST. A plan for its "study of WTC Buildings 1 and 2 ('The Twin Towers') and WTC Building 7" was formulated by NIST between October 2001 and August 2002. NIST then filed progress reports on its WTC investigation in December 2002 and May 2003.[19] In June 2004, it published an *Interim Report on WTC 7*.[20] But after that report appeared (according to an account given by NIST in 2006),

> the NIST investigation team stopped working on WTC 7 and was assigned full-time through the fall of 2005 to complete the investigation of the WTC towers. With the release and dissemination of the report on the WTC towers in October 2005, the investigation of the WTC 7 collapse resumed.[21]

In April 2005, however, NIST released another preliminary report on WTC 7.[22]

This history is important because, when NIST issued its final WTC 7 report in 2008, as we will see later, it claimed—in response to the charge that it had deliberately delayed publication of its report, perhaps because of orders from the Bush administration—that it had worked on it only since 2005 and hence for only three years. In reality, however, it had worked on it for almost six years.

In any case, although NIST's theory as to what caused WTC 7's collapse changed over the years, one element remained constant: the denial that the building was brought down by explosives. As the preliminary report of April 2005 put it: "NIST has seen no evidence that the collapse of WTC 7 was caused by... controlled demolition."[23]

How, then, did NIST intend to explain the building's collapse? Between June 2004 (when it published its *Interim Report on WTC 7*) and August 2008 (when it put out a tentative version of its final report as a Draft for Public Comment), NIST suggested that its argument would be that WTC 7 collapsed because of damage of two types: damage caused by the fires and damage caused by debris from the collapse of the North Tower (which was considerably closer than the South Tower).

Popular Mechanics Interprets NIST's Work

As to why the fires were hot enough and long-lasting enough to cause significant structural damage, NIST was during that period carrying forward the suggestion, made earlier by the FEMA report, that the fires were fed by the building's diesel fuel. An article about 9/11 in the March 2005 issue of *Popular Mechanics* magazine, which strongly supported the official account of 9/11, said (with reference to NIST):

> Investigators believe the fire was fed by tanks of diesel fuel that many tenants used to run emergency generators. Most tanks throughout the building were fairly small, but a generator on the fifth floor was connected to a large tank in the basement via a pressurized line.[24]

Popular Mechanics then quoted NIST's lead investigator, Shyam Sunder, as saying: "Our current working hypothesis is that this pressurized line was supplying fuel [to the fire] for a long period of time."[25] In a slightly revised and expanded version of its article issued as a book in 2006, *Popular Mechanics* repeated this point, saying that "long-burning fires" may have been supplied by fuel tanks in the building "for up to seven hours."[26]

Whereas this appeal to the diesel fuel repeated FEMA's hypothesis, NIST introduced a novel element by suggesting, in the words of the *Popular Mechanics* book, that "WTC 7 was far more compromised by falling debris than the FEMA report indicated." In describing this damage, *Popular Mechanics* quoted Shyam Sunder as saying: "On about a third of the face to the center and to the bottom—approximately 10 stories—about 25 percent of the depth of the building was scooped out." Given this discovery, *Popular Mechanics* claimed, critics could no longer cast doubt on the official explanation by pointing out that "there were no other examples of large fire-protected steel buildings falling because of fire alone."[27]

This allegedly massive damage to WTC 7 caused by debris was treated by *Popular Mechanics* as parallel to the damage to the Twin Towers caused by the airplane impacts, as shown by the following statement:

> The conclusions reached by [hundreds of experts from academic and private industry, as well as the government] have been consistent: A combination of physical damage from the airplane crashes—or, in the case of WTC 7, from falling debris—and prolonged exposure

to the resulting fires ultimately destroyed the structural integrity of all three buildings.[28]

Although in 2006, when this statement was published, this view was simply NIST's "working hypothesis," *Popular Mechanics* rashly treated it as one of the "conclusions" reached by "hundreds of experts."

Popular Mechanics was even ready to announce that NIST's working hypothesis, which involved both debris-induced damage and long-burning fires fed by diesel fuel, had solved the mystery of WTC 7's collapse. Although this collapse had been "initially puzzling to investigators," *Popular Mechanics* told the public in 2006, these investigators "now believe the building failed from a combination of long-burning fires in its interior and damage caused from the North Tower's collapse."[29]

Popular Mechanics was treating this working hypothesis as settled fact even though, it admitted, NIST had not decided how the two elements in this hypothesis were related. "Sunder says," *Popular Mechanics* wrote, that "NIST has not determined whether [the fires or the damage from debris] was the primary instigator of the collapse."[30] While admitting that this rather important question had not been settled, *Popular Mechanics* claimed that NIST was, nevertheless, in position to rule out the possibility that explosives contributed to the collapse, saying:

> [T]he NIST report is definitive on this account. The preliminary report states flatly: "NIST has seen no evidence that the collapse of WTC 7 was caused by... controlled demolition."[31]

The fact that *Popular Mechanics* could treat a *preliminary* report as *definitive* suggests that it was guided by a rather strong will to believe.

NIST's 2008 Solution to the Mystery

NIST itself, in any case, was evidently not so certain during that period that it had solved the mystery of WTC 7. When asked early in 2006 why this building had collapsed, Sunder replied: "[T]ruthfully, I don't really know. We've had trouble getting a handle on building No. 7."[32]

The fact that NIST's statements during this period should not have been treated as definitive was demonstrated in 2008 when NIST issued its final report on WTC 7 (with the Draft for Public Comment being issued in August and the Final Report in November).[33] In this report, NIST no longer affirms the two elements that, according to *Popular*

Mechanics, had provided a satisfactory solution to the mystery of WTC 7's collapse. That is, (1) NIST no longer claims that the diesel fuel in WTC 7 explained why the fires burned so long, saying instead that "fuel oil fires did not play a role in the collapse of WTC 7."[34] And (2) NIST no longer claims that the collapse of WTC 7 was significantly caused by damage inflicted on it by North Tower debris, saying instead: "Other than initiating the fires in WTC 7, the damage from the debris from WTC 1 had little effect on initiating the collapse of WTC 7."[35]

The second of these two reversals means that, contrary to what *Popular Mechanics* had said in its 2006 book, NIST does make the claim that a steel-framed high-rise building had, for the first time in history, been brought down by fire alone.

This reversal also undermines an essential element in *Popular Mechanics'* argument against the idea that WTC 7 was brought down with explosives. In a 2006 BBC documentary entitled *The Conspiracy Files: 9/11,* Davin Coburn, a research editor for *Popular Mechanics,* was asked about the fact that the collapse of WTC 7 "does look exactly like a controlled demolition." He replied:

> I understand why people may think that…, but when you learn the facts about the way the building was built and about the way in which it supported itself and the damage that was done by the collapsing towers that preceded it, the idea that it was demolition simply holds no water.[36]

Now that NIST has said that debris from the collapsing towers did *not* play a role in the collapse of WTC 7, it would seem that *Popular Mechanics* should reverse itself, saying that perhaps the controlled demolition theory *does* hold some water.

Such a complete reversal has not, however, been suggested by NIST itself: In spite of changing its position on some matters, it continues to insist in its final report that explosives played no role in the collapse of WTC 7. In fact, in his opening statement at the press conference on August 21, 2008 (at which NIST's final report on WTC 7 was unveiled as a Draft for Public Comment), Shyam Sunder seemed to suggest that this was NIST's most important finding about WTC 7. "Before I tell you what we found," he said, "I'd like to tell you what we did not find. We did not find any evidence that explosives were used to bring the building down."[37]

Besides appearing confident about this point, Sunder also seemed unjustifiably certain of the truth of NIST's new answer to the question of what did bring WTC 7 down. Declaring that "the reason for the collapse of World Trade Center 7 is no longer a mystery,"[38] he assured his listeners that "science is really behind what we have said." He even added: "The obvious stares you in the face."[39]

In the remainder of this book, I will demonstrate that NIST's report on WTC 7, far from being supported by science, is an unscientific document, violating various principles of accepted scientific practice.

Part I provides reasons to consider NIST a political, rather than a scientific, agency; it discusses some basic principles of scientific method; and it shows that NIST has violated two of these principles: (1) that scientists should begin with the most likely hypothesis (in this case, controlled demolition), and (2) that scientists must take into account *all* the relevant evidence (in this case, all the evidence, both physical and testimonial, suggesting that WTC 7 was brought down by explosives).

Part II of the book examines NIST's alternative theory, according to which WTC 7 was brought down by ordinary building fires. I will show that it is a thoroughly unscientific theory, resting on a combination of observation-free speculation, implausible claims, fudged data, and even outright fabrications. In Chapter 10, I show that NIST, in the final (November) version of its 2008 report on WTC 7, even violates one of science's most fundamental principles: Explanations must not imply that miracles have occurred.

Readers of NIST's report on WTC 7 will indeed, as Shyam Sunder says, find the obvious staring them in the face—except that "the obvious" is not the report's truth, as he suggested, but its falsity.

Terminological Notes

Explosive: The term "explosive" refers to any substance that, being energetically unstable, can produce explosive effects. In this book, however, the focus is on a particular class of explosives: those that can be used to cut steel or otherwise cause it suddenly to lose its weight-bearing strength. In fact, of these two capacities—to produce explosive effects and to cause steel suddenly to fail—the latter is primarily in view. This means, for example, that if a substance classified as an "incendiary," such as ordinary thermite,[40] is used to make a "shaped charge," it is here considered an explosive even if it does not produce some of the effects, such as loud noises and blast waves, generally associated with powerful explosions. (An *explosive* charge is a particular quantity of explosive material. A *shaped* charge is a "charge shaped so as to concentrate its explosive force in a particular direction."[41])

Final Report, final report: NIST's use of "final report" in reference to its WTC 7 reports can be confusing. This term serves, in the first place, to distinguish the WTC 7 report that appeared in 2008 from NIST's preliminary reports, which appeared in earlier years. But this 2008 "final report" came in two versions: a draft report for public comment, which was issued in August, and then a (truly) final report, which was issued in November. Matters are further complicated by the fact that NIST, in both August and November, issued two versions of its final report: a brief version, which is titled *Final Report on the Collapse of World Trade Center Building 7*, and a long version, which—although it is NIST's definitive final report on WTC 7—does not have the words "final report" in its title, instead being called *Structural Fire Response and Probable Collapse Sequence of World Trade Center Building 7*.

To avoid confusion, this book employs the following conventions: The lowercase title "final report" is used for NIST's final report on WTC 7, which was issued in 2008 (in both brief and long versions), in distinction from its preliminary reports, which were issued in earlier years. The uppercase title "Final Report" is used to designate the truly final version, which was released in November 2008, in distinction from the first version, which was released in August 2008 and is called the "Draft for Public Comment," or sometimes simply the "Draft Report" or the "Draft version." When there is no need to distinguish the Final Report from the Draft Report, the lowercase "final report" is used.

PART ONE

NIST's Unscientific Rejection of the Most Likely Theory

I
NIST AS A POLITICAL,
NOT A SCIENTIFIC, AGENCY

This chapter provides introductory reasons to believe that NIST, while preparing its reports on the World Trade Center, was functioning as a political agency of the Bush–Cheney administration, rather than as a scientific agency. Before making this case, I discuss the fact that suspects in a crime are usually not put in charge of investigating that crime; I then point out that all of the official investigations of 9/11, including the NIST investigation, were carried out by representatives of the Bush–Cheney administration.

Suspects, Investigations, and 9/11

When a crime has been committed, both common sense and the law dictate that persons suspected of committing that crime should not be put in charge of the investigation. The two major suspects for having committed the 9/11 crimes are Osama bin Laden and al-Qaeda, on the one hand, and members of the Bush–Cheney administration, on the other. It obviously would have been outrageous if the task of investigating the 9/11 attacks had been assigned to representatives of bin Laden's al-Qaeda organization. And yet all official investigations have been carried out by representatives of the other chief suspect: the Bush–Cheney administration.

It might be thought that the official account of 9/11 is considered questionable by only a small number of people, mainly cranks, so that the fact that the investigations have been carried out by representatives of the Bush–Cheney administration does not constitute a serious problem.

However, the number of people who question the official account is significant. According to the 2006 Zogby poll mentioned earlier, less than half—only 48 percent—of the American public expressed confidence that the government and the 9/11 Commission had not engaged in a cover-up.[1] Another poll taken that year was even more revealing because it specifically asked people whether they believed 9/11 to have been, at least in part, an inside job. Citing the claim that "federal officials either participated in the attacks on the World Trade Center and the Pentagon or took no action to stop them 'because they wanted the United States to go to war in the Middle East,'" a Scripps Howard/Ohio University poll found that 36 percent of the public endorsed this claim.[2] A story in *Time* magazine commented: "Thirty-six percent adds up to a lot of people. This is not a fringe phenomenon. It is a mainstream political reality."[3]

Besides constituting a significant portion of the American population, people who reject the official account of 9/11 constitute an even larger percentage of the population in other countries. Polling in seventeen countries during the summer of 2008, WorldPublicOpinion.org found that in eight of those countries, fewer than 50 percent of the citizens accepted the view that al-Qaeda was responsible for the attacks. These countries even included allies of America, such as Mexico, where only 33 percent of the people identified al-Qaeda as the guilty party, and Jordan, where a mere 11 percent did. Even in Great Britain, America's main ally in the post-9/11 "war on terror," only 57 percent said they believed al-Qaeda to have been behind the attacks.[4]

Among people who rejected the view that al-Qaeda was responsible, a significant percent opined that the attacks were arranged by the United States itself. This view was most widespread (among the seventeen countries polled) in two of America's allies, Turkey and Mexico, in which it was endorsed by 36 and 30 percent of the people, respectively. The figures for two more allies, Germany and South Korea, were 23 and 17 percent, respectively. In China, the United States was blamed by nine percent of the people. Although that is a lower percentage than in most countries, it translates into over 90 million Chinese.[5]

Those who believe that there is no good evidence against the official story about 9/11 may assume that it is rejected primarily by poorly educated people, so that the more education people have, the more likely they are to accept the official story. The poll found, however, that having less education did not make people significantly more likely to attribute the 9/11 attacks to al-Qaeda.[6]

Another widespread assumption is that the 9/11 truth movement—defined here as consisting of all the people who have publicly expressed skepticism about the official story, at least to the point of saying that a new investigation is needed—consists of "kooks" and "crackpots." But the falsity of this assumption is demonstrated by the existence and membership of various scholarly and professional organizations that have emerged. These organizations include Architects and Engineers for 9/11 Truth,[7] Firefighters for 9/11 Truth,[8] Lawyers for 9/11 Truth,[9] Intelligence Officers for 9/11 Truth,[10] Medical Professionals for 9/11 Truth,[11] Pilots for 9/11 Truth,[12] Political Leaders for 9/11 Truth,[13] Religious Leaders for 9/11 Truth,[14] Scholars for 9/11 Truth,[15] Scholars for 9/11 Truth and Justice (which includes a large number of scientists),[16] Veterans for 9/11 Truth,[17] and S.P.I.N.E.: The Scientific Panel Investigating Nine-Eleven.[18] (To get an overview of well-known and well-credentialed people from various fields who have called for a new investigation, consult Patriots Question 9/11.[19])

As these polls and organizations show, large numbers of people in the United States and around the world—many of whom are well educated and some of whom have professional expertise specifically relevant to evaluating the official account of 9/11—believe that the Bush–Cheney administration did not tell the truth about the attacks. A significant portion of these people believe that the attacks were, in fact, orchestrated or at least facilitated by members of that administration.

Given this context, no one can responsibly dismiss as irrelevant the fact that people who are suspected of facilitating, or at least of covering up, a crime are normally not allowed to run the investigation of that crime. Any investigation of 9/11 run by representatives of the Bush–Cheney administration must be considered illegitimate in principle (just as would any investigation run by al-Qaeda). And yet every official investigation of 9/11 thus far has been carried out under the direction of representatives of this administration.[20]

The FEMA–ASCE Report

The first investigation into the destruction of the World Trade Center, mentioned in the Introduction, was headed by FEMA, the full name of which—the Federal Emergency Management Agency—makes clear that it is an agency of the federal government. This means that in 2001 and 2002, when the report was being prepared, FEMA was an agency of the Bush–Cheney administration. FEMA's pathetically inadequate response to Hurricane Katrina made Americans painfully aware of the fact that the director of FEMA is appointed by, and serves at the pleasure of, the president.

The FEMA report was actually prepared by the American Society of Civil Engineers (ASCE). But the ASCE's work was carried out on behalf of, and under the limits imposed by, FEMA as well as other federal agencies. The seriousness of these limits was revealed when ASCE investigators told the House Committee on Science that they did not even have the authority "to impound pieces of steel for examination before they were recycled."[21] The magazine *Fire Engineering* wrote in 2002:

> [T]he "official investigation" blessed by FEMA… is a half-baked farce that may already have been commandeered by political forces whose primary interests, to put it mildly, lie far afield of full disclosure. Except for the marginal benefit obtained from a three-day, visual walk-through of evidence sites conducted by ASCE investigation committee members—described by one close source as a "tourist trip"—no one's checking the evidence for anything.[22]

As these statements illustrate, no real *investigation* was allowed.

Moreover, even if the FEMA and ASCE personnel themselves, as thinking individuals, rejected the administration's claim—according to which the airplane impacts and resulting fires sufficed to bring down all three buildings—they could not have published a FEMA–ASCE report challenging that claim.

The 9/11 Commission

Although it was widely called an "independent" commission, the 9/11 Commission was, in reality, not at all independent from the Bush–Cheney White House.

This commission was run by its executive director, Philip Zelikow (not by its co-chairmen, Thomas Kean and Lee Hamilton, and the other eight Commissioners we saw on television). The Commission's work was done by Zelikow and the 85 members of his staff, all of whom worked directly under him. This meant that, as *New York Times* reporter Philip Shenon wrote, none of the commissioners had "a staff member of their own, typical on these sorts of independent commissions." Zelikow thereby prevented "any of the commissioners from striking out on their own in the investigation."[23]

Besides directing the staff's work, telling them what to investigate (and hence what *not* to investigate), Zelikow was largely responsible for the Commission's final product, *The 9/11 Commission Report*. Moreover, Shenon reported, Zelikow had secretly outlined this book, and hence had determined its conclusions, in advance—before the Commission's staff had even begun its work.[24]

Why is this important? Because Zelikow was essentially a member of the Bush White House. He was especially close to Condoleezza Rice: He had served with her in the National Security Council during the presidency of the senior George Bush; when the Republicans were out of power during the Clinton years, he co-authored a book with her; then, when Rice was appointed National Security Advisor to the second President Bush, she brought on Zelikow to help with the transition to the new National Security Council (after which Zelikow was appointed by Bush to the president's Foreign Intelligence Advisory Board); finally, in 2002, when Rice had the responsibility of producing "The National Security Strategy of the United States of America" (NSS 2002), she turned this task over to Zelikow.[25]

This last fact is especially important, because NSS 2002 used the 9/11 attacks to justify a new doctrine of preemptive war, which was desired by Cheney and other hawks in the administration. In enunciating this new doctrine, the United States, using 9/11 as the justification, gave itself permission to attack other countries even if they posed no imminent threat.[26] This was a fateful document because, as Shenon pointed out, it was used to "justify a preemptive strike on Iraq."[27]

Given the possibility that the 9/11 attacks were orchestrated or at least assisted by the Bush–Cheney administration—in part to have a pretext to attack Afghanistan and Iraq—the 9/11 Commission should have asked whether there was evidence to support this alternative account. (The alternative account of 9/11 had been widely explored on the internet and publicly rejected by the Bush administration, so it cannot be claimed that the Commission was not aware of it.) The Commission, therefore, should have been run by someone who was completely independent of this administration. Seen in this light, Philip Zelikow, who was essentially a member of this administration and had used 9/11 to develop a doctrine that was employed to justify the attack on Iraq, was one of the worst possible choices to direct the Commission. With him in charge, the White House, insofar as it was investigated, was investigated by itself, just as if the Commission had been run by Condoleezza Rice or Karl Rove—two members of the Bush administration with whom Zelikow remained in touch, in spite of his promise to the contrary, while he was directing the Commission.[28]

That his directorship left the Commission without a shred of independence is made especially clear by the fact that Zelikow, in making assignments to the various teams into which the staff was organized, simply presupposed the truth of the Bush–Cheney administration's claim that 9/11 was orchestrated by al-Qaeda. Although Kean and Hamilton said that the Commission, unlike conspiracy theorists, started with the facts, not with a conclusion—"we were not setting out to advocate one theory or interpretation of 9/11 versus another"[29]—they admitted that Zelikow gave one of the teams the task of "tell[ing] the story of al Qaeda's most successful operation—the 9/11 attacks."[30] There could be no clearer example of starting with a theory.

The staff assignments, we now know, were based on an outline of the Commission's final report that Zelikow had prepared in advance. This startling fact, mentioned by Kean and Hamilton, was revealed more fully by Philip Shenon, who reported that it was "a detailed outline, complete with 'chapter headings, subheadings, and sub-subheadings.'" Shenon also revealed that Kean and Hamilton conspired with Zelikow to conceal the existence of this outline—for fear that the staff would regard this outline "as evidence that they—and Zelikow—had predetermined the report's outcome."[31]

How could they possibly have concluded anything else? In fact, when the staff did learn about this outline a year later, some of them began circulating a parody entitled "The Warren Commission Report—Preemptive Outline." One of its chapter headings was: "Single Bullet: We Haven't Seen the Evidence Yet. But Really. We're Sure."[32] The point, of course, was that Zelikow's outline could have been entitled: "Osama bin Laden and al-Qaeda: We Haven't Seen the Evidence Yet. But Really. We're Sure."

NIST: An Agency of the Bush–Cheney Administration

If both FEMA and the 9/11 Commission were controlled by representatives of the Bush–Cheney administration, what about NIST? It was, if anything, even worse.

The most obvious problem is simply the fact that NIST is an agency of the US Department of Commerce. During the years in which its reports on the Twin Towers and WTC 7 were produced, therefore, NIST was an agency of the Bush–Cheney administration. Accordingly, if the scientists working on NIST's report personally concluded that the buildings were brought down by explosives, the NIST reports themselves could not have said this, because to say this would be to imply that the attacks had been facilitated by insiders. Why? Because only insiders could have secured the access to the buildings that would have been required to plant the explosives.

As to how insiders could have gotten this access, the 9/11 truth movement has pointed out that Marvin Bush, one of the president's brothers, was a principal of Securacom, a company that provided security for the World Trade Center, and that Wirt Walker III, a cousin, was its CEO.[33]

In any case, given the fact that NIST was an agency of the Bush–Cheney administration while it was preparing its WTC reports, we must be alert to the possibility that its reports were at least partly political, and hence not purely scientific, in nature.

Bush Administration Distortions of Science: This is especially the case in light of the Bush administration's record of forcing its agencies to distort science in order to advance the administration's agenda. In 2003, the minority staff of the House Committee on Government Reform published a document, "Politics and Science in the Bush Administration," which described "numerous instances where the Administration has manipulated the scientific process and distorted or suppressed scientific findings."[34] In 2004, the Union of Concerned Scientists published a document entitled *Scientific Integrity in Policy Making: An Investigation into the Bush Administration's Misuse of Science.*[35] It provided detailed documentation of charges that had been made in a briefer statement, "Restoring Scientific Integrity in Federal Policymaking," which accused the Bush administration of engaging in "distortion of scientific knowledge for partisan political ends." By the end of 2008, this statement had been signed by over 15,000 scientists, including 52 Nobel Laureates and 63 recipients of the National Medal of Science.[36]

One especially well-known and deadly example of scientific distortion ordered by the Bush–Cheney White House involved Ground Zero after the 9/11 attacks. On September 14, 2001, the *Boston Globe* reported that scientists had determined that the air had "levels of asbestos up to four times the safe level, placing unprotected emergency workers at risk of disease."[37] On September 18, however, the Environmental Protection Agency issued a statement saying that the "air is safe to breathe," specifically assuring New Yorkers that the air did *not* contain "excessive levels of asbestos."[38]

Why did the EPA lie—as Dr. Cate Jenkins, one of its scientists, later testified that it had?[39] EPA Inspector General Nikki Tinsley reported that pressure from the White House "convinced EPA to add reassuring statements and delete cautionary ones." Specifically, Tinsley said, statements were deleted about the potential harmful effects of airborne dust containing asbestos, lead, glass fibers and concrete.[40]

On the basis of the EPA's assurance, many of the Ground Zero workers did not take even minimal precautions—let alone the extreme precautions that should have been mandatory, given the very toxic air. As a result, thousands of the workers—reportedly 60 or 70 percent of them[41]—now suffer from various debilitating illnesses, including cancer, which have already led to some deaths. A lawyer for victims has predicted that "[m]ore people will die post 9/11 from these illnesses, than died on 9/11."[42] These facts, which have been discussed in stories with titles such as "Death by Dust," "Dust and Disease," and "Dust to Dust,"[43] have led one writer to refer to the aftereffects of the EPA's lie as "9/11's Second Round of Slaughter."[44]

If the White House would force the EPA to tell such a lie, even though this lie would endanger the lives of thousands of Ground Zero workers, would it not also, if it had arranged the controlled demolition of the Twin Towers and WTC 7, have made sure that NIST would issue reports covering up this fact? Given the record of the Bush–Cheney administration, one can reject this possibility out of hand only if one presupposes, circularly, that the White House was not complicit in the destruction of the WTC buildings.

Testimony from a Former NIST Employee: The Bush–Cheney White House's record of distorting scientific facts for political purposes is, moreover, not the only basis for suspecting that NIST's WTC reports are political, rather than scientific, documents. We also have the testimony of a former NIST employee who had held "a supervisory scientist position at the top civil service grade" until 2001, after which he worked as a part-time contractor until 2006.[45] Although this man wishes to remain anonymous, for fear of possible retaliation, he is known to physicist Steven Jones, who has confirmed that he is indeed who he says he is.[46]

According to this former employee, NIST in recent years has been "fully hijacked from the scientific into the political realm." This politicization of NIST, he said, began in the mid-1990s, during the Clinton presidency, but had "only grown stronger to the present" (he made this statement in October 2007). As a result, he said, scientists working for NIST "lost [their] scientific independence, and became little more than 'hired guns.'"[47]

Speaking in particular about the implications of NIST's politicization for its work on 9/11-related issues, he wrote:

> When I first heard… how the NIST "scientists" involved in 9/11 seemed to act in very un-scientific ways, it was not at all surprising to me. By 2001, everyone in NIST leadership had been trained to pay close heed to political pressures. There was no chance that NIST people "investigating" the 9/11 situation could have been acting in the true spirit of scientific independence, nor could they have operated at all without careful consideration of political impact. Everything that came from the hired guns was by then routinely filtered through the front office, and assessed for political implications before release.

In addition to being examined by NIST's front office, he added, all of the documents produced by NIST's scientists were also scrutinized by "the HQ staff of the Department of Commerce" ("which scrutinized our work very closely and frequently wouldn't permit us to release papers or give talks without changes to conform to their way of looking at things"), the National Security Agency, and the Office of Management and Budget—which is "an arm of the Executive Office of the President" and "had a policy person specifically delegated to provide oversight on [NIST's] work."[48]

If everything produced by NIST about 9/11 had to be approved not only by the Bush–Cheney administration's Commerce Department but also by its (now notorious) National Security Agency and a "policy person" from the president's Office of Management and Budget, it would seem that the White House was very concerned about what NIST might report.

Philip Shenon reported that the 9/11 Commission had been a focus of Karl Rove's attention: Rove led the fight to prevent the formation of such a commission; after the 9/11 Commission was forced into existence by public pressure, he was involved in the selection of its chairman (Thomas Kean, who was contacted by Rove, said that he found this strange, wondering why "membership on the panel [had] been shopped around by Bush's political guru"); he then became the White House's "quarterback for dealing with the Commission"; and finally, Rove (as well as Rice) had continuing contact with Zelikow while the Commission was doing its work.[49]

The statement by the former NIST employee suggests that the White House was equally concerned with NIST.

Conclusion: In light of the above facts, we have strong reasons to suspect that NIST, while producing its reports on the Twin Towers and WTC 7, was functioning as a political, rather than a scientific, agency. NIST's lead investigator, Shyam Sunder, explicitly denied this, saying: "We conducted this study without bias, without interference from anyone, and dedicated ourselves to do the very best job possible."[50] Evidence that this description was far from the truth, however, is suggested not only by the former NIST employee's statement but also by NIST's reports themselves, which violate various principles of sound scientific methodology. In previous books, I have shown this to be true of NIST's report on the Twin Towers.[51] In the present book, I show that it is at least equally true of its report on WTC 7.

The next chapter discusses some of the principles of scientific method that are violated in NIST's WTC 7 report.

2
SOME PRINCIPLES OF SCIENTIFIC METHOD

President Barack Obama has promised that his administration will put an end to the Bush administration's policy of ignoring and distorting science to advance political ends. In his inaugural address, Obama said: "We will restore science to its rightful place."[1] Within the first 50 days of his presidency, he issued a memorandum aimed at insulating the federal government's scientific reports from political influence.[2] This policy implies that, if some federal agencies during the Bush administration issued reports on important topics in which good science was overridden by political considerations, those reports would need to be corrected.

The Introduction and Chapter 1 of this book have already provided reasons to suspect that one such report is the NIST report on WTC 7, because in writing it, NIST acted as a political rather than a scientific agency. The present chapter provides specific bases for confirming this suspicion by discussing principles of scientific method.

This chapter does not, however, provide a discussion of scientific method in general. It merely discusses some basic principles of scientific method that, the scientific community agrees, should not be violated. There is, moreover, no attempt here to provide an exhaustive list of such principles. The focus is much narrower, dealing only with principles of this type that are violated by NIST's report on WTC 7.

If the authors of this NIST report violated these principles deliberately, they were guilty of scientific fraud.

1. SCIENTIFIC FRAUD

At one time, most people may have assumed that scientists, being devoted to the disinterested pursuit of truth, were seldom if ever tempted to engage in fraud. Several decades ago, however, we learned that scientists hired by tobacco companies had deliberately obscured the evidence that smoking causes cancer. More recently, as mentioned in the Introduction, we have become aware that scientists working for the Bush administration were willing to distort scientific data to support the administration's political agenda.

It may be supposed, however, that these were exceptions—that for the most part, scientists do not engage in fraud. Unfortunately, the evidence does not support this optimistic assumption. A recent story in the *International Herald Tribune* was titled "Scientific Fraud: There's More of It Than You Think." It began:

> A wide-ranging study of the incidence of scientific fraud in the United States has just been published, and the results are alarming: Scientists resort to fraud more commonly than we think.[3]

Within the scientific world, the fact of scientific fraud has been the subject of some book-length studies. In 1985, for example, William Broad and Nicholas Wade published a book titled *Betrayers of the Truth: Fraud and Deceit in the Halls of Science.*[4] In 2004, Horace Freeland Judson published *The Great Betrayal: Fraud in Science.*[5]

In discussing the nature of scientific fraud, we can distinguish between fraud in the strict sense and fraud in a broader sense. Scientific fraud in the broad sense occurs when scientists, in order to make their case, violate any of the basic principles of scientific method. Scientific fraud in the strict sense is constituted by those violations that have been explicitly identified as "fraud" by the scientific community. After discussing the principles that are violated by scientific fraud in this strict sense, I will discuss some additional principles, the violation of which constitutes fraud in the broader sense.

A document entitled "What is Research Misconduct?" which was issued by the inspector general of the National Science Foundation (NSF), says: "Research Misconduct is defined as fabrication, falsification, or plagiarism in proposing, performing, or reviewing research, or in reporting research results." This document then defines these three types of misconduct thus:

> Fabrication is making up results and recording or reporting them. Falsification is manipulating research materials, equipment, or processes or changing or omitting data or results such that the

research is not accurately represented in the research record.
Plagiarism is the appropriation of another person's ideas, processes, results or words without giving appropriate credit.[6]

These three types of "scientific misconduct" are identical with the three types of "scientific fraud" identified in Judson's book. We can say, therefore, that fabrication, falsification, and plagiarism constitute scientific fraud in the strict sense.

In an examination of NIST's WTC 7 report, the third type of fraud—plagiarism—is not relevant. Our focus will, therefore, be on the first two types: fabrication and falsification.

Scientific fraud in the strict sense is considered very serious. The above-quoted document of the National Science Foundation urges anyone aware of scientific fraud to contact the NSF's inspector general; it even supplies an anonymous hotline.[7]

The importance of exposing fraud has been explained by eminent biologist Richard Lewontin in his review of Judson's book. While acknowledging that scientists might disagree about many things, he declared:

> [E]very scientist must agree that outright fraud is beyond the pale. Putting aside the issue of morality, scientific investigation would be destroyed as a useful human endeavor and scientists would lose any claim on social resources if deliberate falsifications were not exposed. So scientists must be on the alert, ready to detect lies arising from within their institution.[8]

The present book shows that the NIST report on WTC 7 should be exposed by the scientific community for committing scientific fraud in the strict sense.

2. PRINCIPLES VIOLATED BY SCIENTIFIC FRAUD IN THE STRICT SENSE

Various principles relevant to fraud in the broad sense will be discussed in the next section. The present section deals with three principles that, if violated by NIST, would make it guilty of fraud in the strict sense.

Evidence Should Not Be Fabricated

Richard Lewontin, in his review of Judson's book, wrote: "Fabrication is the creation of claimed observations and facts out of whole cloth. These are just plain lies." By contrast, he said: "Falsification is the trimming and adjustment of the results of genuine experiments so that they come to be in agreement with a desired conclusion."[9] As this distinction shows, Lewontin and Judson were thinking primarily of experimental sciences.

In preparing its report on WTC 7, however, NIST did not perform physical experiments. It instead relied on computer-based simulations. Insofar as it did experiments, these were carried out on computers, with simulated fires, simulated steel beams, simulated shear studs, and so on. This entire procedure, in which NIST based its theory on computer-generated models, could have been used for almost unlimited fabrication. As architect Eric Douglas wrote with regard to NIST's 2005 report on the Twin Towers:

> [A] fundamental problem with using computer simulation is the overwhelming temptation to manipulate the input data until one achieves the desired results. Thus, what appears to be a conclusion is actually a premise. We see NIST succumb to this temptation throughout its investigation.[10]

That NIST continued this practice in preparing its report on WTC 7 is illustrated by its admission, discussed below in Chapter 9, that in creating its models of the spread of fires on the various floors, "The observed fire activity gleaned from the photographs and videos was not a model input."[11]

Given the fact that, insofar as NIST performed experiments, these were carried out on computers, not with physical materials, it is difficult to draw a clear distinction between (mere) falsification and outright fabrication. As we will see, nevertheless, NIST does appear to be guilty of practices that would most accurately be classified as fabrication, given the definition provided by the National Science Foundation: "making up results and recording or reporting them."[12]

A common term for fabrication, which is used below in Chapter 10, is "dry labbing." Originally used to refer to the practice by scientists of reporting experiments that they had not actually performed in the laboratory, it is now used more broadly to refer to any type of fabrication.

Evidence Should Not Be Falsified

Falsification is, to repeat the NSF definition, "manipulating research materials, equipment, or processes or changing or omitting data or results such that the research is not accurately represented in the research record."

Although it is not always clear whether particular violations of scientific principles should be classified as falsifications or fabrications, we will see that NIST's report does contain several claims that clearly appear to be one or the other. These include claims, discussed in Chapters 8 and 9, involving the location and duration of fires, the temperatures reached by fires, and the temperatures reached by steel. They also include claims, discussed in Chapter 10, about thermal expansion, failed shear studs, missing shear studs, and column failures.

Relevant Evidence Should Not Be Ignored

Horace Judson defined falsification as "altering the data or tendentiously selecting what to report."[13] The second type of falsification mentioned in this definition—"tendentiously selecting what to report"—is echoed by the NSF definition quoted above, which includes "omitting data." This type of falsification is so important, especially in relation to NIST's report, that it deserves to be treated as a distinct principle: *None of the relevant evidence should be ignored.*

Some philosophers of science believe that "inference to the best explanation" lies at the heart of scientific methodology.[14] Although there are valid debates about whether this phrase describes the actual process of scientific investigation, there can be no denying that an investigation should aim to reach the *best explanation.*

What is the *best* explanation, from a strictly scientific or philosophical point of view? It is the one that best fulfills the criteria of self-consistency and adequacy. The scientific method can be summarized as *rational empiricism.* Its rational dimension is oriented around the goal of self-consistency, its empirical dimension around the goal of adequacy to all of the relevant facts. The best explanation for any phenomenon, then, is the one that, while being self-consistent, best explains or otherwise takes account of all of the relevant evidence.

Of these two criteria, it is the empirical criterion—adequacy to all of the relevant evidence—that is most often violated. Scientific explanations are not usually marred by instances of obvious inconsistency (although NIST's report on WTC 7 is thus marred, as Chapter 10 shows). Rather, scientists are often tempted to achieve self-consistency by simply ignoring part of the relevant evidence. "It is easy enough to find a [logically harmonious] theory," wryly observed philosopher of science Alfred North Whitehead, "provided that you are content to disregard half your evidence."

Although it is sometimes thought that science is an enterprise to which morality is irrelevant, this is not true, because a habit of ignoring evidence while producing purportedly scientific reports is a moral failing. "[T]he moral temper required for the pursuit of truth," Whitehead said, is "[a]n unflinching determination to take the whole evidence into account."[15]

We will see, especially in Chapters 4 and 5, that NIST repeatedly failed to manifest this moral temper.

3. PRINCIPLES VIOLATED BY SCIENTIFIC FRAUD IN A BROADER SENSE

Having discussed principles violated by scientific fraud in the strict sense, I next discuss several additional principles, the violation of which constitutes scientific fraud in a broader sense. If committed, these additional violations reveal that, although a report may claim to be scientific, it really is not. NIST clearly claimed the mantle of science for its WTC 7 report. As we saw in the Introduction, Shyam Sunder, NIST's lead investigator for this report, said: "science is really behind what we have said."[16] But if this report violates a number of commonly accepted principles of scientific method, it should not, even aside from the charge of fraud in the strict sense, be considered a scientific report. I turn now to some of those additional principles.

Extra-Scientific Considerations Should Not Be Allowed to Determine Conclusions

In saying that scientists' conclusions should not be *determined* by extra-scientific considerations, this principle is not saying that the practice of science should not be *influenced* by extra-scientific factors, because this would be unrealistic.

For example, Richard Lewontin observed, in his review of Judson's book, that scientists are sometimes led to commit fraud by "the drive for economic success, personal power, and the gratification of one's ego." Although these are clearly extra-scientific motives, they have also played a significant role in most scientific discoveries. Likewise, although aesthetic and religious considerations are generally considered extra-scientific, they have sometimes played positive roles in scientific breakthroughs.

Rather than insisting that extra-scientific considerations should not *influence the work* of scientists, this principle simply says that they should never be allowed to *determine their conclusions.* The dominant motive must be the intent to discover the truth about the subject being investigated.

For example, religious motives may have originally led a person to become a scientist and to do research on a particular topic. But the dominant motive underlying the research, if it is to be truly scientific, cannot be the intent to support a pre-existing religious belief. Some scientists may have this desire. But if their work is to be considered science rather than pseudo-science, they must follow the evidence where it leads, even if it ends up refuting the belief that they had hoped to support.

Likewise, scientific work may at times be influenced by political motives, as scientists may hope to support their own political party's policy on some medical or environmental issue. This is natural and may be fine. But if this motive leads them to ignore or distort evidence, then their work cannot be considered scientific.

An especially common extra-scientific motive is the desire of employees in a company to please their employers, if only to keep their jobs or be promoted. Such desires often reflect economic motives and concerns with social status. These motives are natural and may cause no problems, as the employees may please their employers by doing good work. But if their employers order them to doctor their data, so as to reach different conclusions than they would have reached on the basis of the undoctored data, then the desire to please their employers may lead them to commit scientific fraud.

The NIST report on WTC 7, as we will see, contains many reasons to conclude that its approach and conclusions were determined by extra-scientific considerations—probably in the form of orders from above, based on political considerations, that were followed by scientists at NIST because they wanted to keep their jobs. The former NIST employee, in fact, said that at least some of his friends still working at NIST have been "unhappily and often unwillingly involved in some of the politicization."[17]

An Investigation Should Begin with the Most Likely Hypothesis

The attempt to find an explanation of some event necessarily begins with a hypothesis—perhaps after an initial period of somewhat neutral, open-minded, gathering of data. Our second principle says that, if more than one explanation seems possible, scientists should begin with the most likely hypothesis.

In some situations, to be sure, no hypothesis stands out as clearly the most likely. (In some murder cases, for example, the immediately available facts do not point to some particular suspect.) In other situations, however, the facts available at the beginning of the investigation do suggest one hypothesis as much more likely than others. In these cases, the investigation should begin with this hypothesis. A more complete statement of the principle, therefore, would be: *When there is a most likely explanation for some phenomenon, the investigation should begin with the hypothesis that this possible explanation is indeed the correct one.*

Starting with such a hypothesis is not, however, the same as dogmatically presupposing its truth. Rather, having begun with this hypothesis, the investigators should then see if there is any evidence that disconfirms it. Indeed, the practice of referring to one's initial assumption as merely a "hypothesis" is a way of indicating that it is, for the time being, held tentatively.

But even though scientists should hold it tentatively, they should begin with the hypothesis that, at the time, seems the most likely explanation of the phenomenon in question. Doing otherwise would suggest that their work is being determined by some extra-scientific motive, rather than the simple desire to discover the truth.

As we will see in Chapter 3, although one possible explanation for the destruction of WTC 7 stood out from all others as easily the most likely one, NIST insisted on orienting its labors around a different hypothesis.

When Two or More Hypotheses Seem Equally Adequate, the Simplest One Should Be Preferred

In some cases, more than one explanation for some phenomenon might seem equally adequate. It is widely agreed among philosophers and scientists that, in such cases, the simplest explanation should be chosen. There is much disagreement, however, about how this principle should be interpreted.

This principle is often called "Occam's razor," after the fourteenth-century philosopher-theologian William of Occam (or Ockham). One of his own formulations was the principle of economy: "It is futile to do with more things that which can be done with fewer."[18] Francis Heylighen, a present-day scientist at the University of Brussels, prefers to formulate Occam's razor as the principle that "one should not make more assumptions than the minimum needed." This principle, he adds, "admonishes us to choose from a set of otherwise equivalent models of a given phenomenon the simplest one."[19]

Arguably the most important and non-controversial interpretation of this principle would apply to explanations of complex events, in which there are several phenomena to explain. Let us assume that there are seven phenomena (A, B, C, D, E, F, G) and that they can be explained with equal adequacy in two different ways. The first way is to provide a hypothesis that, while explaining A, simultaneously explains B, C, D, E, F, and G. The second way is to provide one hypothesis to explain A, another hypothesis to explain B, another to explain C, and so on. Virtually all scientists would agree that, if both approaches are equally adequate for explaining all seven features of this complex event, then the first approach should be preferred. It would clearly exemplify Heylighen's stipulation that the simplest model be chosen. And it would fulfill the principle of economy, endorsed by Occam, interpreted to mean: *It is futile to explain with several hypotheses a complex occurrence that can be explained equally well with one hypothesis.*

This principle, as we will see later, counts decisively in favor of the demolition hypothesis for the destruction of WTC 7.

Straw-Man Arguments Should Be Avoided

When scientists are less interested in a genuine search for truth than in defending a theory based on extra-scientific considerations, they often deal with arguments presented by critics of their position by attacking "straw-man arguments." That is, rather than answering the arguments actually made by the critics, they construct ones that can easily be defeated, attribute these arguments to the critics, and then demonstrate their falsity. This approach gives the appearance of responding to the critics' arguments while doing no such thing.

When scientists resort to this approach, it provides a good clue that they are not genuinely searching for the truth. If they were, they would use the fact that they could not answer their critics' arguments as a stimulus to revise their position to make it more adequate.

In Chapter 6, we will see that NIST uses straw-man arguments to claim that WTC 7 could not possibly have been brought down by explosives.

Prima Facie *Implausible Claims Should Not Be Made without Good Reasons*

Many scientific advances have often come from scientists who made claims that, at the time, seemed implausible to most of their fellow scientists. This was certainly the case, for example, with quantum theory. It is not, therefore, a basic principle of science that its practitioners should not make implausible claims. The basic principle is that they should not do so without good reason. The founders of quantum theory fulfilled this stipulation by, on the one hand, showing that the basic assumptions of Newtonian physics simply could not deal with the interactions occurring at the quantum level and, on the other hand, showing that their new theory, however weird it might seem, produces very accurate predictions.

Through these means, the founders of quantum theory convinced their peers that, although their claims were *prima facie* (on the surface) implausible, they were, upon deeper inspection, not really implausible after all. This development reflects the fact that "plausibility" is a subjective judgment, existing in the mind of the beholder. A more complete statement of the principle, therefore, would be: "Do not make *prima facie* implausible claims without good reasons."

This principle embodies a well-known dictum: "Extraordinary claims demand extraordinary evidence." This dictum can be stated as a basic principle: *Extraordinary claims should be supported by extraordinary evidence.*

NIST, as we will see in Part II of this book, makes several extraordinary claims. Far from supporting them with extraordinary evidence, however, it provides very weak evidence.

As the example of quantum theory shows, moreover, providing good reasons for making an initially implausible claim may require more than simply providing strong evidence. The founders of quantum theory also showed that the hitherto accepted principles of physics could not handle the new data being discovered at the most elementary levels of nature. The extraordinary, initially implausible, claims were necessary to accommodate this new set of data.

NIST, however, does nothing analogous. Although NIST's theory that WTC 7 was brought down by fire requires it to make several implausible claims, it never gives a good—that is, a *scientific*—reason why it rejected the explanatory principles that have successfully explained the collapses of all steel-framed high-rise buildings that have occurred both before and after September 11, 2001.

Some of the implausible claims made by NIST, moreover, involve violations of two more basic principles, which will be treated next.

Unprecedented Causes Should Not, Without Good Reasons, Be Posited to Explain Familiar Occurrences

Given the regularity of nature—which is both assumed and continually confirmed by science—we properly assume, unless there is extraordinary evidence to the contrary, that each instance of a familiar occurrence was produced by the same causal factors that brought about the previous instances. This expectation is expressed in a dictum: "Like effects imply like causes."

No better example can be supplied than the one at issue in this book. The rapid and complete collapse of steel-framed high-rise buildings has become a familiar occurrence, with dozens of instances, some of which have been shown on television. In each instance prior to and since September 11, 2001, the collapse was caused by explosives in the process known as controlled demolition. In the form of controlled demolition known as implosion, the building typically comes straight down with acceleration close to free fall. Without strong evidence to the contrary, therefore, scientists would naturally and properly presume that the Twin Towers and WTC 7, which came straight down in free fall or close to it, were brought down with explosives.

NIST claims, however, that these three collapses, in spite of their similarity to implosions, were produced by completely different causes. With regard to WTC 7 in particular, the unprecedented cause was said to be the thermal expansion of steel caused by fires in the building.

NIST has thereby provided a perfect example of a claim that is initially, or *prima facie*, implausible. NIST could have changed this *prima facie* implausible claim into a plausible one, only by (1) providing very strong evidence for its contention that explosives were *not* used and (2) providing a plausible alternative theory to account for WTC 7's straight-down, virtually free-fall, collapse. As we will see in Chapters 6 through 10, however, NIST failed on both counts.

Scientists Should Not Make Claims Implying That Laws of Nature Have Been Violated

The most implausible claims scientists can make, aside from those that involve self-contradictions, are those that imply that one or more of the fundamental laws of nature—alternatively called laws of physics—have been violated. An alleged violation of the laws of nature would be a *miracle* in the traditional sense of the term: an interruption of the normal laws of nature by a supernatural cause. It has become almost universally accepted in the scientific community that miracles, thus understood, do not happen. This principle is even accepted by many theologians.[20]

However, in spite of the fact that this principle is widely accepted, some scientists—like some philosophers and theologians—are occasionally tempted, when they encounter difficulties in providing an explanation for some phenomenon, to violate it. This fact is lampooned in a well-known cartoon showing a physicist using a chalkboard to provide a technical explanation. After filling the board with a string of formulae, he wrote at the bottom: "then a miracle happens."[21] The temptation to resort to this solution when no naturalistic explanation seems possible is illustrated by the fact that a well-known philosopher, after referring to this cartoon approvingly, himself implicitly affirmed a miracle in trying to explain the emergence of mind out of matter.[22]

It is perhaps no surprise that NIST succumbed to this temptation, as we will see in Chapter 10. Having developed a theory of WTC 7's collapse that did not allow for the building to enter into free fall, NIST denied in its Draft Report of August 2008 that WTC 7 had done so. But after evidence to the contrary was publicly presented, NIST admitted in its Final Report, issued in November, that the building had entered into free fall for over two seconds—even though NIST's theory, by denying that explosives had been used to remove the steel columns, did not allow for free fall. NIST thereby implied that a miracle had happened.

Scientific Work Should Be Reviewed by Peers Before Being Published

It is accepted practice that, before scientific reports are published, they should be reviewed by fellow scientists who are "peers" in the sense of sharing competence in the subject at hand. Whether the reports are intended to be published as books or as journal articles, editors will typically send them to two or three other scientists who have agreed to be reviewers. If these reviewers indicate that the reports contain serious problems, the editors will hold up publication until the authors have responded satisfactorily to the criticisms.

Although the peer-review process works only imperfectly,[23] it is far better than nothing. Scientists tempted to fabricate, ignore, or otherwise falsify evidence will be less likely to do so if they know that independent experts will be reviewing their work. They will also be more likely to avoid the other unscientific practices discussed above, such as dismissing the most likely hypotheses, attacking straw-man arguments, making implausible claims without good reasons, attributing common occurrences to unprecedented causes, and implying that laws of nature have been broken.

NIST's WTC 7 report was not, however, submitted to a peer-review process. NIST did, as we will see, invite the general public, and thereby fellow scientists, to offer "comments" on it. But there was no neutral adjudicator to require NIST to respond in a responsible way to the criticisms it received. And, as we will see, NIST for the most part simply ignored these critiques—thereby failing to show even *pro forma* respect for the standard review process of the scientific community.

Having flagged in this chapter a number of principles of scientific method, I will in the following chapters show that NIST violated them, thereby suggesting that it was operating as a political rather than a scientific agency.

3
NIST'S REFUSAL TO BEGIN WITH THE MOST LIKELY HYPOTHESIS

n Chapter 1, we saw that there were good reasons to suspect that NIST would not follow the basic formal principle of scientific method discussed in Chapter 2, namely: *Extra-scientific considerations should not be allowed to determine conclusions.* We saw reasons to suspect, in particular, that NIST was functioning as a political (not a scientific) agency. As such, its first concern would not have been to determine the probable truth. Although NIST had to create a report that would appear sufficiently plausible to satisfy the press and the general public, its first priority would have been to produce a report that would be acceptable from the perspective of the Bush–Cheney administration.

If NIST did indeed allow political considerations to determine its conclusions, this would explain why NIST also violated the principle that any scientific attempt to determine the cause of some event should begin with the most likely hypothesis.

The Most Likely Hypothesis
As we saw in the Introduction, the most likely hypothesis, as NIST began its investigation of the collapse of WTC 7, would have been that it was brought down with explosives in the procedure known as controlled demolition.

To repeat the two most obvious reasons to consider this the most likely hypothesis: First, all previous collapses of steel-framed high-rise buildings had been produced by controlled demolition. Prior to 9/11, no building of this type had ever collapsed without the aid of pre-placed explosives. Second, the collapse of WTC 7 exemplified many of the signature features of the type of controlled demolition known as implosion.

This second point was ignored by Shyam Sunder, NIST's lead

investigator, when at the press conference to unveil NIST's report on WTC 7 he said:

> [W]e knew from the beginning of our study that understanding what happened to Building 7 on 9/11 would be difficult. It did not fit any textbook description that you could readily point to and say, yes, that's why the building failed.[1]

Sunder's statement was false. As pointed out in the Introduction, the collapse of this building exemplified seven features of a textbook description of a controlled implosion. To repeat:

(1) The collapse started from the bottom.
(2) The onset of the collapse was sudden.
(3) The collapse was total.
(4) The building came straight down.
(5) Its acceleration approximated that of a free-falling object.
(6) Most of its concrete was pulverized into tiny particles, resulting in a huge dust cloud.
(7) The building ended up as a relatively small pile of debris.[2]

In fact, insofar as there is a "textbook" that the NIST investigation should have followed, it is the *Guide for Fire and Explosion Investigations* put out by the National Fire Protection Association (NFPA). This NFPA manual says that investigators should look for evidence of explosives whenever there is "high-order damage," which is defined thus:

> High-order damage is characterized by shattering of the structure, producing small, pulverized debris. Walls, roofs, and structural members are splintered or shattered, with the building completely demolished. Debris is thrown great distances, possibly hundreds of feet.[3]

The first two sentences in this description apply fully to the destruction of WTC 7. Although the third sentence, which speaks of debris being thrown great distances, does not, it definitely does apply to the destruction of the Twin Towers—which NIST itself admits by claiming that debris from the collapse of the North Tower, which was several hundred feet away, damaged and started fires in WTC 7.

In any case, given the fact that the collapse of WTC 7 as well as that of the Twin Towers manifested many of the features mentioned in the NFPA manual as signs of "high-order damage," NIST was virtually mandated to begin its investigation by looking for evidence that explosives had been used.

Besides following from the fact that the collapse of WTC 7 exemplified many standard features of controlled implosions, including showing signs of "high-order damage," the conclusion that NIST should have begun its investigation by looking for evidence of explosives also follows from another principle discussed in Chapter 2: *Investigators should avoid positing, without good reasons, unprecedented causes for familiar occurrences.* This principle in turn follows from another, which is that *like effects generally imply like causes.*

Prior to 9/11, every total collapse of a steel-framed high-rise building had the same cause: explosives. But NIST asserted that the collapse of WTC 7 had an unprecedented cause, saying: "This was the first known instance of the total collapse of a tall building primarily due to fires."[4]

In a few cases, to be sure, the standard cause for a familiar event might be ruled out, so that it might be necessary to posit an unprecedented cause. This is why the principle in question states that scientists should avoid positing unprecedented causes *without good reasons.*

Did the collapse of WTC 7 present NIST with a phenomenon for which the standard cause was ruled out on scientific grounds? NIST claims that it did. But as we will see in Chapter 6, that is a bogus claim, which NIST is able to make only by violating another principle of scientific discussion: *Straw-man arguments are to be avoided.*

NIST's Alternative to the Most Likely Hypothesis

When NIST began its investigation of the collapse of WTC 7, the most likely hypothesis would have been that it was caused by explosives of some sort. Indeed, as we just saw, NIST was virtually mandated by the NFPA manual to begin its investigation by looking for signs of explosives—which is another way of saying that NIST should have begun by looking for evidence to confirm the hypothesis that the building had been deliberately imploded. And yet the NIST investigators adopted a different working hypothesis. NIST wrote:

> The challenge was to determine if a fire-induced floor system failure could occur in WTC 7 under an ordinary building contents fire.[5]

Why would NIST have assumed that this was "the challenge"? Why would NIST, already knowing that buildings such as WTC 7 can be brought down with explosives—and indeed that this is the only way in which such buildings had ever been caused to collapse—have asked if a collapse caused by an ordinary building fire "could occur"? As physicist Steven Jones has written:

> The likelihood of near-symmetrical collapse of WTC 7 due to random fires (the "official" theory)—requiring as it does near-simultaneous failure of many support columns—is infinitesimal.[6]

Whereas "infinitesimal probability" means *virtually* zero probability, a structural engineer, Kamal Obeid, has bluntly rated the probability to be, simply, zero. Pointing out that the perfectly vertical and hence symmetrical collapse of WTC 7 required all of its 82 steel columns to have failed simultaneously, Obeid stated that for this to have occurred without the use of explosives would have been an "impossibility."[7]

Why would NIST, rather than starting with the hypothesis of controlled demolition—which virtually all scientists, architects, structural engineers, and controlled demolition experts around the world would have considered the most likely hypothesis—have started with a hypothesis that most nongovernmental physicists, architects, and structural engineers would have considered extremely unlikely—so unlikely that physicist John Wyndham called it "the least likely assumption"?[8]

Marshaling evidence to support such an unlikely hypothesis would indeed have been a "challenge." But why would NIST have taken on this difficult challenge instead of simply starting with the most likely hypothesis? This is one of the key questions that should be addressed to NIST about its report on WTC 7. And if NIST spokespersons would answer honestly (as they might do if put under oath), they would surely confess that NIST, as an agency of the Bush–Cheney administration, had to rule out the demolition hypothesis on political grounds. This was the conclusion reached by Wyndham, who wrote: "NIST's failure to seriously consider other causes besides fire for the building collapses strongly suggests government interference in a scientific process."[9]

Speaking as NIST's lead investigator, Shyam Sunder denied this charge in advance, saying: "We conducted our study with no preconceived notions about what happened."[10] That claim is simply not credible, however, given NIST's refusal to begin with the most likely hypothesis—along with, as we will see in the next three chapters, NIST's systematic ignoring of all evidence pointing to controlled demolition as the explanation of WTC 7's collapse.

Sunder in effect denied that NIST allowed political considerations to overrule scientific principles, saying: "Our job was to come up with the best science."[11] A more honest statement would surely have been: *Our job was to come up with the best science consistent with our being an agency of the Bush–Cheney administration.*

Given that task, NIST's challenge was to find a seemingly plausible scenario through which WTC 7 might have come down without the assistance of explosives, and then to assert that, no evidence of explosives having been found, this scenario must describe why and how the building actually came down. NIST, however, could claim that no evidence of explosives was found only by ignoring a great amount of such evidence. I turn next to this issue.

4

NIST'S IGNORING OF PHYSICAL EVIDENCE FOR EXPLOSIVES

As we saw in Chapter 2, one of the most important criteria for determining whether an investigation into some issue has been truly scientific is whether it reflects, in the words of Alfred North Whitehead, an "unflinching determination to take the whole evidence into account." Whitehead added that it is easy to find a theory that is logically harmonious, "provided that you are content to disregard half your evidence," but that such short cuts lead to "a merely illusory success."

It would be difficult to find a more apt description of NIST's report on WTC 7. Even if NIST's theory about the collapse of this building were logically harmonious and otherwise impeccable—and we will see in Part II that it is not—it would still be inadequate, because it simply ignores half of the relevant evidence. For this reason alone, any of NIST's apparent success in dealing with the mystery of WTC 7's collapse would be "merely illusory."

The ignored evidence points to explosives as the cause of the collapse of WTC 7. The evidence for explosives that NIST ignored consists of two general types, testimonial and physical. Whereas the next chapter will be devoted to testimonial evidence that explosives were used, the present chapter deals with physical evidence for this conclusion.

1. SQUIBS AND BLOWN-OUT WINDOWS

In the Introduction and Chapter 3, we saw seven features of the collapse of WTC 7 that are also common features of controlled implosions—namely, that the collapse began at the bottom, started suddenly, was total, was vertical, occurred in virtual free fall, involved the pulverization of much of the concrete, and resulted in a relatively small pile of debris.

These features, which can all be seen in videos of WTC 7's collapse,[1] are acknowledged by NIST. But there are two other features, which can also be seen on videos, that NIST does not acknowledge: apparent demolition squibs and windows that were blown out at the onset of the collapse.

Apparent Demolition Squibs

When explosives are used to implode a building, it is often possible to see sequences of horizontal puffs of smoke and pulverized material, known as "demolition squibs," coming out of various floors of the building before they collapse. Examples of implosions in which squibs are visible can be viewed on the internet.[2]

One of the types of physical evidence for the conclusion that WTC 7 was imploded is that such phenomena—which Kevin Ryan suggests would best be described as "high velocity bursts of debris ejected from point-like sources"[3]—are visible in videos of its collapse. Physicist Steven Jones, referring to some of these videos,[4] said in a 2006 essay:[5]

> [H]orizontal puffs of smoke and debris, sometimes called "squibs," emerge from the upper floors of WTC 7, in regular sequence, just as the building starts to collapse. The upper floors have evidently not moved relative to one another yet, from what one can observe on the videos.... The official reports lack an explanation for these squibs.

Defenders of the official account typically try to claim that these high-velocity ejections of debris were simply caused by compression after the floors began to collapse. In its "Answers to Frequently Asked Questions" about the Twin Towers, published in 2006, NIST gave this explanation as to why the "puffs of smoke," as it called them, did not provide evidence of controlled demolition:

> [T]he falling mass of the building compressed the air ahead of it— much like the action of a piston—forcing smoke and debris out the windows as the stories below failed sequentially.[6]

However, this explanation for the apparent demolition squibs from the Twin Towers does not fit the descriptions given by several witnesses. For example, firefighter James Curran said: "I looked back and... I heard like every floor went chu-chu-chu.... [E]verything was getting blown out of the floors before it actually collapsed."[7] If material was being blown out from floors *before* those floors collapsed, then the ejections cannot be explained as resulting from compressed air caused *by* the collapse.

Moreover, Ryan has pointed out, videos of the collapses of the Twin Towers show that bursts of debris ejected from point-like sources sometimes occurred on floors *long* before the collapse front reached them. Some of the bursts occurred "at levels twenty to thirty floors below a 'collapse' front."[8]

This same problem exists with regard to the bursts of debris ejected during the collapse of WTC 7. As Jones pointed out, the bursts coming from the upper floors of WTC 7 occurred at a time when "[t]he upper floors have evidently not moved relative to one another."[9] There are videos on the internet in which these squibs, moving up the building near the top, can be seen.[10]

The concluding sentence of Jones's 2006 essay—"The official reports lack an explanation for these squibs"—remains true today. NIST, in fact, did not even try to explain the apparent squibs coming out of WTC 7. A search of its long (729-page) report turns up not a single instance of the word "squib" or "puff." The issue is also not addressed in its "Questions and Answers about the NIST WTC 7 Investigation."[11] So, having given an obviously inadequate explanation of the squibs that appeared during the collapses of the Twin Towers, NIST simply ignored the squibs that are visible in videos of the collapse of WTC 7.

A Vertical Row of Blown-Out Windows

In 2008, a video of the collapse of WTC 7 appeared on the internet that evidently had not previously been available to the public. In this video, titled "New 911 Building 7 Collapse Clearly Shows Demolition," a vertical row of approximately eight windows, between (roughly) the 29th and 37th floors, can be seen being blown out as WTC 7 begins to collapse.[12] There would seem to be no way that NIST's theory of this building's collapse, to be discussed in Part II of this book, could explain these blown-out windows. It is not surprising, therefore, that NIST did not mention them.

The apparent demolition squibs and the blown-out windows were evidently part of the physical evidence that NIST was content to ignore in order to find a politically acceptable theory. But they were only a small part. There is much more.

2. MOLTEN METAL IN THE DEBRIS

The existence of molten metal—which has usually been described as "molten steel" but may have actually been molten iron (which is a byproduct when thermite melts steel)—was reported in the Ground Zero rubble by many credible witnesses.

Leslie Robertson, a member of the engineering firm that designed the Twin Towers, reportedly said during a speech in early October 2001: "As of 21 days after the attack, the fires were still burning and molten steel was still running." This statement was reported by James Williams, the president of the Structural Engineers Association of Utah.[13]

Two men in charge of the clean-up operation also reportedly spoke of molten steel in the rubble. Peter Tully, president of Tully Construction, said that he saw pools of "literally molten steel" at the site. Mark Loizeaux, president of Controlled Demolition, Inc., said that several weeks after 9/11, when the rubble was being removed, "hot spots of molten steel" were found "at the bottoms of the elevator shafts of the main towers, down seven [basement] levels." Loizeaux also reportedly said "that molten steel was also found at WTC 7."[14]

Firefighters at Ground Zero also reportedly spoke of having "encountered rivers of molten steel."[15] One of these firefighters was Captain Philip Ruvolo, who said: "You'd get down below and you'd see molten steel, *molten* steel, running down the channel rails, like you're in a foundry, like lava."[16] Joe O'Toole, a Bronx firefighter who worked on the rescue and clean-up efforts, reported that one beam lifted from deep below the surface "was dripping from the molten steel."[17]

Other people at the site reported that steel beams had become molten. Greg Fuchek, vice president of a company that supplied computer equipment employed to identify human remains, said: "[S]ometimes when a worker would pull a steel beam from the wreckage, the end of the beam would be dripping molten steel."[18] Tom Arterburn, writing in *Waste Age,* reported that the New York Department of Sanitation removed "everything from molten steel beams to human remains."[19]

Health professionals who visited the site gave similar testimonies. One of these was Dr. Ronald Burger of the National Center for Environmental Health, who spoke of "[f]eeling the heat, seeing the molten steel."[20] Dr. Alison Geyh of the Johns Hopkins School of Public Health, who headed up a scientific team that went to the site shortly after 9/11 at the request of the National Institute of Environmental Health Sciences, said: "Fires are still actively burning and the smoke is very intense. In some pockets now being uncovered they are finding molten steel."[21]

This body of testimony creates a problem for the official account, defended by NIST, according to which the only source of energy (beyond gravity) for bringing down the WTC buildings was fire (along with, in the case of the Twin Towers, the impact of the airplanes). Could the fires have melted steel?

Structural steel does not begin to melt until it reaches about 1,482°C (2,700°F).[22] NIST does not suggest that any of the steel in WTC 7 came anywhere close to this temperature. Its most extravagant claim is that some of the beams reached 675°C (1,250°F).[23] The fires, which would have been considerably hotter than the steel, would themselves not have been close to 1,482°C (2,700°F). NIST's most extravagant claim for fires, as we will see in Chapter 9, is that they reached 1,100°C (2,012°F) in some places.

If fires did not melt any steel in WTC 7, could the molten steel under WTC 7 have come from the Twin Towers, in which the fires had been fed by jet fuel? MIT's Thomas Eagar, who supports the official account of how the WTC buildings came down, says that the fires in the towers were "probably only about 1,200 or 1,300°F [648 or 704°C]."[24] For those fires to have heated any steel up even to that temperature, they would have had to have been very big and long-lasting fires, which they were not. NIST itself reported that it found "no evidence that any of [the steel in the Twin Towers] had reached temperatures above 600°C [1,100°F]."[25] NIST also explicitly stated that the fires in the towers could not have melted any steel.[26] In response to this situation, physicist Steven Jones wrote:

> [NIST] admits that the fires were insufficient to melt steel beams. That admission raises the obvious question: Where, then, did the molten metal come from?[27]

NIST had three ways of responding to this question. Its first way was simply to dispute the claim that steel had melted. When John Gross, one of the authors of NIST's WTC reports, was asked about the molten steel, he challenged the questioner's "basic premise that there was a pool of molten steel," saying: "I know of absolutely no... eyewitness who has said so."[28] As we have seen, however, many credible witnesses testified to its existence.

A second way in which NIST responded to the molten metal was to say that, if it did exist, it was probably produced in the rubble pile after the collapse. One of the questions raised in response to NIST's 2005 report on the Twin Towers was: "Why did the NIST investigation not consider reports of molten steel in the wreckage from the WTC towers?" NIST replied:

> Under certain circumstances it is conceivable for some of the steel in the wreckage to have melted after the buildings collapsed. Any molten steel in the wreckage was more likely due to the high temperature resulting from long exposure to combustion within the pile than to short exposure to fires or explosions while the buildings were standing.[29]

But there are two problems with this response.

One problem is that this response is simply incredible. Structural steel does not begin to melt, as we saw, until it reaches almost 1,500°C (2,732°F). For a fire to heat steel up to that temperature, it would obviously have to be at least that hot. But a diffuse hydrocarbon fire, even if oxygen is abundant, could never get much above 1,000°C (1,832°F). NIST's answer, therefore, implausibly suggested that combustion in an oxygen-starved pile of rubbish could produce temperatures 500°C (almost 900°F) hotter than the world's hottest forest fire.

A second problem with this answer by NIST is that, as Steven Jones has pointed out, it is a purely speculative—that is, unscientific—answer. In the experimental sciences, a claim, to count as a scientific claim, must be supported either by experimental evidence or historical precedent. Jones wrote:

> It would be interesting if underground fires could somehow produce molten steel, but then there should be historical examples of this effect, since there have been many large fires in numerous buildings. But no such examples have been found. It is not enough to argue hypothetically that fires could possibly cause all three pools of molten metal. One needs at least one previous example.[30]

NIST also could have carried out an experiment to find out whether steel could melt in such an environment. But it provides no evidence of having done so.

NIST's third response to the molten metal was to declare that, even if it existed, it was irrelevant. NIST wrote:

> The condition of the steel in the wreckage of the WTC towers (i.e., whether it was in a molten state or not) was irrelevant to the investigation of the collapse since it does not provide any conclusive information on the condition of the steel when the WTC towers were standing.[31]

This answer, which NIST presumably meant to apply to WTC 7 as well the Twin Towers, is absurd. If molten steel—or molten iron, a byproduct produced when steel is melted by certain substances, such as thermite—was present in the rubble, it *does* provide some information on the condition of the steel when the buildings were still standing. It indicates that during the final moments of the buildings, some of their steel was melted.

As emphasized in Chapter 2, a purported explanation of some event cannot be considered adequate unless it takes into account all of the evidence related to that event. Philosopher of science James Fetzer, responding to NIST's claim that the molten metal was irrelevant to understanding the collapse, has written:

> The presence of molten metal… three, four, and five weeks later cannot be "irrelevant" to the NIST explanation of the "collapse," since it was an effect of that event. If the NIST cannot explain it, then the NIST's account is incomplete and fails to satisfy a fundamental requirement of scientific reasoning, known as the requirement of total evidence, which states scientific reasoning must be based upon all of the available relevant evidence.[32]

NIST's failure to do justice to the squibs, the blown-out windows, and the pools of molten metal would, by themselves, make its theory inadequate. But there are still more things that NIST ignores.

3. SCIENTIFIC REPORTS INDICATING EXTREMELY HIGH TEMPERATURES

Three studies, which were surely known to the scientists at NIST, reported phenomena in the Ground Zero debris that could have been created only by extremely high temperatures.

The RJ Lee Report

In May 2004, the RJ Lee Group issued a report entitled "WTC Dust Signature" at the request of the Deutsche Bank, which had occupied the building at 130 Liberty Street, across from the South Tower. The occasion for this request by Deutsche Bank was its insurer's claim that most of the dust in the building was "either innocuous or, to the extent that it contained contamination, resulted from a pre-existing condition." The purpose of the RJ Lee study was to prove that the building was "pervasively contaminated with WTC Dust, unique to the WTC Event."[33] This study was not, therefore, aimed at determining the cause of the collapses. But it did report findings that bear on this question.

The RJ Lee report of May 2004 represented, incidentally, a revision of an earlier report, entitled "WTC Dust Signature Study: Composition and Morphology," dated December 2003.[34] Why the report was revised is not made clear, but there are some interesting differences between the two versions.

In order to prove the Deutsche Bank's contamination claim, the RJ Lee Group argued in its final report that the dust in the building had characteristics that resulted from "the collapse of the WTC Towers and the subsequent fires at the WTC site which collectively were unique events that produced unique dust." In a statement that explained its title, the RJ Lee report added: "The unique characteristics of this dust are collectively referred to as the WTC Dust Signature," which "differentiate[s] it from other building dust."[35]

The report then listed five main elements in this signature, one of which was: "Spherical iron and spherical or vesicular silicate particles that result from exposure to high temperature."[36] This statement, which implies (without explicitly stating) that iron had melted, is the only statement about the modification of iron by high temperature in the final version of the RJ Lee report.

The earlier version, by contrast, had contained much more about iron. It said: "Particles of materials that had been modified by exposure to high temperature, such as spherical particles of iron and silicates, are common in WTC Dust... but are not common in 'normal' interior office dust."[37] This 2003 version of the report even pointed out that, whereas iron particles constitute only 0.04 percent of normal building dust, they constituted (a whopping) 5.87 percent of WTC dust. This earlier version also explicitly stated that iron and other metals were "melted during the WTC Event, producing spherical metallic particles."[38]

The word "melt" was completely absent, by contrast, from the 2004 version. Only scientifically informed readers would realize that the existence of spherical iron particles implied that iron had melted. Nevertheless, the final version of the RJ Lee report did indicate that the dust contained spherical iron and silicate particles, which had been produced by "high temperatures."

What caused these high temperatures? Making no suggestion that these high-temperature effects had been produced by explosives, the RJ Lee report instead said: "[T]he heat affected particles result from the fires that ensued following the WTC Event."[39] (The earlier report had similarly attributed the particles to "the fire that accompanied the WTC Event."[40])

This explanation, however, does not work. The existence of "spherical iron particles" means—as the 2003 report had explicitly stated—that iron had been melted. Iron does not melt until it reaches 1,538°C (2,800°F),[41] and the building fires, as we saw earlier, could not have heated iron anywhere close to that temperature.

The RJ Lee report, moreover, suggested that some substances must have been heated to still higher temperatures. Lead must have become hot enough to volatilize (boil) and hence to vaporize:

> The presence of lead oxide on the surface of mineral wool indicate [sic] the existence of extremely high temperatures during the collapse which caused metallic lead to volatilize, oxidize, and finally condense on the surface of the mineral wool.[42]

Although the word "vaporize" was never used in the final version of the RJ Lee report, the 2003 version of this passage explicitly referred to temperatures "at which lead would have undergone vaporization."[43] For lead to boil and hence vaporize, it must be heated to 1,749°C (3,180°F).[44] As the report indicates, therefore, the temperatures must have been not merely high but *extremely* high.[45]

The purpose of the RJ Lee report, as stated before, was simply to prove that the Deutsche Bank building had been pervasively contaminated by dust from the destruction of the World Trade Center. For this purpose, the report merely needed to show that the dust in this building had a distinctive signature that identified it as WTC dust. There was no need for the report to explain the origin of all the ingredients in this signature. Insofar as the report did, nevertheless, suggest that all of the effects requiring high temperatures were caused by fire, it was inadequate, because phenomena such as melted iron and vaporized lead could not have been produced by fire.

In spite of this defect, however, the report was commendable from a scientific point of view, precisely because it reported phenomena that it was unable to explain.

NIST's treatment was not equally commendable. It dealt with the RJ Lee report's revelation—that certain ingredients in the WTC dust had been produced by extremely high temperatures—by simply ignoring it. From reading NIST's reports on the Twin Towers and WTC 7, one would never know about the remarkable findings of the RJ Lee Group's extensive study of the WTC dust.

The USGS Report

Another major report, "Particle Atlas of World Trade Center Dust," came out in 2005. Written by Heather Lowers and Gregory Meeker on behalf of the United States Geological Survey (USGS), it was intended to aid the "identification of WTC dust components."

For our present purposes, the most significant feature of this report was its statement that the WTC dust signature included "trace to minor amounts" of "metal or metal oxides" (which its methods could not clearly distinguish). It said, in particular: "The primary metal and metal-oxide phases in WTC dust are Fe-rich [iron-rich] and Zn-rich [zinc-rich] particles."[46] One must, however, wonder at its suggestion that there were at most "minor" amounts of iron-rich particles, given the statement by the 2003 version of the RJ Lee report that these particles constituted almost 6.0 percent of the WTC dust.

In any case, the existence of the iron-rich particles was even emphasized by the inclusion of micrographs for two of them, one of which was labeled "iron-rich sphere."[47]

How do these iron-rich spherical particles or "spherules," as they are sometimes called, come about? As indicated earlier, iron must be melted and then—as explained by Steven Jones and several coauthors in an article to be discussed below—"sprayed into the air so that surface tension draws the molten droplets into near-spherical shapes."[48]

This means that the USGS's report mentions the existence of particles in the dust that should not have been there, given the official explanation of the collapses (according to which they were produced by a combination of airplane impacts, fire, and gravitation, without the aid of explosives). And yet the USGS report, like the RJ Lee report, provides no explanation as to how those iron-rich spheres could have been created. But at least the USGS report, like the RJ Lee report, did mention these phenomena.

By contrast, just as NIST did not mention the RJ Lee report's findings, it also did not mention those of the USGS report, even though this report had been produced by another agency of the federal government (the USGS is an agency of the US Department of the Interior). NIST thereby avoided the need to explain how these iron-rich particles could have been created without explosives to produce the requisite temperature.

The failure of the NIST scientists to mention these iron-rich particles, it should be emphasized, was not based on ignorance of them. It was a simple refusal to mention them—a refusal that could be defended only by a pretense not to understand a basic principle of scientific method. After the release of NIST's Draft report on WTC 7 in August 2008, a member of the 9/11 truth movement asked NIST about the iron-rich spheres. NIST replied with one sentence: "The NIST investigative team has not seen a coherent and credible hypothesis for how iron-rich spheres could be related to the collapse of WTC 7."[49] In giving this answer, the NIST scientists pretended not to understand that the scientific method works the other way around. Scientists cannot legitimately refuse to mention some phenomenon until they have found a "coherent and credible hypothesis" to account for it (and certainly not until they have found a politically acceptable hypothesis). The empirical dimension of scientific methodology demands that empirical data be reported, whether or not a hypothesis is currently on hand to explain them. To refuse to report the data is to commit scientific fraud.

The Report by the Steven Jones Group

NIST also ignored a third scientific report describing phenomena in the WTC dust that could have been produced only by extremely high temperatures. Entitled, in fact, "Extremely High Temperatures during the World Trade Center Destruction," this report, published by Steven Jones and seven other scientists early in 2008, pointed out the existence of particles in the dust that required even higher temperatures than those implied by the reports of the RJ Lee Group and the USGS.

Using their own samples of WTC dust, which had been collected on or shortly after 9/11—either right after the collapse of the WTC buildings or inside some buildings near the WTC site—which means that the dust could not have been contaminated by clean-up operations at Ground Zero—Jones and his colleagues ran their own tests. They reported finding "an abundance of tiny solidified droplets roughly spherical in shape (spherules)," which were primarily "iron-rich... and silicates." As stated earlier, the formation of the iron-rich spherules would have required a temperature of 1,538°C (2,800°F). Silicates are compounds of silicon, oxygen, and a metal, which is often aluminum. The formation of aluminosilicate spherules, which were found in abundance, would have required a temperature of 1,450°C (2,652°F).[50]

The most remarkable feature of this study, however, was its discussion of another type of spherule reportedly found in the dust. Having used a FOIA request to obtain data from the USGS that was not mentioned in its "Particle Atlas of the World Trade Center Dust," Jones and his coauthors learned that "the USGS team had observed and studied a molybdenum-rich spherule." This fact is of special significance because molybdenum (Mo) is "known for its extremely high melting point," which is 2,623°C (4,753°F).[51]

Noting that the data about this molybdenum-rich spherule "were not previously released in the public USGS reports," Jones and his coauthors pointed out that this silence was evidently not due to lack of interest, because the number of images and graphs about this spherule in the unpublished material obtained by the FOIA request shows that "considerable study was performed on this Mo-rich spherule." They added: "No explanation of the high temperature needed to form the observed Mo-rich spherule is given in the USGS material (either published or obtained by FOIA action)."[52]

The material obtained through the FOIA request also contained no explanation as to why the USGS's published report did not mention the molybdenum. One might suspect that it was precisely because it is "known for its extremely high melting point." In any case, whatever be the explanation for this silence, the point at hand is that the molybdenum was also not mentioned by NIST, even though it could have obtained the information about its presence in the WTC dust from the article by the Jones group or directly from the USGS.

To summarize: Although NIST claimed that it knew of no evidence that explosives had been used, it ignored evidence, provided by three different sets of scientists, showing that the WTC dust contained particles that could have been created only by extremely high temperatures—temperatures that could not have been produced by fire.

4. THE "DEEPEST MYSTERY": THINNING AND SULFIDATION OF STEEL

NIST also ignored evidence of extremely high temperatures published by a fourth set of scientists. Although the discussion of this report could have been included in the previous section, it is discussed separately for two reasons: first, this report introduces a new factor, the sulfidation of metal; and second, this report was published as an appendix to FEMA's WTC report, which was the predecessor to NIST's reports.

The New York Times on the "Deepest Mystery"

In light of Shyam Sunder's announcement that NIST had solved the mystery of the collapse of WTC 7, we would assume that its report would, at least, have explained a phenomenon that had been called the *deepest* mystery associated with this collapse. But it did not.

In a *New York Times* story published in February 2002, James Glanz and Eric Lipton wrote:

> Perhaps the deepest mystery uncovered in the investigation involves extremely thin bits of steel collected... from 7 World Trade Center.... The steel apparently melted away, but no fire in any of the buildings was believed to be hot enough to melt steel outright.

Glanz and Lipton's final sentence states the mystery: Although fire could not have melted steel, steel had melted. In suggesting a possible solution, Glanz and Lipton wrote:

A preliminary analysis of the steel at Worcester Polytechnic Institute using electron microscopes suggests that sulfur released during the fires—no one knows from where—may have combined with atoms in the steel to form compounds that melt at lower temperatures.[53]

As their statement mentions, sulfur can greatly lower the temperature at which structural steel will melt, as Steven Jones points out.[54]

Far from providing a possible solution, however, this information simply deepened the mystery, for three reasons. First, NIST itself does not claim, as we saw earlier, that any of the steel in WTC 7 was heated even to 700°C, let alone to 1,000°C. So the fact that sulfur can lower steel's melting point to about 1,000°C does not explain why some of the building's steel had melted, if the official explanation, according to which fire brought the building down, is presupposed. Second, as Glanz and Lipton indicate, as long as that explanation is presupposed, the presence of the sulfur constitutes a second mystery. Third, even if the presence of sulfur could be explained, there would still be the mystery of how some of it, as they reported, "combined with atoms in the steel," because that could happen only at extremely high temperatures.

The WPI Report

In mentioning Worcester Polytechnic Institute (WPI), Glanz and Lipton were alluding to the fact that three professors involved in that school's Fire Protection Engineering program—Jonathan Barnett, Ronald R. Biederman, and Richard D. Sisson, Jr.—had analyzed a section of steel from WTC 7 (as well as a section from one of the Twin Towers).[55] Their discoveries were then reported in an article by Joan Killough-Miller entitled "The 'Deep Mystery' of Melted Steel," which appeared in a WPI publication.[56]

This article brought out the implications of the professors' analysis even more fully than did the *New York Times* story. In a statement that is especially significant in light of NIST's conclusion that WTC 7 was caused to collapse by "an ordinary building contents fire,"[57] this article said:

[S]teel—which has a melting point of 2,800 degrees Fahrenheit—may weaken and bend, but does not melt during an ordinary office fire. Yet metallurgical studies on WTC steel brought back to WPI reveal that a novel phenomenon—called a eutectic reaction—occurred at the surface, causing intergranular melting capable of turning a solid steel girder into Swiss cheese.... The New York Times called these findings "perhaps the deepest mystery uncovered in the investigation." The significance of the work on a sample from Building 7 and a structural column from one of the twin towers becomes apparent only when one sees these heavy chunks of damaged metal. A one-inch column has been reduced to half-inch thickness. Its edges—which are curled like a paper scroll—have been thinned to almost razor sharpness. Gaping holes—some larger than a silver dollar—let light shine through a formerly solid steel flange. This Swiss cheese appearance shocked all of the fire-wise professors, who expected to see distortion and bending—but not holes.[58]

As this statement makes clear, the startling discovery was that something had melted the steel so as to reduce its thickness and even produce holes in it. The WPI professors, therefore, had pointed to another phenomenon indicating that effects had been produced in WTC 7 that could not have been produced by "an ordinary building contents fire."

Statements about Vaporized Steel Attributed to Professors Barnett and Astaneh-Asl

In an article that appeared in November 2001, Glanz reported that one of the WPI professors, Jonathan Barnett, said that fire "would not explain steel members in the debris pile that appear to have been partly evaporated in extraordinarily high temperatures."[59] If Glanz (who himself has a Ph.D. in physics) was correctly reporting Barnett's statement, so that Barnett had said that some steel had *evaporated*, then we would be talking about very high temperatures indeed, because the normal boiling point of structural steel—apart from a reaction involving sulfur—is roughly the same as that of iron, namely 2,861°C (5,182°F).

The claim that some steel had evaporated was also attributed to Abolhassan Astaneh-Asl, a professor of civil engineering at the University of California at Berkeley. Immediately after 9/11, he received a National Science Foundation grant to spend two weeks at Ground Zero studying steel from the buildings. One of his discoveries involved a horizontal I-beam from WTC 7. According to a *New York Times* story by Kenneth Change, Astaneh-Asl reported that "[p]arts of the flat top of the I, once five-eighths of an inch thick, had vaporized."[60]

If both of these professors meant that steel had literally evaporated or vaporized, then they were both implying that some steel in WTC 7 had reached its boiling point, which is a temperature—2,861°C (5,182°F)—even higher than that needed to melt molybdenum. But even if the words "evaporated" and "vaporized" were used loosely, to mean only that the melting had caused some of the steel to disappear from view, these professors were reporting phenomena that NIST's fire theory could not come close to explaining.

The Barnett–Biederman–Sisson Appendix to the FEMA Report

Barnett and the other two WPI professors reported their discoveries in an essay entitled "Limited Metallurgical Examination," which was included as an appendix to FEMA's report on the WTC buildings.[61]

Two Mysteries: In the summary of their analysis of a piece of steel from WTC 7, Barnett, Biederman, and Sisson made the following statement:

1. The thinning of the steel occurred by a high-temperature corrosion due to a combination of oxidation and sulfidation.

2. Heating of the steel into a hot corrosive environment approaching 1,000°C (1,832°F) results in the formation of a eutectic mixture of iron, oxygen, and sulfur that liquefied the steel.

3. The sulfidation attack of steel grain boundaries accelerated the corrosion and erosion of the steel.

Having mentioned sulfidation in each of these three points, they then, under the heading "Suggestions for Further Research," added: "The severe corrosion and subsequent erosion of Samples 1 and 2 are a very unusual event. No clear explanation for the source of the sulfur has been identified."[62]

NIST, as we will see later, said that it did not bother to test for sulfur because its presence in the debris would mean nothing, as it could be explained by the fact that the wallboard of the WTC buildings was made of gypsum, which is calcium sulfate.

What the WPI professors reported, however, was not merely that there was sulfur in the debris. They reported that the steel had been *sulfidized,* which means that sulfur had entered into the *intergranular structure* of the steel (which Glanz and Lipton had indicated by saying that sulfur had "combined with atoms in the steel"). As chemist Kevin Ryan has said, the question NIST would need to answer is: "[H]ow did sulfates, from wallboard, tunnel into the intergranular microstructure of the steel and then form sulfides within?"[63] Physicist Steven Jones has added:

> [I]f NIST claims that sulfur is present in the steel from gypsum, they should do an (easy) experiment to heat steel to about 1000°C in the presence of gypsum and then test whether sulfur has entered the steel... [I]f they actually do scientific experiments like this, they will find that sulfur does not enter steel under such circumstances.[64]

Once again, Jones pointed out that NIST, which claims that its conclusions are based on good science, should not have answered crucial questions by merely offering speculative hypotheses. Insofar as a hypothesis suggested by NIST was amenable to empirical testing, NIST needed, in order to claim the mantle of science, to perform the test.

Jones stated, moreover, that if NIST *had* performed the test, the result would have been negative. Niels Harrit, a chemist at the University of Copenhagen, has explained why this can be known in advance: Although gypsum contains sulfur, this is not elemental sulfur, which can react, but sulfur in the form of calcium sulfate, which cannot.[65]

We have seen, in any case, that the WPI professors were puzzled by two mysteries: the source of the sulfur in the steel and the intergranular melting caused by a "eutectic" reaction.[66]

The Thermate Solution: There is a well-known possible answer for both mysteries, namely, *thermate*, which results when (elemental) sulfur is added to thermite. Steven Jones has written:

> The thermate reaction proceeds rapidly and is in general faster than basic thermite in cutting through steel due to the presence of sulfur. (Elemental sulfur forms a low-melting-temperature eutectic with iron.)[67]

Besides providing an explanation for the eutectic reaction, thermate can also, Jones pointed out, explain the melting, oxidation, and sulfidation of the steel studied by the WPI professors:

> When you put sulfur into thermite it makes the steel melt at a much lower temperature, so instead of melting at about 1,538°C [2,800°F]

it melts at approximately 988°C [1,820°F], and you get sulfidation and oxidation in the attacked steel.[68]

Although the WPI professors did not mention this possible explanation of the phenomena they reported, they did speak of the possibility that the corrosion and erosion "started prior to collapse and accelerated the weakening of the steel structure." In light of that possibility, moreover, they concluded: "A detailed study into the mechanisms of this phenomenon is needed."[69]

NIST's Response to the FEMA Appendix

Given the presence of this statement in an appendix to FEMA's WTC report, which came out in 2002, we would assume that NIST would have studied this phenomenon. This is especially the case in light of the fact that Arden Bement, who was the director of NIST when it took on the WTC project, said that NIST's projected report would address "all major recommendations contained in the [FEMA] report."[70]

That, however, would not be the case. NIST's report on WTC 7—like its earlier report on the Twin Towers—did not even mention the discovery of the three WPI professors, which had been reported in the appendix to the FEMA report and elsewhere. It ignored, therefore, what the *New York Times* had called "perhaps the deepest mystery uncovered in the investigation."

In spite of this fact, Shyam Sunder, as we saw, declared that NIST had solved the mystery of the collapse of WTC 7.

NIST had said in its 2005 preliminary report on this building that it had "seen no evidence that the collapse of WTC 7 was caused by bombs or... controlled demolition."[71] In its final report, it says: "NIST found no evidence of a blast or controlled demolition event."[72] In an alternative formulation, which evidently used "blast event" for any kind of explosion occurring as part of a controlled demolition, NIST said that it "found no evidence whose explanation required invocation of a blast event."[73]

The authors of the NIST report, however, clearly knew about the thinned and sulfidized steel reported in the FEMA report's appendix. They also surely knew about the report by Professor Astaneh-Asl, which had been discussed in a *New York Times* story.[74] They also knew, on the one hand, that fire could not have produced these phenomena and, on the other hand, that thermate, which is thermite to which sulfur has been added, *could* produce them. As Kevin Ryan has pointed out: "The thermite reaction, available in several useful variations for the purposes of cutting steel, can explain this thinning and sulfidation quite readily."[75] The NIST authors knew, therefore, that these phenomena provided *prima facie* evidence that explosives or steel-cutting incendiaries with sulfur, perhaps thermate, had gone off in WTC 7.

It would seem, therefore, that a more candid statement by these authors would have been: *NIST, being an agency of the Bush–Cheney administration's Commerce Department, could not report any evidence whose explanation required invocation of a "controlled demolition event."* But these NIST authors were clearly not being paid to be candid.

NIST's Denial of Recovered WTC 7 Steel: Besides ignoring the startling discoveries of Professor Astaneh-Asl and the three WPI professors, NIST's reports even claimed that no recovered steel from WTC 7 existed to be studied. Its "Questions and Answers" document of August 2008 included the following question: "Why didn't the investigators look at actual steel samples from WTC 7?" In its answer, NIST wrote:

> Steel samples were removed from the site before the NIST investigation began. In the immediate aftermath of Sept. 11, debris was removed rapidly from the site to aid in recovery efforts and facilitate emergency responders' efforts to work around the site. Once it was removed from the scene, the steel from WTC 7 could not be clearly identified. Unlike the pieces of steel from WTC 1 and WTC 2, which were painted red and contained distinguishing markings, WTC 7 steel did not contain such identifying characteristics.[76]

This statement was clearly intended to give the impression that no steel from WTC 7 had been recovered. NIST had even made this claim explicitly in a 2005 report.[77] In light of the experiments on pieces of WTC 7 steel reported by the four professors, how could we avoid concluding that this statement was simply a lie?

The falsity of NIST's claim was pointed out by a critic in one of the "Comments" posted at NIST's website in response to its Draft for Public Comment, issued in August 2008. Referring to NIST's 2005 report stating that no steel from WTC 7 was recovered, this critic, using the pseudonym "Skeptosis," wrote:

NIST seems to have made no effort to obtain or examine existing steel samples (such as the heavily corroded beam featured in FEMA 403, Appendix C) known to have come from WTC 7, choosing instead to estimate the properties of the steel "completely from the literature."

Being required by NIST's protocol to explain the reason for his comment and to provide a suggested revision of the passage, Skeptosis added these statements:

Reason for Comment: Surely the theoretical steel described in the literature would not show any signs of sulfidation and erosion (as were found on the actual steel recovered from WTC 7), ensuring that NIST would not be required to investigate or identify the cause of this bizarre phenomenon.

Suggestion for Revision: "While steel from WTC 7 was, in fact, recovered, NIST made no efforts to obtain or examine this steel. Despite the failures of previous examinations to determine the cause of the sulfidation and erosion of steel samples from WTC 7, NIST felt that an investigation into the potential causes of this deterioration could threaten the Institute's ability to arrive at a conclusion that would not implicate domestic saboteurs."[78]

Whether this letter made the NIST authors smile, I do not know. But it did not, in any case, lead them to revise their report.

Sunder's Oral Acknowledgment of the Sulfidized Steel: NIST's defenders cannot, incidentally, suggest that NIST may have failed to mention the sulfidized steel simply because it did not know about it. Besides the fact that this steel was mentioned in the appendix to the FEMA report on WTC 7, Shyam Sunder himself mentioned it during a "technical briefing" on WTC 7 that he gave on August 26, 2008, shortly after the release of NIST's Draft for Public Comment. In response to a question by attorney James Gourley as to whether NIST had tested "any WTC 7 debris for explosive or incendiary chemical residues," Sunder said:

With regard to the issue of the residue, there is reference often made to a piece of steel from Building 7 that is documented in the earlier FEMA report that deals with some kind of a residue that was found, sulfur-oriented residue. And in fact that was found by a professor who was then at the Worcester Polytechnic Institute, Professor Jonathan Barnett. But that piece of steel has been subsequently analyzed by Professor Barnett and by Professor Rick Sisson, who is also from the Worcester Polytechnic Institute, and they reported in a BBC interview that aired on July 6 [2008][79] that there was no evidence that any of the residue in that… piece of steel had any relationship to an undue fire event in the building or any other kind of incendiary device in the building.[80]

This response raises five questions.

First, it reveals that NIST's lead investigator knew about this "piece of steel from Building 7," and yet NIST, besides not mentioning it in its Draft for Public Comment, which was released five days before this technical briefing, also did not mention it in its Final Report, which was issued three months later.

Second, NIST continued to claim in its public documents that no steel from WTC 7 had been recovered: In an updated version of its "Questions and Answers" document about WTC 7, which appeared in December 2008, NIST repeated the statement quoted above from the first version of this document, in which it had claimed that "the steel from WTC 7 could not be clearly identified"—even though this was almost four months after Sunder's acknowledgment that he knew about at least one piece of steel recovered from WTC 7.[81] There can be no doubt, therefore, that NIST was guilty of scientific fraud by deliberately failing to report, and even denying the existence of, evidence that contradicted its theory.

Third, Sunder acknowledged knowing about this piece of steel only after two of the professors who had reported it—Jonathan Barnett and Richard Sisson—had stated on a BBC program about WTC 7 (to be discussed in the next chapter) that, in Sunder's paraphrase, "there was no evidence that any of the residue in that… piece of steel had any relationship to an undue fire event in the building or any other kind of incendiary device in the building." Why had he not acknowledged it earlier, before he had a statement from them that could be used to suggest—even if deceptively—that it no longer posed a threat to NIST's theory? This is not how science is supposed to operate.

Fourth, the Barnett–Sisson–Sunder statement did not really lessen the threat to the official story posed by this piece of steel, which had been melted, oxidized, and sulfidized—processes that would take extremely high temperatures. If these changes in the steel were not caused by fire (as everyone agrees) or some kind of "incendiary device" (such as one made of thermate) or by an explosive, then how were they brought about? Neither Barnett, Sisson, nor Sunder answered this question. For people who accept the official account of the destruction of the World Trade Center, this melted, oxidized, and sulfidized piece of steel still remains a deep mystery.

Fifth, given the fact that this piece of steel had been publicly acknowledged as a deep mystery, it clearly demanded a thorough investigation and discussion. And yet NIST's only public treatment of it consisted of Sunder's paraphrase of a statement made on a television show. If this is how the present staff at NIST believes that science should be done, then it would seem that a thorough housecleaning (among other things) is in order, if President Obama's commitment to good science is to be fulfilled.

5. HEAT AND UNUSUAL EMISSIONS AT GROUND ZERO

Two more features of the Ground Zero rubble pile pointed to the use of explosives: (1) long-lasting heat, produced by inextinguishable fires, and (2) periodic emissions of unexpected substances.

Long-Lasting Heat, Inextinguishable Fires

Engineer Roger Fulmer was at Ground Zero from the middle of October until the middle of November 2001, as part of the Sacramento Debris Removal Team of the US Army Corps of Engineers. He gave the following account of the temperature of the debris pile during the first two months after 9/11:

> Temperatures in the pile were over 1,200°F [649°C]. Every time an area was opened, fire started in any buried combustible debris. Water trucks and fire engines were used continually. The high temperature debris and water created steam.... The dust and other hazardous materials from the debris required sprayers to be set up to wash all trucks exiting the site. These sprayers were also used to cool the high temperature debris before it left the site. Several trucks were returned to the site for additional cooling because the law enforcement officers would not let them through the tunnels leaving Manhattan until they stopped steaming.[82]

The fact that Ground Zero remained hot for several months after 9/11 was widely reported. A *New Scientist* article in December (2001) was titled "Ground Zero's Fires Still Burning."[83] Then in January (2002), Herb Trimpe, an Episcopal deacon who served as a chaplain at Ground Zero, wrote: "On the cold days, even in January, there was a noticeable difference between the temperature in the middle of the site [and that] two blocks over on Broadway. You could actually feel the heat."[84] According to Greg Fuchek—who was mentioned above as the vice president of a company that supplied computer equipment to identify human remains at the site—the working conditions were "hellish," partly because the ground temperature varied between 600° and 1,500°F (315° and 815°C) for six months.[85]

This heat existed because very hot fires continued to burn in the Ground Zero debris piles, even though heavy rains occurred, millions of additional gallons of water were sprayed onto the piles, and a chemical suppressant was pumped into them.[86] Why the fires could not be extinguished was a mystery.

Periodic Emissions of Unexpected Substances

The mystery of Ground Zero was increased by the fact that two separate projects to monitor the air after 9/11 discovered high levels of substances in the air that, given the official account of the destruction of the Twin Towers and WTC 7, should not have been there.

Thomas Cahill, a professor at the University of California at Davis, monitored the air about a mile from Ground Zero during the month of October 2001. Having discovered various coarse particles, Cahill declared: "These particles simply should not be there."[87] With regard to *fine* particles, he said: "We see very fine aerosols typical of combustion temperatures far higher than [expected in] the WTC collapse piles."[88] These very fine particles, some of which "were found at the highest levels ever recorded in air in the United States,"[89] contained high levels of sulfur and extremely high levels of silicon.[90]

Cahill also found high concentrations of various metals, including iron, titanium, vanadium, nickel, copper, and zinc.[91]

The other project to monitor the air was carried out over several months by the Environmental Protection Agency (EPA). It dealt extensively with a fact noted by Cahill: that the air contained high levels of rare organic compounds. By far the most prevalent of these was one that is called 1,3-diphenylpropane, abbreviated 1,3-DPP. The EPA had monitored countless building fires in which many toxic substances had been emitted. And yet, an EPA scientist stated, although the EPA had never previously reported finding 1,3-DPP in the air, this chemical was present in the air at Ground Zero during the first three weeks at levels that "dwarfed all others." The EPA's Erik Swartz said that "it was most likely produced by the plastic of tens of thousands of burning computers."[92] Experiments could surely be performed to see if that is an adequate explanation, but NIST did not report doing this.

Another fact that could be learned from the EPA monitoring was that violent fires occasionally flared up at Ground Zero long after all normal combustible materials would have been consumed. This fact was discovered from material released by the EPA in 2007 in response to a FOIA request instigated by chemist Kevin Ryan. This information was then made public in a paper published in the *Environmentalist*, on which the present section of this chapter is based, "Environmental Anomalies at the World Trade Center: Evidence for Energetic Materials," by Kevin Ryan, Steven Jones, and James Gourley (who is a chemical engineer as well as an attorney).

These scientists discovered, moreover, that the occasional flare-ups produced spikes in the release of several toxic substances classified as "volatile organic chemicals" (VOCs), including benzene, propylene, styrene, toluene, and ethylbenzene. Although the EPA's reports to the general public in 2002 mentioned these chemicals, it did not reveal the levels at which they had been detected, and they were, Ryan and his coauthors learned, "far above the levels published by EPA in their reports." Indeed, "these spikes in VOCs [were] at levels thousands of times higher than seen in other structure fires."[93] I repeat: *thousands of times higher.*

One of the most significant facts about the occasional spikes in the emissions of these volatile organic chemicals is that they continued long after the ordinary fuel sources at the site would have disappeared. Although most of the typical combustible materials were "largely burned off by mid to late October,... the most striking spike in toxic air emissions... occurred on 9-February, 2002," almost five months after 9/11.[94] There clearly had to be something in the debris that could remain volatile for several months.

Energetic Nanocomposites: A Possible Explanation

Accordingly, Ryan and his coauthors argued, these spikes "point not to other sources of typical combustible materials but to other forms of combustion," namely, to "chemical energetic materials, which *provide their own fuel and oxidant and are not deterred by water, dust or chemical suppressants.*"[95] Fires fed by these energetic materials could not, therefore, be extinguished until these materials had exhausted their reactivity.

Ryan and his colleagues suggested that these materials were "energetic nanocomposites," such as "nanothermites," sometimes called "superthermites." An exploration of this suggestion requires a brief discussion of nanotechnology.

Nanotechnology is based on "nanoenergetics," which is research into ways to "manipulate the flow of energy… between molecules."[96] The nanoworld, with which nanotechnology works, deals with things that are very small—only slightly larger than ordinary molecules. This means that nanotechnology deals with particles between 10 and 100 nanometers in size, and a nanometer is only one millionth of a millimeter.

The significance of the tiny size of these particles follows from the fact that, the smaller something is, the larger is its surface area relative to its volume. (For example, a mouse has a much greater surface area relative to its volume than does an elephant.) This means that, compared to a larger particle, a nanoparticle has a larger percentage of its atoms on its surface, which in turn means that its atoms can react with other atoms much more rapidly.[97]

An essential part of nanotechnology is the creation of nanometals, such as ultra-fine-grain aluminum (nanoaluminum).

Nanometals can then be used to create nanocomposites, one type of which is nanothermite (superthermite), which is a collective name—there are many forms of nanothermite. A nanothermite is a composite of a nanometal, which is usually nanoaluminum, with an ultra-fine-grain metal oxide, commonly iron oxide (rust). By contrast, ordinary thermite—now sometimes called macrothermite—combines a standard metal oxide with standard aluminum.

Because of the presence of aluminum in all (or at least virtually all) forms of thermite, they are often called "aluminothermic" mixtures.

Compared with ordinary thermite, nanothermite (superthermite) releases "greater amounts of energy much more rapidly." In fact, "Superthermites can increase the (chemical) reaction time by a thousand times." An article in *Technology Review*, from which these quotations were taken, explained why this is the case, employing the previously mentioned point about the surface area:

> Nanoaluminum is more chemically reactive because there are more atoms on the surface area than standard aluminum. ... Standard aluminum covers just one-tenth of one percent of the surface area (with atoms), versus fifty percent for nanoaluminum.[98]

Because of the very high rate of energy release, which is made possible by the high surface area of the reactants, nanothermite explosives are classified as *high explosives*.[99] The difference has been explained by Jim Hoffman thus:

> The reaction rate... determines the destructive character of the material. Whereas a cup of conventional thermite will melt a hole clear through a car's engine block, the same quantity of nano-thermite will blow the car apart.[100]

Whereas the enormous explosive power of nanothermites is one reason to suspect that they were used in the destruction of the Twin Towers and WTC 7, understanding how they could account for the chemical emissions at Ground Zero requires that we look at their chemical composition.

Although the most common type of nanothermite uses ultra-fine iron oxide (along with nanoaluminum), the oxidizer can be formed from many other metals, such as barium, copper, molybdenum, nickel, potassium, titanium, vanadium, or zinc. One type of nanothermite, for example, mixes nanoaluminum with copper oxide, another with molybdenum oxide, another with barium nitrate, still another with potassium permanganate.[101]

Two more essential factors about nanothermites involve the way in which the ingredients are mixed and how the resulting mixture is stored. Kevin Ryan, with reference to a 2000 article entitled "Nanoscale Chemistry Yields Better Explosives,"[102] explained:

> The mixing is accomplished by adding these reactants to a liquid solution where they form what are called "sols," and then adding a gelling agent that captures these tiny reactive combinations in their

intimately mixed state. The resulting "sol-gel" is then dried to form a porous reactive material that can be ignited in a number of ways.

Silicon compounds, Ryan added, are often used to create the porous structural framework.[103]

With regard to the question of how sol-gel nanothermites could have been used to cut the steel columns of the World Trade Center buildings, Ryan quoted a 2002 article entitled "Energetic Nanocomposites with Sol-gel Chemistry," which says:

> The sol-gel process is very amenable to... spray-coating technologies to coat surfaces. ... The energetic coating dries to give a nice adherent film. Preliminary experiments indicate that films of the hybrid material are self-propagating when ignited by thermal stimulus.[104]

One or more types of sol-gel nanothermite could, in other words, have been sprayed onto the steel.

Elsewhere, Ryan has suggested that "spray-on nano-thermite materials may have been applied to the steel components of the WTC buildings, underneath the upgraded fireproofing."[105] The fact that the steel was coated with explosive material would not, therefore, have been detectable by WTC employees.

Ryan supported this suggestion with the fact that there was "a remarkable correlation between the floors upgraded for fireproofing in the WTC towers, in the years preceding 9/11/01, and the floors of impact, fire and failure." This correlation is important, Ryan pointed out, because the "fireproofing upgrades would have allowed for shutdown of the affected floors, and the exposure of the floor assemblies and the columns for a significant period of time."[106] In this way, all the explosive material could have been added beyond the view of ordinary WTC employees.

I turn now to the ways in which Ryan, Gourley, and Jones suggested that their hypothesis—that the buildings were brought down by the use of thermitic materials, involving both thermate and nano-thermite—can also explain the long-lasting fires and chemical emissions at Ground Zero.

Because nanothermites (superthermites) provide not only their own fuel but also their own oxidant, as stated earlier, they can burn underground and "are not deterred by water, dust or chemical suppressants."[107] They could, therefore, account for the long-lasting fires in the rubble.

The occasional spikes in the emissions of volatile organic chemicals (VOCs), usually lasting only "one day or less," can also be explained by the hypothesis that nanothermite was employed to bring the buildings down:

> If energetic nanocomposite materials, buried within the pile at GZ [Ground Zero], were somehow ignited on specific dates..., violent, short-lived and possibly explosive fires would result. Such fires would have quickly consumed all combustible materials nearby. The combustible materials available, after a month or two of smoldering fires in the pile, might have been more likely to be those that were less likely to have burned completely on earlier dates, like plastics. Later combustion of such plastic materials, in violent but short-lived fires, could explain the spikes in VOCs seen on those dates.[108]

The spikes in benzene, 1,3-DPP, and other organic chemicals could perhaps have been produced in this way.

The extreme level of 1,3-DPP might also be partly explainable by the fact that "[t]he synthesis of novel nanostructured materials has involved the use of 1,3-DPP to functionalize mesoporous silicas through control of pore size."[109] Then, after the 1,3-DPP was released from the nanothermite's silica microstructure, it would in turn have broken down into some of the other chemicals found at unusually high levels, including styrene, toluene, and benzene.[110]

Some of the chemicals could also have come from the nanothermite materials. For example, high levels of silicon would follow from the use of silica in the liquid used to mix the nanoaluminum with an oxidant to create the "sol," and high levels of sulfur can be explained by the addition of sulfur to thermite mixtures to create thermates.[111]

Furthermore, the various metals found in the dust in surprisingly high concentrations can also be explained by this hypothesis. Take, for example, the extremely high percentage of iron-rich particles in the WTC dust, said by the 2003 RJ Lee report to constitute 5.87 percent of the dust—which, as Jones and his coauthors emphasized, is "nearly 150 times" the amount found in ordinary office building dust.[112] This extremely high concentration of iron-rich particles can be explained by the aforementioned fact that iron oxide is the most commonly used oxidant in nanothermites. Also, the unusually high concentrations of barium, copper, molybdenum, nickel, titanium, vanadium, and zinc, which were found by the RJ Lee, Cahill, and/or USGS studies, can be explained by the fact that oxidants based on these metals are sometimes used in the production of nanothermites.

Finally, still another phenomenon supporting the hypothesis proposed by Ryan, Gourley, and Jones was the simultaneous spiking of emissions of chemicals commonly used in aluminothermic mixtures. For example, the EPA data showed that the top nine days for iron emissions were also the top nine days for aluminum emissions—which is precisely what would be expected if nanothermite composed of aluminum and iron oxide had been used to demolish the buildings.

Eight of those same days, moreover, were also the top days for emissions of barium, another common ingredient in thermitic materials.[113]

The unusual amount of barium in the WTC dust, incidentally, might provide a clue as to the provider of at least some of the thermitic material. The film *Zero* has footage in which Steven Jones says:

> [B]arium nitrate and sulfur are part of the military patent on what is known as thermate. This is thermite with sulfur and barium nitrate added to make this material cut more rapidly through steel. Now barium is a very toxic metal, so one would not ordinarily expect this to be present in the large concentrations that we see. Well, the fact that we see it… in the dust is a very strong indication to me that the military form of thermite has been used.[114]

In any case, December 19, 2001, provided another example of simultaneous emissions, being the top day for both iron and vanadium emissions and the second highest day for aluminum and barium emissions. A spike in nickel emissions also occurred on that day.[115]

Nickel also spiked on March 7, which was the highest day for barium emissions.[116]

Still another correlation involved silicon. During October, which was the only month that Cahill monitored emissions, the top two days for silicon emissions were October 5 and 11, which were also this month's days with the highest emissions of benzene, ethylbenzene, propylene, styrene and toluene.[117]

In sum: The long-lasting fires at Ground Zero, along with the unusual emissions noted by Professor Cahill and the EPA, provide further evidence that WTC 7 and the Twin Towers were brought down with explosives. NIST could have contested this conclusion by providing an alternative explanation for the long-enduring heat at Ground Zero and for the emissions of chemicals and metals that should not have been present. Instead, NIST's WTC 7 report dealt with these phenomena in the same way it dealt with the reported pools of molten metal, the scientific reports of particles that could have been produced only by extremely high temperatures, and the pieces of steel that, according to the WPI professors, had undergone oxidation, sulfidation, intergranular melting, and perhaps even vaporization: by simply ignoring them. Once again NIST illustrated Whitehead's observation that if, when formulating a theory, scientists are "content to disregard half [the] evidence," any apparent success of their theory is merely illusory.

6. RED/GRAY CHIPS: MORE EVIDENCE FOR THE USE OF NANOTHERMITE

Early in 2009, the *Open Chemical Physics Journal* published a paper, "Active Thermitic Material Discovered in Dust from the 9/11 World Trade Center Catastrophe," which provides additional, and still more definitive evidence that nanothermite was used to destroy WTC 7 as well as the Twin Towers. Written by Niels Harrit, who teaches in the University of Copenhagen's chemistry department, along with Steven Jones, Kevin Ryan, and six more coauthors, this paper reports results of experiments on very small but visible bi-layered chips, red on one side and gray on the other, that Jones had found while studying dust that had been recovered from the World Trade Center site.[118]

Initially suspecting that these red/gray chips might simply be dried paint chips, this team of scientists tested this possibility through two methods. First, paint chips and red/gray chips were soaked for 55 hours in methyl ethyl ketone, which is an organic solvent known to dissolve paint. Although the paint chips partially dissolved, the red/gray chips did not.[119] Second, both types of chips were subjected to a hot flame. Although the paint chips were "immediately reduced to fragile ashes," the red/gray chips were not.[120]

Having found two facts counting against the paint hypothesis, these scientists then employed a scanning electron microscope, an X-ray energy dispersive spectroscope, and a differential scanning calorimeter to determine the chemical composition of the red/gray chips. This composition provided further evidence against the paint hypothesis.

The gray sides were found to consist of "high iron and oxygen content including a smaller amount of carbon,"[121] but what the scientists found to be most interesting was the composition of the red sides, because they were found to have various features suggestive of thermite.

Evidence of Thermite: One such feature is that the red sides are composed primarily of "aluminum, iron, oxygen, silicon, and carbon."[122] The first three of these ingredients are suggestive of thermite because, as we saw in the previous section, thermite is commonly made by combining aluminum with iron oxide. The analysis showed, moreover, that "iron and oxygen are present in a ratio consistent with Fe_2O_3 [iron oxide]."[123]

The presence of iron was also suggested by the red color and the fact that the chips were subject to magnetic attraction.[124] However, Harrit and his colleagues realized, although the red layer has the same chemical signature as thermite, it might "not really be thermitic." The crucial test would be whether, when heated, it would "react vigorously." They performed this test in two ways. First, using the differential scanning calorimeter, they found that "the red/gray chips from different WTC samples all ignited in the range 415–435°C." They also produced "highly energetic reactions," the details of which produced "evidence for active, highly-energetic thermitic material in the WTC dust [that] is compelling."[125]

A second test occurred when they tested the paint hypothesis by applying a flame to the red/gray chips to determine their response to heat. The results of this test will be reported below.

Evidence of Nanothermite: Several features of the thermitic material suggested to this team of scientists that it is nanothermite, rather than ordinary (macro) thermite.

For one thing, the primary ingredients in the red side are ultra-fine grain, typically being "present in particles at the scale of tens to hundreds of nanometers." Commenting on this fact, Harrit—an expert on nanochemistry—and his colleagues wrote: "The small size of the iron oxide particles qualifies the material to be characterized as nano-thermite or super-thermite."[126]

A second piece of evidence supporting the presence of nanothermite in the WTC dust was that, when a flame was applied to a red/gray chip, as a further test of the paint hypothesis, the result was "the high-speed ejection of a hot particle," suggesting that the chip's red side consisted of "unreacted thermitic material, incorporating nanotechnology"—in other words, nanothermite. This test rather dramatically, in conjunction with the other evidence, ruled out the paint hypothesis.[127]

A third reason to call it nanothermite, rather than ordinary (macro) thermite, is the temperature at which it reacted. As the test in the calorimeter revealed, it reacted at about 430°C, whereas ordinary thermite does not ignite until heated above 900°C (1,650°F). In a statement combining this third reason with the first, Harrit and his colleagues wrote: "The low temperature of ignition and the presence of iron-oxide grains less than 120 nm [nanometers] show that the material is not conventional thermite... but very likely a form of super-thermite."[128]

Fourth, these scientists found that the ingredients of the red sides of the chips were intimately mixed. Pointing out that the intimate mixing of these ultra-fine ingredients belongs to the chemical signature of nanothermite, they wrote: "The red layer of the red/gray chips... contains aluminum, iron and oxygen components which are intimately mixed at a scale of approximately 100 nanometers (nm) or less."[129]

A fifth sign of nanothermite is the red material's carbon content, which "indicates that an organic substance is present"—which is what "would be expected for super-thermite formulations in order to produce high gas pressures upon ignition and thus make them explosive."[130]

Finally, this team of scientists observed, the hypothesis that the red material contains nanothermite is supported by the twofold fact that it is porous and that silicon was one of its main ingredients.[131] As we saw in the previous section, when nanothermite is mixed in a sol-gel, silicon compounds are often used so that, when the mixture dries, it forms a porous reactive material.

Various facts about the red sides of the red/gray chips, therefore, support the conclusion that they are unreacted nanothermite. The gray sides, composed primarily of iron and oxygen, required further study, Harrit and his colleagues said. But they speculated that the existence of the gray side may indicate "that the unreacted material was in close contact with something else, either its target, a container, or an adhesive."[132]

In any case, the conclusion that the red side of these chips is unreacted nanothermite suggests the further conclusion that someone had put nanothermite in the buildings. How else could the large quantity of this material be explained?

An innocent explanation would be possible, to be sure, if the WTC dust might have been contaminated with these ingredients during the clean-up operations at Ground Zero. This hypothesis was, however, excluded by the fact that the four dust samples were collected at times and places that ruled out such contamination. One sample was collected on 9/11 itself about ten minutes after the collapse of the North Tower. The other three samples were collected from nearby apartments into which dust had come through open windows. In two of these cases, moreover, the dust was collected the day after 9/11.[133]

Also, Steven Jones was not the only one to receive samples of WTC dust from those who had collected it. "I have two samples in Copenhagen which were sent to me directly from the collectors, and they contained the chips as well," Harrit reported. "There is a handful of other scientists who can bring the same testimony."[134]

Another question is whether the red/gray chips necessarily mean that nanothermite was used to bring down the WTC buildings. Could not red/gray chips with the ingredients of nanothermite have been produced by conventional explosives? Besides regarding this idea as *a priori* implausible, Harrit and his colleagues wrote:

> No red/gray chips having the characteristics delineated here were found in dust generated by controlled demolition using conventional explosives and methods, for the Stardust Resort & Casino in Las Vegas (demolished 13 March 2007) and the Key Bank in Salt Lake City (demolished 18 August 2007).[135]

The red/gray chips, therefore, present compelling evidence that nanothermite was employed—perhaps along with other thermitic and explosive materials—in the demolition of WTC 7 as well as the Twin Towers.[136]

During a TV interview after his essay was published, Harrit made clear that he and his colleagues were not excluding the use of other materials as well: "We found nanothermite in the rubble. We are not saying only nanothermite was used."[137]

Harrit *was* saying, however, that he and his colleagues had found active thermitic material in the WTC dust. To the interviewer's question as to whether he had any doubt about this, he replied: "You cannot fudge this kind of science. We have found it. Unreacted thermite."[138] As to how much nanothermite was used to bring the three buildings down, given the amount of residue found in the WTC dust, Harrit estimated that it would have been over ten tons.[139]

Harrit also expressed no doubt about whether it was, in fact, used to bring down the buildings. When asked why he thought this substance, which he and his fellow scientists had found in the WTC dust, contributed to the collapse of the WTC buildings, he replied: "Well it's an explosive. Why else would it be there?... This [unreacted thermite] is the 'loaded gun,' material that did not ignite for some reason."[140]

With regard to the question of *how* the nanothermite was used, Harrit replied:

> I cannot say precisely, as this substance can serve [two] purposes. It can explode and break things apart, and it can melt things. Both effects were probably used, as I see it. Molten metal pours out of the South Tower several minutes before the collapse. This indicates the whole structure was being weakened in advance. Then the regular explosives came into play. The actual collapse sequence had to be perfectly timed, all the way down.

Finally, making clear that the discovery of nanothermite in the dust is not the first strong evidence for the demolition of the WTC buildings, Harrit said:

> [T]he article may not be as groundbreaking as you think. Hundreds of thousands of people around the world have long known that the three buildings were demolished. This has been crystal clear. Our research is just the last nail in the coffin. This is not the "smoking gun," it is the "loaded gun."[141]

7. DID NIST TEST FOR THERMITE RESIDUE?

As we have seen in the previous three sections, evidence found in the WTC dust is consistent with the hypothesis that forms of thermite, including thermate and nanothermite, had been employed to bring down WTC 7 as well as the Twin Towers. If NIST had carried out a scientific investigation, truly seeking the cause of the collapses, it would have tested the dust for residues of thermite reactions. By its own admission, however, it did not.

In NIST's 2006 document giving "Answers to Frequently Asked Questions" about its 2005 report on the Twin Towers, we find the following question: "Was the [WTC] steel tested for explosives or thermite residues? The combination of thermite and sulfur (called thermate) 'slices through steel like a hot knife through butter.'" NIST replied:

> NIST did not test for the residue of these compounds in the steel.... Analysis of the WTC steel for the elements in thermite/thermate would not necessarily have been conclusive. The metal compounds also would have been present in the construction materials making up the WTC towers, and sulfur is present in the gypsum wallboard that was prevalent in the interior partitions.[142]

NIST's argument, in other words, was that even if they had found sulfur and thermite residue, this would not have proved that thermate had been used to bring the buildings down, because sulfur and the other elements in thermate might have come from the building materials.

Simultaneously with its release in August 2008 of the Draft version of its WTC 7 report, NIST put out a document entitled "Questions and Answers about the NIST WTC 7 Investigation." One of the questions was: "Is it possible that thermite or thermate contributed to the collapse of WTC 7?" As part of its answer, NIST repeated almost verbatim its previous statement as to why it did not bother to check for thermate, saying:

> Analysis of the WTC steel for the elements in thermite/thermate would not necessarily have been conclusive. The metal compounds also would have been present in the construction materials making up the WTC buildings, and sulfur is present in the gypsum wallboard used for interior partitions.[143]

By repeating its earlier answer, NIST implied that it was a good explanation. But it was not.

One problem is that NIST's statement—that such a test "would not necessarily have been conclusive"—entails that it *might possibly have been conclusive.* This point was made in a "Request for Correction," which was submitted to NIST in 2007 by a group of scholars that included Steven Jones and Kevin Ryan. In their letter, they pointed out several problems in NIST's report on the Twin Towers. With regard to the question at hand, they wrote:

> A chemical analysis for explosive residue on the steel or in the dust... could put to rest... the theory that explosives were responsible for the collapses of the Twin Towers.[144]

In other words, even if a positive result would not have been conclusive, a negative result, showing that there was *not* any residue from explosives in the Ground Zero dust, *would* have been conclusive. It would have conclusively disproved the theory that explosives had been used. As the group of scholars pointed out in a later "Appeal" to NIST, this would have required only "a very simple lab test."[145] Why would NIST's scientists not have performed this test? Was it because they knew that the test would *not* have provided this negative result?

A second problem with NIST's claim is that a positive result, showing the presence of thermite residue, might indeed have been conclusive. The group of scholars made this point in their "Request for Correction" by quoting a statement from Materials Engineering, Inc. (a company that "provides assistance in arson investigations"),[146] which says:

> When thermite reaction compounds are used to ignite a fire, they produce a characteristic burn pattern, and leave behind evidence. These compounds are rather unique in their chemical composition, containing common elements such as copper, iron, calcium, silicon and aluminum, but also contain more unusual elements, such as vanadium, titanium, tin, fluorine and manganese. While some of these elements are consumed in the fire, many are also left behind in the residue.... The results [of Energy Dispersive Spectroscopy on minute traces of residue], coupled with visual evidence at the scene, provide *absolute certainty* that thermite reaction compounds were present, indicating the fire was deliberately set.[147]

Accordingly, these scholars said:

> [I]t is difficult to imagine a scenario in which a test for explosive residues would not be conclusive.... Unless NIST can explain a plausible scenario that would produce inconclusive explosive residue test results, its stated reason for not conducting such tests is wholly unpersuasive.[148]

At the press briefing of August 21, 2008, on the occasion of NIST's release of its Draft Report on WTC 7, Shane Geiger of the 9/11 truth movement tried to confront NIST's lead investigator, Shyam Sunder, with evidence for the use of explosives provided by materials that have been found in the WTC dust. No sooner had he started his point than Sunder and Ben Stein (NIST's director of media relations) tried to silence him, saying that it was time to "move on" (to another question). Here is how the exchange went:

GEIGER: [Y]ou reiterated from your Twin Towers report that NIST has stated that it found no corroborating evidence to suggest that explosives were used to bring down the buildings. Now, in the very next sentence you...
SUNDER: OK. Well, let's, let's...
GEIGER: ...admit that NIST did not conduct tests for explosive residue. So of course it's very difficult to... to find what you're not looking for. But in...
STEIN: OK, we're going to move on.
GEIGER: ... iron spheres which are characteristic of the dust and can be seen on the United States Geological Survey website. These are found in every single sample of the dust to date, including all the samples that RJ Lee group took a look at. I actually have...
STEIN: OK, we're gonna move on ...
GEIGER: I have a friend who's found these in his sample of dust....
STEIN: I think....
GEIGER: ...and I think this is—there's enough of these out there—there's a billion pounds of World Trade Center dust in the landfill on Staten Island. I think it's pretty fair to say that NIST could, if NIST were interested in doing so, that NIST take a look at these spheres.
STEIN: Do you have a question, sir?
GEIGER: Inside these spheres, Dr. Steven Jones is claiming that there is evidence of a thermite reaction.
VOICE: OK, move on.
GEIGER: I certainly would like to hear about your research on this, other than bare assertions.
STEIN: Could you comment on what was said?
SUNDER: Yes, very quickly, there are a thousand pages of reports right there. It's on the website. I urge you to read it, understand it, and when you've understood it, we can have a discussion.
GEIGER: How may I go about discussing this with you in the future?
SUNDER: Well, you can submit your questions in writing and we will look at what you have to say.[149]

So, although Sunder had been happy to answer all the other questions raised at the briefing, Geiger's question did not deserve a reply until he had read the "thousands of pages of reports." Also

Geiger's questions had to be submitted in writing. These two conditions meant that Sunder did not need to reply while reporters were listening and video cameras were running. They also meant, in fact, that Sunder would not need to answer the question at all. In any case, Sunder concluded his response to Geiger with these words:

> But I will reassert what I've said all along, that the findings that we have got, we are very comfortable with. It's based on sound science, it is consistent with the observations.[150]

However, as we have seen and will continue to see in the following chapters, NIST's report, far from being *consistent* with the observations, is based on *ignoring* a wide range of relevant observations. For this and other reasons to be explored in the second part of this book, Sunder's claim that his report is based on "sound science" could hardly be further from the truth.

Sunder's systematically unscientific treatment of the question of thermitic materials in the dust was continued a week later during his "technical briefing" of August 28, 2008. A question submitted by Steven Jones asked: "Did NIST have available to it samples of dust from the WTC catastrophe? And if so, did NIST examine the dust for red or gray chips?" Sunder replied:

> [W]e went through a pretty rigorous screening process to figure out which were the credible hypotheses that we would pursue and how we went about pursuing them, and we did not believe that the possible hypothesis that you just mentioned fell into the realm of a credible hypothesis.[151]

Jones, however, had not suggested a hypothesis. He had only asked whether NIST had checked WTC dust for the presence of red or gray chips. Sunder simply dodged that question by calling it a hypothesis that could not be deemed credible.

It is true, of course, that the question posed by Jones *implied* a hypothesis, namely, that nanothermite was used to bring down WTC 7. Sunder began the statement quoted above by saying, "As I said just a moment ago,…" In that earlier statement, he had said:

> [W]hen we started the investigation we considered a whole range of possible hypotheses. And from that, based on our technical judgment, we decided what were credible hypotheses that we should

pursue further. Among them, of course, was the… diesel fuel fire, the transfer girders,… and, of course, the most obvious, which is the normal building fires.… In addition to that, because of the concern expressed by several people about blasts and blast-oriented sounds, we decided to include that as a hypothetical scenario to also evaluate. We judged that other hypotheses that… were suggested really… were not credible enough to justify a careful investigation.[152]

It was this statement that lay behind Sunder's answer to Jones, namely, that NIST did not believe that the hypothesis Jones was suggesting "fell into the realm of a credible hypothesis" the kind that would "justify a careful investigation."

So, although no steel-framed high-rise building had ever been brought down by diesel fuel fires, normal building fires, or girder failures, NIST thought that hypotheses about the collapse of WTC 7 based on these causes *were* credible enough to justify careful investigations. And although nanothermite could have helped bring the building down and could, moreover, explain the melted steel and the "blast-oriented sounds," NIST found the hypothesis that nanothermite was used to bring down WTC 7 so lacking in credibility that checking the WTC dust for unreacted nanothermite would not have been justified!

Sunder's reply shows that, besides refusing to begin, as we saw in the previous chapter, with the most likely hypothesis—namely, that WTC 7 was brought down by explosives of some sort—NIST even refused to do a simple test to confirm or disconfirm the most strongly supported version of that hypothesis. Whatever the NIST report was, it was not a scientific report.

Besides giving a completely inadequate rationale for not testing the dust to see if it contained the red/gray chips that Steven Jones and his colleagues had reported, NIST gave an equally lame excuse for not testing the dust for the presence of sulfur. NIST claimed, as we saw, that finding sulfur would not prove anything because the gypsum wallboard contained sulfur. But if that might provide an adequate explanation, why had the three professors from Worcester Polytechnic Institute been so puzzled by the fact that the piece of steel they studied from WTC 7 had been sulfidized? Are we to assume that these professors, all experts in the field, did not know that gypsum wallboard contains sulfur? If that fact might have provided a satisfactory answer, surely these "fire-wise professors" would not have stated at the end of their appendix to the FEMA report: "No clear explanation for the source of the sulfur has been identified."[153]

At least one likely reason why they would not have considered the gypsum a possible source has been explained in the previously discussed paper, "Extremely High Temperatures during the World Trade Center Destruction," by Steven Jones and other scientists. Gypsum is calcium sulfate, so if the only sulfur discovered were from gypsum wallboard, it would be matched by about the same percentage of calcium. Given the fact that the sulfur at Ground Zero was not matched by a corresponding amount of calcium, it could not have been from gypsum.[154]

Could NIST simply have been unaware of this fact? That would be possible only if its scientists were unfamiliar with the most common building materials. Also, Jones had made the point about calcium and sulfur in a 2007 paper entitled "Revisiting 9/11/2001,"[155] and this paper was presented to NIST in December 2007 by architect Richard Gage and placed on NIST's own website.[156] We can be confident, therefore, that NIST, rather than being ignorant of this fact—that the absence of a correspondingly high percentage of calcium in the Ground Zero dust shows that the sulfur did not come from gypsum—simply ignored it.

A third problem is that NIST's answer about sulfur is a straw-man argument. The question NIST answers by referring to gypsum in the wallboard is: *Why was there sulfur in the WTC dust?* As we saw earlier, however, the real question is: *How did sulfur enter into the intergranular structure of the steel?* As Steven Jones indicated in a passage quoted earlier, if scientists at NIST "heat steel to about 1000°C in the presence of gypsum,… they will find that sulfur does *not* enter steel under such circumstances."[157] NIST, however, ignored this issue.

A fourth problem with NIST's position is that it is circular. On the one hand, as we saw in the Introduction, NIST's lead investigator, Shyam Sunder, said at NIST's press briefing in August 2008: "We did not find any evidence that explosives were used to bring the building down."[158] That statement implies that NIST looked for possible evidence and found that it was absent. On the other hand, as we have also seen, NIST said in its "Answers to Frequently Asked Questions," published in 2006: "NIST did not test for the residue of these [thermite] compounds." Although this admission was not repeated in NIST's 2008 documents about WTC 7, it was implied by its statement that finding such residues would not necessarily have been conclusive. NIST's statement that it "did not find any evidence that explosives were used" is, therefore, deceptive. As the group of scholars observed in their "Appeal" to NIST: "[I]t is extremely easy to 'find no evidence' when one is not looking for evidence."[159]

The circularity in NIST's position was pointed out by journalist Jennifer Abel of the *Hartford Advocate* in a story in which she discussed an interview she had with Michael Newman, spokesman for NIST's Department of Public and Business Affairs. Abel asked: "[W]hat about that letter where NIST said it didn't look for evidence of explosives?" Newman replied: "Right, because there was no evidence of that." In response to this strange answer, Abel asked the obvious question: "But how can you know there's no evidence if you don't look for it first?" Newman then responded with a still stranger statement: "If you're looking for something that isn't there, you're wasting your time… and the taxpayers' money."[160]

Newman's obviously circular position illustrates in a humorous fashion—or at least it *would* be humorous if so much were not at stake—NIST's refusal to follow the scientific method's empirical dimension, which entails that a theory, to be truly scientific, must do justice to *all* of the evidence that might be relevant.

NIST's failure to test for signs that thermite had been used is even more inexcusable in light of the fact that the *Guide for Fire and Explosion Investigations,* which is put out by the National Fire Protection Association (NFPA), says that, in seeking to determine the cause of a fire, investigators should look for evidence of *accelerants,* which are any substances that could be used to ignite, and/or accelerate the progress of, a fire. (Dogs that are employed to detect such substances are known as "accelerant detection canines.") In its section on "undetermined fire cause," this NFPA *Guide* says:

> In the instance in which the investigator fails to identify all of the components of the cause of the fire, it need not always be classified as undetermined. If the physical evidence establishes one factor, such as the presence of an accelerant, that may be sufficient to establish the cause even where other factors such as ignition source cannot be determined.[161]

Thermite mixtures constitute one of the most common types of accelerants.[162] By admitting that NIST had not checked for evidence of thermitic materials, therefore, Newman admitted that NIST had violated one of the basic principles of fire investigations.

Also, as we have seen, nanothermites would be sufficient to account for at least many of the unusual ingredients in the WTC dust and also for at least some of the fires in WTC 7. (Although NIST treated it as self-evident that the fires in WTC 7 were caused by burning debris from the collapse of the North Tower, this explanation is not at all self-evident, as we will see in Chapter 8.)

There can be no doubt, therefore, that NIST should have performed tests to check for thermitic materials. In light of the fact that its purported reason for not doing so—that such tests would not necessarily have been conclusive—is unpersuasive, must we not suspect that NIST's real reason was its knowledge that such tests *would* have been conclusive, showing that such materials had indeed been used?

As we saw earlier, Alfred North Whitehead noted that the pursuit of truth requires an "unflinching determination to take the whole evidence into account."[163] In preparing its WTC 7 report, however, NIST appears to have been possessed of unflinching determination to *ignore* much of the relevant evidence.

5
NIST'S IGNORING OF TESTIMONIAL EVIDENCE FOR EXPLOSIVES

I n its final report on WTC 7, as we have seen, NIST claims that it "found no evidence of a… controlled demolition event."[1] In making this claim, NIST implies not only that it found no physical evidence to support the controlled demolition hypothesis, but also that it knew of no reliable testimonial evidence. However, just as NIST simply ignores several kinds of physical evidence, it also ignores various sources of testimonial evidence.

In ignoring relevant testimony, NIST continues a precedent it set in its report on the Twin Towers. In preparation for examining NIST's treatment of testimonial evidence about explosions in WTC 7, therefore, I will review its treatment of testimony about explosions in the towers.

1. NIST'S TREATMENT OF TESTIMONIAL EVIDENCE ABOUT EXPLOSIONS IN THE TWIN TOWERS

In its 2005 report on the Twin Towers, NIST claimed that it had "found no corroborating evidence for alternative hypotheses suggesting that the WTC towers were brought down by controlled demolition using explosives planted prior to Sept. 11, 2001."[2] In accordance with this claim, NIST wrote its report as if no credible witnesses had spoken about explosions occurring before or during the destruction of the Twin Towers. In reality, however, there were dozens of such witnesses.

In 2005, the City of New York was forced to release 503 oral testimonies by members of the Fire Department of New York (FDNY), which had been recorded shortly after 9/11. These testimonies, which were available to NIST, were made publicly available by the *New York Times*.[3]

Even prior to this development, testimonies about explosions in the towers had been available from WTC employees, police officers, and journalists, some of which I quoted, along with several of the FDNY testimonies, in an essay entitled "Explosive Testimony."[4]

One of the WTC employees was engineer Mike Pecoraro, who was working in the sixth sub-basement of the North Tower. He said that, after an explosion that occurred at about the time this building was hit, he and a co-worker went up to the C level, where there had been a small machine shop. "There was nothing there but rubble," said Pecoraro. "We're talking about a 50 ton hydraulic press—gone!" On the B level, he and his co-worker found a steel-and-concrete fire door, which weighed about 300 pounds, wrinkled up "like a piece of aluminum foil."[5]

One police officer who reported explosions was Sue Keane of the New Jersey Fire Police Department. After speaking of an explosion that occurred during the collapse of the North Tower, she said:

> [There was] another explosion. That sent me and the two firefighters down the stairs.... I can't tell you how many times I got banged around. Each one of those explosions picked me up and threw me.... There was another explosion, and I got thrown with two firefighters out onto the street.[6]

Two of the journalists who reported explosions were from the *Wall Street Journal*, which occupied a building next to the WTC. One of them wrote:

> I... looked up out of the office window to see what seemed like perfectly synchronized explosions coming from each floor.... One after the other, from top to bottom, with a fraction of a second between, the floors blew to pieces.[7]

The other WSJ reporter said that, after seeing what appeared to be "individual floors, one after the other exploding outward," he thought: "'My God, they're going to bring the building down.' And they, whoever they are, had set charges.... I saw the explosions."[8]

Surely, one would think, NIST would have considered such reports credible. But it did not mention these or any other testimonies from journalists, police officers, or WTC employees.

With regard to the testimonies from the Fire Department of New York, Professor Graeme MacQueen, in a thorough study, found that 118 of the 503 FDNY testimonies referred to phenomena indicating that explosions had occurred.[9] For example, Chief Frank Cruthers, speaking of the South Tower, said:

> [T]here was what appeared to be at first an explosion. It appeared at the very top, simultaneously from all four sides, materials shot out horizontally. And then there seemed to be a momentary delay before you could see the beginning of the collapse.[10]

Firefighter Richard Banaciski said:

> [T]here was just an explosion. It seemed like on television [when] they blow up these buildings. It seemed like it was going all the way around like a belt, all these explosions.[11]

NIST was not unaware of these FDNY testimonies. It had been given access to the oral histories prior to their public release and even referred to them in its report on the Twin Towers.[12] But it wrote its report on the Twin Towers as if these testimonies did not exist.

NIST's Limited Denial

In response to a question about its failure to mention testimonies about explosions, NIST even specifically denied that any relevant testimonies had been collected by the FDNY. In its 2006 document responding to "frequently asked questions," NIST wrote:

> There was no evidence (collected by... the Fire Department of New York) of any blast or explosions in the region below the impact and fire floors.[13]

While not explicitly saying that the FDNY had not collected *any* testimonies about explosions in the towers, this statement, by saying that NIST had collected none that referred to explosions "in the region below the impact and fire floors," implied that it had collected no *relevant* testimonies. NIST's rationale for this limited denial was apparently that, unless explosions occurred below the floors with fires, they could be explained as resulting from the jet fuel that had been released into the buildings when the airplanes crashed into them.

This rationale was not justifiable. For one thing, explosions *above* the impact floors also could not be explained by the jet fuel, because this fuel could not have gone *up* the elevator shafts. NIST would have had no justification, accordingly, for considering irrelevant the above-quoted testimony of Chief Frank Cruthers, who reported what seemed to be an explosion that "appeared at the very top, simultaneously from all four sides."

A second factor is that the jet fuel, NIST itself admitted, would have "lasted at most a few minutes."[14] Given the fact that the vast majority of the testimonies suggestive of explosions referred to phenomena that occurred during or just before the collapses, long after all the jet fuel would have been exhausted, NIST could not have justified dismissing them as irrelevant.

Moreover, even NIST's limited denial—that the FDNY did not collect any testimonies of explosions *below* the fire and impact floors—is incorrect. Firefighter Timothy Burke, for example, said:

> Then the building popped, lower than the fire.... I was going oh, my god, there is a secondary device because the way the building popped. I thought it was an explosion.[15]

Firefighter Edward Cachia reported:

> [T]he South Tower... actually gave at a lower floor, not the floor where the plane hit... [W]e originally had thought there was like an internal detonation, explosives, because it went in succession, boom, boom, boom, boom, and then the tower came down.[16]

Assistant Fire Commissioner Stephen Gregory said:

> I saw low-level flashes.... I saw a flash flash flash and then it looked like the building came down.... [It was at] the lower level of the building. You know like when they demolish a building, how when they blow up a building, when it falls down? That's what I thought I saw.[17]

Firefighter Kenneth Rogers reported:

> [T]hen there was an explosion in the South Tower.... Floor after floor after floor. One floor under another after another and when it hit about the fifth floor, I figured it was a bomb, because it looked like a synchronized deliberate kind of thing.[18]

And firefighter Howie Scott said:

> I just happened to look up and saw the whole thing coming down, pancaking down, and the explosion, blowing out about halfway up.[19]

If one form of scientific fraud is, in the words of Horace Freeland Judson quoted in Chapter 2, "tendentiously selecting what to report," then NIST, which not only failed to mention this evidence but even specifically denied its existence, is clearly guilty of this form of scientific fraud.

NIST's Response to a "Request for Correction"

The aforementioned "Request for Correction," which was sent to NIST by Steven Jones and other scholars in 2007, was based on a federal law known as the Data Quality Act, which required NIST to respond to charges that their report was biased. Jones and his colleagues quoted many of the FDNY testimonies about explosions in the towers, including some that spoke specifically of explosions "in the region below the impact and fire floors," and then stated:

> An unbiased NIST investigation would consider these multiple, credible, mutually supporting, publicly available reports of explosions inside the Twin Towers.... [T]he entire WTC Report is clearly biased in favor of finding that the airplane impacts and resulting fires were the only cause of the collapses of the Twin Towers.[20]

In its letter of reply, sent several months later, NIST wrote:

> Your letter... asserts that NIST failed to take into account interviews of emergency personnel that suggested the presence of bombs in the towers. NIST reviewed all of the interviews conducted by the FDNY of firefighters (500 interviews) and in addition conducted its own set of interviews with emergency responders and building occupants. Taken as a whole, the interviews did not support the contention that explosives played a role in the collapse of the WTC Towers.[21]

The second sentence of this statement made clear that NIST's claim about the absence of testimonies about explosions was not based on ignorance of the FDNY oral histories.

The third sentence constituted, in effect, a correction of NIST's previous claim, implicit in its 2005 report on the Twin Towers, that the FDNY did not report *any* testimonies about explosions in the towers. NIST's revised claim seemed to be that, although there were *some* testimonies about such explosions, there were not *enough* "to support the contention that explosives played a role in the collapse of the WTC Towers." This was a significant modification of NIST's stance, which should have been published as a correction on its website and stated in a press release, not simply put in a letter to a few scholars.

In any case, what exactly NIST meant by this statement is not clear. Did it mean that the oral histories did not provide evidence worth mentioning unless *all* of the oral histories, or at least a *majority* of them, mentioned explosions? If so, that would be an incredible response. Almost 25 percent of the members of the FDNY provided testimony suggestive of explosions. This was a very high proportion, especially given the fact that these men and women had not been asked whether explosions had been going off—they had simply volunteered this information.

With regard to NIST's limited denial—that none of the FDNY testimonials spoke of explosions "in the region below the impact and fire floors"—NIST's "taken as a whole" statement in this letter seemed to admit that there were *some* testimonies of this type while claiming, in an attempt to justify its silence about them, that there were *not enough* of them to be worth mentioning.

NIST, however, had not simply failed to mention them. It had specifically stated that the FDNY collected "no evidence... of any blast or explosions in the region below the impact and fire floors." *No evidence* would mean no testimonies of this sort whatsoever. Accordingly, insofar as NIST admitted that the FDNY oral histories did include some testimonies of this sort, it admitted that its limited denial had been false. And yet NIST has never publicly retracted it, so we have here another example of scientific fraud.

By admitting, in effect, that there were some testimonies about explosions, including several specifically referring to the region below the fire and impact floors, while claiming that these testimonies "taken as a whole" did not provide evidence that explosives played a role in the collapse of the Twin Towers, NIST demonstrated that it had been determined—whatever the effect on its credibility as a scientific agency—to avoid mentioning evidence for explosives in its report.

NIST's wording, it should be noted, was that, taken as a whole, the FDNY testimonies *"did not support the contention* that explosives played a role in the collapse of the WTC Towers" (emphasis added). The phrase "support the contention" is ambiguous. It can mean "provide some support for the contention, albeit not sufficient support to prove it (because additional evidence would be required to have proof)." This is surely how most people would understand the phrase. But NIST, in saying that the FDNY interviews did not support the contention that explosives played a role, meant that they did not provide *sufficient* support for it (which means that the testimonies suggestive of explosives did not serve, all by themselves, to *prove* it—even though no one had claimed they did). It used this very strong, even aberrant, meaning of the phrase to justify the fact that it had not even mentioned the testimonies suggestive of explosions, even though it knew about them.

NIST was clearly employing a double standard. With regard to evidence supportive of its own position, NIST did not demand that this evidence be sufficient to prove it. Indeed, as we will see in the second part of this book, NIST cited extremely weak evidence in support of its explanation of the collapse of WTC 7. But when dealing with a type of evidence supportive of the controlled demolition hypothesis, NIST implied that this type of evidence can be ignored if it is not sufficient, all by itself, to prove the truth of this hypothesis.

What the proponents of the controlled demolition hypothesis claim, however, is merely that the testimonial evidence about explosions is part of a *cumulative case*—which also includes evidence for pulverized concrete, melted steel, oxidized-and-sulfidized steel, squibs, and other types of physical evidence—that provides sufficient support for their hypothesis. As such, the testimonial evidence for explosions is clearly part of the total evidence, which any scientific study of the destruction of the WTC buildings would need to consider.

Accordingly, if NIST had been carrying out a truly scientific investigation of the destruction of the Twin Towers, thereby considering the whole of the evidence, it would have mentioned the massive body of testimonial evidence that explosions were going off before and during the collapses of the Twin Towers.

NIST's dismissive attitude to testimonial evidence about explosions in the buildings was also illustrated by its response to a WTC employee who tried to inform NIST about an explosion he had experienced.

NIST's Response to the Testimony of William Rodriguez

William Rodriguez, who was employed as a janitor in the North Tower, was named a "national hero" for helping many people escape from that building. As such, he was invited to the White House and had his picture taken with President Bush.[22] But Rodriguez was not treated like a hero by NIST.

Rodriguez said that while he was reporting for work in an office on the first sub-level floor, he and others, at 8:46AM, heard and felt an explosion below them. In his words:

When I heard the sound of the explosion, the floor beneath my feet vibrated, the walls started cracking and everything started shaking.... Seconds [later], I hear another explosion from way above.... Although I was unaware at the time, this was the airplane hitting the tower.

Co-worker Felipe David, who had been in front of a nearby freight elevator, then came into the office, Rodriguez reported, with severe burns on his face and arms and yelling, "Explosion! explosion! explosion!" Rodriguez said: "He was burned terribly. The skin was hanging off his hands and arms. His injuries couldn't have come from the airplane above, but only from a massive explosion below."[23]

Rodriguez's testimony that he had witnessed an explosion *before* the attack on the North Tower was reported by the BBC.[24]

His account was also corroborated by José Sanchez, who was in the workshop on the fourth sub-level. Sanchez said that he and a co-worker heard a big blast that "sounded like a bomb," after which "a huge ball of fire went through the freight elevator."[25]

When Rodriguez later learned that NIST was doing the official investigation of the destruction of the Twin Towers, he wanted to let its researchers know about his experience. But, he discovered, NIST was unreceptive:

I contacted NIST... four times without a response. Finally, [at a public hearing] I asked them before they came up with their conclusion... if they ever considered my statements or the statements of any of the other survivors who heard the explosions. They just stared at me with blank faces.[26]

Clearly, given the fact that Rodriguez was reporting something that NIST did not want to hear, his "national hero" status did not count for much. NIST treated his testimony with the same lack of respect that it would show for that of Barry Jennings (to be discussed below).

NIST's unscientific treatment of testimonial evidence for explosions in the Twin Towers illustrates the fact that, by the time it started working on its reports on the World Trade Center, it had become a political agency, whose employees with science degrees had lost all scientific independence. We should not be surprised, therefore, to find that these employees treated the testimonial evidence for explosions in WTC 7 in the same unscientific way. I turn now to this evidence.

2. TESTIMONIES ABOUT EXPLOSIONS IN WTC 7 FROM WITNESSES OUTSIDE THE BUILDING

Although we do not have nearly as many recorded testimonies about explosions in WTC 7 as we have for the Twin Towers, there are some very clear statements from people who witnessed such explosions from either outside or inside the building. The present section quotes a few people who reported witnessing such explosions from outside.

One of these witnesses was reporter Peter Demarco of the *New York Daily News*, who said:

> [T]here was a rumble. The building's top row of windows popped out. Then all the windows on the thirty-ninth floor popped out. Then the thirty-eighth floor. Pop! Pop! Pop! was all you heard until the building sunk into a rising cloud of gray.[27]

Another witness was former NYPD officer Craig Bartmer, who reported:

> I was real close to Building 7 when it fell down.... That didn't sound like just a building falling down to me.... There's a lot of eyewitness testimony down there of hearing explosions.... [A]ll of a sudden... I looked up, and... [t]he thing started pealing in on itself.... I started running... and the whole time you're hearing "boom, boom, boom, boom, boom."[28]

Still another witness was a New York University medical student, who had been serving as an emergency medical worker that day. He gave this report:

> [W]e heard this sound that sounded like a clap of thunder.... [T]urned around—we were shocked.... [I]t looked like there was a shockwave ripping through the building and the windows all busted out.... [A]bout a second later the bottom floor caved out and the building followed after that.[29]

All of these statements had long been on the public record when NIST published its report on WTC 7. But NIST, claiming that it "found no evidence of a blast or controlled demolition event,"[30] simply ignored them.

3. STATEMENTS ABOUT EXPLOSIONS IN WTC 7 FROM WITNESSES INSIDE THE BUILDING

In addition to the foregoing statements from people who witnessed explosions from outside of WTC 7 as it started to collapse, we have testimonies from two men who reported experiencing explosions while they were in the building early in the morning. These two testimonies are of special importance, not only because they referred to explosions early in the day, but also because they were given by two city officials.

The Testimony of Michael Hess

One of these officials was Michael Hess, who at the time was New York City's corporation counsel. As such, he was the chief lawyer for the city, supervising its law department, which had over 600 attorneys. When he was appointed to this position in 1997, he was already, as a *New York Times* story reported, one of Mayor Rudy Giuliani's "old friends from the legal profession."[31] This friendship was illustrated in a 2002 book by Giuliani, in which he referred to Hess simply as "Mike." In that book, in fact, Giuliani pointed out that Hess, along with Jennings, was in WTC 7 on the morning of 9/11.[32] As we will see, however, Giuliani gave an account that differed greatly from the accounts given by Hess and Jennings themselves.

Hess provided his own account while being interviewed before noon on 9/11 by Frank Ucciardo of UPN 9 News. The interview began at 11:57.[33] And it occurred, Ucciardo reported, "on Broadway about a block from City Hall," which is several blocks from the WTC site. So Hess had to have been rescued early enough to get there before noon. During this live interview, Hess said:

> I was up in the emergency management center on the twenty-third floor [of WTC 7], and when all the power went out in the building, another gentleman and I walked down to the eighth floor [sic] where there was an explosion and we were trapped on the eighth floor with smoke, thick smoke, all around us, for about an hour and a half. But the New York Fire Department... just came and got us out.[34] [Although Hess said they had "walked down to the eighth floor," they actually walked down to the sixth floor, then went back up to the eighth floor after the explosion; see the endnote.]

While clearly stating that there had been "an explosion," Hess did not indicate the time at which it occurred. We can infer from his testimony, however, that it must have been no later than 10:00AM. That is, if he had been trapped for "about an hour and a half" and then, after being rescued, had made his way to City Hall, several blocks away, close to two hours must have passed between the explosion and the interview. Accordingly, if the interview began at 11:57AM, then the explosion that trapped the two men must have happened no later than 10:00AM.

Giuliani, however, gave a very different account of this episode in the life of his old friend Michael Hess. Giuliani wrote:

> When he got to the 8th floor [of WTC 7], Tower 1—the North Tower—collapsed, part of it falling on top of the southern part of 7 World Trade Center. Luckily, Mike was in the northern section of the building. Unluckily, he was now trapped, as the stairs were impassable.

> Mike went into an office on the 8th floor, joined only by a fellow from the Housing Authority. The building was filling up with smoke and dust from the collapsed towers, but since the men were facing north they had no way of knowing the towers had fallen.[35]

Like Hess, Giuliani stated that Hess was trapped on the 8th floor and that the building was filling up with smoke. Otherwise, however, Giuliani's account diverged from that of his friend. He made no mention of "an explosion." And whereas Hess simply said that he and the other man were surrounded by "smoke, thick smoke," Giuliani spoke of "smoke and dust" and claimed that it had come "from the collapsed towers" (rather than from an explosion within WTC 7). Giuliani said, moreover, that the two men had become trapped because WTC 7 had been damaged by debris from the collapse of the North Tower, which did not occur until 10:28. According to Giuliani, therefore, Hess and his companion became trapped on the 8th floor at about 10:30.

But this timeline created a problem. Although Giuliani did not indicate how long the two men were trapped, he surely would not have contested Hess's statement that he and his companion had been trapped "for about an hour and a half." If they were not rescued until an hour and a half after 10:30, then they could not have been rescued until noon. How, then, could Hess have been giving an interview several blocks away *before* noon? The timing as well as the content of the Hess interview, therefore, contradicted Giuliani's claim that the event Hess called "an explosion" had really been produced by the 10:28 collapse of the North Tower.

Giuliani's account was also problematic because of his claim that the men became trapped because "part of [the North Tower fell] on top of the southern part of 7 World Trade Center." As a result of the debris from the collapsing North Tower, he implied, "the stairs were impassable." But Giuliani also acknowledged that the two men were in "the northern section of the building"—a fact that allowed Giuliani to say that, although the event that had filled the building with smoke and trapped the two men was really just the collapse of the North Tower, Hess and Jennings themselves did not know this: "since the men were facing north they had no way of knowing the towers had fallen." But Giuliani's second point—that they were trapped on the north side of WTC 7—undermined his main claim—that they had become trapped when debris from the North Tower fell "on top of the southern part of 7 World Trade Center." The north side of WTC 7 was 50 yards—half the length of a football field—from the south side. Debris striking the south side would not have made the stairs on the *north* side impassable.

Giuliani's account, published in 2002, was evidently the first attempt by a spokesperson for the official story about 9/11 to deal with the potentially problematic fact that two city employees, Michael Hess and Barry Jennings, had become trapped in WTC 7 on the morning of 9/11. I have dealt with this account at some length partly because of its intrinsic interest, as the account provided by the then mayor of New York City, and partly because NIST would later give essentially the same account, which would, in turn, be echoed in 2008 by the BBC.

Before turning to the treatments by NIST and the BBC, however, we need to look at the testimony of the other city official, Barry Jennings, which is much more extensive.

The Testimony of Barry Jennings

Barry Jennings was the emergency coordinator/deputy director of the Emergency Services Department of the New York City Housing Authority. In June 2007, he agreed to do an interview with Dylan Avery, who planned to include segments from it in his forthcoming documentary, *Loose Change Final Cut*. Prior to the completion of the film, however, portions of the interview were released on the internet.[36] This release evidently led to developments at the New York City Housing Authority that caused Jennings, only two years from retirement, to fear that he would lose his job and hence his pension. For this reason, he requested that his interview be omitted from the film, and Avery reluctantly agreed. This occurred late in 2007, shortly before the release of *Loose Change Final Cut* in November of that year.

On July 6, 2008, however, the BBC aired a program on WTC 7 that featured an interview with Jennings.[37] During this interview, Jennings repeated many of the things he had told Avery. But he suggested that Avery's film had distorted his testimony on one issue (to be discussed below). At that point, Avery decided to put the entire interview, labeled "Barry Jennings Uncut," online,[38] which he did on July 9, 2008.[39]

Jennings had also been interviewed by NIST, as both Jennings and NIST reported.[40] Although the transcript of this interview has not been made public, Jennings' statements in his interviews with Avery and the BBC surely provide a good idea of what he told NIST. Jennings, in fact, said to Avery: "They asked me the same questions that you guys are asking me," and, in response to Avery's comment, "And yet you told them pretty much the same things you just told us," Jennings said "Yes." He later added: "I don't know if they liked the answers I gave. I could care less. I gave… my account of it, the truth, and that was that."[41]

We can conclude, therefore, that insofar as NIST's account of Jennings' experiences differs greatly from what he said in those other interviews, NIST has probably distorted what it heard from him.

The following summary of Jennings' testimony is based primarily on "Barry Jennings Uncut," supplemented with statements he made in his interview for the BBC.

"[S]hortly after the first plane hit [the North Tower]," Jennings said, he received a call to go to WTC 7. Like Hess, whom he had not previously known, he was going to see Mayor Giuliani, who, they both assumed, would be in the Office of Emergency Management's emergency command center on the 23rd floor. As Hess later explained: "In an emergency, we were supposed to go and huddle and plan and strategize with Mayor Giuliani in the Emergency Management Center on the 23rd floor. That was the plan."[42]

When did they arrive? The North Tower had been struck at

8:46AM, so Hess and Jennings should have arrived at about 9:00. Jennings said, in fact, that he "got in the building... a little before 9:00, a little after 9:00."[43] He also said that he "had to be inside on the 23rd floor when the second plane hit,"[44] which was at 9:03. That they arrived "shortly after the first plane hit" and before the second plane hit, as Jennings said, was stated two days after 9/11 in one of London's leading newspapers, the *Independent*, which wrote:

> Up in the command centre on the 23rd floor, two men felt the building rock with the second explosion. Housing Authority worker Barry Jennings, 46, had reported there after the initial blast. So had Michael Hess, the city's corporation counsel. After the second plane hit they scrambled downstairs.[45]

As we will see below, the *Independent's* account, which stated that it was "[a]fter the second plane hit" that Hess and Jennings "scrambled downstairs," would become more important after Hess, in an interview for the BBC in 2008, claimed that it was much later.

In any case, although the two men had expected to find Giuliani and other people on the 23rd floor, they did not. Jennings said:

> [W]e noticed that everybody was gone. I saw coffee that was on the desks still, the smoke was still coming off the coffee. I saw half-eaten sandwiches. Only me and Mr. Hess was up there. And after I called several individuals, one individual told me to leave and to leave right away.[46]

Then, finding that the elevator would not work, they went down the stairs as fast as they could. Jennings told the BBC: "I wanted to get out of that building in a hurry, so I started, instead of taking one step at a time, I'm jumping landings."[47] But when they got to the 6th floor, Jennings said:

> The landing that we were standing on gave way—there was an explosion and the landing gave way. I was left there hanging. I had to climb back up, and now I had to walk back up to the 8th floor.[48]

When later asked where the explosion originated, Jennings said: "Under us. It was definitely under us, it was definitely under us." When asked if it lifted them up, he said: "Yeah, it blew us back."[49] He later repeated the point, saying: "The explosion was beneath me."[50]

The account by Jennings differs from that of Hess on one point:

Whereas Hess, as we saw earlier, said that the explosion occurred when they reached the 8th floor, Jennings said that it was when they reached the 6th floor, after which they "went back up to the eighth floor." However, it may be that Hess did not consider that detail important enough to mention in the very brief account he was giving. Or perhaps he simply misspoke—in a later interview, in fact, Hess said that it occurred when they got to the 6th floor.[51] (Also, Jennings himself on one occasion spoke of the explosion as having occurred when they were on the 8th floor, although he later corrected this statement.[52])

In any case, Jennings expressed no doubt about his statement that what they experienced was an explosion in WTC 7. Besides *calling* it "an explosion," he specified that it happened "beneath" him and that it was powerful enough to cause the landing on which he was standing to give way.

Jennings was also certain that what he considered an explosion beneath him could not have been simply effects from the collapse of one of the towers. During the interview, Dylan Avery pointed out that, according to defenders of the official story, "the whole reason that Building 7 collapsed… is because the North Tower fell onto it and caused damage. And what people are going to say is… that Barry was hit by debris from the North Tower." Jennings replied: "No. What happened was, when we made it back to the 8th floor, as I told you earlier, both buildings were still standing."[53] Jennings clearly rejected Giuliani's claim, therefore, that it was debris from the North Tower collapse that caused him and his companion to become trapped.

After getting back up to the 8th floor, Jennings said, he used a fire extinguisher to break a window, after which he was able to catch someone's attention with his cries for help.[54] He and Hess, however, were not rescued immediately, as Jennings explained:

> I was trapped in there several hours. I was trapped in there when both buildings came down. The firefighters came…. And then they ran away. See, I didn't know what was going on. That's when the first tower fell. When they started running, the first tower was coming down. I had no way of knowing that. Then I saw them come back. Now I saw them come back with more concern on their faces. Instead, they ran away again: the second tower fell. So, as they turned and ran the second time, the guy said, "Don't worry, we'll be back for you. And they did come back.[55]

Jennings repeated this explanation of how he knew that the Twin Towers were both still standing when the explosion occurred, saying:

> When I got to the 6th floor, there was an explosion. That's what forced us back to the 8th floor. Both buildings were still standing. Keep in mind, I told you the fire department came and ran. They came twice. Why? Because Building Tower One fell, then Tower Two fell. And then when they came back, they came back all concerned to get me the hell out of there, and they did.[56]

In other words, although firefighters were ready to rescue them before 10:00, the firefighters had to leave because of the collapse of the South Tower, which occurred at 9:59. Then, although firefighters returned to the site, they had to leave again at 10:28, when the North Tower collapsed.

Also notable is Jennings' statement that they were trapped "several hours." This assertion suggests that Hess's estimate that they were trapped for "about an hour and a half" may have been somewhat conservative. For example, if the period was closer to two hours, then, if they were rescued by 11:30AM (allowing Hess 25 minutes to talk to people and walk to the location of his 11:57 interview), then the explosion would have occurred at about 9:30.

In any case, the most important point is that, whereas Giuliani had claimed that the two men were trapped because of damage caused by the collapse of the North Tower, Jennings stated that the North Tower and even the South Tower collapsed only *after* an explosion had caused them to become trapped. What Jennings called "an explosion" beneath him could not, therefore, have simply been some effects created in WTC 7 by the collapse of the North Tower. He and Hess were clearly describing an explosion that occurred in WTC 7 approximately an hour before the 10:28 collapse of the North Tower.

Moreover, besides reporting the big explosion that knocked the landing out from under them, Jennings spoke of further explosions. Referring to the time the two men were trapped, waiting for firefighters to rescue them, Jennings said: "All this time, I'm hearing all type of explosions. All this time, I'm hearing explosions."[57]

Jennings also reported that, when he was taken down to the lobby of WTC 7, he was amazed by what he saw:

When they finally got to us and they took us down to what they called the lobby—'cause I asked them when we got down there, "Where are we?" he said, "This *was* the lobby," and I said, "You got to be kidding me." It was total ruins, total ruins. Now keep in mind, when I came in there, the lobby had nice escalators, it was a huge lobby, and for me to see what I saw, it was unbelievable.[58]

He later added: "[T]he lobby was totally destroyed. It looked like King Kong had came through and stepped on it. And it was so destroyed I didn't know where I was. And it was so destroyed that they had to take me out through a hole in the wall."[59]

In the course of describing his experience while walking through this lobby, Jennings contradicted the official account of the collapse of WTC 7 on still another point. According to that account, no one died in this building. NIST wrote: "No lives were lost in WTC 7."[60] Jennings, however, suggested otherwise, saying:

[T]he firefighter that took us down kept saying, "Don't look down." I asked, "Why?" And he said, "Do not look down." We were stepping over people, and you know you can feel when you're stepping over people.[61]

Jennings' account of the destroyed lobby is given added credibility by the fact that he (and perhaps also Hess) evidently reported it shortly after the event. The previously cited *Independent* story, published two days after 9/11, said that Hess and Jennings went "downstairs to the lobby, or what was left of it."[62] It cannot be claimed, therefore, that Jennings' statement to Avery about the destruction of the lobby was a later elaboration.

Before completing his narrative, Jennings spoke of still more explosions, saying:

They took us out through a hole in the wall.… And this big giant police officer came to me, and he says, "You have to run," and I said, "I can't run, my knees are swollen." He said, "You'll have to get on your knees and crawl, then, because we have reports of more explosions."[63]

As to why his knees would have been swollen, this is probably explained by the above-quoted statement by Jennings—a big, heavy-set man—that while rushing down the stairwell he had been "jumping landings." Be that as it may, the police officer's meaning was evidently that Jennings needed to leave the premises quickly because more explosions were expected.

The testimony of Michael Hess and Barry Jennings was clearly threatening to the official account of WTC 7, according to which its collapse was not caused or even aided by explosives. I turn now to the way in which NIST dealt with this threat in its 2005 report, which would be repeated in its 2008 report on WTC 7. I will then deal with the BBC's attempt in 2008 to popularize and bolster NIST's account.

NIST's Treatment of the Hess–Jennings Episode

Prior to its 2008 report on WTC 7, NIST had referred twice to the fact that Hess and Jennings were trapped in this building.

The first mention of this episode was in a progress report that NIST put out in 2004.[64] Although most of this report dealt with the Twin Towers, it included as an appendix the earlier-mentioned *Interim Report on WTC 7*, for which NIST staff person Therese McAllister was evidently the lead author.[65] In this document, NIST said that the men had been rescued "[a]t 12:10 to 12:15PM."[66] But if Hess was being interviewed several blocks away at 11:57, they must have been rescued, as we saw earlier, no later than 11:30AM.[67] The assertion that they were not rescued before 12:10PM is, therefore, clearly false.

Why would NIST have made this false assertion? Apparently because this assertion allowed NIST to claim—as had Giuliani in his 2002 book—that the event called "an explosion" by Hess and Jennings was really caused by debris from the collapse of the North Tower. NIST made this claim in its 2005 report on the Twin Towers, which consisted of a main report and 42 supporting volumes.[68] One of those supporting volumes, entitled *The Emergency Response Operations*, described the rescue of Hess and Jennings from WTC 7. In an account that referred to Hess simply as a "New York City employee" and misidentified Jennings as "a WTC building staff person," the authors of this volume, Randall Lawson and Robert Vettori, wrote:

> With the collapse of the two towers, a New York City employee and a WTC 7 building staff person became trapped inside of WTC 7. The two had gone to the OEM center on the 23rd floor and found no one there. As they went to get into an elevator to go downstairs the lights inside of WTC 7 flickered as WTC 2 collapsed. At this

point, the elevator they were attempting to catch no longer worked, so they started down the staircase. When they got to the 6th floor, WTC 1 collapsed, the lights went out in the staircase, the sprinklers came on briefly, and the staircase filled with smoke and debris. The two men went back to the 8th floor broke out a window and called for help. Firefighters on the ground saw them and went up the stairs.... [They] shined their flashlight through the staircase smoke and called out. The two trapped men on the 8th floor saw the flash-light beam and heard the firefighters calling and went down the stairway. The firefighters took the men outside and directed them away from the building.[69]

This account radically changed the timeline of the Hess–Jennings episode from the one Jennings himself gave.

First, Jennings said that it was shortly after the South Tower was *struck*, and hence shortly after 9:03, when he and Hess had started down the stairs. As to why they went down the stairs instead of taking the elevator, Hess had said during his interview on 9/11 that it was because the power had gone out in WTC 7. But Lawson and Vettori suggested that the building's electric power was lost when the South Tower *collapsed*, which did not occur until 9:59. It was only then, according to NIST, that the two men started down the stairs.

Second, the event that blocked their descent at the 6th floor, accord-ing to Jennings, was an explosion, powerful enough to knock the landing out from under them. His account suggested that this explosion would have happened no later than 9:30. But NIST claimed, as had Giuliani in 2002, that the stairwell became blocked because of debris from the North Tower's collapse, which did not occur until 10:28.[70]

Third, Jennings said that, "want[ing] to get out of that building in a hurry," he was "jumping landings," which suggests that it would have taken him only a few minutes to descend from the 23rd to the 6th floor, once he had received word that they should get out of the build-ing. But NIST's timeline implied, implausibly, that it took Jennings and Hess almost a half hour—from about 9:59, when the South Tower collapsed, until 10:28, when the North Tower collapsed—to get down those seventeen flights of stairs.

Fourth, Jennings reported that, after the explosion, "both [towers] were still standing." He knew this because, after the firemen came to rescue them, they ran away (which was when the first tower collapsed);

then the firemen came back, but again ran away (when the second tower collapsed). NIST's timeline, by contrast, entailed that both towers had already collapsed by the time Jennings first called for help.

It appears that NIST's 2004 claim that the rescue of Hess and Jennings occurred at "12:10 to 12:15PM" was a result of NIST's timeline—according to which they had became trapped at 10:28—combined with Hess's statement that they were not rescued until about 90 minutes after they were trapped.

NIST's claim that the two men did not become trapped until 10:28 created yet another problem. Jennings had provided an explanation as to why it took so long for him and Hess to be rescued: Although the firefighters had come twice, they had to leave each time one of the Twin Towers came down. But NIST, as we saw, simply said: "The two men went back to the 8th floor [and] broke out a window and called for help. Firefighters on the ground saw them and went up the stairs." NIST thereby portrayed Jennings as having broken the window at about 10:30. Why would it have then taken the firefighters over 90 minutes—from roughly 10:30AM until 12:10 or 12:15PM—to rescue the men, given the fact that both towers had already collapsed? NIST offered no explanation.

Besides contradicting many statements by Jennings and creating the two problems just mentioned—why it took Hess and Jennings so long to reach the 6th floor and then why it took the firefighters so long to rescue them—NIST's timeline also contradicted the fact that Hess gave an interview several blocks away that started before noon, which means, as we have seen, that he and Jennings must have been rescued no later than 11:30AM.

Having distorted Jennings' testimony on many points by changing the timeline of the events he reported, NIST then completely omitted the final part of his testimony, in which he reported that the lobby of WTC 7 had been destroyed, that he felt himself "stepping over people," and that the "big giant police officer" said that there were "reports of more explosions." NIST again simply omitted whatever evidence did not fit its story.

Is it possible that Jennings had not told NIST the things he told Avery? Although this is not likely—especially given the fact that Jennings, as we saw earlier—explicitly said that he had been asked the same questions and had given the same answers—it is possible. Assuming for the sake of argument that it is true, is it also possible that NIST did not know about Avery's interview of Jennings? That would be very unlikely simply from the fact that this interview, titled "Barry Jennings Uncut," was made available on the internet in the second week of July 2008, over a month before NIST issued its Draft Report on WTC 7. Beyond that, moreover, Avery notified NIST about the interview, he has reported.[71] We can safely conclude, therefore, that NIST was not ignorant of this interview; it simply ignored it.

I turn now to the way in which the BBC, which supported NIST's explanation of the collapse of WTC 7, treated the testimony of Hess and Jennings in its documentary about WTC 7.

The BBC's Treatment of the Hess–Jennings Testimony

Dealing with the BBC's treatment of this testimony is complicated by the fact that it put out two versions of its documentary on the collapse of WTC 7: one that included testimony from Barry Jennings but none from Michael Hess and, in fact, even ignored the fact that Hess had been present; and a later one that, in addition to acknowledging Hess's presence, included testimony from him.

The First Version of the BBC's Program on WTC 7: On July 6, 2008, the BBC aired a documentary entitled *The Conspiracy Files: 9/11—The Third Tower*,[72] which supported the official view of the collapse of WTC 7. It described Barry Jennings as "the key witness in the controversy over what really happened inside Tower 7." It could thus describe him, while supporting the official view, because it distorted the meaning of his statements by placing them within the timeline provided by NIST.

For example, right after showing Jennings recounting the fact that, while on the 23rd floor, he was told to exit WTC 7 quickly (an exit that, according to Jennings, occurred not long after 9:03), the BBC narrator said: "At 9:59, the 1,300-foot South Tower collapses."[73] The BBC thus made it seem as if Jennings did not start down the stairs until after 9:59.

Next, after showing Jennings' account of rushing down the stairs to the 6th floor, at which point the staircase landing was knocked out from under him (which would have probably have been between 9:15 and 9:30), the BBC narrator said: "At 10:28, the North Tower collapses…. This time, Tower 7 takes a direct hit from the collapsing building."[74] The BBC thus made it seem as if Jennings himself had said that this was when he became trapped.

These timeline distortions then allowed the narrator to conclude: "Early evidence of explosives were just debris from a falling skyscraper."[75]

Having drawn this false conclusion, the BBC could then misuse Jennings' account of the destructiveness of the explosion in WTC 7— "When we got to the 8th floor," Jennings said, "I thought of walking to one side of the building. That side of the building was gone!"—as evidence that debris from the North Tower's collapse had caused great damage to WTC 7.[76] The BBC also used Jennings' account of fire caused by the explosion—he said, "I could smell fire; you know, you could smell the smoke, and I felt the heat; it was intense"—as evidence that fires had been set in WTC 7 by debris from the North Tower.[77]

To complete the timeline distortion, the BBC, after showing Jennings describing how he finally got outside the building, showed a clock with its hands at 12:03 (which came close to the rescue time— "12:10 to 12:15PM"—stated in NIST's 2004 *Interim Report on WTC 7*).

Here, however, the BBC slipped up, saying that Jennings was finally rescued "after surviving for three hours, trapped inside an inferno."[78] This was a slip, because if Jennings had been trapped in the building for three hours before being rescued at 12:03, he would have been trapped since 9:03. The BBC thereby inadvertently stated the truth: that Jennings (and Hess) had started down the stairs shortly after the South Tower *was struck* (which occurred at 9:03), *not* shortly after the South Tower *collapsed* (which occurred at 9:59).

This slip aside, the most important issue is how the BBC handled the problematic fact that Michael Hess, who had been with Jennings and was rescued at the same time, had given an interview several blocks away before noon. If Hess and Jennings had not been rescued until *after* noon, as the BBC suggested, Hess could not have been giving this interview *before* noon.

The BBC dealt with this problem by simply making no mention of Hess, giving the impression that Jennings experienced these events all by himself. The BBC did this even though Jennings had sometimes, in statements included in the BBC program, used the word "we." In describing explosions, for example, he said: "The first explosion I heard when we were on the stairwell landing, when we made it down to the

6th floor."[79] Bizarrely, however, the BBC narrator consistently spoke only of Jennings, never uttering Hess's name or even mentioning that Jennings was with another man.

In addition to distorting Jennings' timeline and pretending that he had experienced these events all by himself, the BBC also engaged in another type of dishonesty: It sought to discredit the *Loose Change* producers by suggesting that *they* had distorted Jennings' testimony—even though footage played by the BBC clearly showed that they had not.

The controversy, such as it was, revolved around Jennings' statement that, when he was being taken through the lobby by a firefighter, they were "stepping over people." After declaring, "There is no evidence that anyone died in Tower 7 on 9/11," the BBC tried to make it seem as if the *Loose Change* producers, by saying that Jennings had indicated otherwise, had mischaracterized his testimony. To do this, the BBC first showed Dylan Avery saying: "He [Jennings] says he was stepping over dead bodies in the lobby." The BBC then said: "Trouble is, Barry Jennings himself disagrees with their interpretation of his words." It then showed Jennings saying:

> I didn't like the way, you know… they portrayed me as seeing dead bodies. I never saw dead bodies.… I said it felt like I was stepping over them, but I never saw any.[80]

As we can see, this was at most a quibble about words. The central issue raised by the BBC in its statement introducing this segment was whether Jennings had suggested that there were bodies in the lobby. He clearly had. Whether he had *seen* them or merely *felt* them was a secondary matter, to which the BBC should not have devoted any time. But it clearly wanted to use this quibble to suggest that the *Loose Change* producers had misrepresented Jennings' testimony on this subject.

Moreover, the BBC provided no evidence that the *Loose Change* producers had ever claimed that Jennings had *seen* bodies. In the statement quoted above, Avery had said: "He [Jennings] says he was stepping over dead bodies in the lobby." When the BBC confronted Avery on camera with the charge that he had taken Jennings' statement out of context, Avery played the portion of the *Loose Change* interview in which Jennings said:

[T]he firefighter that took us down kept saying, "Don't look down." I asked, "Why?" And he said, "Do not look down." We were stepping over people, and you know you can feel when you're stepping over people.[81]

So, although the BBC had introduced this segment by saying that Jennings disagreed with the *Loose Change* producers' interpretation of his words, it showed no actual disagreement. Indeed, this segment of the interview even explained why Jennings would not have "seen" any bodies—because he had been told by the firefighter not to look down.

Was this supposed disagreement between Jennings and the *Loose Change* producers manufactured by the BBC? We do not know. What does seem clear, however, is that the BBC unfairly used it to create the impression that the *Loose Change* producers had distorted Jennings' testimony. The BBC was thereby able to appear to have supported the claim with which it began this segment, namely: "There's no evidence that anyone died in Tower 7 on 9/11."

It was clearly the BBC, however, that had distorted Jennings' testimony on this subject, because he had supplied such evidence. And this, as we have seen, is simply one of many ways in which the BBC, in the interests of supporting NIST's claim that there were no explosions in WTC 7, distorted Jennings' testimony.

The BBC rightly called Jennings "the key witness in the controversy over what really happened inside Tower 7." His testimony, undistorted, provided evidence that a very powerful explosion occurred within WTC 7 fairly early that morning, followed by other explosions, and that, at some point, people in the building were killed.

Jennings, however, would not personally be able to correct the distortions of his record by NIST and the BBC. Although only 53 years old, he reportedly died, after several days in a hospital, on August 19, 2008.[82] This was just two days before NIST had its August 21 press briefing to announce the Draft version of its final report on WTC 7.

As this book was going to press, those who have tried to obtain any additional information from authorities, even about the reported cause of Jennings' death, have been unable to do so. In April 2009, for example, Dylan Avery hired a private investigator—reputed to be one of the best in the state of New York—to find out what she could. Within 24 hours, however, Avery received a message from her, saying:

Due to some of the information I have uncovered, I have determined that this is a job for the police. I have refunded your credit card. Please do not contact me again about this individual.

This sounded like the response of a person who had been frightened. It is, in any case, not the response one would expect, as Avery observed, if she had merely found that Jennings had passed away "innocently in a hospital."[83]

Whatever its actual cause, Jennings' death at that time was undeniably convenient for NIST. There would now be no chance that Jennings would be asked—perhaps again by Avery, perhaps by a mainstream reporter who had watched "Barry Jennings Uncut," perhaps by a grand jury—what he thought about NIST's report on WTC 7. Jennings' death was also convenient, as we will see next, for the BBC.

The Second Version of the BBC's Program on WTC 7: On October 26, 2008—almost 10 weeks after Jennings died—the BBC aired a revised version of its WTC 7 program, entitled *The Conspiracy Files: 9/11—The Truth behind the Third Tower.*[84] This version was significantly different. In the first version, as we saw, Jennings was portrayed as having been alone and, accordingly, was described in the singular as the "key witness." In this new version, by contrast, Michael Hess's presence with Jennings is acknowledged; the BBC now uses the plural, referring to the two of them as the "key witnesses"; and several statements from Hess are included, among them his assertion that "there were no explosions."[85]

The addition of Hess is, in fact, the major way in which this second version of the BBC program differs from the first. The statements from Hess, which are interspersed throughout the program, were taken from a BBC interview with him. Producer Mike Rudin, in his blog of October 21, 2008, called it Hess's "first interview since 9/11," adding that it was "recently recorded."[86]

By including Hess in this second version of its documentary, the BBC was able to shore up its chronology. In his blog, Rudin acknowledged that some critics, whom he called "self-styled truthers," had charged that the first version of the BBC's program, in presenting Barry Jennings' testimony, had "misrepresented the chronology." Rudin was able to reply to this charge by referring to the BBC's "recently recorded" interview with Michael Hess, saying: "In his first interview since 9/11 he confirms our timeline."[87]

Although "confirms" is a loaded word, implying the correctness of the BBC timeline, it is certainly true that Hess *endorsed* this timeline, at least on the crucial issue of the time of the event that Jennings had called an "explosion." While now claiming that "there were no explosions" in WTC 7, Hess admitted that, at the time, he had "assumed that there had been an explosion in the basement." He also acknowledged that the lights had gone out, that the stairwell had filled with smoke and soot, that the sprinklers had come on, and that he had felt "the building shake." But, he claimed: "I know now this was caused by the northern half of Number 1 [the North Tower] falling on the southern half of our building."[88]

This interpretation would mean, of course, that the event did *not* occur before either of the Twin Towers had collapsed, as Jennings had said, but instead at 10:28, as NIST and the BBC had claimed. Besides including these statements by Hess in the second version of its program, the BBC had its narrator emphasize their significance by introducing Hess with these words: "One witness who first thought there was an explosion is now clear that it was something else."[89]

The BBC hence used Hess to refute what was said in the *Loose Change* interview by Jennings, who can no longer defend his account (except posthumously, by means of that interview, which is widely available on the internet and also in a new [2009] version of *Loose Change*[90]).

Back on 9/11 itself, Hess evidently gave the same account as Jennings. In his interview with UPN 9 News, as we saw, he said that there had been an explosion. At that time, Hess clearly had no idea what Giuliani's account of WTC 7 would be. But after he became aware of this account—which would likewise become the account given by NIST and the BBC—Hess would not have wanted to contradict it: Besides being an old friend of Giuliani's, he had since 2002 been a founding partner and vice chairman of the former mayor's consulting business, Giuliani Partners LLC.[91]

Hess also, however, probably would not have wanted to contradict the account given by Barry Jennings, which had become somewhat well known on the internet. Indeed, if Hess had contradicted Jennings' account and then Jennings had publicly disputed Hess's account, implying that Hess was either lying or seriously confused, this dispute could have resulted in considerable publicity for something that Giuliani and other defenders of the official story surely wanted kept quiet—the fact that Jennings had testified to an enormous explosion in WTC 7 on the morning of 9/11 and that Hess had originally supported that testimony.

It is not surprising, therefore, that Hess's "first interview since 9/11" occurred only after Jennings was dead.

The BBC apparently tried to suggest that the second version of its program, and hence its interview with Hess, had been made before Jennings had died. At the end of the program, the following statement appears on the screen: "Since this program was filmed Barry Jennings has sadly passed away."[92] That would most likely be true only if by "this program," the BBC meant the first version of it, which was aired July 6, 2008. If Jennings died on August 19, the second version, which was not aired until October 26 and hence almost ten weeks later, was probably filmed *after* Jennings' death. This assumption seems confirmed in Mike Rudin's own blog of October 26, in which he said that the interview with Hess had been "recently recorded."

A second thing that is not surprising about Hess's interview, when he finally did allow one, is that his account agrees point by point with Giuliani's 2002 account (which can be reviewed on pages 85–86, above).

Giuliani had written: "When [Hess] got to the 8th floor [of WTC 7], Tower 1—the North Tower—collapsed, part of it falling on top of the southern part of 7 World Trade Center." Hess similarly, as we just saw, told the BBC that "the northern half of Number 1 [fell] on the southern half of our building."

Giuliani then wrote: "Luckily, Mike was in the northern section of the building." Hess told the BBC: "We were in the northern half of our building so luckily we weren't crushed."[93]

It was almost as if Hess had reviewed Giuliani's account before doing the interview. In any case, by virtue of agreeing with Giuliani, Hess's 2008 statement also agreed with NIST and thereby the BBC. Accordingly, as we saw, the BBC's Mike Rudin said that Hess's testimony "confirms" the BBC's chronology. It could have confirmatory value, however, only if it were plausible. But it is problematic in many ways.

One problem is that Hess's BBC account is contradicted by Barry Jennings' account on two points: First, Jennings said that he and Hess ran down the stairs following the attack on the South Tower, hence not long after 9:03, but Hess now implies that they started down the stairs almost an hour later, right after 9:59, when the South Tower collapsed. Second, Jennings explicitly said that he heard explosions, stating: "The first explosion I heard when we were on the stairwell landing, when we made it down to the 6th floor. Then we made it back to the 8th floor, and I heard some more explosions." When he was asked by the BBC interviewer what it sounded like, Jennings said: "Like a boom, like an explosion."[94] But when Hess was asked whether he heard "any sounds, like explosions," he replies: "No, nothing.... My position, and I'm quite firm on it, there were no explosions."[95] If Hess really disagreed with Jennings on these points with regard to what the two of them had experienced, why did he wait until after Jennings was dead to give his contradictory account?

A second problem with Hess's new testimony involves the first of the above points of disagreement: the time at which the two men started down the stairs. As we saw earlier, an *Independent* story two days after 9/11 echoed Jennings' account, saying: "After the second plane hit they [Hess and Jennings] scrambled downstairs."[96] This story shows, therefore, that what Jennings told Dylan Avery is what he— and possibly Hess—had told the press immediately after the event.

A third problem involves the second point of disagreement. When Hess was interviewed by UPN 9 News on 9/11, he did not express the slightest doubt about there having been an explosion. He did not, for example, speak of an event that *might* have been an explosion, or that he *assumed* to have been an explosion. He simply stated, as a matter of fact, that "there was an explosion." Would he have spoken with such certainty if he had not *heard* an explosion? And given how certain he appeared to have been at that time, before he knew what the official story was going to be, how can we believe his present claim, according to which he heard nothing and is now quite certain that no explosions occurred?

A fourth problem with Hess's statement to the BBC is that, in this statement, he implies that he and Jennings had arrived at WTC 7 shortly after the attack on the North Tower. He said: "In an emergency, we were supposed to go and huddle and plan and strategize with Mayor Giuliani in the emergency management center on the 23rd floor. That was the plan."[97] If that was the plan, Hess and Jennings should have arrived shortly after the first attack and hence around 9:00, as Jennings had said, not almost an hour later, shortly before the 9:59 collapse of the South Tower. But if they arrived at about 9:00AM and found that the emergency management center was empty, as Hess as well as Jennings said,[98] then why would they still have been up there at 9:59, when the South Tower collapsed? Why would they have remained in this empty building for almost an hour—especially after two World Trade Center buildings had been hit by airplanes? The idea is completely implausible.

A fifth problem was discussed earlier in relation to NIST's account: If Hess and Jennings started down the stairs right after the collapse of the South Tower and hence at about 10:00AM, why would it have taken them 28 minutes to descend the 17 flights from the 23rd to the 6th floor? Jennings said that they were running down the stairs (saying that he was "jumping landings"), so it certainly would not have taken them over 90 seconds per floor.

A sixth problem, which was mentioned earlier in discussing Giuliani's account, involves Hess's statement to the BBC that he and Jennings were in the *northern* part of WTC 7 (so that, when they went back up to the 8th floor, they could not see whether the Twin Towers had collapsed). If so, then why did the debris from the North Tower, which struck the *south* part of WTC 7, cause their stairwell, on the north side of the building, to become blocked? The account by Hess and the BBC, like that by Giuliani, is simply self-contradictory on this issue.

A seventh problem for Hess's new story concerns his own interview with UPN 9 News: If the event that he had earlier called "an explosion" had really been caused by the collapse of the North Tower, which occurred at 10:28, and if he and Jennings had then been trapped for "about an hour and a half" before they were rescued, as he reported on that day itself, then how did he get back to City Hall, several blocks away, in time to be interviewed before noon?

Accordingly, every part of Hess's new story is either inherently implausible or contradicted by the testimony of Jennings, who—unlike Hess—had no obvious motive to lie. The BBC cannot credibly claim, therefore, that the truth of its chronology was "confirmed" by Hess's testimony.

To conclude this discussion of the BBC's effort to bolster NIST's attempt to neutralize Barry Jennings' testimony about explosions in WTC 7: Far from bolstering NIST's account, the BBC succeeded only in making it more obviously problematic. It did this by allowing

Jennings to tell his story on a mainstream television program while revising Jennings' chronology in a way that could be easily exposed as a distortion; by first trying to pretend that Jennings was by himself, even though he repeatedly spoke of "we"; by only later, after Jennings was dead, admitting that he had been accompanied by Michael Hess, who was now used by the BBC to support the official account; and by making public an interview with Hess that is so riddled with problems as to leave little doubt that it is a tissue of falsehoods from beginning to end.

As a result, the testimony of Barry Jennings stands: There were explosions in WTC 7 on the morning of 9/11, with a huge one occurring not long after 9:03, hence prior to the collapse of both of the Twin Towers.

NIST's Implicit Account of the Rescue Time

According to the scenario suggested by Hess and Jennings on 9/11, as well as by Jennings subsequently, they were trapped not long after 9:03AM (probably sometime between 9:15 and 9:30), and rescued no later than 11:30AM. Further support for the truth of this account is provided by the fact that NIST itself implies, while describing the Hess–Jennings rescue in its WTC 7 report of 2008, that it took place at about 11:00AM.

This report's account of the rescue of Hess and Jennings is contained in a passage that focuses primarily on a security officer who was said also to have been in the building:

> A security officer for one of the businesses in the building headed back up to a floor in the 40s after WTC 2 collapsed [i.e., after 9:59am] to see if all his personnel were out of the building.... The security officer had reached the 30th floor when the building shook as WTC 1 collapsed, and the stairwell became dark. He began to descend and stopped at the 23rd floor to see if anyone was on the OEM floor. He opened the door to check for staff that might have been present and saw the area was filled with smoke. He made it down to the 7th floor, where he stopped because he could not see or breathe at this point. He broke a window near the center of the north face to yell for help. A ladder truck pulled up, but could not reach the window because of the Con Edison building extension at the lower floors. Firemen came up the stairwell right away.... As the

firefighters went up, they vented the stairway and cleared some of the smoke. They first met the security officer on the 7th floor, and firefighters escorted him down the stairs. Other firefighters from the group continued up the stairs, shined their flashlights through the staircase smoke and called out. The two trapped men on the 8th floor [i.e., Hess and Jennings] saw the flashlight beams, heard the firefighters calling, and went down the stairway. The firefighters took the men outside and directed them away from the building.[99]

According to this account, a security officer was on the 30th floor at 10:28, when the North Tower collapsed. Then, after descending to the 23rd floor and opening the door to the Office of Emergency Management, to make sure no one was still there, he descended to the 7th floor. Even if we assume he was, because of the darkness, going down the stairs slowly, he surely would have reached the 7th floor by 10:40. He then broke a window and yelled for help. After firefighters found that they could not get a ladder to his window, they came up the stairs "right away"—which means that they probably would have reached him by 11:00. Then while some of the firefighters led the security officer out of the building, others continued up toward the 8th floor, found Hess and Jennings, and led them out of the building.

The conclusion that this account implies that Hess and Jennings were rescued at about 11:00AM is reinforced by another fact: The section of the NIST report *after* this description of the rescue is headed "Activity from 11:02 to approximately 2:30PM EDT."[100]

Moreover—to bring up a remarkable fact not mentioned earlier—this rescue account in NIST's 2008 report on WTC 7 is essentially the same as the rescue account provided in its 2005 report, which was quoted earlier. In my previous discussion of that 2005 account, however, I interpreted it in light of the statement, found in NIST's 2004 *Interim Report on WTC 7*, that the rescue did not occur until "12:10 to 12:15PM." But nothing in that 2005 rescue account itself—which had different authors than the 2004 report[101]—suggested that the rescue occurred so late. Instead, like the account provided in NIST's 2008 report, it suggested that Hess and Jennings were rescued at about 11:00AM. This is not surprising, given the fact that the same person—J. Randall Lawson—was the first-listed author of each document.[102]

In Lawson's 2005 version, however, he and his coauthor, Robert Vettori, were somewhat vague about how quickly the firefighters started up the stairs to rescue the three men (Hess, Jennings, and the security officer).[103] One could, therefore, not say for certain that their account contradicted NIST's statement, made in its 2004 *Interim Report on WTC 7*, that they were not rescued until "12:10 to 12:15PM."

But in Lawson's account in NIST's 2008 report, he and his coauthor, Richard Gann, are more explicit about this point. Their account, quoted above, says that when the security officer broke a window on the 7th floor (following the 10:28 collapse of WTC 1) and yelled for help, the firefighters, after unsuccessfully trying to get a ladder to his window, "came up the stairwell right away." This Lawson–Gann account could not reasonably be read as the description of a rescue effort that, by not succeeding until 12:10 to 12:15PM, took close to an hour and a half. It is clear, therefore, that this account contradicted the 2004 *Interim Report*'s claim—a claim also made by the BBC[104]—that Hess and Jennings were not rescued until after noon.

The conclusion that NIST gave two mutually inconsistent versions of the rescue of the three men is confirmed by its treatment of the security officer, and in this case the inconsistency occurs within the pages of NIST's 2008 WTC 7 report itself.

In its fifth chapter, written by William M. Pitts, we read that "a witness saw a fire on the southwest corner of the 7th floor at about 12:15PM, before being rescued (Chapter 6)."[105] Pitts thereby agreed with NIST's 2004 *Interim Report on WTC 7* with regard to the question of when the men were rescued.

However, when we follow Pitts' suggestion to turn to Chapter 6, which is the chapter in which Randall Lawson and Richard Gann describe the rescues, we find that this "witness" is the security officer we discussed above. The statement about his seeing a fire on the 7th floor is in a sentence that was omitted, for the sake of brevity, in my earlier quotation of Lawson and Gann's 2008 account of the rescue. A portion of that passage, with the omitted sentence reinserted and italicized, reads:

> He broke a window near the center of the north face to yell for help. A ladder truck pulled up, but could not reach the window because of the Con Edison building extension at the lower floors. Firemen came up the stairwell right away. *Soon after WTC 1 collapsed, the security officer saw a fire on the west side of Floor 7 that he attempted to put out with an extinguisher, but he was unable to do so. As the*

firefighters went up, they vented the stairway and cleared some of the smoke. They first met the security officer on the 7th floor, and firefighters escorted him down the stairs.[106]

In this Chapter 6 account by Lawson and Gann, the security officer observed the fire "shortly after WTC 1 collapsed," meaning shortly after 10:28AM—not at "about 12:15PM," as the Chapter 5 account by William Pitts states. Pitts even, as we saw above, referred readers to Chapter 6, evidently not realizing that its account contradicted his own.

These two contradictions within the 2008 report—regarding the time at which the security officer observed a fire on the 7th floor and the time at which the three men were rescued—show that the various authors of the NIST report had not settled upon a consistent story. Obviously, both sets of stories cannot be true. And, as we have seen, the "12:10 to 12:15PM" rescue time contradicts not only the testimony of Jennings but also the fact that Hess gave an interview before noon. Of the two NIST stories, therefore, the Lawson–Gann account, which suggests that the men were rescued at about 11:00, is surely closer to the truth.

However, to suggest that this element in the Lawson–Gann rescue account is true, or at least close to the truth, is not to suggest that this account is true in its entirety. It is, in fact, almost certainly not.

One problem is that this account—by indicating that firefighters were available to rescue the men when the security officer called for help shortly after the 10:28 collapse of the North Tower—implies that firefighters stayed at the WTC site after that collapse, or at least returned within a few minutes. This would have been impossible, because the collapse of each of the Twin Towers produced an enormous dust cloud that blocked out all light and made breathing virtually impossible.

For example, the transcription of Captain Karin Deshore's account of her experiences after the collapse of the South Tower reads thus:

Total darkness, total noise.... Can't tell you how long it was before it died down.... Not being able to breath—there was no air whatever. This explosion... simply sucked all the oxygen out of the air.... Sudden[ly] it was all over and... you could open your eyes. It was pitch black.... Can't give you time periods.... [A] man said "I'm over here; can't see." That's when [I] opened my eyes; said "can't see either." He said, "Okay, I'm going to talk. . . we will find each other.... And we held onto each other like little kids. By then we were coughing, vomiting, spitting. It was just, we were trying to breathe.[107]

Paramedic Louis Cook had a similar experience after the collapse of the North Tower. Having just returned to the site after surviving the South Tower's collapse by running away, Cook said that when he heard the North Tower start to rumble:

> I didn't look up. I figured I've been through this once. I know what's coming now. I started running north on West Street. Stuff just kept hitting it seemed like right behind me.... This time fire was coming down, because I could feel the heat. I grabbed a firefighter's turnout coat... I threw it over my shoulders.... I ended up diving down next to some kind of truck.... I just waited there. I just covered up.... The heavy stuff was really hitting the ground.... I just waited there for everything to stop.... I couldn't breathe. I'm breathing in my shirt.... I figured, all right, now you've got to find a way out of here because you're going to suffocate. So I start crawling—because I can't see, I start crawling and doing one of these sweeps in front of me so I don't hit anything. Somebody yells, "Is there anybody out there?" I was like, "Yeah. It's Cook."... The response was, "Yeah, this is Chief McCarthy.... So I yelled, "Just keep yelling. I'll find you." He started just calling back and forth his name. I remember crawling up to him, and... I grabbed him by the arm.... We latched onto each other's arms. We were crawling, and we stood up. He said to me, "All right. As long as we make it to the water, we'll be all right."... I had an idea where the water is. You still can't see it because it's dark as a mother. You can't breathe. It's so heavy with smoke and dust and ash. I can't breathe. I have... dust impaction in my ears, in my nose. I was coughing it out of my mouth. It felt like I had a baseball in my mouth.[108]

As these accounts show, the idea that firefighters could have remained at the site, or could have returned within ten minutes, is quite implausible. (The fact that the firefighters had to leave—indeed, to run for their lives—was reflected in an earlier-quoted account by Barry Jennings, in which he said: "The fire department came and ran. They came twice. Why? Because Building Tower One fell, and then Tower Two fell."[109])

An equally serious problem is created by the idea, suggested by the Lawson–Gann account, that Hess and Jennings were rescued about 30 minutes after they had become trapped. This suggestion is implicit in both the 2005 and the 2008 versions of Lawson's account of the rescue, because both versions say that it was the collapse of the North Tower at 10:28 that trapped the two men. This means that, if they were rescued at about 11:00, they would have been trapped for only about half an hour.

Hess and Jennings themselves, as we have seen, said that they had been trapped for much longer: Hess said "about an hour and a half"; Jennings said "several hours." They surely would not have made these estimates if they had really been trapped for only about half an hour.

It would appear that Lawson's rescue account, with its difficulties, resulted from combining the account given in Rudy Giuliani's 2002 book—in which he said that Hess and Jennings were trapped at 10:28 by damage caused by the North Tower collapse—with the testimony given to NIST in 2004 by Hess and Jennings themselves, who probably reported that they had been rescued at about 11:00.[110] (Lawson was one of two NIST staff members who handled "first person interviews" for the reports on emergency response operations,[111] so he was probably involved in the interviews of Hess and Jennings.) Lawson and Gann evidently combined these two sources without realizing, or perhaps caring, that the resulting account radically contradicted what Hess and Jennings themselves had said.

Given the fact that we have no reason to doubt the statements by Hess and Jennings that they had been trapped for an hour and a half or longer, we can conclude that one of the two claims in the rescue account by Lawson and Gann—that Hess and Jennings first became trapped at 10:28 and that they were rescued at about 11:00—is false. As to which of these claims must be false, the fact that the Lawson–Gann account implicitly suggests that Hess and Jennings were rescued at about 11:00—in spite of the existence of a prior NIST document putting the time at over an hour later—suggests that they obtained this information from the 2004 interviews with Hess and Jennings themselves. The false claim, therefore, must be the one derived from Giuliani—that the men were not trapped until the collapse of the North Tower damaged WTC 7 at 10:28. And there are, as we have seen, other reasons to consider this claim false.

To conclude this discussion about timing: If Hess and Jennings were rescued at about 11:00 and if this was at least an hour and a half after they had become trapped, then they had become trapped no later than about 9:30. NIST's rescue account, therefore, has inadvertently supplied evidence in favor of Jennings' report that the event that trapped them occurred prior to the collapse of either tower, so it must have been an explosion within WTC 7 itself.

Other Possible Testimonial Evidence about Interior Damage to WTC 7

Barry Jennings, as we have seen, reported that extensive damage had been done to the interior of WTC 7 on the morning of 9/11. Besides reporting that the 6th floor landing of the stairwell that he and Hess were descending was destroyed, he told the BBC, as we saw earlier: "When we got to the 8th floor, I thought of walking to one side of the building. That side of the building was gone!" He also told Avery that, as he was being rescued, he found that the lobby was in "total ruins." If Jennings was telling the truth, other people, we might assume, would have reported some of this damage. If so, did they report it to NIST?

The question about witness reports of damage came up during the "technical briefing" of August 2008. A question submitted by Jake Pauls asked: "Did NIST use interviews with occupants to learn what they saw of the damage to WTC 7 when the Towers fell, when and how they evacuated from WTC 7, and if you did not seek such information, why not?" Although the primary part of this question was about reports of damage, Shyam Sunder deferred it until later, when he would be ready to "talk about the evacuation process." When the question was repeated later, Sunder responded only to the part about the evacuation, ignoring the question as to whether NIST had used "interviews with occupants to learn what they saw of the damage to WTC 7." After completing his rather long answer, Sunder asked Richard Gann if he had anything to add. Gann said:

> Recall that virtually the entire population of the building that morning was out of the building before the Towers collapsed.... So the evacuating people didn't have very much to say about damage to the building that occurred later in the day.[112]

Jake Pauls, I should add, did not seem to have in mind the issue of whether WTC 7 might have been damaged *prior* to the collapse of the towers. It is interesting to note, however, that Gann's answer, by speaking of damage that had occurred "later in the day," avoided the question of damage that might have occurred in the morning.

Pauls, in any case, did not give up. Later reformulating his question so that it focused only on reports of damage, he asked: "What interior direct observation reports of WTC 7 damage were available for your analysis for the post-Tower collapse period, and where in WTC 7 were those interior observations made?" Sunder turned for a response to Therese McAllister, who said:

> We interviewed a number of emergency responders that were in and around WTC 7 after the collapse of the Towers. They generally were walking up and down the building on the lower floors up to about Floor 10. And they did report the conditions that they saw from walking around the core and the floor areas on the lower floors. And we did use that information as part of our assessment of the interior damage.[113]

That was her total answer, and this "answer," it should be noted, completely dodged the question of the nature of the damage reported.

It appeared that this was a subject that NIST did not want to discuss.

In sum: NIST's treatment of testimonies about explosions in WTC 7 clearly involves serious falsification, in which NIST both ignored and distorted testimonial evidence about explosions—evidence that is directly relevant to the reason for the collapse of WTC 7.

4. TESTIMONIES ABOUT FOREKNOWLEDGE OF WTC 7'S COLLAPSE

Although direct testimony about explosions is the most relevant type of testimonial evidence for the question of why WTC 7 collapsed, it is not the only type. Also relevant are reports that some people knew in advance that this building was going to come down. These reports are relevant because, prior to that day, no steel-framed high-rise building had ever collapsed because of fire alone, so there should have been no reason for anyone to expect WTC 7 to collapse, especially given the absence of fires except on a few floors.

It might be thought, to be sure, that the fact that the Twin Towers had collapsed would have provided a good reason to suspect that WTC 7 would also collapse. But many people at the time assumed that the towers had come down because they had been hit by airplanes, and WTC 7 had not been hit by a plane. Also, there were four other buildings in the World Trade Center complex, and there were no reports that these buildings were expected to collapse, even though some of them were considerably closer to the Twin Towers, and were damaged much more severely by debris from them, than was WTC 7.

One of the interesting facts about WTC 7 is that, because it was expected to collapse, there was little effort to put out its fires. This little-reported fact was even mentioned by NIST. One of its documents stated:

> According to the FDNY first-person interviews,... firefighting was never started in [WTC 7]. When the Chief Officer in charge of WTC 7 got to Barclay Street and West Broadway, numerous firefighters and officers were coming out of WTC 7. These firefighters indicated that several blocks needed to be cleared around WTC 7 because they thought that the building was going to collapse.[114]

One such firefighter was Captain Ray Goldbach. In discussing events taking place in the afternoon, he said:

> There was a big discussion going on… about pulling all of our units out of 7 World Trade Center. Chief [Daniel] Nigro didn't feel it was worth taking the slightest chance of somebody else getting injured. So at that point we made a decision to take all of our units out of 7 World Trade Center because there was a potential for collapse…. Made the decision to back everybody away, took all the units and moved them all the way back toward North End Avenue, which is as far I guess west as you could get on Vesey Street, to keep them out of the way.[115]

This process of establishing a safety zone was described by many members of the FDNY. Firefighter Vincent Massa said:

> [L]ater on in the day as we were waiting for seven to come down, they kept backing us up Vesey, almost like a full block. They were concerned about seven coming down, and they kept changing us, establishing a collapse zone and backing us up.[116]

Decosta Wright, an emergency medical worker, said:

> [B]asically they measured out how far the building was going to come, so we knew exactly where we could stand…. Five blocks. Five

blocks away.... Exactly right on point, the cloud just stopped right there.[117]

As to when people were moved away from WTC 7, witnesses differed. Chief Daniel Nigro said: "[A]pproximately an hour and a half after that order [to move away] was given,... 7 World Trade Center collapsed completely."[118] That would mean that the collapse zone was established at about 3:50PM. Firefighter Kevin McGovern put it earlier, saying: "It took about three hours [after the order] for Seven World Trade Center to actually come down," which would have meant about 2:20.[119] Captain Robert Sohmer said that the evacuation occurred still earlier, "at approximately maybe 2:00 roughly."[120] Chief Frank Fellini, one of the men who made the decision, said that, after it was made, "for the next five or six hours we kept firefighters from working anywhere near that building"—which would mean that the collapse zone was established by about noon.[121]

In any case, whenever the decision not to fight the fires in WTC 7 was made, it was not a decision with which everyone agreed. The expectation of imminent collapse was, therefore, not universal. For example, Chief Thomas McCarthy said:

[The firefighters at the site] were waiting for 7 World Trade to come down.... They had... fire on three separate floors..., just burning merrily. It was pretty amazing, you know, it's the afternoon in lower Manhattan, a major high-rise is burning, and they said "we know."[122]

In stating that there was "fire on three separate floors," McCarthy indicated that, from his perspective, there was no objective basis for expecting the building to collapse. A similar statement was made by Decosta Wright, who said:

I think the fourth floor was on fire.... [W]e were like, are you guys going to put that fire out? I was like, you know, they are going to wait for it to burn down—and it collapsed.[123]

Puzzlement about the failure to fight the fires in WTC 7 was also reported by Deputy Chief Nick Visconti, who said: "Now, World Trade Center 7 was burning and I was thinking to myself, how come they're not trying to put this fire out?" Then, after he started implementing Chief Fellini's order to "get these people out of... 7 World Trade Center," he encountered resistance from some other chiefs, one of whom said: "Oh, that building is never coming down, that didn't get hit by a plane, why isn't somebody in there putting the fire out?"[124]

Similarly, Fire Commissioner Thomas Von Essen reported that, while walking past hundreds of firefighters who were being held away from WTC 7, he heard comments such as, "Why don't they let us in there?"[125]

To summarize: Whereas some firefighters, in line with the fact that fire had never caused a steel-framed high-rise building to come down, did not expect WTC 7 to collapse, some senior fighters did expect it to collapse, and correctly so. The question arises, therefore, as to why the latter group had this expectation.

According to Captain Michael Currid, the Uniformed Fire Officers Association's sergeant at arms, he and other FDNY officers at some point went into WTC 7, where four or five fire companies were battling its flames, and yelled up the stairwells: "Drop everything and get out!" He did this, he said, because "[s]omeone from the city's Office of Emergency Management" had told him that WTC 7 was "basically a lost cause and we should not lose anyone else trying to save it."[126]

The fact that the idea that WTC 7 was a lost cause came from Giuliani's Office of Emergency Management is significant. As I reported elsewhere, this same office had told some firefighters in advance that the Twin Towers were going to collapse.[127] Mayor Giuliani himself, in fact, told Peter Jennings on ABC News that he had been told that the towers were going to collapse shortly before the first of them actually did.[128] How could Giuliani's people have known that these three buildings—and *only* these three buildings—were going to collapse? The only possible answer seems to be their knowledge that explosives were going to bring these three buildings down.

NIST, of course, failed to point out that the decision to stop fighting the fires in WTC 7 must surely have been based on such knowledge, not on any evidence that could have been discerned by firefighters lacking such knowledge.

5. PREMATURE MEDIA REPORTS OF WTC 7'S COLLAPSE

Further evidence of foreknowledge of WTC 7's collapse was provided by premature news reports, in which this building's collapse was announced before it actually occurred. These reports evidently began "at about 4:15," when CNN's Aaron Brown said: "We are getting information now that… Building 7… has either collapsed or is collaps-ing."[129] This was over an hour before the building actually did collapse (at 5:21).

Additional premature announcements came from the BBC. At 4:53PM, the BBC's Radio Five Live said it had reports "that another large building has collapsed just over an hour ago." At 4:54, the BBC's domestic television news channel announced the collapse. Then at about 5·10, BBC World repeated this announcement. It even provided an explanation of why the building had collapsed, saying: "[T]his wasn't the result of a new attack but because the building had been weakened during this morning's attack." Finally, at 5:14, BBC reporter Jane Standley was seen announcing the collapse of the Salomon Broth-ers building—the other name for WTC 7—while it could still be seen standing in the background.[130]

In February 2007, a video containing some of this news footage, especially of the BBC's premature reporting, was placed on the inter-net. After it had evoked an enormous amount of discussion and "lots of emails" to the BBC, Richard Porter, the head of news for BBC World, responded on his blog, writing:

> We're not part of a conspiracy. Nobody told us what to say or do on September 11th. We didn't get told in advance that buildings were going to fall down. We didn't receive press releases or scripts in advance of events happening…. If we reported the building had collapsed before it had done so, it would have been an error—no more than that.[131]

This was a manifestly inadequate response (as shown by viewers' responses to it, which numbered almost 600 by the end of 2007). It was obvious that the BBC's announcement was "an error." The question was: How could such an error—announcing the collapse almost 30 minutes before it happened—have occurred? Rather than offering some explanation, Porter simply exclaimed that the BBC was not part of any conspiracy.

The suspicion that the BBC's premature announcement reflected something more than simply an inexplicable "error" was not entirely unreasonable, given some of the BBC's previous coverage of 9/11. On September 13, 2001, it published an article on its website entitled

"How the World Trade Center Fell," which quoted two experts making the obviously false assertion that the buildings collapsed because the jet fuel–fed fires had melted their steel columns.[132] Then in February 2007, just over a week before Porter's blog entry was published, the BBC aired one of the worst, most-biased television programs ever produced on the subject, *The Conspiracy Files: 9/11*.[133]

In March 2007, Porter wrote another blog entry on the subject in which he said that, on the afternoon of 9/11, there had been "a fairly consistent picture being painted of Building 7 in danger of collapse." But how did the transition get made to the declaration that the building *had* collapsed? Referring to the fact that three BBC channels reported the collapse "in quick succession," Porter was "inclined to believe that one or more of the news agencies was reporting this, or at least reporting someone saying this." But why would such agencies have been reporting the collapse approximately 30 or even—in the case of CNN—60 minutes before it happened? Porter's only explanation was to "point to [the] confusing and chaotic situation on the ground."[134] This second blog entry by Porter evoked over 600 responses, most of which found his explanation inadequate.

Porter could have offered a somewhat plausible explanation by suggesting that the rumor that WTC 7 was *going to* collapse, which had been circulating for several hours, at some point became changed, through misunderstanding, into the rumor that it had *already* collapsed.

If we accept this explanation, which the BBC could have offered, we might conclude that the premature announcement of the collapse by the news media adds nothing to what we have already established, namely, that Giuliani's Office of Emergency Management had spread the word several hours in advance that WTC 7 was going to collapse.

Even with that interpretation, however, the premature announcements were not insignificant, because they revealed in a dramatic and memorable fashion the fact that *someone* knew in advance that Building 7 was going to collapse. This is important because, given the salient facts—that WTC 7 had not been hit by a plane, that no steel-framed high-rise building had ever collapsed because of fire alone, that WTC 7 had fires on only a few floors, and that some of the other still-standing WTC buildings had suffered far worse damage—there should have been no reason to expect WTC 7 to collapse.

6. REPORTS OF INTENTIONS TO BRING WTC 7 DOWN

Besides the fact that some people knew in advance that WTC 7 was going to *come* down, there were reports that some people had said that it was going to be *brought* down.

Indira Singh's Report: One person giving such a report was Indira Singh, a senior consultant for JP Morgan Chase. On 9/11, while serving as a volunteer emergency medical worker, she was put in charge of setting up triage sites. In 2005, Singh said during an interview on Bonnie Faulkner's *Guns and Butter* radio show:

> [P]retty soon after midday on 9/11 we had to evacuate [the site where we had been working] because they told us Building 7 was coming down.... I do believe that they brought Building 7 down because I heard that they were going to bring it down because it was unstable because of the collateral damage. That I don't know; I can't attest to the validity of that. All I can attest to is that by noon or one o'clock, they told us we need to move from that triage site up to Pace University, a little further away, because Building 7 was gonna come down or be brought down.

In response to this statement, Faulkner asked: "Did they actually use the word 'brought down' and who was it that was telling you this?" Singh replied: "The fire department. The fire department. And they did use the words 'we're gonna have to bring it down.'"[135]

Additional Statements from "Seven Is Exploding": Most of Indira Singh's testimony as quoted above can be heard on a video entitled "Seven Is Exploding" (which is a segment from a program aired on Italian television in April 2007). After playing Singh's statement, this video shows police officers saying: "Keep your eye on that building, it'll be coming down.... This building is about to blow up; move it back." We then hear the sound of loud explosions, after which a firefighter says: "We gotta get back. Seven is exploding."[136]

Kevin McPadden's Report: Additional testimony has come from Kevin McPadden, a former Air Force officer involved with Special Operations for Search and Rescue. In 2006, he gave the following account of what he experienced on 9/11 while stationed at a Red Cross operations center:

They said you know you've got to stay behind this line because they're thinking about taking this building down, they're not sure if it's stable or not, so they were holding a line off because they had knowledge that something was gonna happen. Well, they pushed us back a little bit.... [A] couple of minutes later... people started coming back out to the street, I watched five New York City buses jam packed with people wanting to do search and rescue head down there towards Building 7... and right then Building 7 came down.[137]

Larry Silverstein's Statement: A different type of report came from WTC leaseholder Larry Silverstein. It was different in being a self-report, in which he stated, at least apparently, that he himself had made the suggestion to bring the building down. During a PBS program in 2002, while discussing events leading up to the collapse of WTC 7, Silverstein said:

I remember getting a call from the fire department commander, telling me that they were not sure they were gonna be able to contain the fire, and I said, "We've had such terrible loss of life, maybe the smartest thing to do is pull it." And they made that decision to pull and we watched the building collapse.[138]

Acknowledging that Silverstein made the first part of this statement, NIST tried to handle it by quoting an interpretation issued by Silverstein Properties, which said:

In the afternoon of September 11, Mr. Silverstein spoke to the Fire Department Commander on site at Seven World Trade Center. The Commander told Mr. Silverstein that there were several firefighters in the building working to contain the fires. Mr. Silverstein expressed his view that the most important thing was to protect the safety of those firefighters, including, if necessary, to have them withdraw from the building. With respect to Mr. Silverstein's statement, when recounting these events for a television documentary, that "I said, you know, we've had such terrible loss of life. Maybe the smartest thing to do is to pull it," [a Silverstein Properties spokesman] has said that by "it," Mr. Silverstein meant the contingent of firefighters remaining in the building.[139]

By simply quoting this interpretation from Silverstein Properties without comment, NIST implied that it was correct, or at least plausible. In so doing, it ignored several facts that show it to be so implausible as to be almost certainly false.

First, the statement from Silverstein Properties, in ending the quotation with the phrase "pull it," omitted the remainder of Silverstein's statement, in which he said: "And they made that decision to pull and we watched the building collapse." This final sentence indicated pretty clearly that he was talking about pulling the building, not the contingent of firefighters.

Second, Larry Silverstein himself undermined the attempt by the Silverstein Properties spokesman to claim that he had been talking about pulling the firefighters out of the building. He did this inadvertently by stating that his conversation with the fire department commander had occurred after all firefighters had left the building. The statement by the Silverstein Properties spokesman, as we saw, simply said that this conversation occurred "in the afternoon," which left open the possibility that it had occurred in the very early afternoon, before the firefighters had been ordered out of the building. It was widely agreed, as we have seen, that this order had been given around 2:00. But Silverstein, in response to a question from a "We Are Change" group in March 2008, said that the decision to pull was made "around 3:30 or 4:00PM."[140] NIST, in implying that the interpretation suggested by the Silverstein Properties spokesman was true, failed to point out that Silverstein himself had undermined that interpretation.

NIST itself, moreover, furthered this undermining. On the page after its quotation of the interpretation from the Silverstein Properties spokesman, NIST wrote:

> [A]t approximately 2:30pm, FDNY officers who had evaluated the condition of WTC 7... decided that it was not worth the additional risk to human life. They decided to abandon the building completely, and the final order was given to evacuate the site around the building.[141]

If this is what happened, "the Fire Department Commander on site at Seven World Trade Center" definitely would not have told Silverstein at "about 3:30 or 4:00" that "there were several firefighters in the building working to contain the fires." Accordingly, NIST itself, evidently without knowing it, helped Silverstein inadvertently undermine the official interpretation of his problematic "pull it" statement—an interpretation that had been endorsed by *Popular Mechanics*[142] and even the US State Department.[143]

Moreover, given the fact that Silverstein did make the statement and that its meaning had been publicly debated, we would assume that NIST would have interviewed him about this. Did it? At the August 2008 technical briefing, 9/11 widow Lorie Van Auken asked: Did NIST interview Larry Silverstein to find out why he said, "There was so much loss of life we decided to pull it," regarding WTC 7?

NIST's lead investigator, Shyam Sunder, replied: "No, we did not interview Larry Silverstein."[144]

Although that admission—parallel to Sunder's admission that NIST had not examined the WTC dust for sulfur or thermite residue—was bad enough, his justification for not interviewing Silverstein only made the problem worse. He said:

> And let me kind of explain why we... did not do that. We are a technical scientific investigation. So what we place the most importance on, credence on, are the scientific facts, to the extent that we can get them. And of course what helps us most in this complex reconstruction are... documents, documentary evidence—that is, plans, specifications, structural plans, architectural plans, connection-framing-detailed fabrication drawings and so on. We then look for visual information—again, information from photographs and videos that actually tell us what actually happened on 9/11. We then try and go in depth and talk to people who actually were in charge of emergency response on the site. And we go and talk to people who... were actually occupants of the building. So, again, we do that not by just anecdotal conversation. We actually do it in a very structured format, where the information we obtain from that analysis can be useful to make robust findings and then conclusions and recommendations. So that's how we approached this investigation. What people say, what they said on TV, why they say it, when they say it, for us is really the least important from the point of view of trying to carry out a scientific investigation.... [W]hat was said doesn't really matter. What happened really matters. And we have the science behind our findings and recommendations, and that's important.[145]

Sunder said, in other words, that given NIST's very rigorous understanding of the nature of scientific method, the fact that the owner of WTC 7 said that he and others had agreed to "pull it" was irrelevant. As scientists, Sunder and his team were only concerned with "what happened," and they knew that they would not discover that by listening to "what people say" and finding out "why they say it." Presumably, if Sunder were a forensic scientist investigating a fire and a young man came forward and said, "It's my fault; I set the fire; I'm sorry," Sunder would say: "Don't bother us, kid. We're scientists."

A little later, in any event, Sunder gave the same kind of answer to the following question from Lorie Van Auken: "Many people who were near WTC 7 on 9/11 did hear explosions. Some even heard a countdown on police radio. Did you speak with these people?" Sunder replied:

> No, we did not speak with those people, again for the same reason I just mentioned, so I won't repeat the whole argument, which is that the science speaks for itself and it's pretty robust.[146]

As we will see in the second part of this book, the science behind NIST's theory is anything but robust. But even if it were, Sunder's excuse for not interviewing these people would be absurd—as if forensic scientists investigating a crime would eschew all testimonial evidence in order to concentrate solely on physical evidence.

In any case, besides uncritically reporting the interpretation offered by Silverstein Properties (showing that NIST considered *some* testimonial evidence acceptable) NIST failed to report any of the other statements in which an intention to demolish WTC 7 was expressed. We have here one more illustration of NIST's ignoring or distorting all evidence that would contradict its politically driven report on WTC 7's collapse.

7. EXPERT TESTIMONY THAT EXPLOSIVES BROUGHT WTC 7 DOWN

In addition to these reports of statements expressing the intention to bring down WTC 7, statements that WTC 7 was indeed brought down with explosives have been made by many people, some of whom can be considered experts. One person sometimes quoted in this regard is Dan Rather, who at the time was the CBS News anchor. Right after WTC 7 came down, Rather said:

> Amazing, incredible pick your word. For the third time today, it's reminiscent of those pictures we've all seen too much on television before, where a building was deliberately destroyed by well-placed dynamite to knock it down.[147]

Rather was not an expert, and he did not say that WTC 7 was actually a controlled demolition; he said only that its collapse was "reminiscent" of such demolitions. But several people with relevant expertise *have* said the building was deliberately brought down.

Hugo Bachmann and Jörg Schneider, both emeritus professors of structural analysis and construction at the Swiss Federal Institute of Technology, have stated that, in their opinion, WTC 7 was "with great probability" professionally demolished.[148]

Jack Keller, emeritus professor of engineering at Utah State University (who had been named by *Scientific American* as one of the world's leaders in using science and technology to benefit society), was even more definite, saying of this building's destruction: "Obviously it was the result of controlled demolition."[149]

Another expert who has stated this was Danny Jowenko, a controlled demolition expert in the Netherlands with his own firm.[150] As mentioned in the Introduction, he was asked in 2006 by a filmmaker to comment on a video of the collapse of WTC 7 without knowing what it was—he had not realized that a third building had collapsed on 9/11. After viewing the video, he said: "They simply blew up columns, and the rest caved in afterwards.... This is controlled demolition." When asked if he was certain, he replied: "Absolutely, it's been imploded. This was a hired job. A team of experts did this." When he was told that this happened on September 11, he was incredulous, repeatedly asking, "Are you sure?" When he was finally convinced, Jowenko said: "Then they worked very hard."[151]

In 2007, Jowenko was asked whether he stood by his statement that it must have been controlled demolition. He replied: "Absolutely.... I looked at the drawings, the construction and it couldn't be done by fire... absolutely not."[152]

Jowenko also explained why controlled demolition experts in the United States have not stated this obvious fact. When the interviewer mentioned that he had phoned the US company Controlled Demolition, Inc., which said: "Oh, it's possible it came down from fire," Jowenko replied: "When... you have to earn your money in the States as a controlled demolition company and you say, 'No, it was a controlled demolition,' you're gone."[153]

NIST, as a political rather than a scientific agency, did not report any of this expert testimony.

SUMMARY

Just as NIST ignored all physical evidence that WTC 7 was brought down by explosives, it ignored all testimonial evidence supporting this hypothesis. Besides failing to mention testimonies about explosions in WTC 7 from people outside of the building, it also ignored the testimony of two city officials, Michael Hess and Barry Jennings, who were inside. To try to neutralize this testimony by Hess and Jennings, NIST distorted it by changing the timeline, as had Rudy Giuliani in his 2002 book, so as to claim that the "explosion" they had reported was really damage caused by debris from the North Tower collapse. NIST thereby ignored what Hess and Jennings actually said. NIST's distortion of their testimony was then amplified and popularized by a BBC documentary, a second version of which employed Hess himself, after Jennings was dead, to "confirm" the Giuliani–NIST–BBC timeline.

NIST also ignored the fact that some senior members of the FDNY knew several hours in advance that the building was going to come down and that the source for this information seemed to be Giuliani's Office of Emergency Management.

With regard to testimonies reporting statements expressing the intention to bring WTC 7 down, NIST ignored all of them except the famous one from Larry Silverstein, which NIST sought to dismiss by repeating an innocuous interpretation of it, while ignoring the fact that this interpretation had been undermined by Silverstein himself.

NIST ignored, finally, the testimony of experts who have declared that WTC 7 was brought down by explosives.

Having ignored all of this evidence, NIST stated, in the December 2008 version of its "Questions and Answers about the NIST WTC 7 Investigation," that "the possibility that an explosion caused or contributed to the collapse of WTC 7" had been "investigated carefully" and that NIST had "found no evidence supporting the existence of a blast event."[154]

And not a single mainstream reporter publicly ridiculed this statement.

6
NIST'S STRAW-MAN ARGUMENTS AGAINST EXPLOSIVES

hapter 3 showed that the most likely starting point for an investigation of WTC 7's collapse would have been the hypothesis
that explosives of some sort were used to bring it down in the
procedure known as controlled demolition. That chapter also showed,
however, that NIST did not begin with this hypothesis, choosing instead
to accept the "challenge" to see if WTC 7's collapse might have been
caused by an ordinary building fire. Chapters 4 and 5 then showed that
NIST, in order to argue that explosives played no role in WTC 7's
demise, had to ignore and distort an enormous amount of physical and
testimonial evidence. The present chapter looks directly at NIST's
arguments for excluding the hypothesis that explosives were used.

NIST's arguments begin with a particular scenario as to the kind
of explosive that might have been used—a scenario that NIST purportedly determined to be the most likely one. NIST then argues that this
scenario could not have occurred because the explosive material could
not have been placed without detection and, even if it had been, it
would have caused sounds and window breakage that did not occur.

After laying out NIST's arguments, I will show that they are
riddled with problems, the central one being that they are perfect
examples of the kind of straw-man arguments discussed in Chapter 2.

1. NIST'S "PLAUSIBLE BLAST SCENARIO"

"As part of assessing alternative hypotheses for initiation of the collapse of
WTC 7," NIST writes, "[s]cenarios of a hypothetical blast event that could
have occurred in WTC 7 on September 11, 2001, were assessed."[1]
However, although NIST speaks here of "scenarios" in the plural, it actually
discusses only one scenario. NIST write: "In particular, a plausible scenario
with the minimum amount of required explosive was identified."[2]

Suggesting that the most plausible scenario would be the one that required the least amount of explosive material to be hauled into WTC 7, NIST claims to have determined that this scenario would minimally require sufficient explosive material to sever one of the building's crucial columns. This requirement would best be fulfilled, NIST further claims, by RDX explosives: "The lowest mass of explosive needed to sever any of the six column or truss sections was found to be 4 kg (9 lb) of RDX explosives in linear shaped charges."[3]

2. NIST'S THREEFOLD ARGUMENT AGAINST ITS "PLAUSIBLE" SCENARIO

After suggesting that this was the most plausible of all the possible scenarios through which WTC 7 might have been brought down by explosives, NIST then proceeds to argue that it was not really plausible after all. NIST bases this conclusion on a threefold argument involving window breakage, sound, and detection. I will examine each of these arguments in order.

Window Breakage

One problem with this scenario, NIST argues, is that it would have caused window breakage that did not, in fact, occur. Claiming that the critical column that would have needed to fail would have been Column 79, NIST writes:

> [T]he minimum charge… required to fail [Column 79] would have produced a pressure wave that would have broken windows on the north and east faces of the building near Column 79. The visual evidence did not show such a breakage pattern on any floor of WTC 7 as late as about 4:00pm or above the 25th floor at the time of the building collapse initiation.[4]

There appear to be two dimensions to NIST's argument here—an implicit as well as an explicit dimension.

The Explicit Argument: Explicitly, NIST argues that, given the scenario it has in mind, according to which explosives would have been placed to bring down Column 79, the windows that these explosives would have broken did not break.

The statement quoted above, however, does not actually say this, as one can see by focusing on the final sentence: "The visual evidence did not show such a breakage pattern on any floor of WTC 7 as late as about 4:00PM or above the 25th floor at the time of the building collapse initiation." This statement leaves open the possibility, and even seems to imply, that there *was* "such a breakage pattern" *below* the 25th floor *after* 4:00PM.

Moreover, even if NIST's argument were true, it would prove nothing. NIST's assumption that explosives would have been focused especially on Column 79 is based solely on its own argument—to be discussed in Part II of this book—that this was the critical column, the failure of which would have caused the entire building to collapse. Prior to NIST's report, the notion that anyone planning to bring down WTC 7 would have concentrated the explosive material on this particular column had apparently not occurred to anyone. Accordingly, even if NIST's argument here is correct—that the windows that would have been broken if NIST's scenario had been enacted were *not* broken—it is a circular argument, based solely on NIST's own scenario, not that of people who have claimed that WTC 7 was brought down with explosives. It is thereby a straw-man argument, disproving an unlikely hypothesis of its own creation that diverts attention from the more likely hypothesis proffered by critics of the official account. NIST's argument does not, therefore, do anything to undermine the contention that the building was deliberately demolished.

The Implicit Argument: In making its explicit argument, NIST also seems to imply that, at the time that WTC 7 began to collapse, no windows whatsoever broke. Insofar as this claim is indeed implicit in NIST's report—which in speaking of window breakage refers *only* to breakage caused by fire—it is false.

As noted in Chapter 4, a video available on the internet shows a vertical row of approximately eight windows, from roughly the 29th to the 37th floor, being blown out as WTC 7 begins to collapse.[5]

As pointed out in Chapter 5, more than one witness described windows as breaking at the time the building started to come down. Peter Demarco of the *New York Daily News* said: "The building's top row of windows popped out. Then all the windows on the thirty-ninth floor popped out. Then the thirty-eighth floor. Pop! Pop! Pop!"[6] A New York

University medical student said that "it looked like there was a shockwave ripping through the building and the windows all busted out."[7]

NIST's argument about window breakage is clearly bogus.

Sound

NIST's second reason for rejecting the plausibility of what it portrayed as the most plausible "blast event" scenario is that it would have produced sounds that did not occur. The explosion of nine pounds of the RDX material, NIST says,

> would have resulted in a sound level of 130 to 140 decibels (a sound level consistent with a gunshot blast or a jet plane that is 10 to 20 decibels louder than a rock concert in front of speakers), at a distance of at least half a mile (if unobstructed by surrounding buildings...).

But no such sound level, was reached, says NIST: "There were no witness reports of such a loud noise, nor was such a noise heard on audio tracks of video tapes that recorded the WTC 7 collapse."[8]

NIST's argument again seems to have an implicit as well as an explicit dimension.

The Explicit Argument: What NIST argues explicitly is that "such a loud noise"—meaning one that reached 130 to 140 decibels—was neither reported nor caught on tape.

This argument depends entirely on NIST's assumption that if WTC 7 had been brought down by explosive material, the most plausible scenario would have involved nine pounds of RDX, which would have produced a very loud concussive sound.

But RDX was emphatically *not* the most plausible type of explosive material for someone to use to bring down WTC 7. Indeed, among those who have argued that WTC 7 was brought down by controlled demolition, RDX has seldom if ever been named as the most likely explosive.

Rather, as we have seen, the prime suspect has been nanothermite. As we saw in Chapter 4, the leading scientists who have worked on this issue have suggested that, in addition to the use of thermate, which is an incendiary, the perpetrators used nanothermite, which is classified as a high explosive. They regard it as the most likely candidate, partly because its signature has been repeatedly and independently discovered in the World Trade Center dust, and partly because of other virtues to be mentioned below.

We can see, therefore, that NIST, in arguing against the feasibility of the controlled demolition of WTC 7 by means of arguing against controlled demolition using RDX, has engaged in one of the best-known of the fallacious forms of argumentation: attacking a straw man. That is, rather than responding to the real argument employed by proponents of the controlled demolition thesis, it attacked an argument of its own creation. Then, having knocked down this straw-man argument, which it had erected on the pretense that RDX would have been employed in the most plausible of the controlled demolition scenarios, NIST could claim to have shown that WTC 7 was not brought down by controlled demolition.

This RDX straw man is, as we have seen, especially vulnerable to the argument from sound. However, if NIST had engaged the scenario actually proposed by the leading scientific exponents of the controlled demolition hypothesis, this argument would not have worked, because explosions produced by nanothermite would not be as loud. Indeed, this fact had been pointed out to NIST before it issued its Final Report.

In August 2008, as we saw in the Introduction, NIST issued a Draft for Public Comment. Before it issued its Final Report in November 2008, it was able to revise its report, to the extent it desired, on the basis of comments it had received. Problems in NIST's argument against controlled demolition were mentioned in several of these comments, some of which dealt specifically with NIST's argument about sound.

One such comment came from attorney and chemical engineer James Gourley, who would become one of the nine coauthors, along with Niels Harrit, of the 2009 paper, discussed in Chapter 4, reporting the discovery of unreacted nanothermite in the WTC dust. "[W]riting on behalf of a group of scientists, scholars, engineers, and building professionals, in 2008" Gourley pointed out that "NIST only considers blast events using RDX, an extremely high explosive." Then, referring to the existence of "nanoenergetic compounds, or nanothermites, that have the potential to be used for building demolitions," Gourley stated:

> Because nanothermites are primarily high-temperature incendiaries rather than explosives, they could cause damage to steel structures without producing the sound... levels associated with RDX.

Finally, following the proper protocol of telling NIST what revision he was recommending, Gourley wrote: "NIST should revise its report to specifically analyze whether such nanoenergetic materials could have been used as a component in a 'hypothetical blast scenario' at WTC 7."[9]

However, in spite of this and other calls for NIST to revise its discussion of this issue, no revisions were made. Indeed, a search of both versions of NIST's Final Report on WTC 7—both the brief and the long versions—reveals not a single instance of the word "thermite" (or "thermate") or any word beginning with "nano." It appears that NIST, after inviting the public to comment on the Draft version of its final report on WTC 7, simply ignored the comments that pointed out the straw-man nature of its RDX scenario.

The Implicit Argument: Beyond NIST's explicit argument that no explosive sounds of 130 to 140 decibels were either reported or recorded, it implicitly seemed to suggest that no explosive sounds whatsoever were reported or recorded at the time just before WTC 7 came down. Any such suggestion, however, would be false.

As pointed out in Chapter 5, the sound of explosions was both reported and captured on videotape. Former NYPD officer Craig Bartmer said:

> I was real close to Building 7 when it fell down.... That didn't sound like just a building falling down to me.... There's a lot of eyewitness testimony down there of hearing explosions.... I started running... and the whole time you're hearing "boom, boom, boom, boom, boom."[10]

The New York University medical student whose testimony was quoted above reported that, just before WTC 7 started coming down, he and others "heard this sound that sounded like a clap of thunder."[11] And the video called "Seven Is Exploding" contains footage of police officers saying, "Keep your eye on that building, it'll be coming down.... This building is about to blow up," followed by the sound of very loud explosions, which frighten people, after which a firefighter says: "We gotta get back. Seven is exploding."[12]

NIST was not—or at least should not have been—unaware of this video, because a correspondent named Michael Smith told them about it. The occasion for his doing so was the following statement by NIST, which described phenomena that would have resulted from a "blast" caused by nine pounds of RDX but that, NIST claimed in its Draft Report, did not occur:

> The sound from such a blast in an urban setting would have been reflected and channeled down streets with minimum attenuation. The sound would have been attenuated behind buildings, but this would have also generated multiple echoes. These echoes could have extended the time over which the sound could have been detected and could possibly have had an additive effect if multiple in-phase reflections met.[13]

After quoting this passage in his letter to NIST, Smith wrote:

> There is a video with this exact effect recorded on the soundtrack, available at the following link: www.youtube.com/watch?v=0 YvrKfWkxdw. While the firefighters are talking on the phone, a very loud blast startles them, and another firefighter comes running up and tells them that they "gotta get back seven is exploding."… [I]t is a very loud sound. After listening again, I clearly heard multiple echoes that slowly died out, which precisely matches the description of reflection and attenuation given in the report.[14]

Smith added that the NIST's Draft Report report claimed that "the soundtracks from videos being recorded at the time of the collapse did not contain any sound as intense as would have accompanied such a blast."[15] Smith then concluded: "This statement is clearly incorrect, given the clear soundtrack of the above video and the criteria described immediately prior to this statement in the report."[16]

Now it may be that, technically, NIST was correct to say that none of the videos contained "any sound as intense" as that which, according to NIST, would have been produced by nine pounds of RDX, namely, a sound of 130 to 140 decibels. But insofar as NIST was implicitly claiming that no videos captured any very loud explosive sound—of perhaps 120 decibels—at the initiation of WTC 7's collapse, NIST was clearly wrong. NIST, however, responded to Smith's comment in the same way that it did to Gourley's—by simply ignoring it, thereby continuing to imply that no explosions were either reported or recorded at the outset of WTC 7's collapse.

To summarize: Insofar as NIST makes technically correct statements about explosive sounds that did not occur, these statements are part of a straw-man argument based on its claim that, if WTC 7 had been brought down by controlled demolition, the saboteurs would have used RDX rather than, say, nanothermite. Insofar as NIST implicitly claims that the controlled demolition hypothesis is disproved by the fact that no explosive sounds whatsoever—perhaps not quite as loud as 130 decibels—were reported or captured on tape, NIST's claim is simply false.

A more complete discussion of the falsity of NIST's denial of reports of explosions in WTC 7 would need to include, of course, the reports to which the most space in Chapter 5 was devoted: those of Michael Hess (in 2001) and Barry Jennings.

Detection

NIST's third argument against the controlled demolition hypothesis is that explosives could not have been planted without detection. In developing this claim, NIST offers two possibilities: either the explosive material would have been planted prior to 9/11, or it would have been planted on 9/11 itself, "during approximately a 6 h[our] time frame, i.e., between the time WTC 7 had been evacuated and the time at which collapse occurred."[17] In either case, NIST argues, the RDX material could not have been deployed without detection:

> Prior to preparing a column for controlled demolition, walls and/or column enclosures and SFRM [fire-proofing material] would have to be removed and replaced without being detected. Preparing the column includes steps such as cutting sections with torches (which produces noxious and odorous fumes) and careful placement of charges and an initiation device. Controlled demolition usually prepares most, if not all, interior columns in a building with explosive charges, not just one column. It is unlikely that… such activity could have taken place without being detected.[18]

There are at least two problems with this argument. One of them is that it presupposes that the people in charge of security at WTC 7 would necessarily have been concerned to prevent explosives from being planted. This is problematic because, as trial lawyer Earl Staelin wrote in his comment to NIST:

The [NIST] report fails to mention that the security firm for WTC 7, as for WTC 1 and 2, Securacom (later called Stratesec) had connections to George W. Bush…, which may have made it possible for agents of our government to place explosives in the buildings and escape "detection."[19]

The connections to which Staelin alluded were close ones: Marvin Bush, one of the president's brothers, had been one of Securacom's principals in the 1990s, during which the fireproofing upgrades to be mentioned below were made, and Wirt Walker III, one of the Bush brothers' cousins, was the CEO through 2001 (and hence on 9/11 itself).

Although the point made by Staelin was an important one, NIST ignored it. In putting out its Final Report in November 2008, NIST simply repeats the statement in question, as if Staelin's comment had never been received.

A second problem with NIST's argument is that it seems to assume that, if explosives were indeed planted in WTC 7, they would have been planted during working hours. But there is no reason to assume this. As we saw in Chapter 4, the explosive material could have been added to the Twin Towers during periods when the floors in question were closed to have the fireproofing upgraded. Perhaps the same thing occurred in WTC 7. If not, the explosive material could have been added during evening hours and weekends. In 1978, for example, after the owners of the new Citicorp Tower learned that it was likely to fall over during a hurricane, they had it retrofitted during the evening hours, without the building's tenants ever knowing.[20]

In light of the previous point about the Bush-family connections to WTC security, moreover, those who had the job of planting the material may have had no problem getting into the buildings during off hours.

A possible objection to this point would be that, if the explosive materials had been planted during evening hours and weekends, employees would have noticed them when they returned to work. This objection, however, would presuppose that the explosive material would necessarily be visible. As we saw in Chapter 4, the advance of technology in this field may mean that this is not necessarily true.

As Jim Hoffman has pointed out, the argument about detection presupposes that a demolition would have necessarily been "set up like a conventional commercial one, with fuses and large numbers of cutting charges." In reality, he points out, "the demolitions could have been controlled using wireless detonators, which have been commercially available for decades." Also, he adds, the use of nanothermite would have given the planners "much more leeway in the placement of charges required to totally destroy the buildings." It would have been easy "to surreptitiously install devices in hidden portions of the cores. Any such job would have been far simpler than the structural retrofit of the CitiCorp Tower."[21]

Once again, NIST's arguments against the controlled demolition hypothesis presuppose its own scenario, in which the saboteurs would have used RDX or some other conventional explosive, rather than one or more explosives made possible by the emergence of nanotechnology.

A Fourth Argument

On the basis of the above threefold argument, NIST's report on WTC 7 says, with apparent confidence: "NIST concluded that blast events could not have occurred." Then, apparently using "blast events" to refer to any kind of controlled demolition whatsoever, NIST declares: "blast events did not cause the collapse of WTC 7."[22]

In its document providing "Questions and Answers," NIST adds a fourth argument in its response to the following question: "An emergency responder caught in the building between the 6th and 8th floors says he heard two loud booms. Isn't that evidence that there was an explosion?" This question obviously refers to the testimony of Barry Jennings, although his name is not mentioned. Here is NIST's answer:

> If the two loud booms were due to explosions that were responsible for the collapse of WTC 7, the emergency responder—located somewhere between the 6th and 8th floors in WTC 7—would not have been able to survive the near immediate collapse and provide this witness account.[23]

NIST's argument here depends on the fallacious assumption that if an emergency responder had heard explosions that contributed to the destruction of WTC 7, these explosions would necessarily have occurred immediately before the collapse.

NIST's scientists knew, however, that in controlled demolitions of large buildings, explosives are used to eliminate some of the columns in advance, prior to the final set of explosions that actually bring the building down (see Appendix A). They also knew that Barry Jennings was trapped in the morning; they themselves reported his rescue. Their answer is, therefore, dishonest as well as fallacious.

The fallaciousness involved one of the logical fallacies taught in elementary logic classes. Called the "complex question fallacy," it is committed "when a single question that is really two (or more) questions is asked and the single answer is then applied to both questions."[24] The fallaciousness of this approach can be seen by imagining the following courtroom conversation between a defense attorney and his client, who is accused of murdering his wife:

> Attorney: Did you murder your wife this past August 25 and then go play tennis?
> Client: No, as my doctor will testify, I have been physically unable to play tennis for several years now.
> Attorney: The defense rests.

That would, of course, be an absurd argument. Structurally, however, it is the same as NIST's argument that, if Barry Jennings had heard explosions in WTC 7, he would have died that day.

NIST here commits the complex question fallacy in order to create a straw-man argument.

3. THE MOST PLAUSIBLE OR LEAST PLAUSIBLE SCENARIO?

In describing its "plausible blast scenario," NIST implies that it was the *most* plausible way in which WTC 7 could have been brought down by controlled demolition. In a comment sent to NIST in response to its Draft Report, however, one critic suggested that it was actually the *least* plausible scenario. What NIST gave us, he argued, "is the epitome of a straw man argument," which "shows that NIST was determined to avoid examining all but the most implausible of theoretical scenarios, so as to easily disprove the plausibility of such a scenario."[25]

In explaining the reason for his comment, this critic pointed out that an appendix to the FEMA report on WTC 7 "found that steel from WTC 7 had melted, due to a corrosive attack by a liquid slag containing high levels of sulfur. Several chemical compounds… could potentially have caused this phenomenon." In response to NIST's protocal question of how the passage could be made more accurate, this author suggested that NIST add the following statement:

> In its evaluation of alternate hypotheses re[garding] the collapse of WTC 7, NIST chose to ignore the likelihood of chemical compounds having been used to amplify the effects of fire on the steel structure, and instead focused exclusively on the least plausible of these alternate theories, the use of high explosives.[26]

As scientists and private citizens, the authors of the NIST report may have responded to this suggestion with a smile of recognition. As NIST employees, however, they made no change in their report.

Although this critic did not mention thermites, including thermates (thermites with sulfur) in particular, they are the chemical compounds that have most often been proposed as the substances used to demolish the towers. Niels Harrit, Steven Jones, Kevin Ryan, and their colleagues have suggested, in particular, that those who brought down WTC 7 (as well as the Twin Towers) employed thermitic materials involving at least thermate—which, because of its sulfur content, could account for the sulfidized piece of steel from WTC 7 mentioned by the above-quoted critic—and nanothermite. Neither one or the other by itself is deemed capable of accounting for the various phenomena. I turn now to the way NIST responded to this discussion.

4. NIST ON THERMITE/THERMATE

As we saw earlier, neither "thermite" nor "thermate" appears anywhere in NIST's WTC 7 reports—either in its brief (87-page) or its long (729-page) report. From reading those reports alone, one might assume that the scientists at NIST did not know about thermite.

However, NIST did finally discuss thermite in a document entitled "Questions and Answers about the NIST WTC 7 Investigation." As pointed out above in Chapter 4, one of the questions was: "Is it possible that thermite or thermate contributed to the collapse of WTC 7?" We examined in that chapter one point made in NIST's reply, namely, that if any steel had been recovered from WTC 7—as we saw, NIST claims that none was, thereby ignoring the piece of oxidized and sulfidized steel reported in an appendix to the FEMA report—an analysis of it "would not necessarily have been conclusive." The *main* point made in NIST's answer, however, is that the use of thermite to sever columns in WTC 7 "was unlikely." In explaining why, NIST writes:

To apply thermite to a large steel column, approximately 0.13 lb of thermite would be needed to heat and melt each pound of steel. For a steel column that weighs approximately 1,000 lbs. per foot, at least 100 lbs. of thermite would need to be placed around the column, ignited, and remain in contact with the vertical steel surface as the thermite reaction took place. This is for one column... presumably, more than one column would have been prepared with thermite, if this approach were to be used. It is unlikely that 100 lbs. of thermite, or more, could have been carried into WTC 7 and placed around columns without being detected, either prior to Sept. 11 or during that day.[27]

Of special interest in this statement is NIST's point that the thermite would need to "remain in contact with the vertical steel surface as the thermite reaction took place." As to *how long* this contact would need to be maintained, NIST had said in an earlier document:

Thermite burns slowly relative to explosive materials and can require several minutes in contact with a massive steel section to heat it to a temperature that would result in substantial weakening.[28]

It is clear that NIST, in speaking of thermite, is referring only to ordinary (macro-) thermite, not nanothermite. As we have seen, whereas ordinary thermite is an incendiary, nanothermite is an explosive (as well as an incendiary). Accordingly, as Steven Jones has pointed out, nanothermite is "not an incendiary that would need to 'remain in contact with the vertical steel surface as the thermite reaction took place.'"[29]

Nanothermite is so different from ordinary thermite that it is, as pointed out in Chapter 4, classified as a *high explosive.* The degree to which it reacts both more quickly and hence more powerfully than ordinary thermite was partly indicated by comparing the numbers of atoms on the surfaces of their ingredients, such as aluminum: "Standard aluminum covers just one-tenth of one percent of the surface area (with atoms), versus fifty percent for nanoaluminum." As a result, nanothermites "can increase the (chemical) reaction time by a thousand times."[30] Besides being far more powerful than ordinary thermite, nanothermite is even more powerful than conventional high explosives such as RDX.[31]

NIST's argument that ordinary thermite (including thermate) could not have, all by itself, brought down the WTC buildings does not, therefore, say anything about whether nanothermite—perhaps in conjunction with ordinary thermite (including thermate)—could have done the trick.

NIST has here clearly engaged in deception. It had been asked to address the following question: "Is it possible that thermite or thermate contributed to the collapse of WTC 7?" However, rather than responding to this question—which asked merely whether thermite (of some sort) could have *contributed to* the collapse—it answers a quite different question, namely, whether ordinary thermite (including thermate) could have, all by itself, brought the buildings down.

Accordingly, just as NIST's refutation of the controlled demolition hypothesis by refuting an RDX version of that hypothesis is irrelevant, so is its refutation of a version of that hypothesis based on ordinary thermite alone. Once again, NIST has responded to a straw-man position rather than to the position taken by the leading scientists who have argued in favor of the controlled demolition hypothesis.

Given the fact that NIST has consistently failed to discuss the possibility that nanothermites were used to bring down WTC 7 (as well as the Twin Towers), mentioning them neither in its official reports nor even in its answers to commonly asked questions, one might suppose that the scientists who worked on these reports for NIST were simply unaware of nanothermites. Is it possible that they ignored the qualitative difference between nanothermite and ordinary thermite because they were simply not aware of the nanotechnology revolution? I turn next to this question.

5. MIGHT NIST HAVE BEEN UNAWARE OF NANOTHERMITES?

Any claim that NIST did not mention nanothermites because its scientists were unaware of their existence would not be plausible. Far from being unaware of the work being done in nanoscience and nanotechnologies, NIST has been closely connected to this work in multiple ways. I will summarize several of these ways so that readers will have some idea about how fully conversant scientists at NIST must have been with the existence and characteristics of nanothermites.[32]

NIST's Directors 2001–2008

The directors of NIST during the years that it has been working on the World Trade Center reports have all been conversant with nanotechnology.

Arden Bement, NIST's Director 2001–2004: In December 2001, President Bush selected Arden Bement, a metallurgical engineer, to be the director of NIST. Bement had previously been employed by organizations that would later become leaders in nanotechnology: Battelle,[33] the Department of Defense (DOD), and, in particular, DARPA (the Defense Advanced Research Projects Agency), an agency of the DOD assigned to develop new technology for the military.[34] Having worked for Battelle in the late 1960s, Bement worked for the DOD in the late 1970s, being the director of DARPA's office of materials science and then the deputy undersecretary of defense for research and engineering in the late 1970s. After being appointed the director of NIST in 2001, Bement remained in this position until November 2004 (at which time he became the director of the National Science Foundation).[35] Accordingly, the person who was in charge of NIST during the first three years of its work on the destruction of the World Trade Center was well connected with organizations that were doing pioneering work in nanotechnology.

During Bement's tenure as director, moreover, NIST was doing its own work in nanotechnology. In a speech he gave shortly after becoming director, Bement said: "NIST is providing tools and research to probe, manipulate, and ultimately, master the world of nanotechnology."[36]

Hratch Semerjian, NIST's Acting Director 2004–2005: NIST's next director, Hratch Semerjian, was even more obviously in a position to be well informed about nanotechnology. In the 1980s, he coauthored several papers with Michael Zachariah, who in the following two decades became known as one of the world's leading experts on nanoscience, and who is now associate editor of the *Journal of Nanoparticle Research.*[37] Semerjian had worked for NIST since 1977 (when it was called the National Bureau of Standards), and had been the director of its Chemical Science and Technology Laboratory from 1992 until 2003. In November 2004, when Arden Bement resigned as NIST's director, Semerjian was appointed its acting director.[38] He remained in that role until after NIST published its report on the Twin Towers in 2005.[39]

William Jeffrey, NIST's Director 2005–2007: In July 2005, William Alan Jeffrey became NIST's director. He had previously worked at DARPA (Defense Advanced Research Projects Agency) as deputy director of its Advanced Technology Office and chief scientist for its Tactical Technology Office, after which he became the senior director for homeland and national security at the US Office of Science and Technology Policy (within the Executive Office of the President). His interest in nanotechnology was shown during an interview shortly after his move to NIST in 2005. In response to the question as to what he viewed as the "most promising research priority at NIST," he mentioned "measurement needs for nanotechnology and nanomanufacturing" as one of the things to which NIST was giving high priority.[40] His commitment was revealed most fully by the fact that, the following year, he created the NIST Center for Nanoscale Science and Technology (described below).[41]

James M. Turner, Acting Director, 2007–: Upon Jeffrey's resignation in September 2007, James M. Turner, who had been NIST's deputy director, was named the acting director. During his testimony on behalf of NIST before a Senate subcommittee in March 2008, he mentioned nanotechnology many times.[42]

NIST Advisors

For its work on the World Trade Center, NIST had an advisory committee comprised of nine "prominent building and fire experts." One of these advisors was Forman A. Williams, director of the Center for Energy Research and also professor of engineering physics and combustion at the University of California at San Diego.[43] Williams has written about the ignition of porous energetic materials[44]—a description that applies to nanothermites.

NIST's Partnerships for Nanotechnology Research

NIST has also been directly involved in nanotechnology research in conjunction with organizations that have pioneered this research.

Lawrence Livermore National Laboratories: The previously discussed sol-gel nanothermites, which can be sprayed onto steel, were developed in the 1990s by the Lawrence Livermore National Laboratories (LLNL).[45] From at least as early as 1999, NIST was working with LLNL to test these nanothermites, as shown by a paper entitled "Nanostructure High Explosives Using Sol-gel Chemistry," which described a 1999 experiment on "energetic nanocomposites" that was "conducted at the National Institute of Standards and Technology."[46]

NASA: In 2003, "NIST and NASA researchers started… sponsoring a series of workshops devoted to nanotube measurements."[47]

University of Maryland, College Park: Also in 2003, NIST signed a memorandum of understanding with the University of Maryland, College Park, to develop a cooperative program in nano-metrology and nano-manufacturing (Hratch Semerjian, as the director of the Chemical Science and Technology Laboratory, signed this document for NIST).[48] This agreement led to the Co-Laboratory for Nanoparticle Based Manufacturing and Metrology, directed by Michael Zachariah (whose co-authorship of papers with Semerjian was mentioned above).[49] That development led in turn to the Center for Nano Manufacturing and Metrology, which is "a joint venture between the University of Maryland and the National Institute of Standards and Technology" and is funded by NIST and NASA.[50]

College of Nanoscale Science and Engineering: In April 2008, NIST signed a cooperative agreement with the College of Nanoscale Science and Engineering of the State University of New York at Albany.[51]

NIST's Own Center for Nanoscience and Nanotechnology
In addition to having these partnerships, NIST in 2006 created the NIST Center for Nanoscale Science and Technology.[52] Being "the federal government's lead laboratory for work on nanoscale measurements and standards," a NIST fact sheet says, the Center "features a large Nanofabrication (Nanofab) Facility," which is "equipped with a still-growing array of state-of-the-art—and, sometimes, unsurpassed—tools for making, testing, and characterizing prototype nanoscale devices and materials."[53]

Accordingly, given NIST's directors and advisors, its various partnerships for research in nanotechnology, and its own center for nanoscience and nanotechnology, the idea that its scientists could have been unaware of the existence and capabilities of nanothermites is implausible. Insofar as the NIST authors implied ignorance of nanothermites, we can only conclude that they were dissembling.

6. NIST'S IMPLICIT ACKNOWLEDGMENT THAT EXPLOSIVES DESTROYED THE TWIN TOWERS

NIST's denial that explosives were used to bring down WTC 7, in spite of the multiple types of evidence pointing to this conclusion, was preceded by a similar denial with regard to the Twin Towers. One of the many types of evidence that explosives were used to bring down the towers was the fact that the destruction of these buildings began with massive explosions near the top, which ejected material out horizontally. Included in this material were massive sections of steel columns, weighing hundreds of tons, which were hurled out 500 or 600 feet. A few of them implanted themselves in neighboring buildings, as can be seen in videos and photographs.[54]

This feature of the destruction of the Twin Towers provides apparently irrefutable evidence against the official account, according to which the only force available, beyond that supplied by the airplane impacts and the resulting fires, was gravitational attraction, which pulls things straight down. One scientific critic of the official story who has emphasized this feature as especially compelling evidence is Dwain Deets, the former director of the research engineering division at NASA's Dryden Flight Research Center. The "massive structural members being hurled horizontally," he has said, is one of the factors that "leave no doubt" in his mind that "explosives were involved."[55]

Deets' point is well grounded, because, as we saw in Chapter 3, the NFPA *Guide for Fire and Explosion Investigations* points to "high-order damage" as a sign that explosives had gone off, and lists as one of the features of high-order damage: "Debris is thrown great distances, possibly hundreds of feet."

In its report on the Twin Towers, NIST avoided the need to explain what could have caused these horizontal ejections by its usual method: simply refusing to acknowledge them.

In its reports on WTC 7, however, NIST does acknowledge them, at least implicitly. As we saw in the Introduction, NIST in earlier years suggested that the damage caused by the debris from the North Tower would likely play a major role in its account of WTC 7's collapse. This stage of NIST's thinking was reflected in the 2006 book by *Popular Mechanics*. Saying NIST had found that "WTC 7 was far more compromised by falling debris than the FEMA report indicated," the *Popular Mechanics* authors wrote that NIST's investigators "now believe the building failed from a combination of long-burning fires in its interior and damage caused from the North Tower's collapse."[56]

Later, as we have seen, NIST abandoned this twofold explanation, saying that WTC 7 was brought down by fire alone. But it still, as we will see, needed to appeal to debris from the North Tower's collapse to explain how the fires in WTC 7 got started. And it could hardly deny all the debris damage that had been described in its *Interim Report on WTC 7*, which said, among other things, that the "middle one-fourth to one-third width of the south face was gouged out from Floor 10 to the ground."[57]

Here, in any case, is what NIST says in its 2008 report on WTC 7:

> When WTC 1 collapsed at 10:28:22AM, most of the debris landed in an area not much larger than the original WTC 1 building footprint. However, some fragments were forcibly ejected and traveled distances up to hundreds of meters. Pieces of WTC 1 hit WTC 7, severing six columns on Floors 7 through 17 on the south face and one column on the west face near the southwest corner. The debris also caused structural damage between Floor 44 and the roof.[58]

Debris that caused such extensive damage, including the severing of seven steel columns, had to be quite heavy. NIST seemed implicitly to be admitting that sections of steel columns, after being forcibly ejected, had been hurled at least 650 feet (because "hundreds of meters" would mean at least 200 meters, which would be about 650 feet). Actually, NIST could have made its point without acknowledging that debris had traveled so far, because the North Tower was only 375 feet (about 115 meters) from WTC 7.

Nevertheless, whether we are talking about 650 or only 375 feet, enormous force would be needed to eject large sections of steel that far out, so as to strike WTC 7. It would seem, therefore, that NIST's report on WTC 7, while explicitly denying that explosives were used to bring down this building, has implicitly admitted that they were used to demolish the Twin Towers. And if explosives were used in the towers, who could doubt that they were also used in WTC 7?

Conclusion: In any case, even if the authors of the NIST report on WTC 7 were fully aware of the straw-man character of their arguments against thermitic explosives, they publicly use this set of arguments as a pretext to offer a theory of how WTC 7 could have come down—in the manner in which it did come down—without the aid of explosives. Part II of this book examines the major elements in that theory.

PART TWO

NIST's Unscientific Arguments for Its
Own Theory

7
NIST'S THEORY OF AN UNPRECEDENTED COLLAPSE: AN OVERVIEW

Having discussed in Part I what NIST denies—that WTC 7 was brought down by explosives—I turn now to NIST's own theory of the collapse of WTC 7. This theory is quite complex, involving several elements, and it is riddled with many problems, requiring extensive discussion. It would be easy for readers, therefore, to lose sight of the forest because of all the trees. In the present chapter, therefore, I provide an overview of NIST's theory, pointing out its main elements and the chief problems in these elements.

At the heart of the problems in NIST's theory is its claim that the collapse of WTC 7 was an unprecedented occurrence, in that the cause of this collapse was different from the cause of all previous collapses of steel-framed high-rise buildings. This claim raises the possibility that NIST has violated the principle, widely presupposed in the physical sciences, that scientists should not, without very good reasons, posit unprecedented causes to explain familiar occurrences.

The first section of this chapter is devoted to an examination of this issue. The second section then provides an overview of the main elements in NIST's theory of this collapse.

1. THE UNPRECEDENTED NATURE OF WTC 7'S COLLAPSE

According to NIST, the collapse of WTC 7 was "the first known instance of the total collapse of a tall building primarily due to fires."[1] WTC 7 was, of course, not merely a "tall building": It was a *steel-framed* tall building. NIST's claim, therefore, is that WTC 7 was the first steel-framed high-rise building ever to be brought down by fire alone.

Although NIST here says "primarily due to fire" rather than "due to fire alone," the role played by the only other alleged cause—structural damage produced by debris from the North Tower collapse—is so minimal in NIST's account that there is no real distortion involved in saying "fire alone." Indeed, Shyam Sunder himself sometimes referred to fire as the sole cause. In his "Opening Statement" at the press conference on August 21, 2008, for example, he spoke of a "fire-induced progressive collapse"; said that NIST had shown for the first time that "fire can induce a progressive collapse"; and added that "WTC 7 collapsed because of fires fueled by office furnishings." And in the "Technical Briefing" held five days later, he referred to "the fires that caused the collapse of World Trade Center 7" and also said: "WTC 7 collapsed due to uncontrolled fires with characteristics that are similar to previous fires in tall buildings."[2]

The Twin Towers, according to NIST, had been the first steel-framed buildings in history to suffer total collapse from any cause other than controlled demolition. They were not, however, brought down by fire alone, according to NIST, but by fire in conjunction with structural damage caused by the impact of the airplanes.

WTC 7 was not hit by a plane. And although NIST had at one time, as we saw earlier, planned to claim that this building's collapse was partly due to damage inflicted by debris from the North Tower's collapse, it ended up not making this claim. "Other than initiating the fires in WTC 7," NIST says in its final report, "the damage from the debris from WTC 1 had little effect on initiating the collapse of WTC 7."[3] Accordingly, whereas the Twin Towers were unique—for a few hours—in being the only steel-framed high-rises to collapse without the aid of explosives, WTC 7, according to NIST, was (and still is) unique in being the only steel-framed high-rise building in which total collapse was induced by fire alone.

But how could a steel-framed high-rise building have been brought down by fires—indeed, not even jet-fuel fires but merely fires "fed by ordinary office combustibles"? How could "ordinary fires," to use NIST's language, have resulted in this "extraordinary outcome"?[4]

NIST's short answer is that its scientists "identified thermal expansion as a new phenomenon that can cause structural collapse."[5] This statement was made by NIST's lead WTC investigator, Shyam Sunder, in his August 2008 press briefing, on the occasion of the release of the Draft version of NIST's final WTC 7 report. This statement led many critics to point out that the thermal expansion of steel is hardly a "new phenomenon." Sunder had, however, simply worded his statement poorly. He meant that NIST had learned that thermal expansion, a well-known phenomenon, could cause structural collapse. The "new phenomenon," in other words, is that structural collapse, which we had known all along could be caused by explosives, can also be caused by the thermal expansion of steel. Sunder expressed himself more clearly when he said: "[WTC 7] fell because thermal expansion, a phenomenon not considered in current building design practice, caused a fire-induced progressive collapse."[6]

But how could this very common phenomenon, thermal expansion, have produced such an uncommon—indeed, unique—result: the total collapse of a steel-framed building without the aid of explosives? As physicist John Wyndham wrote in his letter to NIST:

> [Your theory] runs contrary to 100 years of experience with the behavior of steel-framed buildings that have caught on fire. Every one of them was subjected to thermal expansion, but never before has there been such a collapse.[7]

The same point had previously been made in a letter to NIST by architect Richard Gage, who wrote: "In more than 100 steel-framed, high-rise fires (most of them very hot, very large and very long-lasting), not one has collapsed, ever."[8]

As I have emphasized, NIST could have easily avoided making its unprecedented claim: It could have begun its research with the assumption that WTC 7 was probably, like all previous steel-framed high-rise buildings that have suffered total collapse, deliberately brought down with explosives. It could then have confirmed the probable truth of this assumption by acknowledging the various types of evidence that explosives of some sort were used to bring this building down.

NIST could have done this easily, that is, from a *scientific* point of view. From a *political* point of view, however, NIST could not say the obvious, because it was an agency at the time of the Bush–Cheney Department of Commerce. As such, it had to come up with a non-demolition theory of how the building came down, because to say "demolition" would be to imply complicity by domestic—most likely government—agents. NIST was thus led to violate the scientific method by affirming, when it scientifically could have done otherwise, an unprecedented cause for a familiar phenomenon. In doing so, NIST affirmed a *unique* occurrence, which Sunder described as "a new kind of progressive collapse… a fire-induced progressive collapse."[9]

The violation might arguably have been less egregious, to be sure, if NIST had been able—without falsifying data and otherwise committing scientific fraud—to come up with a plausible explanation for WTC 7's collapse. As we will see, however, NIST did not even come close to doing this.

In the remainder of this chapter, I provide an overview of the main elements of NIST's theory, pointing out some of its problematic claims. In the following chapters, I will show in detail that each element of this theory is implausible—a fact that makes the theory as a whole implausible in the extreme.

2. THE MAIN ELEMENTS OF NIST'S THEORY

NIST's theory about the collapse of WTC 7 involves five major elements. The first is NIST's claim about the way in which fires started and then spread in this building.

(1) How the Fires Started and Spread

NIST says: "The fires in WTC 7 were ignited as a result of the impact of debris from the collapse of WTC 1 [the North Tower]."[10] In his press briefing of August 2008, Shyam Sunder elaborated on this point, saying: "The debris from Tower 1… started fires on at least 10 floors of the building. The fires burned out of control on six of these ten floors for about seven hours."[11] The six floors on which there were reportedly out-of-control fires were Floors 7, 8, 9, 11, 12, and 13.[12]

As to why the fires on those floors burned out of control, Sunder said: "The city water main had been cut by the collapse of the two WTC Towers, so the sprinklers in Building 7 did not function for much of the bottom half of the building."[13] This lack of water was said to have been crucial:

> Had a water supply for the automatic sprinkler system been available and had the sprinkler system operated as designed, it is likely that fires in WTC 7 would have been controlled and the collapse prevented.[14]

Given this absence of an operating sprinkler system, the fires were able, NIST claims, to spread from the south side and southwest corner of the building, where the debris from the North Tower struck, to the building's northeast region, where they caused the thermal expansion that initiated the building's collapse.

An important element of NIST's account is its statement that "there was no evidence of floor-to-floor fire spread."[15] This means that the fires on each of the ten floors with fire had to have been ignited separately by debris from the North Tower.

Another important element of NIST's account is a claim that it did *not* make in its final report. Supporters of the fire theory of the collapse of WTC 7, as I mentioned in the Introduction, had generally assumed that the fires had been spread and intensified by diesel oil contained in the building. NIST's final report on WTC 7, however, said that "fuel oil fires did not play a role in the collapse of WTC 7."[16] Gone, therefore, was the possibility of claiming that the diesel fuel had played a role in WTC 7 analogous to that played by jet fuel in the Twin Towers. In those two buildings, NIST said, there was "widespread spraying of jet fuel to ignite numerous workstations or offices simultaneously." In WTC 7, by contrast, "the fire would have spread from one individual workstation or office to another."[17]

Nevertheless, as Chapter 8 will show, NIST claimed that the fires spread from the south side and the southwest corner of WTC 7 to the northeast region, where they burned with sufficient intensity, and for a sufficient length of time, to cause enough thermal expansion to start a chain of failures that would result in the building's total collapse.

(2) Fire Temperatures and Durations

NIST's theory, as we will see in Chapter 9, requires that fires on some of the floors burned at 1,000°C (1,832°F); it even suggested that they in places reached 1,100°C (2,012°F). But independent scientists, as we will also see, believe that the fires could not have been burning at temperatures even close to this.

In addition, in order to have caused the damage required by NIST's theory, the fires on some floors, as we will also see in Chapter 9, must have lasted up to four hours. But NIST's claim that fires on some of the floors burned that long is purely speculative, unsupported by empirical evidence. Indeed, as we will see, some of NIST's claims about the fires are *contradicted* by facts contained in its own reports.

Another problem involves the fact that big, intense, long-burning fires on the floors in question would have been possible only if those floors had contained large quantities of combustible material. NIST claims that this was indeed the case on the 11th, 12th, and 13th floors—the floors that, according to NIST, had the fires that were primarily responsible for bringing down WTC 7. As we will see, however, the claim that these floors had extraordinarily high amounts of combustible material is unfounded.

(3) Steel Temperatures

The role of the fires in NIST's theory, of course, was to bring steel up to temperatures at which it could change in ways that could have produced global collapse. Unlike NIST's report on the Twin Towers, however, its report on WTC 7 does not claim that fire damaged the (vertical) columns. NIST's theory about WTC 7 is, instead, based on the heating of (horizontal) beams.

The fire-induced effects in these beams that led to collapse, according to NIST, were of two types: expansion and weakening. The thermal expansion of beams—generally alleged by NIST to have been the primary cause of WTC 7's collapse—was said to have occurred at steel temperatures below 400°C (750°F). So this part of NIST's theory is not obviously outlandish. Equally essential to the theory, however, is the idea that the beams on some of the floors became hot enough to lose most of their strength, which happened, according to NIST, when they reached temperatures of 600°C to 675°C (1,100°F to 1,250°F)—temperatures that, as we will see in Chapter 9, are clearly implausible.

Beyond overestimating the temperatures and durations of the fires, NIST had two other methods for trying to make its claims about steel temperatures seem plausible. One of these methods was to base its calculations on temperatures ten percent higher than its own simulations suggested. The second method was to avoid the implications of its own finding that each cubicle or office would have provided sufficient fuel for fires lasting only 20 to 30 minutes. As we will see, both of these methods are invalid—a fact that further discredits the claim that office fires caused the high steel temperatures required by NIST's theory.

(4) How Thermal Expansion Caused Floor and Column Failures

According to NIST, the high temperatures reached by the steel beams supporting Floors 6 through 13 on the northeast side of WTC 7, near Column 79, weakened them so much that they were ready to collapse. At the same time, the thermal elongation of a beam on Floor 13 caused the steel girder connecting Column 44 to Column 79 to disconnect from the latter, so that it was no longer supporting it. This loss of support for Column 79, along with other damage, caused Floor 13 to collapse, and its collapse triggered a cascade of collapses down to the 5th floor. Then Column 79, having lost support from the girder and the floors, buckled, and this started a chain reaction of column failures, leading eventually to the collapse of the entire building.

One problem with this theory, already mentioned, is that it depends on greatly overestimated steel temperatures.

A second problem is that, even if those temperatures were correct, the claim that the steel would have elongated sufficiently to produce the effects described by NIST appears to be unsupported by the relevant calculations, as we will see in Chapter 9.

A third problem is that NIST's claim that steel beams expanded enough to cause such damage is dependent on a finding of its computer simulation, according to which the shear studs connecting the steel beams to the concrete floor slabs failed because the steel beams expanded further and more quickly than the concrete slabs. This was a surprising result, given the fact that steel and concrete, when heated, expand virtually the same amount. The result becomes less surprising, however, when we learn that NIST, while running its simulation, "heated" only the simulated steel, not also the simulated concrete, even though an actual fire in the real building would have heated the actual concrete as well as the actual steel. It was only through this chicanery, evidently, that the simulation predicted the failure of the shear studs.

A fourth problem involves a second instance of fraud involving shear studs. NIST's finding in its computer simulation that the girder connecting Columns 44 and 79 failed is dependent on its claim that, although shear studs were used to connect the beams to the floor slabs, they were not also used to connect the girders to the slabs. But NIST's *Interim Report on WTC 7*, released back in 2004, stated that shear studs *were* used to connect the girders (as well as the beams) to the floor slabs.

Once we are aware of this and the previous three problems in NIST's theory of how the global collapse of WTC 7 began, we can see that it is completely unworthy of credence.

(5) How a Failed Column Led to Total Collapse

The final element of NIST's theory—which, of course, presupposes the correctness of the previous four elements—is that the collapse of Column 79, which NIST calls the "initial local failure," eventually led to the global collapse of WTC 7. The theory is that the failure of Column 79 caused Columns 80, 81, and, eventually, all the interior columns to fail, so that the building was simply an empty shell; then the exterior columns failed, causing the descent of the exterior façade—a descent that, from the perspective of external witnesses and video cameras, appeared to be the sudden collapse of the whole building. With this account, NIST attempted to reconcile its theory of a progressive collapse, which would have taken considerable time, with the fact that the building appeared to collapse at virtually the rate of a free-falling object.

But this part of NIST's theory is, like the previous parts, riddled with problems, as we will see in Chapter 10. One of these problems involves a claim NIST makes concerning Column 79: that after losing support from a critical girder and eight floors, which had collapsed, it started moving downward with a high rate of acceleration within a fifth of a second, even though it had not lost the supports it had from the remaining floors. This would have been impossible.

A second problem is that although NIST claims that its simulation-based graphics of the collapse of WTC 7 match the building's behavior as seen in the videos "reasonably well," these graphics really—as can most easily be seen by comparing the rooflines—show a completely different kind of collapse.

A third problem is that careful measurements of the building's descent as seen in videos show the upper portion of the building coming down in free fall for over two seconds. NIST's theory does not allow for such an occurrence, a fact that was reflected in the first version of NIST's final report, the Draft for Public Comment, which was issued in August 2008. In that version, NIST denied that free fall had occurred. But public discussion, especially by high-school physics teacher David Chandler, forced NIST to admit, in its Final Report, issued in November, that there had been a stage in the collapse, lasting for over two seconds, during which free fall had occurred. NIST's theory was not revised, however, to allow for this, so NIST ended up with a contradiction between its *description of,* and its *theory about,* the collapse. This contradiction dramatically illustrates, more clearly than any of the other problems in NIST's theory, the falsity and unscientific character of its entire approach.

Having given this overview of the five main elements of NIST's collapse theory, along with the chief problems in them, I will provide in the following three chapters a detailed exposition and critique of these elements and problems.

8
THE INITIATION AND SPREAD OF FIRES: NIST'S UNEMPIRICAL ACCOUNT

I n Shyam Sunder's opening statement at the August 2008 press briefing to announce the release of NIST's final report on WTC 7, he said: "The debris from Tower 1... started fires on at least 10 floors of the building. The fires burned out of control on six of these ten floors for about seven hours."[1] Both claims in this statement are highly problematic.

Although Sunder stated the first claim—that the fires in WTC 7 were *ignited by debris from the North Tower*—as if this were beyond doubt, NIST's WTC 7 report itself shows otherwise. It says that the cause of the fires is "unknown,"[2] which means that NIST could only call the idea that they were ignited by debris from the North Tower "likely."[3]

The press, however, simply reported Sunder's seemingly confident statement at the briefing, without pointing out that NIST's report did not back it up. Eric Lipton of the *New York Times*, for example, wrote: "The investigators determined that debris from the falling twin towers... ignited fires on at least 10 floors at 7 World Trade Center."[4] In light of NIST's report, Lipton's term "determined" should have been replaced by "speculated." The Associated Press repeated Sunder's speculation in an even more matter-of-fact manner, writing that WTC 7 "was set on fire by falling debris from the burning towers."[5] But that claim, as we will see, is not supported by evidence and is—in light of evidence reported by NIST itself—highly *un*likely.

The press also failed to challenge Sunder's second claim—that fires on six floors "burned out of control... for about seven hours." The press thereby let stand the impression, created by this statement, that the fires on those floors were such that they could have greatly increased the temperature of the building's steel. NIST's report, however, provides no evidence of any seven-hour fires—let alone seven hours of the raging-inferno fires suggested by the expression "out of control." The fires were out of control only in the sense that no one was trying to control them.

In the following discussion, I focus primarily on problems with NIST's claim that the fires in WTC 7 were ignited by debris from the collapse of the North Tower. I deal secondarily with the question, important for the following chapter, of the spread and duration of the fires.

1. REQUIREMENTS OF NIST'S THEORY

If NIST's theory of the initiation of the fires in WTC 7 was to be consistent with the official view of this building's collapse—that it was *not* caused by explosives—there were several requirements that had to be met.

One requirement was that the fires in this building began when the North Tower collapsed at 10:28:22 (henceforth designated simply as "10:28"). NIST might have claimed, to be sure, that one or more fires had started at 9:59, when the South Tower (WTC 2) collapsed. But NIST pointed out evidence that "large and heavy debris did not reach WTC 7 from the collapse of WTC 2," which was 675 feet (206 meters) away. (By contrast, WTC 1, the North Tower, was only about 370 feet [113 meters] away.)[6] NIST, accordingly, dismissed the possibility that any fires began before 10:28.

Given the recognition that no fires could have been started by the 9:59 collapse of the South Tower, any evidence that fires began *before* 10:28 would threaten NIST's theory, because the existence of such fires could be used to support the contention, reported by both Barry Jennings and Michael Hess on 9/11 and reiterated by Jennings several years later, that explosions occurred in WTC 7 prior to the collapse of either of the Twin Towers.

Evidence that fires had begun *after* 10:28 would also be problematic from NIST's perspective, because it could be used to support the idea that fires had been deliberately started by means of incendiary devices of some sort.

Strictly speaking, NIST could have accommodated evidence of late-starting fires by positing that they were caused by electrical shorts that, although ultimately caused by the North Tower debris damage, had developed some time later. The possibility that electrical shorts started fires was even mentioned. However, this was not a possibility that NIST took seriously. It is mentioned only once, and then only in passing, in a chapter in the long version of NIST's final report written by a single author, Richard Gann.[7] It is not mentioned in the final chapter, in which NIST's theory is summarized, or in any of the other chapters co-authored by NIST's lead investigator, Shyam Sunder. The possibility that fires might have been started by electrical shorts is, moreover, not mentioned even once in the brief version of NIST's report, which was intended for the press and the general public.

Why did NIST not take seriously the possibility of late-starting fires caused by electrical shorts? Perhaps because acknowledging this possibility would have undermined the claim that fires on some of the floors had "burned out of control for about seven hours." It could even have undermined NIST's claim, which (as we will see later) was essential to its theory, that some of the fires had burned for four hours.

Perhaps for these reasons, therefore, NIST wrote—with one strange exception, to be mentioned later—as if all the fires in WTC 7 had begun at 10:28, due to debris from the North Tower's collapse. NIST seemed to consider this claim to be a requirement for giving full support to the official view of WTC 7's collapse, according to which it was *not* brought about deliberately.

A second requirement followed from NIST's acknowledgment, pointed out in the previous chapter, that "there was no evidence of floor-to-floor fire spread."[8] Given this fact, NIST had to maintain that the fires on all ten floors on which fires were observed had been started directly by debris from the collapse of the North Tower. It needed to maintain, therefore, that the fires on each of those floors began at 10:28. This means that if fires were not observed on some of those floors until later on in the day, NIST could not suggest that they had migrated from floors on which fire had been observed earlier. It had to claim that fires had been burning on each of the ten floors since 10:28.

These two requirements entailed a third. Most of the debris damage to WTC 7 was on its south face, with a little on its west face near the southwest corner, so "[t]here was no superficial or structural damage to the north and east faces."[9] NIST had to maintain, therefore, that the fires on all ten floors began on either the south side or the south end of the west side. Therefore, if fire was first observed on the north or east face of a particular floor—and this was indeed the case for some floors—NIST had to claim that the fire had migrated there unnoticed from the south or southwest part of the building. NIST's theory, moreover, claims that WTC 7 was caused to collapse by fires on its north and east sides. Accordingly, whereas floor-to-floor migration of fires was ruled out, side-to-side migration of fires on the floors was essential to the theory.

With these requirements in mind, let us compare NIST's theory with the evidence, as reported by NIST itself.

2. WHERE, WHEN, & HOW DID THE FIRES START?

Physical chemist Frank H. Greening has written that one of the most significant problems with NIST's theory is "the question of where and how fires started in building 7."[10] If, as NIST claims, fires were started on ten floors at 10:28 by debris from the North Tower's collapse, we would assume that fires would have been observed on those floors shortly thereafter. And this is what NIST suggests, writing: "Shortly after the towers collapsed, fires began to appear at multiple locations in WTC 7."[11] But whether this statement is true depends on the meaning of "shortly" and "multiple."

After the collapse of the North Tower, as we will see below, photographers and camera crews returned to the site and started capturing imagery, according to NIST, at about 11:00AM. And yet, NIST says, the earliest that any fires in WTC 7 were captured by photographs or videos was at 12:10PM, when fires were visible in two windows on the southwest corner of Floor 22.[12] Fires were then seen at the south end of the west face of the 29th and 30th floors at 12:28.[13] Accordingly, NIST's statement that fires began to appear "[s]hortly after the towers collapsed" means that fire appeared on one floor about one hour and 40 minutes after the collapse of the North Tower and on two other floors about two hours after the collapse. Most people would probably not consider this a reasonable interpretation of "shortly."

The fact that cameras did not capture fires on those floors until almost two hours after 10:28 creates a plausibility problem for NIST's theory: It requires us to believe that, although the fires were supposedly started near the building's south and southwest faces, and hence near the windows, they remained invisible from outside the building for all that time. NIST's theory that all of the fires began at 10:28 is, in any case, speculative, not based on any empirical evidence.

NIST's claim that fires began appearing shortly in "multiple locations" is also problematic. Given NIST's assertion that debris from the collapse ignited fires on ten floors, the word "multiple" would most naturally suggest that fires soon began appearing—in imagery captured by cameras—on most, or at least many, of these floors. NIST, however, reports that, prior to 2:08PM, fires were photographed on only three floors: the 22nd, the 29th, and the 30th.[14] On all the other floors, fires did not appear in imagery until 2:08 or later. Fires that did not appear until 2:08 or later—three and a half hours or more after the collapse of the North Tower—certainly cannot be said to have appeared "shortly after" that collapse.

The fact that fires first became visible on the 11th and 12th floors at 2:00 make it very difficult to believe NIST's claim that all fires began at 10:26.

Equally implausible are NIST's claims about the 7th and 13th floors. NIST wrote: "Early indications of a developing fire were observed on the west side of the 7th floor shortly after 2:00PM.... The first visual evidence for burning on the 13th floor was seen on the east face around 2:30PM."[16] According to NIST, therefore, these fires remained invisible from outside the building for three and a half to four hours.[17]

NIST's theory moves completely beyond the realm of plausibility in relation to the 8th, 9th, and 14th floors, on which fires were first photographed at about 3:40, 4:00, and 5:00PM, respectively, and hence about five, five and a half, and six and a half hours after the collapse of the North Tower.[18] Can anyone really believe, for example, that a fire had been burning on Floor 14 since 10:28AM, even though "the first and only visual indication of a fire on this floor" was a picture of it taken at 5:03?[19]

3. ALLEGED EYEWITNESS TESTIMONIES OF EARLIER FIRES

The plausibility of NIST's claim that the fires in WTC 7 all originated when the North Tower collapsed at 10:28 is seriously threatened, as we have seen, not only by the fact that imagery of fires on some floors was not captured until three to six hours later, but also by the fact that imagery of no fires whatsoever were captured until 12:10PM. If fires had been initiated at 10:28 near the south and southwest faces of ten different floors, and if cameras had resumed capturing images at 11:00, then surely at least one of the fires would have become visible much earlier than 12:10PM. This supposition could lead to the suspicion that none of the fires began before noon. To overcome this problem, NIST claims that eyewitnesses saw fires on some floors in before any cameras captured them.

An Earlier Fire on the 7th Floor?

NIST claims that a security officer saw a fire on the 7th floor shortly after the North Tower collapsed at 10:28. Although NIST's statement about this security officer—which occurs in a chapter written by Lawson and Gann—was quoted in Chapter 5, I have repeated it here, with the statement about the security officer's observation italicized:

> A security officer... headed back up to a floor in the 40s after WTC 2 collapsed [i.e., after 9:59AM].... The security officer had reached the 30th floor when the building shook as WTC 1 collapsed [i.e., at 10:28AM], and the stairwell became dark. He began to descend and stopped at the 23rd floor to see if anyone was on the OEM floor. He opened the door... and saw that the area was filled with smoke. He made it down to the 7th floor, where he stopped because he could not see or breathe at this point. He broke a window near the center of the north face to yell for help. A ladder truck pulled up, but could not reach the window.... Firemen came up the stairwell right away. *Soon after WTC 1 collapsed, the security officer saw a fire on the west side of Floor 7 that he attempted to put out with an extinguisher, but he was unable to do so.* As the firefighters went up, they vented the stairway and cleared some of the smoke. They first met the security officer on the 7th floor, and firefighters escorted him down the stairs. Other firefighters from the group continued up the stairs, shined their flashlights through the staircase smoke and called out. The two trapped men on the 8th floor [i.e., Hess and Jennings] saw the flashlight beams... and went down the stairway.[20]

With this account, NIST apparently meant to avoid having to claim that, although the fires began at 10:28AM, there was no evidence of a fire until 12:10PM. By means of this Lawson–Gann account of the security officer, NIST has shown that a fire was seen in WTC 7 shortly after the collapse of the North Tower (WTC 1), hence at about 10:30. Or rather, NIST has shown this if, and only if, its account of the security officer's observation is plausible. But it is not, for five reasons.

One problem is that the sentence about the fire being seen by the security officer breaks the line of thought: After describing firemen going up the stairwell, the passage describes the observation of a fire, which had occurred several minutes earlier, and then returns to the account of the firefighters going up the stairwell. If the sentence about the observation of the fire is eliminated, the passage reads much more smoothly: "Firemen came up the stairwell right away. As the firefighters went up, they vented the stairway and cleared some of the smoke." It seems, therefore, that the sentence about the security officer's observation of the fire was inserted after the description of the rescue had been written.

A second problem is that, if he had come down the staircase that Hess and Jennings were on, he would have encountered them before he reached the 7th floor.

A third problem with this alleged observation is that it is not mentioned in any previous NIST document about the WTC. The footnote to it, giving the source of its information, says, "SSB [Salomon Smith Barney] Interview 5, April, 2004,"[21] which suggests that the security officer had given this account to NIST in April 2004. But, in NIST's 2005 account of the rescue—which was written by Lawson with Robert Vettori—the relevant footnote referred only to the interviews with Michael Hess and Barry Jennings. The account does mention a security officer, but there is no indication that he had been interviewed.[22] Are we to believe that, although this interview was recorded in April 2004, Lawson and Vettori, while writing their 2005 account of the rescues, would have made no reference to it?

A fourth problem is one that I mentioned in Chapter 5, when discussing the Lawson–Gann account of the rescue of Hess and Jennings. As we saw, this account implies that firefighters either remained at the WTC site after the 10:28 collapse of the North Tower or else returned only a few minutes thereafter. This conclusion is implied by the fact that the security officer appears to have called for help as soon as he reached the 7th floor, which the account suggests would have been no later than 10:40AM. But due to the huge dust cloud caused by the collapse of the North Tower, as we saw in Chapter 5, firefighters would not have been able to remain at the site, or even to return to it within a few minutes.

Moreover, even if they had been standing around outside, barely able to breathe, they would not have been able to see Hess, Jennings, and a security officer signaling for help. The brief version of NIST's report says that the time at which visibility allowed firefighters to see the building again was "estimated to be 11:00AM to 12:00PM."[23] And a chapter in NIST's long report written by William Pitts says: "During [the] first hour following the collapse of WTC 1, emergency responders… and professional photographers and film crews began to work their way slowly back to the WTC site," with the latter starting to obtain imagery "around 11:00AM."[24] Accordingly, NIST's reports contain evidence contradictory to the idea that a security officer could have signaled to firefighters at about 10:40AM.

For these reasons, the claim that the security officer became trapped when WTC 1 collapsed is implausible. If the story reflects actual events, it seems more probable that the security officer would have been trapped, like Hess and Jennings, around 9:30, when the huge explosion occurred that prevented Hess and Jennings from going below the 6th floor. If so, the security officer would have signaled for help shortly after that, as did Hess and Jennings. (However, these would still be a problem with the claim that he had descended to the 7th floor on the same staircase.) But then firefighters, after failing to reach the three men with a ladder, would have been unable to rescue them until 11:00 or so, due to the collapses. (Jennings, as we saw in Chapter 5, said: "The fire department came and ran. They came twice. Why? Because Building Tower One fell, and then Tower Two fell."[25]) Accordingly, if a security officer really reported seeing a fire on the 7th floor shortly after the first damage to WTC 7 occurred, it probably would have been a fire he observed closer to 9:30 than to 10:30.

I will return to this possibility after discussing a fifth reason for doubting Lawson and Gann's claim that, "Soon after WTC 1 collapsed, the security officer saw a fire on the west side of Floor 7." This fifth reason is that NIST provides contradictory versions of the claim.

As we saw above in Chapter 5, an account in NIST's final WTC 7 report written by William Pitts says: "[A] witness saw a fire on the southwest corner of the 7th floor at about 12:15PM, before being rescued (Chapter 6)."[26] Chapter 6, to which Pitts refers the reader, is the chapter written by Lawson and Gann. His "witness," therefore, is the security officer discussed by them. Pitts, however, was apparently unaware that, according to their chapter, this security officer saw the fire at about 10:30, not at about 12:15.

Another version of the alleged observation that contradicts the Lawson–Gann version occurs in Chapter 9 of the report, which says: "There was a direct observation of a workstation fire in the southwest corner of Floor 7 around noon." On the following page, the time is stated more precisely: "A cubicle fire was observed on Floor 7 at about 12:15PM, near the southwest corner of the building."[27] This chapter was co-authored by Kevin B. McGrattan, William L. Grosshandler, and, amazingly, Richard G. Gann.[28] One chapter that Gann helped write, therefore, claimed that a 7th floor fire was observed at about 10:30, whereas another chapter co-authored by Gann says, like Pitts's chapter, that it was observed at "around noon" or, more precisely, "at about 12:15PM."

There is yet another version of this alleged observation. The "summary" at the end of Chapter 6, written by Lawson and Gann, says: "Soon after WTC 1 collapsed, and thus about 10:30AM, FDNY observed a fire on the west side of the 7th floor."[29] This chapter had not previously discussed any such observation by the FDNY, so this claim, stated in the summary, cannot be a reference to a second observation of the fire (in addition to the one made by the security officer). Accordingly, besides contradicting other authors of NIST's WTC 7 report on the question of when the 7th floor fire was observed, Lawson and Gann even contradict themselves on the issue of who observed the fire at "about 10:30AM"—a security officer or the FDNY. Did they, after deciding to report an observation of fire at 10:30, change their minds about details and then forget to make the entire chapter consistent with regard to this issue?

In any case, given all of these contradictions, there is no reason to credit NIST's claim that a 7th floor fire was observed at about 10:30.

It appears likely that this claim is a distortion or even a complete fabrication, created to support NIST's theory that the fires in WTC 7 were started by debris from the collapsing North Tower.

Doubt about NIST's claim could easily be cleared up if NIST would provide proof that it did indeed interview a security officer who reported what NIST claims. But NIST refused a FOIA request to release the text of the alleged interview—thereby increasing the doubt that it actually took place.[30]

An Earlier Fire on the 8th Floor?

No fire was filmed on Floor 8, as we saw above, until 3:40PM. NIST, however, claims that eyewitnesses reported seeing a fire on the south face of this floor sometime "[b]etween 12:15PM and 2:30PM" (which would make it somewhat more believable that a fire had started on this floor at 10:28). In the chapter by McGrattan, Grosshandler, and Gann, NIST states:

> At 12:15PM, when the cubicle fire was observed on Floor 7, people being led from Floors 7 and 8 out of the building reported no fires, heavy dust, or smoke on Floor 8. Between 12:15PM and 2:30PM, fire activity on Floor 8 was observed at the south face by eyewitnesses near the southwest corner of the building.[31]

The first of these two sentences is quite remarkable: Even though NIST claims that the fire on Floor 8—like the fires on all the other floors—began at 10:28AM, this sentence seems to imply that people had remained on this floor until 12:15PM. Can we imagine that people would have remained on a floor for almost two hours after a fire had started on it?

The sentence clearly states, in any case, that people being led out of the building from the 8th floor at 12:15 saw no fires or even smoke on this floor. I will return to this statement later. For now I wish to point out that we have several reasons to be suspicious of the entire passage.

One problem is the statement that a security officer observed a 7th floor fire at 12:15PM. As we saw earlier, this statement, made by McGrattan, Grosshandler, and Gann, is contradicted by other NIST authors, who claim that the security officer made this observation at about 10:30AM, shortly after the North Tower collapsed.

A second problem is that, as we saw in Chapter 5, the claim that the security officer spotted a 7th floor fire at around noon, just before he was rescued, appears to have been motivated by the desire to support the claim, made in NIST's 2004 *Interim Report on WTC 7*, that Michael Hess and Barry Jennings, who were rescued at the same time as the security officer, were rescued at "12:10 to 12:15PM." And that claim, as we saw, runs contrary to many facts, most obviously the fact that Hess gave an interview before noon several blocks from the WTC site.

A third problem involves this passage's main claim—that an 8th floor fire was observed between 12:15 and 2:30PM "by eyewitnesses." Not only are these alleged eyewitnesses unnamed, their existence is not even supported by a footnote referring to interviews with any of them.

Accordingly, NIST's claim about eyewitness testimony to an 8th floor fire early in the afternoon is no more credible than its claim about an early observation of a 7th floor fire.

NIST's Claims for Earlier Fires: Conclusion

On the basis of these alleged eyewitness reports of fires at 10:30AM on Floor 7 and sometime between 12:15 and 2:30PM on Floor 8, NIST created computer simulations (to be discussed in the following chapter) in which "the fires on these two floors were assumed to have initiated at a time designated as noon."[32] This is puzzling: If NIST believes that the fires began at 10:28, why did it have its computer simulations based on the assumption that they did not begin until noon?

The more serious question, however, is whether NIST even had evidence that the fires began as early as noon. The only evidence NIST offers is alleged eyewitness testimonies and, as we have seen, they are too problematic to be considered credible evidence. The earliest good evidence of fires on these floors, therefore, is the first set of images captured by cameras, which were captured "shortly after 2:00PM" (Floor 7) and at about 3:40PM (Floor 8).

This conclusion has two important implications. First, it means that NIST'S earliest objective evidence of a fire in WTC 7 remains the photograph of a fire on the 22nd floor taken at 12:10PM. To accept NIST's theory of the initiation of the fires, therefore, we must believe that fires were burning on ten floors for an hour and 40 minutes before we have objective evidence for even one of them.

The second implication is that the objective evidence of fire on any of the lower floors, on which there were said to be "sustained" fires, remains the image showing fires on the 11th and 12th floors, which was captured at 2:08PM (even though "imagery of the WTC 7 faces [had] started to become available around 11:00AM"[33]). This fact creates a problem for NIST's claim that these fires all started at 10:28 and hence for its claim, to be discussed below, that some of these fires endured for seven hours.

Before turning to the question of the duration of the fires, however, we need to look at a report that there was fire in WTC 7 even *earlier* than NIST claimed.

Reports that Fire Began at about 9:30AM

I suggested above that, if a security officer actually did report a fire on the 7th floor, it was probably not at 10:30, as NIST claims, but more like 9:30. (If NIST changed the timeline of the events reported by Michael Hess and Barry Jennings, there is no reason to doubt that it would have done the same for events reported by a security officer.) A reason to believe this, beyond those given earlier, is that three people reported fires in WTC 7 at about 9:30.

Two of these people were Michael Hess and Barry Jennings. As we saw in Chapter 5, they reported an explosion that evidently occurred between 9:15 and 9:30AM. According to Hess's testimony at the time, this explosion produced "thick smoke" on the 8th floor, and where there is smoke, there is usually fire. Jennings told Dylan Avery that when he got back up to the floor, "It was dark. It was also very, very, hot—*very* hot."[34] Jennings told the BBC: "I could smell fire; you know, you could smell the smoke, and I felt the heat; it was intense." The BBC, to be sure, interpreted this to mean fire that was started by the collapse of the North Tower at 10:28, but Jennings was talking about fire that followed upon the big explosion that he experienced approximately an hour earlier.

The third person, an expert on building collapses who otherwise supports the official story about the destruction of the World Trade Center, publicly stated that the fires in WTC 7 began at 9:30 that morning. This expert was structural engineer Matthys Levy, the co-author of a book entitled *Why Buildings Fall Down*[35] and the chairman of Weidlinger Associates, which assisted Larry Silverstein's pursuit of a $7 billion insurance payment for the destruction of the World Trade Center (which he had leased shortly before 9/11).[36] Levy offered expert testimony in support of the official story in a 2002 PBS documentary, *Why the Towers Fell,* and also in a 2007 History Channel documentary, *9/11 Conspiracies: Fact or Fiction?*

While discussing WTC 7 during the second of these programs, Levy said: "The initial fires started around 9:30 in the morning, so the building was allowed to burn for eight hours."[37] Levy's intent to support the official account, according to which fires brought the building down, is shown by his statement that "the building was allowed to burn for eight hours." That statement also shows that he did not simply misspeak—that he had not meant to say that the initial fires had started "around 10:30": Only if the fires had burned from 9:30AM until 5:21PM, when WTC came down, would they have burned for (almost) eight hours.

In stating in 2007 that the fires in WTC 7 began at 9:30, Levy probably did not realize that he was contradicting in advance what NIST was going to say in its 2008 report, namely, that no fires began until 10:28.

In any case, Levy's statement provides independent support for the account given by Barry Jennings and Michael Hess—before the latter changed his story after Jennings' death in 2008, as discussed in Chapter 5—according to which a fire-producing explosion occurred as they were trying to leave the building shortly after the 9:03 attack on the South Tower. The independent support from Levy makes it seem even more likely that if a security officer did report having observed a 7th floor fire, this observation would have been made closer to 9:30 than 10:30.

It might be thought, to be sure, that if a fire had been started on one or more lower floors at that time, there would be photographs showing this fire. However, images captured from cameras at a distance from the site did not show the lower floors of WTC 7, as they were blocked by surrounding buildings. And the attention of the photographers and camera crews who had arrived at the site by 9:30 would surely would have been focused on the Twin Towers, which had been struck by airplanes and were burning very visibly. Subsequently, the dust clouds created by the collapses of the Twin Towers at 9:59 and 10:28 would have prevented imagery of WTC 7's lower floors from being captured until about 11:00, when visibility returned (as we saw above). By then, any fire that had started at 9:30 would have likely burned out—as did fires, as we will see below, on several other floors.

To summarize: Whereas NIST claims that all the fires in WTC 7 began at 10:28, this claim appears to be purely speculative. The empirical evidence seems to be more consistent with the idea that some fires began before 10:21 and other fires began after that time. I turn next to NIST's claims about the spread and endurance of the fires.

4. THE SPREAD AND ENDURANCE OF THE FIRES

As we saw at the outset of this chapter, NIST claims that "fires burned out of control on six… floors for about seven hours." The claim that fires burned for many hours on some of the floors is an essential part of NIST's theory, according to which the fires burned long enough to increase the temperature of steel beams sufficiently to cause significant thermal expansion. This claim, however, is not supported by NIST's own evidence.

If fires burned for (almost) seven hours before WTC 7 came down at 5:21, they would have needed to start at about 10:30. But once NIST's claims about early eyewitness observations of fires are dismissed, its earliest evidence of fires in WTC 7 consists of images of fires on Floors 22, 29, and 30, which were captured by cameras at 12:10 and 12:27PM.

These images, moreover, do not even lend support to the notion that fires on some floors lasted for about five hours, because, as NIST acknowledges: "These [fires] were short-lived."[38] Spelling this out, NIST says that the fires on these three floors "generally did not spread far before dying out."[39] NIST also says: "There are no images showing flames or other evidence of active fires above the 14th floor after about 1:00PM."[40] In other words, these fires all died out in less than an hour.

As to why the fires on Floors 22, 29, and 30 died out rather than continuing to spread, NIST suggested that they were put out by WTC 7's sprinkler system, which remained intact above the 20th floor:

> Water for Floors 1 through 20 was supplied directly from the NYC water distribution system through two service lines.… [T]he water

supply tanks located in the upper part of the building did not service the lower floors. Therefore, there was no source of water for controlling fires on the lowest 20 floors when the NYC system became inoperable following the collapse of WTC 1.... The water supplies for Floors 21 through 47 included large capacity storage tanks and direct connections to the NYC water distribution system. These supplies provided redundant sources of water for the standpipe and sprinkler system infrastructures.... This might explain why some fires on and above Floor 20 did not spread into the afternoon.[41]

This would seem plausible, except for one problem: There was also evidence of fire on the 19th floor, which was one of the floors on which the sprinkler system was *not* supplied with water. And yet the fire on this floor had also died out by 1:00.[42] Why so? NIST wrote: "NIST was unable to obtain evidence to indicate why this fire did not spread."[43] Perhaps the area where this fire began simply did not have sufficient combustible material to keep it going.

Be that as it may, the 19th floor exception prevented NIST from claiming that, once a fire was started on a floor, it would spread unless it was put out by sprinklers. The fact that Floor 19's fire did not spread, even though its sprinklers could not have been operating, suggests that fires on other floors may have been unable to spread for a reason unrelated to the question of whether those floors had functioning sprinklers—with such a possible reason being the absence of sufficient combustible material. The fire on Floor 19, therefore, provides one more reason to be skeptical of NIST's theory that fires started on some of the lower floors at 10:28 and continued to spread until the building collapsed.

In any case, NIST's claim about long-burning, out-of-control fires was restricted to six lower floors: "Sustained fires occurred on Floors 7, 8, 9, 11, 12, and 13."[44] These are the floors on which Shyam Sunder claimed that fires burned "for about seven hours." But NIST's own evidence fails to support this claim. I will look at these six floors in reverse order, starting with Floor 13.

Floor 13

NIST says, as we saw earlier: "The first visual evidence for burning on the 13th floor was seen on the east face around 2:30PM."[45] So, although NIST claims that this fire started on the south or southwest part of building at 10:28, it provides no evidence to support this claim. The empirical evidence would be compatible with the assumption that the fire on this floor originated on the east face shortly before 2:30. At best, therefore, NIST has provided evidence that the fire on the 13th floor lasted about three hours. This is important because, as we will see in the next chapter, Floor 13 is one of the three floors on which fire is said to have caused the greatest damage.

Floors 12 and 11

The fires on the 11th and 12th floors are the other ones said to have caused the most damage. With regard to Floor 12, NIST says: "The first observation of a fire on the 12th floor was on the east face around 2:08."[46] NIST's evidence, therefore, would be consistent with the assumption that the fire on this floor began on the east face at about 2:00PM. At best, therefore, NIST's evidence supports the existence of a fire on this floor lasting about 3 hours and 20 minutes.

The same is true of the 11th floor, about which NIST states: "A fire was first observed on this floor at 2:08PM on the east face." NIST, however, makes additional comments about this floor, saying:

> Shortly after the flames first appeared on the north face [at 4:34PM], a photograph showed intense burning…. By around 4:52PM, the flames in the area had apparently died down, and flames on this floor were not observed again until around 5:10PM…. NIST found no evidence regarding the pathway that the fire took to reach the north face.[47]

So although NIST claims that the fire on Floor 11 began on the south or southwest side at 10:28, then migrated to the east face by 2:08 and to the north face by 4:34, it presents no evidence to support this claim. Its evidence would be consistent with the assumption that one fire began on Floor 11's east face at about 2:00, another began on its north face at about 4:30, and still another began at about 5:00. Moreover, even if we accepted NIST's speculation of a continuous, migrating fire on Floor 11 from 2:08PM until the building collapsed, this would be evidence for a fire lasting only a little over 3 hours.

Floor 9

NIST's evidence for a "sustained fire" on the 9th floor is even weaker.

NIST states:

> There was no indication of fire in the available imagery on this floor until… [shortly] before 4:00PM.… There are no images suggesting how fire reached [the west side of the north face]. Views of the floor as little as 10 min[utes] earlier provided no indication that a fire was present. Once the fire appeared, it grew rapidly and spread to the east.… NIST found no evidence regarding fire behavior after 4:40PM.[48]

In other words, NIST had evidence that a fire on the 9th floor was "sustained" for a total of 40 minutes—from about 4:00 until about 4:40PM. It was "out of control" in the sense that no one was controlling it. But it seemed to control *itself* quite well, perhaps because this floor—possibly like the 19th floor—simply did not have enough combustible material to keep a fire going.

Floor 8

"The earliest observation of a fire present on the 8th floor," NIST says, occurred at about 3:41PM.[49] This statement is made in the chapter written by William Pitts, who was perhaps unaware of the above-discussed claim, made in the chapter by Kevin McGrattan, William Grosshandler, and Richard Gann, that eyewitnesses had reported "fire activity on Floor 8… at the south face" sometime between 12:15 and 2:30PM. The fact that Pitts was apparently unaware of this claim is another reason, beyond those discussed above, to consider it poorly supported.

But even if we accepted the alleged eyewitness testimony, NIST would still not have provided a credible account of a long-lasting fire on the 8th floor.

One problem is that the alleged eyewitness testimony does not support NIST's general narrative about the fires in WTC 7, according to which they began on the south or southwest face of the building at 10:28 and then moved toward the other faces. The fire on the 8th floor, according to these reported eyewitnesses, was still on the south face when it was spotted sometime between 12:15 and 2:30PM, and hence two, three, or even four hours after it had supposedly started.

A second problem is the claim that this fire remained in the same area for such a long period. As will be seen in the next chapter, NIST acknowledged that the combustibles in any given area would be burned up within approximately 20 minutes. If so, how could fire have kept burning on Floor 8's south face for several hours?

A third problem is implicit in a statement by McGrattan, Grosshandler, and Gann that follows their claim about eyewitnesses to an 8th floor fire:

> At 3:15PM, fire was observed on Floors 7 and 12 at the north face, but not Floor 8. At about 3:40PM, fire was observed near the center of the north face of Floor 8 at roughly the same time fires were burning on the west face and in the northeast corner.[50]

So, after having remained on the south face for several hours, the 8th floor fire suddenly appeared "near the center of the north face" at roughly the same time that it appeared "on the west face and in the northeast corner."

Far from suggesting a fire that migrated from the south face to other parts of the 8th floor, the evidence would be more consistent with the hypothesis that fires were somehow started separately in these four locations.

In its computer simulation of the fires on this floor, in fact, NIST itself needed to assume the existence of at least two independently started fires. Its account of this simulation is quite remarkable. In the chapter entitled "Fire Simulations," McGrattan, Grosshandler, and Gann say:

> Fire spread [in general] was predicted by the model as a natural consequence of surrounding objects heating and burning. The exception was that, for the simulation of the 8th floor, a second specified fire was needed to spread the fire to the north face of the building.[51]

NIST admits, in other words, that it could not explain how fire could have migrated from the south face to the north face of the 8th floor. In seeking to overcome this problem by positing a second, separately ignited, fire on this floor, NIST has violated its claim that all of the fires in this building were started by the collapse of the North Tower at 10:28.

This violation is made even clearer in the longer account by McGrattan, Grosshandler, and Gann, which begins:

> In the simulation, a 2 MW[52] fire was prescribed near the middle

of the south face at about 12:30PM, 30 min[utes] after the start of the fire on Floor 7. Although there is no direct photographic evidence for it, in the model, windows were intentionally broken out along the west face, starting from the southwest corner, as a means of directing the simulated fire spread in the observed clockwise direction.[53]

These authors then admit that, even after they had broken windows (in the simulation) to direct the fire from the south face up the west face toward the north face (although photographs provided no warrant for doing this), they could not get the simulated fire to move to the north face:

> The fire did not spread to the north face in preliminary simulations. The cause was a partition (shown in the architectural drawing of the floor) that partially blocked the path from the southwest corner to the northwest corner. Thus a second MW fire was prescribed near the northwest corner at 3:00PM, based on the photographic evidence.[54]

The "photographic evidence" to which these authors refer was not evidence of a second fire, but simply the photograph of a fire on the north face taken at about 3:40PM.

Is this not truly remarkable? NIST claims that WTC 7 was brought down by fires, all of which originated at 10:28 when the North Tower collapsed. NIST's lead investigator, Shyam Sunder, said in his technical briefing in August 2008: "Our observations support a single point of fire ignition on any given floor in World Trade Center 7."[55] Nevertheless, to explain the photographic evidence of fires on the 8th floor, McGrattan, Grosshandler, and Gann simply speculate that a second fire originated in the northwest corner at 3:00PM.

Besides contradicting NIST's general theory, this speculation raises the question of how such a fire could have originated. If there was no floor-to-floor fire migration, as NIST acknowledges, this fire could not have come up from Floor 7 or down from Floor 9. Also, no burning debris was flying through the air at this time. To exclude the possibility that this second fire was intentionally set later in the day, therefore, NIST would have needed to insist that it was caused by an electrical short—a possible cause of fires that is mentioned once in NIST's WTC 7 report, in a chapter by Richard Gann.[56] But the chapter in which the second fire is posited, which Gann co-authored, does *not* mention this possibility. It simply posits a second fire, starting about 3:00PM, without any discussion of how it might have been started.

Moreover, if these NIST authors concluded that a fire must have somehow started on Floor 8 at about 3:00PM, what basis did they have for assuming that a previous fire had been initiated on this floor at 10:28AM? As we saw earlier, NIST itself says that at 12:15PM "people being led from Floors 7 and 8 out of the building reported no fires, heavy dust, or smoke on Floor 8."[57] With this statement, NIST provided evidence *against* its claim that a fire had started on Floor 8 at 10:28. Why, therefore, should the NIST authors not simply have assumed that the 8th floor fire started at 3:00?

There is, in fact, no photographic evidence that a fire was present even that early. The earliest objective evidence of fire anywhere on the 8th floor, to recall, is a photograph of a fire on its north face that was taken at about 3:40PM. If NIST was going to speculate about a fire igniting in the afternoon, perhaps because of an electrical short, it could most reasonably have speculated that it arose shortly before that photograph was taken.

Insofar as NIST had empirical evidence of a fire on Floor 8, therefore, it was for one that endured less than two hours.

Floor 7

The 7th floor was the lowest of the six floors said to have had sustained fires. Aside from the claim of an observation of a fire at 10:30AM—which, as we saw, is too problematic to take seriously—the first evidence of fire on this floor is an image captured "shortly after 2:00." Beyond that, here is what NIST says about Floor 7:

> The fire spread north along the west face. By 3:00PM, the fire had progressed... past the halfway point of the north face. Shortly after this time, the fire on the north face appeared to stop.... [A]bout 4:25PM, a fire flared just east of this and died down within another 15 min[utes]. As late as 4:45PM, fire was observed near the middle of the north face on Floor 7.[58]

To reword the final sentence to bring out its point more clearly: No fire was observed on the 7th floor after 4:45PM. It was, therefore, hardly what most people would call a fire that was "out of control." NIST has provided, in any case, good evidence for fire on Floor 7 only from

2:00 until 4:45PM—a duration of less than three hours. And yet, as we will see in the next chapter, NIST claims that this 7th floor fire heated steel up to very high temperatures.

Summary

Although Shyam Sunder, NIST's lead investigator, claimed at his August 2008 press briefing that "fires burned out of control on six… floors for about seven hours," NIST's report at best provides evidence that fires on these six floors had endured for durations ranging from 40 minutes to a little over three hours. NIST has speculated, of course, that all of the fires started at 10:28, which would mean that the fires on some of the floors would have endured almost seven hours. NIST has provided no credible evidence, however, that any of the fires lasted even half that long.

This fact is implicitly acknowledged by NIST in the chapter on "Fire Simulations," written by Kevin McGrattan, William Grosshandler, and Richard Gann. Whereas the short version of NIST's WTC 7 report claims that "[s]ustained fires occurred on Floors 7, 8, 9, 11, 12, and 13,"[59] the chapter by these three authors in the long version says, more accurately, that "sustained and/or late fires were observed on Floors 7 through 9 and 11 through 13 of WTC 7."[60] This statement reflects a major modification, because the "and/or" allows for the possibility that *none* of the six floors had "sustained" fires—that all of them merely had "late" fires. This is, in fact, all that NIST's evidence shows.

Of course, while the statement by McGrattan, Grosshandler, and Gann has the virtue of honesty, it would not have been nearly as impressive at the press briefing as Sunder's claim that "fires burned out of control on six… floors for about seven hours."

Besides not being reflected in the press briefing, the statement by McGrattan, Grosshandler, and Gann is also ignored in NIST's final chapter, titled "Principal Findings," which was written by Sunder along with Therese McAllister, Richard Gann, and John Gross. This chapter states that WTC 7 "withstood fires… on several floors for almost seven hours."[61] So, although Gann was one of the authors of the chapter containing the modest statement about "sustained and/or late fires," he evidently agreed to sign off on the unsupported claim about fires that endured "almost seven hours."

In any case, the great difference between these two durations is of crucial importance for the claim by NIST to be examined in the following chapter—the claim that the fires in WTC 7 not only became hot enough, but also endured long enough, to heat some of the steel to extremely high temperatures.

9
FIRE AND STEEL TEMPERATURES: IMPLAUSIBLE CLAIMS BASED ON DISTORTED DATA

According to NIST's theory, WTC 7 collapsed because of fires fed by office furniture and other ordinary combustibles. These fires did their damage by heating steel beams up to temperatures high enough to cause some of them to expand and others to weaken. This theory requires that fires on some floors became very hot and remained that way for many hours. The first part of this chapter examines NIST's claims concerning the temperatures and durations of the fires; the second part examines its claims about temperatures reached by some of the building's steel. In both parts, we will see, NIST's theory involves implausible claims based on fudged data.

1. FIRE TEMPERATURES AND DURATIONS

As we saw in the previous chapter, NIST claims that fires on six of the floors endured for seven hours. The existence of long-lasting fires on these floors is essential to NIST's theory because its computer simulations indicated that the crucial damage, which caused WTC 7 to collapse, would have occurred when fires had been burning at high temperatures for about four hours. NIST says:

> [I]t appeared likely the critical damage state occurred between 3.5 h[ours] and 4 h[ours].[1]

> The global analysis with fire-induced damage at 4.0 h[ours] most closely matched the observed collapse events.[2]

This theory is rendered extremely dubious by many problems.

No Evidence of Four-Hour Fires

As we saw in the previous chapter, NIST's claim that fires burned for seven hours on six floors is purely speculative, unsupported by empirical evidence. The actual video and photographic evidence provided by NIST would be consistent with fires enduring on these floors from 40 minutes (Floor 9) to three hours and 20 minutes (Floors 11 and 12). The available empirical evidence, therefore, does not support the four-hour fires required by NIST's simulations.

Overestimated Combustibles on Floors 11 and 12

One of the most extraordinary aspects of NIST's WTC 7 report is its estimation of the amount of combustible materials on the 11th and 12th floors. NIST provides only very flimsy support for its claim that these floors had far more combustible fuel than the floors in the Twin Towers and most of the other floors in WTC 7. And yet the fires on these floors—along with the 13th floor, which will be discussed below—are portrayed by NIST as the primary cause of the collapse of WTC 7. We must, therefore, look closely at its evidence for this claim.

For the 7th, 8th, and 9th floors, NIST used the same estimate of combustible fuel load that it had made for the floors of the Twin Towers: 20 kg/m^2 (4 lb/ft^2). For Floors 11 and 12, however, NIST estimated the combustible fuel load to have been more than 50 percent higher: 32 kg/m^2 (6.4 lb/ft^2).[3] Why? In Chapter 3 of the long version of its Draft for Public Comment, put out in August 2008, NIST wrote:

> The U.S. Securities and Exchange Commission (SEC) had occupied the 11th and 12th floors and the north side of the 13th floor.... American Express occupied the southwest sector of the 13th floor.... The furniture [on the 11th and 12th floors] was mostly modular, generally consisting of decorative laminate over particle board. There were some older solid wood pieces scattered among the managers' offices. The combustible load in the offices was described as high by interviewed American Express managers. There was no clean desk policy. Open case files were left on surfaces. There were many bookcases, file cabinets, and cartons of files in the offices.[4]

The key statement here, to which NIST would repeatedly refer, is that the combustible load was "described as high."

Attorney and chemical engineer James Gourley, writing "on behalf of scientists, scholars, engineers, and building professionals" (including scientists Niels Harrit, Steven Jones, and Kevin Ryan, and architect Richard Gage), sent NIST an incisive critique of its Draft Report. Commenting on the passage just quoted, Gourley said:

> Recall that American Express occupied only the southwest sector of the 13th floor. How, then can NIST credibly claim that the combustible load on the entirety of the 11th and 12th floors, both occupied solely by the SEC, was reported to have been high?[5]

Gourley was wrong about one thing here: Besides occupying part of the 13th floor, American Express also occupied Floors 7 and 8. This fact does not, however, affect his point, which was that American Express representatives could not be assumed to be authorities about Floors 11 and 12.

In NIST's Final Report, issued in November 2008, the sentence in question has been changed to read: "The combustible load in the offices [on Floors 11 and 12] was described as high by interviewed SEC managers."[6] Was NIST here, by changing "American Express managers" to "SEC managers," simply correcting a careless error that Richard Gann, the author of Chapter 3, had made in the Draft Report? Probably so, because citing the American Express managers would have made no sense, as Gourley's letter pointed out, and the Draft Report did have a footnote referring to 2005 and 2006 interviews with SEC staff.

With this alteration, in any case, NIST's claim for a much higher fuel load on Floors 11 and 12 is not so obviously baseless. But it is still very weak, for several reasons.

One problem involves NIST's point, made in the statement quoted above, that there was "no clean desk policy" on Floors 11 and 12. In making this point, NIST seems to imply that desks on these floors were probably covered with more combustibles than those on Floors 7 and 8. But NIST had earlier noted that American Express, which occupied Floors 7 and 8 (the combustible loads of which NIST did *not* rate as "high"), also "did not require their employees to clear their desktops at the end of a workday."[7]

Even more serious problems with NIST's claim about Floors 11 and 12, according to which they had far more combustibles than Floors 7 and 8, can be seen by examining its comparison of the layouts of these floors, which is provided in NIST's chapter entitled "Fire Simulations" (written by Gann along with Kevin McGrattan and William

Grosshandler):

> [T]he 7th and 8th floors of WTC 7... were mostly populated by cubicles.... [T]he 11th and 12th floors of WTC 7 were mainly partitioned into offices. The combustible loading of office furnishings was estimated as follows. There were approximately 150 cubicles on the 8th floor and about 120 offices on the 12th floor. NIST assumed that the combustible mass of the furniture was about the same in an office as in a cubicle. Since the loading of other combustibles was reported to have been high on the 11th and 12th floors (Chapter 3), NIST assumed that the total combustible mass in an office was about double that of a cubicle. Thus, the average combustible fuel load on the 11th and 12th floors was estimated as 32 kg/m^2 (6.4 lb/ft^2).[8]

One problem with NIST's argument here is that, if each cubicle had about as much furniture as each office, as NIST says, Floor 8, with its 150 cubicles, would have had considerably more furniture than Floor 12, with its merely 120 offices. Accordingly, if NIST had needed, for some reason, to argue that the 8th floor had more combustibles than did Floors 11 and 12, it could have used the cubicles-versus-offices contrast to make *that* case.

But NIST, which needed the opposite conclusion, interpreted its own statement in Chapter 3—"The combustible load in the [11th and 12th floor] offices was described as high by interviewed SEC managers"—to mean that the quantity of "other combustibles" on those floors was so great that it not only compensated for the furniture deficit but also made the "total combustible mass" on each of these floors *over 50 percent higher* than that on Floors 7 and 8. That is a lot to read into the statement reportedly made by some SEC managers.

There is, moreover, no way to verify whether these managers really made this statement to NIST. And if they did, we have no way to check NIST's interpretation of it. If these managers said that the combustible load on these two floors was "high," were they indicating that it was higher than that of the other floors in WTC 7 and the floors in the Twin Towers? And if so, did they mean that it was over 50 percent higher? We have no way to find out, as we are not told their names. Unlike some of NIST's reported interviews, moreover, these alleged interviews are not even given reference numbers. The footnote simply says: "NIST Interviews with U.S. Securities and Exchange Commission staff, December 2005 through March 2006."[9]

And yet NIST's entire theory about the collapse of WTC 7 is dependent on its highly dubious interpretation of this vague, anonymous, and unverifiable statement.

The claims about Floor 12 are especially important, because NIST uses its computer simulation of fire on this floor as the basis for its description of the fires on the 11th and 13th floors. This fact is reflected in the following statement by NIST about its fire simulations, in which it points out the connection between high fuel loads and intense fires:

> In the computations, the fire on the 12th floor, and thus the derivative fires on the 11th and 13th floors, generated significantly more heat than the fire on the 7th or 8th floor. This was in large part due to the higher fuel load in the simulations.[10]

The fact that NIST's simulated fires on Floors 11 and 13 were derivative from its simulated 12th floor fire—meaning that, rather than working up independent simulations of the fires on those floors, NIST simply assumed that they would have progressed in roughly the same way as the fire on the 12th floor—is of great importance, because NIST claims, as we will see, that the fires on these three floors were primarily responsible for bringing down WTC 7.

In other words, if NIST were not positing extra-high loading of combustible material on Floor 12 and hence Floors 11 and 13, its theory that fires brought down WTC 7 would not have even *prima facie* plausibility. But the basis for NIST's argument for this high loading is, we have seen, far too weak to support NIST's extraordinary claim—that for the first time in history, a steel-framed high-rise building was brought down by fire.

Extraordinary claims, it is often pointed out, require extraordinary evidence. But NIST's evidence for the claim in question—that Floor 12 and hence Floor 11 (and also Floor 13) had 50 percent more combustible fuel than the other floors in the World Trade Center buildings—is extraordinary only in the sense of being extraordinarily flimsy.

It even appears, moreover, to be demonstrably false. NIST's report contains schematic diagrams of Floors 8 and 11. If NIST is correct in saying that the 11th and 12th floors were the same, the schematic of Floor 11 shows that each of these floors had 120 offices. But the schematic diagram for Floor 8 shows that, instead of having only 150 cubicles, as NIST states, it had 249.[11] We saw earlier that, even with only 150 cubicles, the 7th and 8th floors would have had more combustibles per square foot than did the 11th and 12th floors. With 249 cubicles each, Floors 7 and 8 would have had *far* more combustibles than Floors 11 and 12. They may, in fact, have had about 50 percent more combustibles than Floors 11 and 12—just the opposite of what NIST claims.

Exaggerated Combustibles on Floor 13

If NIST's treatment of the quantity of combustibles on the 11th and 12th floors is remarkable for its weakness, its treatment of this issue with regard to Floor 13 is even more so. Here is NIST's main statement: "The density of combustibles on the 13th floor was varied and not well known. The average value was assumed to be the same as the 12th floor."[12]

NIST says, in other words: *Because we had little information about the density of combustible material on the 13th floor, we concluded that we could best estimate this density by assuming that it was the same as that which we postulated for the 12th floor.*

NIST uses this assumption to claim that the fires on Floor 13, like those on Floors 11 and 12, were very hot and long-lasting. There are two problems with this claim.

First, as mentioned above, both American Express and the SEC had offices on the 13th floor. And yet evidently no one from these organizations reported that this floor had a high quantity of combustible material. If there had been, surely the SEC managers with offices on this floor would have mentioned it when making their comment about Floors 11 and 12.

A second problem involves NIST's claim that the "density of combustibles on the 13th floor was… not well known." This claim of ignorance is made in Chapter 9, which was written by McGrattan, Grosshandler, and Gann. But Chapter 3, which was written by Gann, indicates that NIST, in fact, knew quite a lot about Floor 13. We there read:

> Along the central section of the north perimeter was a corridor, with
> a hearing room and multiple testimony rooms facing it. There were

additional testimony rooms on the northern portion of the east side of the floor and a storage room at the northwest corner. The testimony rooms were sparsely furnished, with just a table and a few chairs.[13]

NIST knew, therefore, that at least part of the 13th floor was "sparsely furnished"—which would surely mean that, far from having more than the average amount of combustible material, this portion of the floor would have had less.

Just below Gann's statement, moreover, NIST's report has a revealing schematic of Floor 13, showing the location of the corridor, the hearing room, and the testimony rooms. In his letter on behalf of a group of critics of the WTC 7 report, attorney James Gourley wrote:

> [A]n examination of the schematic diagram... reveals that the hearing room appears similar to a court room. Court rooms [like testimony rooms] are also sparsely furnished, with a few tables and chairs.[14]

This schematic also reveals that almost half the floor space of Floor 13 was taken up by the corridor, the hearing room, and the testimony rooms, along with the elevators and restrooms that filled the center of the floor. About half of the floor, therefore, would have had very few combustible items.

Accordingly, NIST's decision to estimate a combustible loading of 32 kg/m² (6.4 lb/ft²) in its computer simulation of 13th floor fires was completely unrealistic. As Gourley wrote: "NIST has apparently greatly overestimated the fuel loading on the 13th floor."[15] Indeed, this floor, far from having more combustible material than most of the other floors, would surely have had less.

NIST's Admitted Gap between Simulations and Evidence

The amount of combustible material on a floor would have been a crucial factor in determining both the temperature and the duration of any fires on that floor. Accordingly, the reasons to believe that NIST overestimated the amount of combustibles on Floors 11, 12, and 13 undermine the credibility of its claim that the fires on these floors were hot enough and long-lasting enough to have greatly raised the temperature of their steel supports.

NIST even admits that the duration of its simulated fires on these three floors exceeded the duration of the actual fires as indicated by the visual evidence. With regard to the 12th floor, NIST says: "The burning time near the north face was longer in the simulation than in the visual evidence."[16] With regard to the 11th floor—which NIST portrays simply by using its simulation for the 12th floor fires delayed by an hour—it admits: "This resulted in a... burn duration that was longer than observed in the photographs." With regard to Floor 13, NIST states: "The Floor 13 fires were represented by the Floor 12 fires delayed by one-half hour. The... burn duration was longer than in the visual evidence."[17]

NIST, however, does not attribute these discrepancies between its simulations and the visual evidence to the fact that it had exaggerated the amount of combustible material on these floors. It does acknowledge the possibility that this might be true—that the discrepancy might be due to the fact that "the input fuel load was too high." But it rejects this possibility as unlikely, citing an alternative simulation of the 12th floor fires: "Decreasing the combustible load... from 32 kg/m^2 to 20 kg/m^2," NIST claims, "showed little effect on the rate of fire progression."[18]

This claim, however, is hard to believe, especially in light of another simulation, in which the combustible load on the 8th floor was doubled from 20 kg/m^2 to 40 kg/m^2. As to the effect of this doubling, NIST says: "This caused the fires to burn in place longer, until the fuel was consumed, before advancing. As a result, the fires moved distinctly more slowly than in the visual evidence."[19]

Both of these results cannot be correct, at least if NIST's computer simulation has any relation to the real world. If *increasing* the amount of available fuel slows down a fire's movement, so that it will burn longer in a given area, then *decreasing* the amount of fuel will speed up the fire's movement, so that its burn duration in a given area will be shorter. NIST itself implies this by saying, with regard to the simulated fires on Floor 12: "[S]pread rate was about one-third to one-half slower than that on lower floors due to the higher fuel load."[20]

NIST cannot have it both ways: It cannot say that, although raising the fuel load slows down the spread rate, lowering the fuel load would not speed it up.[21]

It would seem, therefore, that NIST's simulations were based on overestimations of the combustibles available as fuel on Floors 11, 12, and 13, and that this is why the duration of the simulated fires exceeds that of the actual fires, as indicated by the visual evidence.

The 5:00 Fire and the 4:45 Photograph

Do the discrepancies between NIST's simulations and the visual evidence indicate a difference between the simulations and *reality*? NIST would deny this. But clear proofs of such differences have been provided by NIST itself.

NIST's simulated fires on Floor 12 are illustrated in Figure 9-11 of its report by graphics that display "hourly snapshots of the upper layer temperatures predicted by the model for the 12th floor." The graphic for 5:00PM shows fires that were very big and very hot—between 500°C and 1,000°C (932°F and 1,832°F)—covering about half of the floor's north side.[22] Such fires would have been highly visible from outside.

These fires would have been visible, that is, if they had existed. A photograph of the north face that had been taken fifteen minutes earlier shows that they did not. This photograph was even described, surely to NIST's present embarrassment, in its *Interim Report on WTC 7*, published in 2004. This report said: "Around 4:45PM, a photograph showed fires on Floors 7, 8, 9, and 11 near the middle of the north face; Floor 12 was burned out by this time."[23]

We have an outright contradiction. On the one hand, NIST's computer simulation, based on its claim that Floor 12's combustible loading was "high," portrayed this floor as the scene of a raging inferno at 5:00PM. On the other hand, photographic evidence shows that, in the real world, this floor's fires had completely burned out at least fifteen minutes earlier—perhaps because all of its combustibles had already combusted.

This contradiction, which existed in NIST's Draft for Public Comment, was pointed out to NIST by Richard Gage (of Architects and Engineers for 9/11 Truth)[24] and also James Gourley, who said: "It appears that NIST's computer fire simulations are not representative at all of the fires actually occurring in WTC 7."[25]

How did NIST respond to having this stark contradiction brought to its attention? It issued its Final Report without making a single change.

Moreover, as Gage's letter pointed out, the contradiction between NIST's simulated Floor 12 fire and the visual evidence of the actual fire was even worse than the contradiction revealed by the 4:45 photograph. NIST's graphic of its simulated 12th floor fire at 4:00PM shows the northeast corner of this floor completely filled with a very hot fire.[26] But photographs in NIST's report tell a different story. A photograph taken "around 2:57PM" shows that the 12th floor fire had already moved across the north face about one-fourth of the way to the northwest corner, leaving the northeast corner dark.[27] A photograph taken "around 3:12:50PM" shows that the fire had continued moving west, being at this time almost to the center of the north face, and the northeast corner was still dark.[28] A photograph taken at "around 3:54" shows that the only fire remaining on Floor 12 was in the northwest corner.[29]

Accordingly, *whereas the graphics of NIST's simulated fire show a raging, very hot fire in the northeast corner of the 12th floor at 4:00PM,* photographs supplied by NIST show that *the actual fire had already left that corner by 3:00PM, never to return.* This is no trivial matter, because one of the central elements in NIST's theory of the collapse of WTC 7 is its claim that, in Sunder's words, "Column 79, which is in the northeast corner, is subjected to the heat from this fire on this particular floor for a pretty long time."[30] NIST's theory clearly hinges, therefore, on *a fire that did not exist.*

Moreover, whereas NIST's 2004 report had pointed out that "Floor 12 was burned out by [4:45PM]," these photographs show that the truth was even worse: the entire floor except for the northwest corner was burned out by 4:00. And yet NIST's 5:00PM graphic shows big, hot fires still going strong.

The stark contradictions between NIST's simulated fire and the available photographs show how we should read statements in which NIST admits that its simulations may involve "mild overestimates." For example, after pointing out that the 11th floor fire's "burn duration was longer [in the simulation] than in the visual evidence," NIST says that this difference "could have led to a mild overestimate of the heating on the north side of the floor." Further down the same page, NIST says the same thing, word for word, about the discrepancy between the simulated fire on the 13th floor and the visual evidence.[31] What does NIST mean by a "mild overestimate"?

We can infer the answer by looking at NIST's statement about the discrepancy regarding the fires on the 12th floor: "The simulations of the 12th floor fires (and thus the derivative 11th and 13th floor fires) may have mildly overestimated the duration of the fires."[32] Accordingly, by portraying 1,000°C (1,832°F) fires at locations at which the fires had actually burned out an hour or two earlier, NIST had, in its own eyes, only "mildly overestimated" the actual durations. We can, therefore, reasonably infer that NIST's derivative models of the 11th and 13th floor fires, each said to have possibly involved a "mild overestimate," had a comparable correspondence to reality—meaning virtually none whatsoever.

Why would there have been such a lack of correspondence between NIST's computer simulations and the visual evidence provided by photographs and videos? NIST provides an answer to this question in the following amazing statement:

> The observed fire activity gleaned from the photographs and videos was not a model input, and thus one should not expect a perfect correspondence between predicted high temperatures and observed fire activity.[33]

By saying that the visual evidence was "not a model input," NIST means that it was not used in constructing NIST's computer-based model of the fire used in its computer simulation.

As we saw in Chapter 2, the form of scientific fraud known as fabrication, in which scientists simply make up their data, is not uncommon. It is unusual, however, for scientists to admit that this is what they have done.

In any case, NIST uses the fact that it simply ignored the visual evidence while constructing its computer models of the fire to explain the lack of "perfect correspondence" between that visual evidence and NIST's models of the fires. As the discrepancy regarding the state of the fire on 12th floor at 5:00PM shows, NIST's admission that there may not be a "perfect correspondence" means that there may be no more correspondence than there is between a raging inferno and a totally burned-out fire.

"Mild Overestimates" of Fires on Floors 11 and 13

As we saw above, NIST states: "The simulations of the 12th floor fires (and thus the derivative 11th and 13th floor fires) may have mildly overestimated the duration of the fires."[34] In referring to the 11th and 13th floor fires as "derivative," to recall, NIST means that, rather than carrying out time-consuming simulations of these fires, its scientists simply modeled them on their simulated 12th floor fires.

In a comment about the significance of this procedure, which had been explained in NIST's Draft for Public Comment, James Gourley wrote: "By using its grossly overestimated 12th floor fire data on both the 11th and 13th floors, it has magnified this error three-fold."[35] The following examination of NIST's portrayal of these other two floors will bear out the correctness of Gourley's criticism of this procedure (which remained unchanged in NIST's Final Report).

NIST's Treatment of Floor 11 Fires: Here is NIST's account of why and how it developed its representation of the 11th floor fires:

> The fire behavior on Floor 11 followed the pattern on Floor 12. The fires on the two floors occurred at similar times on the east face, prior to 2:30PM. The appearance times of the fires on the north face of the 11th floor were about 1 1/2 h[ours] later than those on the 12th floor. Since the floor layouts had the same arrays of partitioned offices, and since it was unknown which office doors were open or closed, the Investigation Team decided that additional simulations of Floor 11 would not have provided any more meaningful results than time-offsetting the temperatures predicted for Floor 12. The Floor 11 fires were represented by the Floor 12 fires delayed by 1 h[our].[36]

If the 12th floor simulation could be trusted, NIST's decision to assume that the 11th floor fire followed the same path might have been reasonable. But then it added an arbitrary twist: Although the 11th floor fire reached the north face an hour and a half later than the 12th floor fire, NIST's model treated it as if it had arrived there only an hour later. Why would NIST have done this?[37]

We can infer the likely answer by looking at NIST's Figure 9-11,[38] which presents graphics showing the progression of the simulated 12th floor fire every hour, on the hour. The graphic for 3:00PM shows the heart of the 12th floor fire still down in the southeast corner. The 4:00 graphic, by contrast, shows big fires along most of the north face. If the 11th floor fire had been portrayed as following the same path 1.5 hours later, by 5:00PM it would have been where the 12th floor fire had been by 3:30, and hence still on the east face. It could not, therefore, have done the damage required by NIST's theory before 5:21, when WTC 7 collapsed.

But by plotting the 11th floor fire as following the path of the 12th floor fire only an hour later, NIST could represent it as burning wildly out of control at 5:00 on the north face (as was the fire on the 12th floor at 4:00 in NIST's simulation). Only by being there at that time could the 11th floor fire do the damage required by NIST's theory. Once again, NIST has simply manipulated the data to produce the result it needed.

NIST's Treatment of 13th Floor Fires: NIST provides the following explanation of its representation of fires on Floor 13:

> The fire on this floor generally followed the pattern of the fire that was observed for the 12th floor. The timing of the fire on the east side was roughly one-half hour behind that of the fire on the 12th floor.... Since the floor layout and fuel load on the east side of the 13th floor were highly uncertain, the Investigation Team decided that additional simulations of Floor 13 would not have provided any more meaningful results than time-offsetting the temperatures predicted for Floor 12.[39]

As we saw earlier, NIST used the claim that the 13th floor combustible content was "not well known" to justify its assumption that it was the same as that of the 12th floor. Here, NIST makes that same claim to ignorance about the 13th floor to justify the assumption that the temperatures on this floor were the same as those calculated for the 12th floor.

As we also saw earlier, however, NIST had more information about the "floor layout and fuel load" of Floor 13 than its claim to ignorance suggests. But if NIST had based its model of the 13th floor fire on this information, it could not have portrayed this fire as it did.

Part of the information NIST possessed, as we saw earlier, is contained in the "Schematic of Floor 13" provided in Chapter 3 of its report.[40] This schematic shows that much of the north part of this floor consisted of a corridor, which ran along the north face, and hearing and testimony rooms, which would have been sparsely furnished. There would not have been enough combustibles to fuel a big, hot, long-lasting fire.

Instead of basing its representation of the 13th floor fire on this information, however, NIST based it on the assumption that this fire had followed the path of its simulated 12th floor fire, except for coming along a half-hour later. We can see the result by looking at NIST's graphics of the simulated 12th floor fire.[41] These graphics show a very big, very hot fire—900°C to 1,000°C [1,650°F to 1,832°F]—covering much of the northern third of Floor 12 at 4:00 and 5:00PM. If the 13th floor fires followed the same path a half-hour later, these big, hot fires would have been covering the same part of this floor from 4:30 until 5:21PM (when WTC 7 collapsed).

However, if we take reality into account by looking at NIST's "Schematic of Floor 13," we can see that the area in which NIST portrays these big, hot, long-lasting fires is precisely the area that was occupied by the corridor and the (sparsely furnished) hearing and testimony rooms. Far from having a combustible fuel loading of 32 kg/m² (6.4 lb/ft²), as NIST proposes, this part of the 13th floor probably had an even lower density of combustibles than that which NIST assigned to most floors, namely, 20 kg/m² (4 lb/ft²). This area, accordingly, would not have had nearly enough combustibles to feed the fires depicted there by NIST.

NIST alludes to this problem by admitting, with regard to its model of the 13th floor fire, that its "burn duration was longer than in the visual evidence."[42] Note that the word "longer" was not qualified with an adverb, such as "mildly" or even "moderately." NIST's statement allows, therefore, for the possibility that the simulated fires might have burned, say, two hours longer than the actual fires.

The evidence, in fact, suggests this conclusion. NIST's theory requires, as we have seen, that the fires on Floors 11, 12, and 13 burned for at least four hours. In the previous chapter, however, we saw that NIST's first visual evidence of fire on the 13th floor is an image captured at 2:30PM. If this fire did indeed move to the north face, as NIST supposes, it would likely not have found enough fuel to sustain it past 4:30PM (which would mean that the fire burned on this floor for at most two hours).

Photographic support for this conclusion is found, interestingly, in NIST's 2004 *Interim Report on WTC 7*. This report displayed a photograph of WTC 7's north face showing fires on the 7th and 12th floors but none on the 13th floor. A note beneath the photograph said: "Around 4:45PM, a photograph showed fires [on] Floors 7, 8, 9, and 11 near the middle of the north face; Floor 12 was burned out by this time."[43] We previously focused on the statement about Floor 12.

But the remainder of the statement is also of interest, because in spelling out the floors on which there were fires on the north face at 4:45, it does *not* mention Floor 13.[44]

According to NIST in 2004, accordingly, *there were no fires on the north face of the 13th floor at 4:45PM.*[45] In its 2008 report, nevertheless, NIST claims that big fires were burning at that location from 4:30 until 5:21PM, when the building collapsed.

Summary of NIST's Treatment of Floors 11 and 13: Given the fact that NIST's computer models of the fires on Floors 11 and 13, like its simulation of the 12th floor fire, completely fails to correspond to the visual evidence, we can fully appreciate the implications of NIST's acknowledgment that such information "was not a model input."

It appears, in sum, that NIST wildly—not merely mildly—overestimated the temperatures and the durations of the fires on Floors 11, 12, and 13. Given the crucial role these fires play in NIST's theory of WTC 7's collapse (which will be explained below), these overestimates alone would render the theory unworthy of credence. There are, however, still further problems.

Could the Fires Have Generated Air Temperatures of 1,000 to 1,100°C?

Another problem with NIST's simulated fires in WTC 7 is that they greatly exceed the temperatures that would have been reached by the actual fires. The air temperatures in some locations of WTC 7, according to graphics in NIST's final report, reached 900°C (1,650°F) to 1,000°C (1,832°F),[46] or even higher.[47] The report also says that "simulated fires on Floors 7, 12, and 13 heated portions of the tops of the floor slabs to over 900°C (1,650°F),"[48] and the fires could have done this in a few hours only if they had been considerably hotter than 900°C (see the Dr. Babravskas quote on page 201). NIST's theory, therefore, clearly requires fires that were 1,000°C (1,832°F) or even higher.

But the idea that there were fires of this temperature is completely implausible. Professor Thomas Eagar of MIT, who supported an early (pre-NIST) version of the official theory about the collapses of the Twin Towers—and who therefore cannot be suspected of distorting the facts in order to support critics of the government's theory—provided a helpful account of the maximum temperatures to be expected in the Twin Towers. Eagar wrote:

> In combustion science, there are three basic types of flames, namely, a jet burner, a pre-mixed flame, and a diffuse flame…. A fireplace is a diffuse flame burning in air, as was the WTC fire. Diffuse flames generate the lowest heat intensities of the three flame types…. The maximum flame temperature increase for burning hydrocarbons (jet fuel) in air is, thus, about 1,000°C [about 1,832°F]… . But it is very difficult to reach [even] this maximum temperature with a diffuse flame. There is nothing to ensure that the fuel and air in a diffuse flame are mixed in the best ratio.[49]

Pointing out that the black smoke being emitted from the Twin Towers indicated that their fires had a less than optimal ratio of fuel to oxidant, being instead starved for oxygen, Eagar estimated that these fires were "probably only about 1,200 or 1,300°F [648 or 704°C]."[50]

Eagar's account would apply all the more to the fires in WTC 7. They also emitted black smoke and, not having been spread by jet fuel, were much smaller. They were, therefore, probably not as hot as those in the Twin Towers. We can say for certain, in any case, that they were no hotter—which means that they would have been at least 300°C (570°F) cooler than the 1,000°C (1,832°F) fires of NIST's simulations. Moreover, NIST even implies in places that the fires may have reached 1,100°C (2,012°F), hence exaggerating their temperature by at least 400°C (750°F).[51]

NIST's collapse theory, therefore, is based on the idea that the fires in WTC 7 were 300 to 400°C (570 to 750°F) hotter than they surely were.

The Adoption of Case B Variables

One method NIST used to obtain such high fire temperatures in its computer models was simply to adopt higher temperatures than those suggested by its own simulations. NIST did so, as I will explain, by falsely supposing that a margin of error can justify an arbitrary adjustment of the results either upward or downward.

NIST's simulations were carried out with the use of the Fire Dynamics Simulator (FDS).[52] However, rather than simply use the results generated by this process, NIST developed two alternative scenarios. Here is NIST's description of its three scenarios, labeled Case A, Case B, and Case C:

> The temperature data for use in the structural analysis of WTC 7 contained thermal data sampled at 30 min[ute] intervals for a 6 hour period. For each time step, a set of thermal data was generated that specified the thermal state of the lower 16 stories of the building. Three different thermal response computations were used, all of which represented a realistic and reasonable range of fire scenarios for WTC 7 on September 11, 2001. Case A used the temperature data as obtained from the FDS simulation. Case B increased the FDS gas temperature by 10 percent and Case C decreased the FDS gas temperatures by 10 percent.

The fact that NIST chose to use the FDS implies that NIST regarded it to be a reliable means for calculating the probable temperatures. It should have assumed, therefore, that the Case A data were the most accurate. NIST claims, however, that it could have reasonably chosen to use any of the three sets of temperature data, writing:

> Given the limited visual evidence, the Investigation Team estimated, using engineering judgment, that a 10 percent change was within the range of uncertainty in the extent and intensity of the fires.[53]

NIST's argument, in other words, is that the FDS calculations might have been 10 percent too high or 10 percent too low, so either Case B or Case C might have been the most accurate. NIST could thereby justifiably use either the Case B or Case C data.

But even if we assume the correctness of NIST's "engineering judgment," it would not justify a choice to use the Case B or Case C, instead of the Case A, data. Even if the Case A data were indeed off by 10 percent, NIST would have had no way of knowing whether they were 10 percent too high or 10 percent too low. If they happened to be 10 percent too high, so that the Case C data were in fact the most accurate, NIST's choice of the Case B data would mean that its figures would be 20 percent too high. Nevertheless, NIST chose to use the Case B data.

A second justification for doing so is proffered by NIST in the following paragraph, which refers to engineering simulation software called ANSYS.[54]

The three thermal response cases (A, B, and C) were used in the ANSYS analysis. Based on ANSYS model results, it became apparent as the analyses progressed that the sequential failures that were occurring were essentially at the same locations and with similar failure mechanisms. However, as might be expected, the failures were shifted in time, i.e., Case C failures occurred at a later time than the same failures in Case A, and Case A failures occurred at a later time than Case B failures. As a result, only the fire-induced damage produced by Case B temperatures was carried forward as the initial condition for the LS-DYNA analysis…, since the damage occurred in the least computational time (about 6 months).[55]

As this statement shows, NIST's second justification for using the Case B temperatures, incredibly, was so that its computer calculations could be carried out more quickly. This was more important, NIST suggested, than using the most accurate data.

NIST would, to be sure, dispute this conclusion, saying that its choice of the Case B data was justified by its "engineering judgment" that the Case A temperatures might have been 10 percent too high or too low. As we have already seen, however, that judgment, even if correct, would not justify choosing the Case B data, because they might well have been 20 percent too high. The only scientifically justifiable approach would have been to stick with the Case A data while warning readers that they might be as much as 10 percent too high or low.

Given the obvious problems with NIST's stated reasons for choosing the Case B data, we can only conclude that its real reason was that these data, with their higher temperatures, would allow NIST's simulated fires to heat up the simulated steel to the temperatures at which it would fail faster than would the Case A temperatures. In NIST's words: "Case B resulted in mildly higher temperatures in the steel," and "Case B failures occurred at the earliest time."[56]

Even with the Case B temperatures, as we will see in the second part of this chapter, the fires would not have been sufficiently hot and long-lasting to heat the steel beams to the temperatures NIST claimed they reached. If NIST had (correctly) employed the Case A temperatures, this problem would have been even more obvious.

To summarize the first part of this chapter: There are very strong reasons to maintain that the fires in WTC 7 neither became nearly as hot, nor endured nearly as long, as the simulated fires on which NIST bases its collapse theory.

2. STEEL TEMPERATURES

The variables in NIST's computer models of the WTC 7 fires appear, we have seen, to have been derived less from the physical facts than from the requirements of its theory as to how this building collapsed. This theory requires fires that would have heated some of the building's steel to temperatures that arguably could have brought about unprecedented structural damage. I turn now to NIST's claims about the temperatures reached by some of WTC 7's steel.

Temperatures Allegedly Reached by Steel Beams

When NIST developed its explanation of why the Twin Towers collapsed, it argued that the (vertical) columns buckled because fires had raised the temperature of their steel to a point at which they had lost most of their strength. In its explanation of the collapse of WTC 7, NIST does not make any such claim about columns. It instead says that, at the temperatures to which the columns in this building were heated, "structural steel experiences relatively little loss of strength or stiffness. Thus, WTC 7 did not collapse due to fire-induced weakening of critical columns."[57]

Fire instead brought down this building, NIST claims, by heating some (horizontal) steel beams and also some floor slabs and connections:

> Being lighter than the columns and with thinner SFRM [spray-applied fire-resistive material], the floor beams, floor slabs, and connections heated more quickly and to higher temperatures than the columns. The elevated temperatures in the floor elements led to their thermal expansion, sagging, and weakening, which resulted in failure of floor connections and/or buckling of floor beams.[58]

The fires, therefore, caused two kinds of damage, referred to in this passage as "thermal expansion," on the one hand, and "sagging" and "weakening," on the other.

Some of NIST's rhetoric misleadingly suggests that it considers thermal expansion to have been *the* cause of the collapse. Shyam Sunder, for example, made this suggestion in his assertion, quoted above in Chapter 7, that NIST had "identified thermal expansion as a new phenomenon that can cause structural collapse."[59]

NIST's report, however, repeatedly refers to thermal expansion, on the one hand, and thermal weakening and sagging, on the other, as two distinguishable phenomena that led to the collapse. Here are some statements in which they are distinguished:

> Elevated temperatures in the floor elements led to thermal expansion, with or without thermal weakening and sagging.[60]

> [T]hermal weakening occurs at temperatures greater than about 500°C [931°F].... The thermal expansion of the WTC 7 floor beams that initiated the probable collapse sequence occurred primarily at temperatures below approximately 400°C (750°F).[61]

> "Better thermal insulation... [would] minimize both thermal expansion and weakening effects."[62]

Thermal expansion is said to have done its damage at relatively low temperatures. When heated, some of the steel beams become sufficiently elongated, NIST argues, to have exerted forces that helped cause a critical column (Column 79) to fail.

The expanded beams could have exerted such force only if they stayed cool enough to remain rigid. "[S]tructural steel," Thomas Eagar has pointed out, "begins to soften around 425°C [797°F]."[63] NIST claims, accordingly, that this particular kind of damage was caused at temperatures low enough for the steel beams to remain rigid: "The thermal expansion of the WTC 7 floor beams that initiated the probable collapse sequence occurred primarily at temperatures below approximately 400°C (750°F)."[64]

NIST could, therefore, make the case for thermal expansion, which it says "initiated the probable collapse sequences," without claiming that any steel reached extremely high temperatures.

But the damage done by thermal expansion was only *one* of the initiating causes of WTC 7's collapse, according to NIST's theory. Another initiating cause was the fact that several floors collapsed because the steel beams supporting them had been severely weakened by fire. NIST sometimes, in fact, seems to give this explanation pride of place. In his technical briefing, for example, Shyam Sunder said: "[T]hermally induced breakdown of the floor system was the determining step in causing collapse initiation."[65]

In any case, these beams had become severely weakened, NIST claims, because they were heated to temperatures of 600°C (1,100°F), even 675°C (1,250°F).

> The temperatures of some sections of the beams supporting Floors 8, 12, 13, and 14 exceeded 600°C (1,100°F).[66]

> [M]any of the floor beams in the southeast half of [Floor 13] reached temperatures around 600°C and remained that hot for over an hour.[67]

> During the course of the simulation, the 8th floor beams heated up significantly due to the fire on the 7th floor.... The temperatures in the northeast corner floor beams were above 675°C [1,250°F] near 5:00pm.[68]

> All floor beams began to buckle [at 675°C].[69]

As made clear in the third of these four quotations, these estimated steel temperatures were based on NIST's computer simulations.

These temperatures were *not* based, it should be emphasized, on an examination of any recovered pieces of steel from WTC 7. NIST claims, as we saw in Chapter 4, that no steel from this building had been recovered. This claim is not true, as we also saw, because the three professors from Worcester Polytechnic Institute and also Professor Astaneh-Asl reported on pieces of steel recovered from WTC 7. NIST, however, had to ignore these pieces of steel, because they had been subjected to temperatures far too high to have been caused by fire. In NIST's calculations of steel temperatures, therefore, information derived from physical reality, in the form of recovered steel, was not a "model input."

It is conceivable, of course, that NIST's estimated steel temperatures, even if not based on any physical evidence, might be plausible. There are strong reasons, however, to conclude that they are not.

Exaggerated Fire Temperatures and Durations

The most obvious problem with NIST's estimated steel temperatures, given the facts discussed in the first section of this chapter, is simply that the fire temperatures and durations used in NIST's simulations appear to have been grossly exaggerated. NIST's simulated fires seem to be 300 to 400°C (570 to 750°F) too hot and to have endured two or more hours too long. As Frank Greening has concluded:

In view of the fact that NIST appears to have overestimated the intensity and duration of the fires in WTC 7,... it follows that the heating of the structural steel is also overestimated.[70]

This problem by itself undermines any credibility that NIST's theory might seem to have. But there are several more problems.

Insufficient Fuel to Heat Beams to 600°C

One reason that the fires in WTC 7 could not have been as hot and long-lasting as NIST suggests, as we have seen, is that they lacked sufficient fuel. Both Greening and Kevin Ryan have concluded from this fact that the steel beams could not have reached 600°C (let alone the 675°C [1,250°F] that NIST claims was reached by beams in at least one location in the building).

Ryan, having noted NIST's claim that the collapse of WTC 7 was initiated by the temperature of five floor beams that had reached 600°C (1,100°F), wrote:

> [R]aising those five floor beams to a temperature of 600°C would require an enormous amount of energy, far more than was available from the burning of the office furnishings underneath the floor beams.[71]

Greening likewise rejected the view that fire could have heated floor beams to 600°C (1,100°F), even expressing doubt that it could have heated them much above 300°C (570°F).

> NIST's collapse initiation hypothesis requires that structural steel temperatures on floors 12/13 significantly exceeded 300°C [570°F]—a condition that could never have been realized with NIST's postulated 32 kg/m₂ fuel loading.[72]

Greening believes, therefore, that NIST's theory requires steel beams to have become twice as hot as they could have been, given the quantity of available combustibles estimated by NIST.

Steel's Thermal Conductivity Ignored

In stating that the fires in WTC 7 could not have increased the temperature of any steel beams to 600°C (1,100°F), Ryan and Greening were taking into consideration the fact that steel is a good conductor of heat (compared with non-metallic substances).[73]

To explain: If a flame is applied to one portion of a long steel beam, that portion will not be quickly heated up to the temperature of the flame, or even close to it, because the heat will be diffused throughout the beam. If this beam is connected to other pieces of steel, the heat will also spread to them (more or less quickly, depending on the nature of the connections). And if these pieces of steel are, in turn, interconnected with hundreds of others, the heat from the flame will be diffused throughout the entire structure.

In doubting that any of the steel beams could have come close to the temperatures posited by NIST, Ryan and Greening were presupposing this fact about the thermal conductivity of steel, plus the fact that WTC 7 had an enormous amount of interconnected steel.

It seems, however, that NIST simply ignores these facts, evidently not factoring in the thermal conductivity of steel in its computer simulations. To ignore it, however, is scientifically illegitimate, because any simulation that does so will necessarily exaggerate the temperature the steel will reach. Dr. Vytenis Babrauskas, an expert on fire temperatures, has written:

> If a flame is exchanging heat with an object which was initially at room temperature, it will take a finite amount of time for that object to rise to a temperature which is "close" to that of the flame. Exactly how long it will take for it to rise to a certain value is the subject for the study of heat transfer.... [T]he rate at which target objects heat up is largely governed by their thermal conductivity, density, and size.[74]

Besides being large and protected by fireproofing insulation, the steel beams conducted heat well and were interconnected with the rest of the steel in this 47-story building, so that "target objects" for the fires to heat up were huge.

Accordingly, given the thermal conductivity of steel and NIST's failure to include it in its calculations, its steel temperature simulations are—even if very hot, long-lasting fires are presupposed for the sake of argument—completely unrealistic.

Fires Burning Too Long in One Place
Still another problem with the simulations of steel temperatures is that they seem to assume that fires remained burning in particular areas of

the building far longer than would have been possible, given the available combustible material.

On the one hand, NIST's computer simulations of the damage the fires would have caused are based almost entirely on damage that would have occurred after four hours of heating. NIST states, for example: "The global analysis with fire-induced damage at 4.0 h[ours] most closely matched the observed collapse events."[75] In a more detailed statement, NIST says:

> At 3.5 h[ours], the floor systems had fire-induced damage and failures of some connections, beams, and girders. After 4.0 h[ours] of heating, there was substantially more damage and failures in the WTC 7 structural floor system, particularly in the northeast region surrounding Column 79. The structural condition at these two times illustrates how the structure developed sufficient fire-induced damage to reach the collapse initiation event.[76]

These statements suggest that the fires continued to heat up particular beams, girders, and connections for four hours. Indeed, in explaining why its simulation showed that a full 4.0 hours of heating was needed, NIST states: "The response of WTC 7 to the fire-induced damage at 3.5 h[ours] was not sufficient to cause an initiating event that would lead to global collapse."[77]

On the other hand, NIST's account of the combustible material available to fuel fires does not allow for four-hour fires in any location. Given the average amount of combustibles on the various floors, NIST says, the fires could have burned at any one spot for only 20 to 30 minutes:

> Fires for the range of combustible contents in WTC 7—20 kg/m² (4.0 lb/ft²) on Floors 7 to 9 and 32 kg/m² (6.4 lb/ft²) on Floors 11 to 13—persisted in any given location for approximately 20 min[utes] to 30 min[utes].[78]

NIST acknowledges, in fact, that its simulations showed the period of intense burning to have been closer to 20 minutes than to 30, saying: "[T]he typical intense flaming peak for most of the fires observed in WTC 7 lasted about 20 min[utes]."[79]

It appears, therefore, that NIST's position is self-contradictory. To increase the temperature of any steel beams to the point at which they would fail, which according to NIST would mean 600°C (1,100°F), or more, the fire would have to affect them continuously for four hours. And yet the fire could have endured at any one spot for only 20 minutes. At the end of a four-hour burning period, the fire would have been 12 offices or cubicles away from its location at the beginning of this period. By that time, the steel that had been heated by the fire at the beginning of this period would have cooled down.

Shyam Sunder, NIST's lead investigator, has offered two quite different solutions to this problem.

Sunder's First Solution: During a 2007 meeting of the advisory committee for NIST's WTC investigation, a committee member asked:

> A 4 lb/ft² fuel load fire moved every 20 minutes; essentially it started and stopped every 20 minutes, so... how could fires burn for as long as they had and taken out this major structure that had good fireproofing?[80]

Sunder replied[81]:

> The fires in the towers did not stop after 20 minutes. The fires moved from location to location, meaning that at any given location the combustibles needed about 20 minutes to be consumed. While the combustibles at a location were being consumed, the fire front would be progressing to adjacent combustibles.... Once the fires had begun heating the air, the overall air temperatures on a floor continued to rise as new combustible material became involved.... The heating of the structure through its protective insulation was a result of both the high air temperatures that were reached and the duration of those high air temperatures, not just the duration of local burning.[82]

In other words, Sunder said, even though the fire kept moving, the air temperature kept rising, and it was the very high air temperature reached after four hours that did the damage.

Sunder's answer presupposed that the fires at that time not only were heating up the objects close to their flames but also had already heated up the entire floor, because otherwise heat from the fire areas would have been going to the still unheated areas of the floor. But each floor was about the size of a football field,[83] and the visual evidence provides no basis for any suggestion that fires covered all or even most of any floor at any time.

Sunder's answer also presupposed that the process of heating up the air temperature was what physicists call an "adiabatic process," in which no heat is lost. His answer presupposed, in other words, that each floor was similar to a furnace, so that the heat, rather than escaping, would keep building up.

But the floors of WTC 7 were nothing like furnaces. Besides being about the size of a football field, each floor would have constantly lost heat through its walls and windows, especially through any broken windows and any holes in the walls caused by debris from the North Tower's collapse.

NIST's own report supports this contention. It says that the floors could *not* have been airtight, or else the fires would never have grown enough to threaten the building:

> If each floor of WTC 7 had been airtight (i.e., no broken windows or breach in the exterior from debris damage), a fire starting on a particular floor would have been limited to the size that would not likely have threatened the building.... [T]hat would have resulted in an oxygen level below which flame spread would slow considerably and soon halt.[84]

NIST's report, moreover, points to extensive window breakage on the south face, which was caused by debris from the North Tower,[85] and to additional window breakage on other faces of Floors 7, 8, 9, 11, 12, and 13, which was caused by the heat of the fires.[86] NIST even reported that it deliberately broke windows in its simulations so as to drive the fires in the proper direction.[87] Sunder's picture of furnace-like floors is, therefore, contradicted by the report prepared by his team.

This contradiction draws attention to the fact that NIST's theory evidently needs to have it both ways. To provide oxygen and direction to the fires, it needs to have broken windows. But to drive the heat up over a four-hour period, even though the combustibles in any particular area would have been exhausted within 20 minutes, it needs the floors to be airtight and otherwise furnace-like, not allowing any heat to escape. Sunder's solution, therefore, did not overcome the apparent self-contradiction in NIST's position. In August 2008, however, Sunder offered a second solution.

Sunder's Second Solution: In his opening statement for NIST's "WTC 7 Technical Briefing" on August 26, 2008, Sunder repeated the point that fires "persisted in any given location for approximately 20 to 30 minutes." During the question period, 9/11 widow Lorie Van Auken asked:

> If building materials typically supply fuel to a fire for 20 minutes, and insulation used on the columns, including Column 79, lasts for two to three hours, how did Column 79 fail? What fueled the fire for that long?[88]

In his response, Sunder did not repeat his earlier answer. Rather, he changed the definition of what would fuel a fire for 20 or 30 minutes, saying:

> [K]eep in mind that the 20 to 30 minutes is the time it takes for a combustible in a particular location to start igniting and then complete the process of completely burning out. But that combustible may be a table. It may be a filing cabinet. It may be a computer workstation. It can be furniture, chairs, and so on. So this is not as though the entire space is all burning concurrently. It is each combustible burns for 20 to 30 minutes.[89]

So, after having earlier said that a fire could persist "in any given location" for only 20 to 30 minutes, Sunder now claimed that a fire could be fueled for 20 to 30 minutes by "a combustible in a particular location"—a combustible such as a table, a chair, a filing cabinet, or a computer workstation. This would imply that a cubicle, if it had all four of these things, could support a fire for an hour and 20 minutes.

But this was *not* what NIST's Draft for Public Comment, which had just been released, said. It said the same thing as an above-quoted passage from NIST's Final Report, namely:

> Fires for the range of combustible contents in WTC 7—20 kg/m² (4.0 lb/ft²) on Floors 7 to 9 and 32 kg/m² (6.4 lb/ft²) on Floors 11 to 13—persisted in any given location for approximately 20 min[utes] to 30 min[utes].[90]

The Draft Report, like the Final Report, also said: "The simulations indicated that the clusters of workstations burned out in about 20 min[utes] to 30 min[utes]."[91]

However, although this is what NIST's documents say, Sunder

tried to rule out this interpretation at the briefing, continuing his answer to Lorie Van Auken by saying:

> [W]hen you look at... the 2,000 square feet of floor area around Column 79, you can have fires moving from combustible to combustible in that vicinity for a long time. So it moves around.... It's just that each combustible takes 20 to 30 minutes to burn, not the entire floor.[92]

In spite of Sunder's claim at this briefing, the fact that the 20-to-30-minute burning period applies to workstations and cubicles, not to individual combustibles, is stated unequivocally in a new passage in NIST's Final Report, which says: "[F]ires moved from one location to the next (e.g., from one office cubicle to the next) and burned intensely in any one location for roughly 20 min[utes] to 30 min[utes]."[93]

In stating during the technical briefing that it was each individual combustible, such as each table or filing cabinet, that burned for 20 to 30 minutes—so that the fire would have remained at each location for an hour or more—Sunder may have inadvertently revealed his awareness that fires moving every 20 to 30 minutes could not have increased the temperature of steel at any particular location to 600°C (1,100°F). Be that as it may, the contradiction remains, constituting yet another fatal flaw in NIST's WTC 7 collapse theory.

Conclusion: NIST's Exaggerated Steel Temperatures

In producing simulations in which steel beams became much hotter than the actual beams in WTC 7 could have been, NIST used various illegitimate means, which included: positing fires that were unrealistically hot; positing fires that endured much longer than the actual fires did; ignoring the thermal conductivity of steel; and positing fires that lasted too long in one place.

Producing exaggerated steel temperatures was nothing new for NIST. It had done this in its report on the Twin Towers. Arguing that these buildings collapsed because steel columns buckled, NIST wrote: "[W]hen bare steel reaches temperatures of 1,000 degrees Celsius, it softens and its strength reduces to roughly 10 percent of its room temperature value."[94] Insofar as NIST was claiming that these columns reached 1,000°C (1,832°F), this was a wild, completely baseless, speculation. NIST's own scientists found that, of the columns from the

North Tower that they examined, none of the core columns, and only three of the sixteen perimeter columns, had "reached temperatures above 250°C [482°F]."[95] And yet NIST implied that some columns in the towers had reached 1,000°C [1,832°F].

Given NIST's extreme exaggeration of steel temperatures in the Twin Towers, we should not be surprised by its similar exaggerations in relation to WTC 7. Whether or not they surprise us, however, these exaggerations would be sufficient to vitiate NIST's report on this building, even if it contained no other problems.

But it does contain other problems—many of them. Some of these problems have been laid out in previous chapters. Still more of them, including some of the most serious, will be discussed in the next and final chapter.

10
FROM THERMAL EXPANSION TO GLOBAL COLLAPSE: FABRICATIONS AND CONTRADICTIONS

In the present chapter, I examine the final two steps in NIST's explanation of the collapse of WTC 7: its claim that thermal expansion caused a crucial column and several floors to fail, and its claim that those failures then led to global collapse.

I begin by quoting NIST's own summary statement of its explanation of how fires in WTC 7 produced a series of *local* failures that quickly led to *global* collapse:

> The heat from [the] uncontrolled fires caused thermal expansion of the steel beams on the lower floors of the east side of WTC 7, primarily at or below 400°C (750°F), damaging the floor framing on multiple floors.... If thermal expansion in steel beams is resisted by columns or other steel members, forces develop in the structural members that can result in buckling of beams or failures of connections.
>
> Fire-induced thermal expansion of the floor system surrounding Column 79 led to the collapse of Floor 13, which triggered a cascade of floor failures. In this case, the floor beams on the east side of the building expanded enough that they pushed the girder spanning between Columns 79 and 44 to the west on the 13th floor.... This movement was enough for the girder to walk off of its support at Column 79. The unsupported girder and other local fire-induced damage caused Floor 13 to collapse, beginning a cascade of floor failures down to the 5th floor.... Many of these floors had already been at least partially weakened by the fires in the vicinity of Column 79. This left Column 79 with insufficient lateral support, and as a consequence, the column buckled eastward, becoming the initial local failure for collapse initiation.
>
> Due to the buckling of Column 79 between Floors 5 and 14, the upper section of Column 79 began to descend. The downward movement of Column 79 led to the observed kink in the east

penthouse, and its subsequent descent. The cascading failures of the lower floors surrounding Column 79 led to increased unsupported length in, falling debris impact on, and loads being re-distributed to adjacent columns; and Column 80 and then Column 81 buckled as well. All the floor connections to these three columns, as well as to the exterior columns, failed, and the floors fell on the east side of the building. The exterior façade on the east quarter of the building was just a hollow shell.

The failure of the interior columns then proceeded toward the west. Truss 2… failed, hit by the debris from the falling floors. This caused Column 77 and Column 78 to fail, followed shortly by Column 76. Each north-south line of three core columns then buckled in succession from east to west, due to loss of lateral support from floor system failures, to the forces exerted by falling debris, which tended to push the columns westward, and to the loads redistributed to them from the buckled columns. Within seconds, the entire building core was buckling. The global collapse of WTC 7 was underway. The shell of exterior columns buckled between the 7th and 14th floors…. The entire building above the buckled-column region then moved downward as a single unit, completing the global collapse sequence.[1]

This theory, as can be seen, contains the following elements:

1. The fires caused sufficient thermal expansion in steel beams on the east side of WTC 7 to force the steel girder connecting Columns 44 and 79 to lose its connection with the latter, and to damage the floor framing on multiple floors near Column 79.

2. The loss of that girder's connection to Column 79, along with fire-induced damage to the floor system around Column 79, caused Floor 13 to collapse.

3. The collapse of Floor 13 caused all the floors below it down to the 5th floor to collapse.

4. Column 79, being left with inadequate lateral support, buckled between Floors 5 and 14.

5. This buckling caused the downward movement of Column 79 (which caused the kink in the east penthouse).

6. Columns 80 and 81, having also lost support, buckled, causing all the floors on the east side of WTC 7, which had been weakened by fire, to collapse.

7. All the other interior columns then failed, leaving the building a hollow shell.

8. After most of the collapse had already occurred in the building's interior, where it could not be seen from outside, the exterior columns failed, completing the global collapse.

Now, presupposing this overview of NIST's theory of global collapse, I focus on problematic details. I first look at various problems in NIST's claims about types of damage caused by thermal expansion. I then turn to problems in NIST's theory of WTC 7's global collapse which are especially severe.

1. NIST'S THEORY OF DAMAGE CAUSED BY THERMAL EXPANSION

The idea that thermal expansion of steel floor beams led to catastrophic damage, which NIST calls the basic element in its theory, contains far too many problems to be even remotely plausible. I will discuss four of them.

Overestimated Steel Temperatures

As we saw in the previous chapter, NIST's claims that steel beams reached temperatures of 600°C (1,100°F), and even higher, is based on exaggerations about the amount of combustible material available on the floors and also about the temperatures and durations of the fires. The claims about steel temperatures are also based on false assertions, such as the assertion that raging fires were burning on the 12th floor at a time when, in fact, the fires on this floor had burned out. NIST's claims about the temperatures of steel beams also seem to ignore the implications of the thermal conductivity of steel and of NIST's own estimate that fires could last in any given area for only about 20 minutes. Insofar as NIST's theory of WTC 7's collapse depends on its claims about steel temperatures, this theory is discredited by the fact that these claims are based on gross exaggerations and even outright falsehoods.

NIST has emphasized, to be sure, that the thermal expansion of steel beams, which (allegedly) initiated the collapse, "occurred primarily at temperatures below approximately 400°C (750°F)."[2] But even raising the temperature of huge, insulated, interconnected pieces of steel close to 400°C (750°F) would have required extraordinary fires.

As we saw in the previous chapter, the idea that steel temperatures significantly above 300°C (570°F) could have been reached on Floors 11, 12, and 13 would be dubious, even if NIST's (unrealistic) fuel loading for those floors were true. As we also saw, NIST itself found only three columns in the Twin Towers that had reached temperatures above 250°C (482°F)."[3] Even NIST's claim that some steel beams in WTC 7 reached almost 400°C (750°F) is, therefore, probably an exaggeration.

And yet its theory requires beams to have reached much higher temperatures. NIST does seek to downplay this fact by portraying thermal expansion, which can occur before steel reaches 400°C, as more important than thermal weakening and sagging, which require much higher temperatures. "In the WTC 7 collapse," NIST says, "the loss of steel strength or stiffness was not as important as the thermal expansion of steel structures caused by heat."[4] NIST's theory, nevertheless, does require that steel beams in some locations reached temperatures of 600°C (1,100°F), even 675°C (1,250°F). Such temperatures, according to NIST, were necessary for the beams to lose enough strength to result in floor failures, which play a central part in NIST's theory.

Accordingly, NIST's theory is shown to be unworthy of credence simply because it requires unrealistic steel temperatures. However, although no further evidence would be required to show NIST's theory of WTC 7's collapse to be unscientific and false, I will examine some additional problems to illustrate more fully just how unscientific and implausible it is.

Vanished Shear Studs

One serious problem involves NIST's claim that the collapse of WTC 7 was due in part to the fact that shear studs were not used to connect its girders to the floor slabs. This claim—that the girders had no shear studs—is stated unambiguously by NIST:

> Floor beams and exterior spandrel beams had shear studs, but the girders that supported the floor beams did not have shear studs.[5]

> In WTC 7, no studs were installed on the girders.[6]

This absence of girder sheer studs, NIST says, was a crucial factor in the movement from thermal expansion to global collapse.

This alleged absence is said to have been most fateful with respect to the girder that connected Column 44 with Column 79. If shear studs had been used to make this girder "composite" with the floor, NIST says, then it could have resisted the thermal expansion of the beams under the 13th floor. But without any shear stud connections, "resistance to the thermal expansion of the floor beams would have been provided primarily by the lateral stiffness of the girder," and the girder simply had far too little stiffness (strength) to offer any significant resistance:

> The lateral stiffness of the girder was about three orders of magnitude smaller than the axial stiffness of the floor beam. Thus… the girder provided almost no lateral resistance to the free thermal expansion of the floor beam.[7]

This lack of resistance due to the absence of girder shear studs, NIST says, allowed—by means of a failure to be described in the next section—the floor beams to expand freely. And it was these processes, rooted in the absence of girder shear studs, that caused the floor system to fail, the girder between Columns 44 and 79 to become disconnected from the latter, and (thereby) Column 79 to fail.

The absence of girder shear studs is, therefore, critical for NIST's answer to one of the most frequently asked questions, namely: *Given the fact that no steel-framed high-rise building had ever collapsed from fire alone, even though some such buildings had bigger and longer-lasting fires, why did WTC 7 collapse?* Here is NIST's answer:

> These other buildings, including Philadelphia's One Meridian Plaza, a 38-story skyscraper that burned for 18 hours in 1991, did not collapse due to differences in the design of the structural system.[8]

These alleged structural differences were spelled out in a longer version of NIST's answer, which said:

> If the fires in First Interstate Bank, One Meridian Plaza, the Cardington Test Building and WTC 7 generated comparable atmospheric temperatures, and of the four buildings cited only the WTC 7 building collapsed, the reason for the different outcomes likely lay in differences in the structural systems and the details of how the steel frames were constructed. Although all four buildings have been described as "steel frame structures," comparison of construction features between the three buildings that did not collapse in an uncontrolled fire and WTC 7 revealed [five] differences.[9]

One of these five claimed differences was the absence of girder shear studs in WTC 7. The Draft version of NIST's final report, released in August 2008, expressed this difference in these words: "Non-composite girders in WTC 7 rather than composite girders (presence or absence of shear studs) in the other three structures."[10]

This made an impressive argument: Although those other buildings had equally big or even bigger fires, all of them had composite girders—meaning that shear studs attached the girders to the floors—and none of them collapsed. Given this perfect correlation, NIST had good reason, it appeared, to suggest a causal relation.

NIST did, in fact, suggest it strongly. In explaining why WTC 7 collapsed, even though other steel-framed high-rise buildings had survived more severe fires, NIST said that one of the factors was "the absence of shear studs on the girders that would have provided lateral restraint."[11] NIST, in fact, made this point repeatedly, with the following sentence appearing twice, verbatim, in its Draft Report: "Additional factors that contributed to the girder failures were the absence of shear studs that would have provided lateral restraint."[12] Applying this general point to, in particular, the girder connecting Columns 44 and 79, NIST wrote: "Additional factors that contributed to the failure of the critical north-south girder were (1) the absence of shear studs that would have provided lateral restraint...."[13]

But in its Final Report, issued in November 2008, NIST admits that the correlation on which it had based this argument in its Draft Report was, in fact, less than perfect. Its list of the structural differences between WTC 7 and the fire-ravaged buildings that did not collapse now has this item: "Non-composite girders in WTC 7 rather than composite girders (presence or absence of shear studs) in two of the other three structures."[14]

This modified version of the statement—the previous version had said "in the other three structures"—makes for a less impressive argument. Although NIST does not draw attention to this fact, it now admits that of the three buildings to which it compares WTC 7, only two had shear studs connecting their girders to the floor slabs. This means that one of the other three buildings remained standing even though it had no girder shear studs. The argument for the causal connection NIST has suggested—between the absence of girder shear studs and global collapse—had become much weaker.

Nevertheless, after making this modification, NIST has continued to suggest the causal connection just as strongly as before. All of the above-quoted statements from the Draft Report, in which NIST called the absence of girder shear studs one of the factors responsible for the collapse of WTC 7, are repeated unchanged in the Final Report. NIST continues to suggest, in other words, that the argument for a causal connection is as strong as ever.

There is, moreover, an even more serious problem with NIST's claim that the lack of girder shear studs was one of the reasons for WTC 7's collapse: In 2004—before NIST had developed a theory around the idea of girder failures—it had stated that shear studs *did* connect the girders to the floor slabs. In its 2004 *Interim Report on WTC 7*, NIST said:

> Most of the beams and girders were made composite with the slabs through the use of shear studs. Typically, the shear studs were 0.75 in[ches] in diameter by 5 in[inches] long, spaced 1 ft to 2 ft on center. Studs were not indicated on the design drawings for many of the core girders.[15]

Whereas the first sentence clearly indicated that shear studs connected most—but not all—of the girders to the floor slabs, the final sentence spelled out the exception: many of the *core* girders did not have shear studs.

This distinction is important because the crucial girder in NIST's 2008 theory—the one connecting Columns 44 and 79—was *not* a core girder. It was instead in the building's eastern region. According to NIST's 2004 report, therefore, this girder would have been anchored to the floor slab with shear studs—-at least 22 of them.

Why at least 22? The above-quoted statement says that the shear studs were placed from one to two feet apart. The girder was 45 feet long.[16] So even if we assume that there was a shear stud only every two feet, there would have been 22 shear studs connecting this girder to the floor.[17]

For its 2008 reports, however, NIST rewrote the above passage to fit its newly developed explanation of why WTC 7 collapsed. Its Draft Report of August 2008 stated:

> Most of the beams were made composite with the slabs through the use of shear studs. Typically, the shear studs were 0.75 in[ches] in

diameter by 5 in[ches] long, spaced 2 ft on center. Studs were not indicated on the design drawings for the girders.[18]

As Chris Sarns, who discovered this contradiction between NIST's 2004 and 2008 reports, has pointed out, two crucial changes were made.[19] First, whereas the 2004 report had said, "Most of the *beams and girders* were made composite with the slabs through the use of shear studs" [emphasis added], the 2008 version deleted "and girders," so only the beams were said to have shear studs connecting them to the slabs. Second, whereas the 2004 report said that the design drawings did not indicate shear studs "for many of the core girders," the 2008 report simply says that shear studs were not indicated "for the girders"—thereby implying that they were not indicated for *any* of the girders, whether they were core girders or not.

It appears, therefore, that NIST, having developed a theory that would seem plausible only if the girders were not connected to the floors with shear studs, has simply made those shear studs vanish. The girder connecting Column 44 and 79, therefore, went from having at least 22 shear studs to having none. How can we avoid the conclusion that NIST, an agency of the US Department of Commerce, is guilty of scientific fraud?

In denying the existence of girder shear studs in its 2008 report, NIST gives the impression that it does so on good authority. In a section headed "Absence of Shear Studs on Girders," NIST says: "In WTC 7, no studs were installed on the girders (Cantor 1985)."[20] NIST thereby implies that the structural design drawings of Irwin G. Cantor, the structural engineer of record for WTC 7, indicated that the girders had no studs. However, besides providing no evidence to support this suggestion, NIST ignores the fact that one of its own earlier state-ments—"The structural design drawings (Cantor 1985) specified design forces for connections and suggested a typical detail, but did not show specific connection designs"[21]—had pointed out that his drawings would *not* have given any such indication.

It appears, therefore, that one of the crucial elements in NIST's explanation of WTC 7's collapse is based on a claim that NIST, by virtue of its 2004 report on WTC 7, knows to be false.

Shear Stud Failure and Concrete's Thermal Expansion

One element of NIST's theory not explained in the previous section is just why the lack of shear studs on the girder connecting Columns 44 and 79 would have led to such catastrophic results. It was stated there that the lack of shear studs on that girder allowed the unrestrained expansion of the floor beams, which in turn led to the processes that caused global collapse.

Why would the expansion of the floor beams, if not restrained by the girder, have left them completely unrestrained? Although the girders, according to NIST, were not connected to the floor slabs by means of shear studs, the steel floor beams *were*. Why did these studs not restrain the beams? NIST's answer is that, once the girder, having become disconnected because of its lack of shear studs, no longer offered resistance to the floor beams, the expansion of these beams broke the shear studs that had anchored them to the floor slabs, because the floor slabs, unlike the beams, did not expand. From then on, the expansion of the beams was completely unrestrained:

> [W]hen a floor beam is not restrained from thermally expanding, while the floor slab to which it is attached with shear studs is restrained due to its in-plane stiffness, the shear studs will fail and the floor beam will have little resistance to thermal expansion or to lateral-torsional buckling.[22]

NIST's theory is based, therefore, on two different types of shear stud failure. Whereas girder shear studs played their role by simply failing to exist, the shear studs connecting the steel beams to the floor slabs failed due to lateral pressure. NIST's claim about this second kind of failure, we will see in this section, is as problematic as its claim about the first.

Is it conceivable that the shear studs making the steel beams composite with the floor slabs would have failed even if the girders had no studs? Kevin Ryan has explained what would have been involved:

> The studs [holding the concrete floor to the beams] were 0.75 inches x 5 inches long, and were positioned every 1 to 2 feet along the beam.… There were 28 of these studs for each of the five beams that supposedly expanded.[23]

So, Ryan pointed out, NIST's theory requires that "those floor beams would have had to not only expand linearly, but also break 28 high-strength shear studs." NIST's theory does require all of this breakage, even though, as Ryan points out, a deceptive media presentation by NIST suggested otherwise by showing only three of these shear studs.[24]

In any case, surprise that such breakage occurred was expressed in a comment to NIST by David Proe and Ian Thomas, a professorial research fellow and the director, respectively, of the Centre for Environmental Safety and Risk Engineering at Victoria University in Melbourne. In a letter to NIST, they said:

> The assessment of WTC 7 appears to conclude that composite beams [i.e., beams connected to floor slabs with shear studs] are extremely susceptible to failure due to thermal expansion. This is not our experience at all.[25]

Why did Proe and Thomas differ so radically with NIST on this issue?

NIST's claim that shear studs failed depends on what it calls the "differential thermal expansion" of the steel beams and the concrete floor slabs. This is simply a technical way of saying that, in response to the heat from the fires, the steel beams expanded more than the floor slabs. This difference is said to have been responsible for the failure of the shear studs connecting the beams to the floor slabs (which then allowed the beams to expand freely). NIST says, for example, that when temperatures in the shear studs became greater than 300°C (570°F), "differential thermal expansion of the floor beams and floor slab resulted in significant shear force in the shear studs and caused them to fail."[26]

NIST suggests, in fact, that this failure of the shear studs is exactly what should have been expected:

> [O]ne would expect that, when a floor beam is not restrained from thermally expanding, while the floor slab to which it is attached with shear studs is restrained due to its in-plane stiffness, the shear studs will fail and the floor beam will have little resistance to thermal expansion.[27]

But why should there have been a significant difference between the expansion of a beam and of the floor slab to which it was connected? Why should one expect the floor slab to have retained its "in-plane stiffness" while the steel beam expanded?

We should, in fact, *not* expect this: The beams and the floor slabs were both subjected to the same fires, and heat causes steel and concrete to expand almost the same amount, with steel being only slightly more expansive. Put technically, the "linear expansion coefficient" of concrete is almost the same as that of steel.[28]

If steel and concrete were not similar in this regard, then reinforced concrete—which is concrete in which steel bars are embedded—would not be useful, because it would fail when subjected to very hot or very cold temperatures. And yet reinforced concrete, which is commonly used in buildings and other structures, works very well, precisely because steel and concrete respond very similarly to changes in temperature. NIST, in fact, acknowledges this similarity, saying that "steel and concrete have similar coefficients of thermal expansion."[29]

On what basis, then, does NIST claim that the shear studs were subjected to intolerable pressure because of differential thermal expansion? Here is its explanation:

> In general, the steel framing heated more quickly than the concrete slab. Thus, even though steel and concrete have similar coefficients of thermal expansion, differential thermal expansion occurred between the steel floor beams and concrete slab when the composite floor was subjected to fire.[30]

Let us focus first on NIST's statement that "the steel framing heated more quickly than the concrete slab."

How much more quickly? Even though this is presumably a scientific document, NIST provides no quantitative assessment. We need to know, however, what NIST had in mind. If its vague statement meant only that the steel heated up 0.5 percent more quickly than concrete, then the difference in the thermal expansion would be too trivial to have mentioned. But if NIST meant that steel heated up much more quickly—say 50 percent more quickly—this would imply, contrary to fact, that reinforced concrete would not be useful. But NIST's report gives no figure.

Nevertheless, NIST's entire case for shear stud failure rests on its vague claim about differential thermal expansion, as the following statement illustrates:

> Shear stud failures in WTC 7 were found to be primarily due to differential thermal expansion effects as the floor beams heated more quickly than the concrete slab.[31]

When we turn to NIST's claim that its computer simulations proved that shear studs would have failed because of the differential thermal expansion, we find this statement:

> The first failures observed were of the shear studs, which were produced by axial expansion of the floor beams, and which began to occur at fairly [sic] low temperature of 103°C.[32]

Is the idea that this could have happened in the real world—which would mean that shear stud failure could be produced by temperatures slightly higher than the boiling point of water—credible? David Proe, in a letter to NIST about its Draft for Public Comment, indicated that it is not, stating:

> We are particularly interested in the finding that the shear studs failed at low temperature. Having conducted numerous fire tests on composite beams, we have never observed this. Was there any physical evidence obtained of this type of failure?[33]

NIST, which did not respond to Proe's question, continues to claim in its Final Report that those shear studs did fail, starting a process that led to the global collapse of WTC 7.

We need an answer, therefore, to the question raised above: Why would NIST's computer simulations have indicated that the floor slabs would have heated up much less quickly, and therefore expanded much more slowly, than the steel beams? Why would the floor slabs have retained their "in-plane stiffness"? The answer is contained in a seemingly innocuous sentence, buried at the end of a paragraph in which NIST describes the variables that were fed into its simulation: "No thermal expansion or material degradation was considered for the concrete slab, as the slab was not heated in this analysis."[34] This remarkable statement bears repeating: "[T]he slab was not heated in this analysis."

This is the reason NIST could tell us that "floor beams heated more quickly than the concrete slab"—enough more quickly to break shear studs. It had nothing to do with the idea that steel expands farther and faster than concrete. It was simply that, when NIST ran its simulation, it "heated" the simulated steel beams but not the simulated floor slabs.

It appears that the authors of NIST's WTC 7 report have made an effort to avoid, at least technically, committing fraud in this case:

Besides admitting that concrete and steel are similarly expansive when subjected to heat, they also explicitly point out that, in their computer experiment, they did not heat the concrete slab.

Nevertheless, these authors do appear to be guilty of fraud in this matter. NIST generally implies in its report that the floor slabs as well as the steel beams were subjected to heat in its simulations. In the passage in which NIST states that "steel and concrete have similar coefficients of thermal expansion," it also says: "differential thermal expansion occurred between the steel floor beams and concrete slab when the composite floor was subjected to fire."[35] The "composite floor," of course, is the floor slab attached to the beams by means of shear studs, so NIST implies here that the floor slab *was* heated in its simulation. And yet NIST's simulation, upon which its explanation was based, assumed that the concrete slab was *not* heated.

Even if NIST had technically protected itself from the charge of fraud, moreover, that would be irrelevant to the question of the credibility of its explanation of the collapse of WTC 7. This explanation, being based on its simulations, could be regarded as credible only insofar as the simulations could be assumed to approximate what actually happened in WTC 7 on September 11, 2001. And insofar as the fires actually heated the steel beams, they would have also heated the floor slabs.

According to NIST's simulations, in fact, the slabs on the 12th and 13th floors reached 675°C (1,250°F).[36] If, for the sake of argument, we accept this estimation, then an "experiment" in which the simulated floor slab was *not* heated, while the simulated steel beams *were* heated, would provide no evidence whatsoever that the actual shear studs connecting the actual slabs and beams to each other would have broken.

The phoniness of NIST's simulation was pointed out by Proe and Thomas, who wrote:

> We do not agree with the calculations... indicating shear stud failure. Under the theory presented,... the W24 beams try to expand, but this is entirely prevented by the slab, producing very high forces at the shear connectors. In reality, the slab is also heated and expands.[37]

Without NIST's unrealistic simulation, in other words, there would have been no reason for the shear studs to fail.

How Much Did the Floor Beams Expand?

Even if NIST's scenario of massive shear stud failure were credible, so that we could imagine that the steel beams were able to expand freely, there would be another question: Could they have expanded sufficiently to cause the kind of damage suggested in NIST's theory?

According to NIST, as we have seen, the process that led to the global collapse of WTC 7 began with the expansion of the floor beams. NIST says:

> [T]he floor beams on the east side of the building expanded enough that they pushed the girder spanning between Columns 79 and 44 to the west on the 13th floor.... This movement was enough for the girder to walk off of its support at Column 79. The unsupported girder and other local fire-induced damage caused Floor 13 to collapse, beginning a cascade of floor failures down to the 5th floor.38

To wreak such havoc, the expansion of those floor beams must have been considerable. How much was it, exactly? In the above passage, which is in the brief version of its 2008 report on WTC 7, NIST does not specify, assuring us only that it was *enough*—"enough that they pushed the girder... to the west," which in turn was "enough for the girder to walk off of its support."

But in light of all the damage allegedly caused by the expansion of these floor beams, we really need to know, in order to assess the plausibility of NIST's theory, just how much they would have expanded. Incredibly, even though NIST's entire theory of a thermal-expansion-induced collapse hinges on its claim about expanding floor beams, NIST never says how much they expanded.

Kevin Ryan, having studied the long version of NIST's report with this question in mind, wrote:

> [I]t appears NIST is telling us that the loose beams... deflected the loose girder a distance of several feet. Even if we believe that WTC 7 was built in such a shoddy manner, is this hypothesis realistic?39

Based on a diagram provided by NIST, Ryan concluded that NIST's claim is that the beams elongated slightly over two feet.40 NIST itself refs in one place to a movement of 6.25 inches.[41] So we can ask if a deflection of two feet, or even half a foot, is realistic.

In trying to make a realistic estimate, Ryan said:

> The floor beams that NIST is speaking of, that supposedly pushed the girder between column 79 and column 44 completely out of place, were each about 52 feet, or 15.8 meters, in length.

Then, employing the relevant mathematical equation, Ryan calculated that "the beams could have expanded 0.019 m[eters] for every 100°C increase in temperature." Finally, pointing out that only half of this expansion would have been on the girder end of the beam, Ryan concluded:

> [A]lthough NIST does not state it clearly in the new report, a 575°C increase in temperature would have caused the girder end of the beams to experience a maximum of 2.2 *inches* of deflection. And if it were only a "section," for example only a third of a beam length, then the increase from thermal expansion would be correspondingly smaller (or 0.7 inches).[42]

Ryan's final sentence referred to the fact that NIST, in claiming that temperatures approaching or exceeding 600°C (1,100°F) had been reached by floor beams, claims only that these temperatures had been reached by "some sections" of the beams.[43]

According to Ryan's analysis, therefore, the heat-induced expansion of the steel beams would have probably increased their length at the girder end no more than an inch. If this is even close to accurate, then we must agree with Ryan's conclusion that a realistic estimate of the beams' thermal expansion "makes NIST's story of all those bolts and studs breaking in unison, and that critical girder buckling, quite unbelievable."[44]

To summarize: There are four reasons to doubt that the thermal expansion of steel beams could have produced the kinds of damage required by NIST's theory: NIST overestimates the steel temperatures; it falsely claims that the girders had no shear studs; it produces a fabricated "differential thermal expansion" in its computer simulation by heating the steel beams but not the concrete floor slabs; and it implies that the beams, once they had broken free from their shear studs, would have expanded much farther than suggested by standard calculations.

2. NIST'S THEORY OF GLOBAL COLLAPSE

Every element of NIST's theory of how thermal expansion induced enormous damage, we have seen, is deeply problematic. Indeed, it is hard to imagine a less credible theory. But even if we accepted this theory, for the sake of argument, NIST's theory of the effect of this damage, namely, WTC 7's global collapse, would be implausible for several reasons. I will examine four.

The Initiation of Column 79's Descent

One of the problems NIST faced was to explain how a building damaged by fire could have come down with about the same acceleration rate as a building that has been deliberately imploded. In the latter case, explosives have removed the building's steel columns, so that there is nothing to prevent it from coming down in free fall. But if a steel-framed high-rise building were somehow caused to collapse by fires, it would come down much more slowly, because the steel columns would impede the collapse.

NIST, however, could not have claimed that the building's exterior came down slowly. Videos of the collapse have long been available, and the descent of the building's roofline (before it disappeared from view) had been very precisely timed. NIST therefore needed to describe a collapse that, while not caused by explosives, appeared to match the acceleration of the collapse revealed by these videos—which is the acceleration that would be expected if explosives had been used to implode the building. Given this impossible task, it would not be surprising to find that NIST has made some implausible claims regarding the collapse of WTC 7. And this is what we do find.

One example is NIST's description of the downward acceleration of Column 79, in which NIST says:

> Once Column 79 buckled, the column section above Floor 14 began to descend downward. Column 79 began moving downward at the roof level approximately 0.2 s[econds] after Column 79 buckled and 0.6 s[econds] before Column 80 buckled.[45]

After examining this and some related statements by NIST, Frank Greening wrote:

> NIST shows... that the vertical displacement of column 79 at the roof level was in fact 0.83 meters in 0.6 seconds. This implies that

within 1 second of buckling column 79 was moving downwards with an acceleration of 4.6 m/s²... which is a very dramatic motion for a column that was restrained by several framing beams and girders on all the undamaged and unheated floors above floor 14 just moments before collapse initiation. I would therefore ask NIST to explain how and why all lateral supports acting on column 79 from more than 30 upper floors, were simply ripped out or otherwise detached from their very secure connections in only 0.2 seconds?[46]

Greening raised this question in response to NIST's Draft for Public Comment. But it went unanswered, and NIST's Final Report simply repeats its above-quoted statement with no added explanation.

Clearly, however, Greening had raised a valid question: Given the fact that Column 79 had been secured on Floors 15 to 47 by beams and girders—ones that, moreover, had suffered no fire damage—how could it have been accelerating downward very rapidly within a fifth of a second? The claim is completely implausible.

The Simulated Versus the Real Roofline

NIST's explanation of the collapse of WTC 7, as we have seen, is based on its computer simulations of various occurrences: the initiation and spread of the fires, the resulting steel temperatures, the thermal expansion of steel beams, the failure of the girder connecting Columns 44 and 79, the failure of Column 79, and the failure of all the other columns. For most of these events, we have no visual information with which to confirm or disconfirm the simulations. With regard to a few matters, however, we do have visual (photographic and video) evidence against which to test NIST's simulations. For NIST's theory to have any plausibility, there must be a close correspondence between its simulations and all such empirical information.

One matter for which we have visual evidence is the initiation and spread of the fires. NIST's simulations, as we saw in Chapters 8 and 9, do not fare well when matched against some of this information, such as the fact that the 12th floor fire had burned out by 4:45PM.

Another matter for which we have visual information is the appearance of the building in the first few seconds of its descent. There are videos, taken from more than one location, which can be closely studied. For NIST's analysis of the collapse of WTC 7 to be credible, therefore, NIST's simulation, on which its analysis is based, must closely correspond to what can be seen on these videos. NIST claims that it does, or at least that it corresponds "reasonably well"— well enough to confirm the accuracy of the simulations. But this is not true.

Three features of the collapse, as revealed by these videos, especially stand out. One is the fact that, before the building as a whole began to collapse, the penthouse on the east side descended below the roofline. A second prominent feature was the development of a "kink" in the roofline of the north face. A third such feature is that, aside from that kink, the roofline remained virtually straight, as the building came down symmetrically.

With regard to the first of these features, NIST appears quite pleased with the results of its simulation, saying that "the calculated and observed times for the descent of the east penthouse below the roofline were quite similar."[47]

But as NIST prepares to discuss the second and third features—the kink and the descent of the building—it seeks to lower expectations, saying:

> Once simulation of the global collapse of WTC 7 was underway, there was a great increase in the uncertainty in the progression of the collapse sequence, due to the random nature of the interaction.... [T]he details of the progression of the horizontal failure and final global collapse were increasingly less precise.[48]

Then, with regard to the kink and the building's "subsequent movement," NIST writes:

> There was another observable feature that occurred after the global collapse was underway. After the exterior façade began to fall downward…, the north face developed a line or "kink" near the end of the core at Column 76.... The kink… occurred 2 s[econds] to 3 s[seconds] after the exterior façade had begun to move downward, as a result of the global collapse. The simulations do show the formation of the kink, but any subsequent movement of the building is beyond the reliability of the physics in the model.[49]

In spite of this caveat, NIST concludes on an upbeat note, saying in a section headed "Accuracy Analysis":

> Given the complexity of the modeled behavior, the global collapse analyses matched the observed behavior reasonably well.... The

global collapse analysis confirmed the leading collapse hypothesis, which was based on the available evidence.[50]

Greening has expressed strong disagreement with NIST's self-evaluation here. After arguing that NIST's estimations of the available combustible materials and hence its simulated steel temperatures were unrealistic, he wrote:

> However, assume for a moment that collapse initiation in WTC 7 did in fact occur as NIST states: by a thermally induced buckling failure of Column 79 on Floors 12/13. It would then be appropriate to ask: Is the collapse propagation mechanism proposed by NIST consistent with the *observed* collapse of WTC 7? If the answer to this question is "Yes," it would add credibility to NIST's account of what happened to Building 7 on 9/11 even if an inappropriate fuel loading was used to arrive at this conclusion. However, I would suggest that NIST's account of the last 1/2 minute of the life of WTC 7… is… at odds with what was observed in the collapse videos of WTC 7.[51]

Focusing on images showing what happened to the core of WTC 7 after the east penthouse collapsed,[52] according to NIST's simulations, Greening wrote:

> What is most significant about these images is that around the time of global collapse initiation NIST's simulation shows that the eastern half of the core had completely collapsed while the western half of the core remained standing and relatively undamaged. This is quite remarkable since videos of the collapse of WTC 7 show that up to *and well beyond* the moment that the roofline of WTC 7 exhibited its first downward movement, the exterior of the building revealed absolutely no signs of NIST's proposed partial collapse of the core even though the core was connected to the exterior walls of Building 7 by dozens of horizontal beams on every floor.
>
> NIST's proposed collapse of the eastern half of the core would have completely removed the lateral restraints normally acting on the eastern exterior columns of WTC 7. Indeed, NIST assert[s] that in the moments before global collapse initiation, "*the exterior façade on the east quarter of the building was just a hollow shell.*" This would have caused the eastern façade to buckle *well before* global collapse ensued. This buckling would have been visible as a bowing of the northeast corner of the building. Needless to say, such pre-collapse buckling or bowing of WTC 7 was not observed.[53]

Greening's observations here highlight one of the fundamental problems with NIST's theory of "progressive collapse." As we saw in the first part of this book, a wealth of evidence shows that explosives were used to make WTC 7 implode. A key piece of this evidence is the fact that the building came straight down. This kind of symmetrical, straight-down collapse of a steel-framed building can occur only if all of its columns fail almost simultaneously. Getting them to do this is, indeed, at the heart of the science, or art, of engineering a controlled implosion. The explosives must be in the right places and go off in the right order.

Insofar as NIST's task was to show how the building could have come down without the aid of explosives, it had an impossible task. Being unable to mention explosives, NIST could not possibly argue that all of the columns failed simultaneously. The best it could do was to develop a theory of "progressive collapse," which it defines as "the spread of local damage, from an initiating event, from element to element, eventually resulting in the collapse of an entire structure."[54] As both the name and this definition make clear, this type of collapse—assuming for the sake of argument that it would even be possible—would take time, with some elements happening later than others.

NIST's impossible task was to try to show that such a collapse, although very different inside the building than a controlled implosion, could look the same from the outside. NIST's attempt to do this involves arguing that most of the collapse occurred inside, invisible to external eyes and cameras, before the exterior façade, which had become a "hollow shell," collapsed. What seemed from the outside to be the total collapse of the WTC 7 was really, NIST says, only the collapse's final phase, which began when "[t]he shell of exterior columns buckled."[55]

But does this makes sense? During NIST's technical briefing in August 2008, Mindy Kleinberg, one of the 9/11 widows, asked: "If Column 79 collapsed and then 80 and 81, all of which are on the same side, why wasn't the collapse asymmetrical?" Although Shyam Sunder gave a long, poorly constructed reply at that time,[56] NIST provided a more concise and precise response in its "Questions and Answers" document, in which it said:

WTC 7's collapse, viewed from the exterior (most videos were taken from the north), did appear to fall almost uniformly as a single unit. This occurred because the interior failures that took place did not cause the exterior framing to fail until the final stages of the building collapse. The interior floor framing and columns collapsed downward and pulled away from the exterior frame. There were clues that internal damage was taking place, prior to the downward movement of the exterior frame, such as when the east penthouse fell downward into the building and windows broke out on the north face at the ends of the building core. The symmetric appearance of the downward fall of the WTC 7 was primarily due to the greater stiffness and strength of its exterior frame relative to the interior framing.[57]

This strategy on NIST's part, however, could not be completely successful. The internal progression of column failures would necessarily have had noticeable effects on the building's exterior. As Greening pointed out, if the core columns in the eastern half of the building had collapsed first, this failure would have removed the support for the eastern exterior columns, causing the eastern façade to collapse before the rest of the building did. But the videos show no such thing.

Moreover, Greening wrote, "the problems with NIST's simulations only get worse *after* global collapse initiation." Following his discussion of two such problems, Greening concluded with "a final blow to the credibility of NIST's collapse simulation," which he stated thus:

> [NIST's computer-based images] reveal a collapsing core with its eastern side a full eight stories... *below* its western side. This would indicate a roofline collapse that started at the eastern end of Building 7 and progressed over a period of about 4 seconds to the western end.[58]

Why was this a fatal problem? Because, Greening explained:

> [I]f NIST's collapse simulations are supposed to accurately reflect what happened to Building 7 on 9/11, one is compelled to ask: *Why did WTC 7 undergo a strictly vertical collapse, with the roofline remaining essentially horizontal throughout the first 5 seconds of its downward motion, when NIST's simulations show the eastern side of the building starting to collapse 4 seconds before the western side?*[59]

Having raised this question in comments on NIST's Draft Report, which were posted by NIST on its website, Greening later submitted a "revised and extended version" of his critique, which NIST did *not* post. In this revised critique, Greening, after pointing out that the available videos "present an unobstructed view of at least the upper third of Building 7 and permit the collapse to be followed for 4–5 seconds," wrote:

> The videos show the upper section of WTC 7 descending very smoothly as an intact structure, with the roofline remaining essentially horizontal until it passes behind buildings in the foreground. The only significant distortion of the boxed-shaped Building 7 that is noticeable after the façade begins its downward motion is the formation of a kink on the eastern side of the north face.[60]

By contrast, he noted, three of NIST's computer-generated images "show very extensive buckling of the exterior columns over much of the building a few seconds into the collapse." Greening then pointed out that two of these images "use lateral and vertical displacement contours that span 2 meters, a level of building distortion that should have been visible in the WTC 7 collapse videos, but was in fact not seen."[61] Two other images, Greening added, "show a localized cave-in of the top ten floors of WTC 7 at its northeast corner about the time of global collapse initiation—another behavior of Building 7 that was never observed."[62] Having pointed out these glaring discrepancies, Greening concluded:

> It is simply astounding that, although NIST's computer generated images of a crumpled and severely distorted Building 7 look nothing like the video images of the real thing, NIST nevertheless concludes: *"the global collapse analyses matched the observed behavior reasonably well."*[63]

Greening was not the only one to complain to NIST about this lack of correspondence. Philip Tompkins wrote:

> I do not see how the pictured object in Figure 12-[70] at all resembles the actual collapse as shown in the videos. In the actual collapse the top of the building is not all crumpled as in Figure 12-[70].[64]

However, in spite of the obvious truth of these statements by Greening and Tompkins, made in criticism of NIST's Draft Report, those same images are reprinted in its Final Report, along with NIST's "astounding" claim that the simulations of the collapse, on which these images were based, "matched the observed behavior reasonably well."

NIST perhaps understood the phrase "reasonably well" broadly enough that it could encompass "hardly at all."

Be that as it may, the fact that the simulated collapse of WTC 7 looks nothing like the actual collapse provides additional reason to conclude that NIST's explanation of that collapse is false.

Did WTC 7 Enter into Free Fall?

One of the most common arguments for the controlled demolition of WTC 7 has been based on the observation that its downward acceleration approximated that of a free-falling object. This could have happened, critics of the official account have pointed out, only if explosives of some sort had removed all of the building's structural columns. Otherwise, even if the upper part of the building had started to come down, the lower part would have stopped or at least slowed down its descent.

NIST's Draft for Public Comment: In its Draft for Public Comment, which was issued on August 21, 2008, NIST countered this argument by claiming that the time that it took WTC 7 to collapse shows that it was not falling freely. NIST wrote:

> The time the roofline took to fall 18 stories was 5.4 s[econds]....
> Thus, the actual time for the upper 18 floors of the north face to collapse, based on video evidence, was approximately 40 percent longer than the computed free fall time and was consistent with physical principles.[65]

NIST repeated this claim in a Q & A document ("Questions and Answers about the NIST WTC 7 Investigation"), which was issued the same day as the Draft Report. One of the questions was:

> In videos, it appears that WTC 7 is descending in free fall, something that would not occur in the structural collapse that you describe. How can you ignore basic laws of physics?

NIST gave the following answer (in a document that has since been removed from its website):

> WTC 7 did not enter free fall. According to NIST analysis of WTC 7 video, the building collapsed 18 stories in 5.3 seconds [sic: NIST usually said 5.4 seconds]. If the building exhibited free fall, this process would have taken just 3.9 seconds. The actual collapse time exceeded the free fall time by 40 percent.[66]

To say "the actual collapse time exceeded free fall time by 40 percent" was to say that the building's acceleration was only 51 percent of that of gravity.[67] Even that would have been an incredibly fast descent in a fire-induced collapse (if such were possible). But by saying that the building's acceleration was "only" 51 percent of that of a free-falling object, NIST was at least able to contradict the widespread claim that it had come down in free fall.

In his technical briefing on August 26, 2008, NIST's lead investigator, Shyam Sunder, explained why WTC 7 could *not* have come down in free fall:

> [A] free fall time would be an object that has no structural components below it.... What the... collapse analysis shows, is that same time [sic] that it took for the structural model to come down from the roof line all the way—for those 17 floors to disappear—is 5.4 seconds. It's about 1.5 seconds, or roughly 40 percent, more time for that free fall to happen [sic]. And that is not at all unusual, because there was structural resistance that was provided in this particular case. And you had a sequence of structural failures that had to take place. Everything was not instantaneous.[68]

Sunder thereby summarized the two main reasons—even if he did not clearly distinguish between them—why NIST could not endorse the idea that WTC 7 had come down in free fall. (1) The upper floors could not have come down in free fall, because that could have happened only if nothing of the lower floors had remained to provide structural resistance. And (2) the collapse could not have been "instantaneous," meaning that all of the supporting columns had failed simultaneously, because NIST espoused a theory of "progressive collapse," in which the failures occurred sequentially over a period of time.

David Chandler's Response to NIST's Draft Report: Sunder's statement at the technical briefing, quoted above, was made in response to the following question from high-school physics teacher David Chandler:

> Any number of competent measurements using a variety of methods indicate the northwest corner of WTC 7 fell with an acceleration within a few percent of the acceleration of gravity. Yet your report contradicts this, claiming 40 percent slower than free fall.... How can such a publicly visible, easily measurable quantity be set aside?[69]

Chandler's question was based on an analysis that he had presented in a video, which he had made available on the internet. In this video, Chandler first explained how he measured the downward acceleration. He then pointed out that "for about two and a half seconds…, the acceleration of the building is indistinguishable from freefall."[70] Finally, explaining the significance of this fact, he said:

> Free fall can only be achieved if there is zero resistance to the motion. In other words, the gravitational potential energy of the building is not available to crush or deform anything. During free fall, all of the gravitational potential energy of the building is being converted into kinetic energy, and nothing else. Any breaking, bending, crushing, or pulverizing of the building components is occurring without the assistance of the free-falling portion of the building. Any force the top portion of the building might exert on the lower portion would be reflected in a reaction force that would produce an observable slowing of the rate of fall.[71]

In other words, the fact that the building was in free fall for over two seconds means that zero resistance, which Sunder had tried to rule out, is exactly what there had been. How, then, had NIST claimed that the building had *not* been in free fall?

NIST did this, Chandler explained, by arbitrarily choosing a starting time that was earlier than the time of the actual beginning of the collapse, and then by "computing only the average acceleration between that point and the disappearance of the roofline." By alleging that the collapse began at a time when the building, in fact, had still been motionless, NIST was able to claim that it took 5.4 seconds for the top 18 floors to collapse. By then computing merely the *average* acceleration—thereby ignoring the fact that the building had been in free fall for over two seconds—NIST could claim that the collapse took 40 percent longer than would a free-falling object.

Pointing out that "[t]his is high school physics we're talking about," Chandler concluded that NIST's approach constituted "either gross incompetence or an attempt to obfuscate the issue." Indicating which of those options he endorsed, he added: "[T]he guys at NIST are not incompetent."[72]

Next, explaining why the authors of NIST's WTC 7 report had tried to obfuscate the issue, he said:

The rate of fall of the building is an embarrassment to the official theory.... Buildings cannot fall at free fall through themselves, because even a weakened building requires energy to break up the pieces, crush the concrete, and push things around. When a falling building pushes things, the fall is not free, the "things" push back, and the reaction forces will measurably slow the descent of the building. This is why one would reasonably expect crumbling structures to come down in a tumbling, halting, irregular manner. In short, the evidence is clear: we are witnessing not the collapse of a building, but its demolition.[73]

In other words, for NIST to admit that the building entered free fall, even for two seconds, would be for it to admit, implicitly, that the building had been intentionally demolished through the use of explosives of some sort.

Finally, evaluating NIST's WTC 7 report in light of this fact, Chandler concluded: "[W]e have received not a report from an independent scientific investigation, but a cover-up by a government agency."[74]

After producing his video and releasing it on the internet on September 4, 2008, Chandler next confronted NIST directly, summarizing his findings in a "Comment" about its Draft for Public Comment, submitted September 13. Stating that his measurement "shows a period of approximately 2.5 seconds, with sudden onset, during which the acceleration was indistinguishable from free fall," Chandler pointed out that the explanation he had provided in his video could easily be repeated "by anyone with a background in elementary physics." Finally, stating that Sunder's answer to his (Chandler's) question at the technical briefing constituted an acknowledgment "that the NIST model is at variance with the observable fact that free fall actually occurred," Chandler concluded: "Acknowledgment of and accounting for an extended period of free fall in the collapse of WTC 7 must be a priority if the NIST is to be taken seriously."[75]

In its Final Report, issued in November 2008, NIST does, amazingly enough, acknowledge a period of free fall. But it does *not* account for it.

NIST's Final Report on WTC 7: In its Final Report, NIST still uses the early start time, thereby claiming that the upper 18 floors took 5.4 seconds to collapse. It also continues to use the average descent rate.

NIST can thereby continue saying that the building took 40 percent longer than free-fall time to collapse. All of these elements are contained in the following summary statement:

> The time that the roofline took to fall 18 stories... was approximately 5.4 s[econds]. The theoretical time for free fall was approximately 3.9 s[econds]. Thus, the average time for the upper 18 stories to collapse, based on video evidence,... was approximately 40 percent longer than the computed free fall time.[76]

Within this unchanged framework, however, NIST goes beyond its former approach by dividing this 5.4-second period into three stages, in which it acknowledges the point on which Chandler had been insisting. After repeating the claim that the descent time of the upper 18 stories "was 40 percent greater than the computed free fall time," NIST says on page 607 of the long version of its Final Report:

> A more detailed analysis of the descent of the north face found three stages: (1) a slow descent with acceleration less than that of gravity that corresponded to the buckling of the exterior columns at the lower floors, (2) a freefall descent over approximately eight stories at gravitational acceleration for approximately 2.25 s[econds], and (3) a decreasing acceleration as the north face encountered resistance from the structure below.[77]

Although this is stated matter-of-factly, as if nothing extraordinary were being said, NIST's three-phase analysis includes, in Chandler's words, "a whopping 2.25 seconds of absolute free fall."[78]

NIST has thereby contradicted its claim, made in its Q & A document of August 2008, that "WTC 7 did not enter free fall." It now acknowledges that WTC 7 not only entered free fall but remained in it for 2.25 seconds—which means that, for over two seconds, the lower floors of the building were offering *zero* resistance.

NIST also admits this point in an updated version of its Q & A document, issued in December 2008. This document's description of the three stages of collapse says: "During Stage 2, the north face descended essentially in free fall, indicating negligible support from the structure below."[79] This is, of course, exactly what Sunder in his technical briefing of August 2008 had said could *not* have occurred. NIST has clearly reversed itself—a point that Chandler emphasized with the title of his next video: "WTC 7: NIST Finally Admits Freefall."

NIST does not, to be sure, admit that the 2.25 seconds of zero resistance implies that explosives had been used to remove all the steel and concrete that would have offered resistance. But neither has NIST continued to insist that its non-demolition collapse analysis, now that it explicitly includes a free-fall stage, is consistent with physical principles.

In its Draft for Public Comment, as we saw earlier, NIST had made that claim, saying:

> [T]he actual time for the upper 18 floors of the north face to collapse… was approximately 40 percent longer than the computed free fall time and was consistent with physical principles.

This claim was reiterated in the next paragraph, which said:

> The actual collapse time of the upper 18 floors of the north face of WTC 7… was 40 percent greater than the computed free fall time. This was consistent with physical principles.[80]

In the list of "Principal Findings" at the end of the Draft Report, NIST again made this claim, saying:

> The collapse time of the upper 18 floors of the north face of WTC 7… was 40 percent greater than the computed free fall time. This is consistent with physical principles.[81]

In NIST's Final Report, however, this claim, so prominent in the Draft for Public Comment, is missing. The claim that NIST's analysis is consistent with physical principles is replaced by NIST's new three-stage analysis. For example, the just-quoted statement from the list of "Principal Findings" has been modified to read:

> The observed descent time of the upper 18 stories of the north face of WTC 7… was 40 percent greater than the computed free fall time. A more detailed analysis of the descent of the north face found three stages: (1) a slow descent with acceleration less than that of gravity that corresponded to the buckling of the exterior columns at the lower floors, (2) a freefall descent over approximately eight stories at gravitational acceleration for approximately 2.25 s[econds], and (3) a decreasing acceleration as the north face encountered resistance from the structure below.[82]

No claim that this three-stage analysis is "consistent with physical principles" is made here or anywhere else in NIST's Final Report on WTC 7.

NIST's Final Report does include a "consistent with" statement, but this statement says nothing about physical principles. Instead, after giving its three-stage analysis, NIST says: "The three stages of collapse progression described above are consistent with the results of the global collapse analyses discussed earlier in this chapter."[83] What NIST asserts, in other words, is that its three-stage analysis on this page is consistent with its three-stage analyses on earlier pages! This tautological statement is a far cry from NIST's earlier claim that its collapse analysis was consistent with physical principles.

In omitting every instance of this earlier claim, NIST has implicitly conceded that its collapse analysis is *not* consistent with physical principles. NIST tries, nevertheless, to disguise this fact by continuing to claim that WTC 7's descent time was 40 percent longer than free fall. In his new video, "WTC7: NIST Finally Admits Freefall," Chandler has explained, more fully than he had before, why this claim is fraudulent.

Chandler on NIST's "40 Percent Greater than Free Fall" Claim: Before looking at Chandler's critique of NIST's claim that the descent of the top 18 floors took 5.4 seconds, it will be helpful to look at the summary of NIST's three-stage analysis of this 5.4-second period, which is provided in its updated Q & A document:

>—Stage 1 (0 to 1.75 seconds): acceleration less than that of gravity (i.e., slower than free fall)
>—Stage 2 (1.75 to 4.0 seconds): gravitational acceleration (free fall)
>—Stage 3 (4.0 to 5.4 seconds): decreased acceleration, again less than that of gravity[84]

Chandler fully agrees with Stages 2 and 3. Stage 2 is, of course, the 2.25 seconds of free fall on which he has insisted. (Although he originally timed it at 2.5 seconds, he has not quibbled about its reduction to 2.25 seconds.) He also agrees that, after this stage of absolute free fall, the descent started to slow. As he said in his critique of NIST's Draft Report:

>[A]bout two and a half seconds after the building drops, the acceleration ceases to be uniform. This indicates that the falling building is starting to offer more resistance. Any measurement of the average acceleration that continues for more than the first two and a half seconds of fall will show a lower average acceleration, masking the

fact that for a significant two and a half seconds the building was in literal free fall.[85]

Chandler agrees, therefore, that the stage of absolute free fall was followed by a stage in which the acceleration decreased. He also agrees that it is important to distinguish clearly between these two stages.

Chandler's point of disagreement with NIST's three-stage analysis involves the period lasting 1.75 seconds, which NIST calls Stage 1 of the collapse. It is this so-called first stage that allows NIST to claim that the collapse of the upper 18 floors required 5.4 seconds and hence took 40 percent longer than free fall. NIST itself even points out this fact in its new Q & A document, saying that "the 40 percent longer descent time—compared to the 3.9 second free fall time—was due primarily to Stage 1."[86] NIST also makes this point in its Final Report, saying that the "increase in time is due primarily to Stage 1, in which column buckling was just beginning and gradual progression in displacement and velocity were observed."[87] Chandler challenged the second half of that statement, pointing out that no significant movement was observed during almost all of this so-called first stage.

Chandler demonstrated this fact by slowing down the video footage, so that the collapse of the upper 18 floors could be analyzed frame by frame. He used a video in which there are 30 frames per second, so that it takes 162 frames to show the 5.4 seconds that, according to NIST, it took WTC 7's roofline to descend to the level where the 29th floor had been (after which the building disappeared from view behind other buildings).

Although NIST said that WTC 7's collapse started exactly 5.4 seconds before the roofline reached that level, Chandler pointed out that there is not "the slightest hint of any collapse until Frame 40."[88] That frame, moreover, merely shows a tiny motion in the corner of the west penthouse, after which the penthouse begins to collapse into the roof. WTC 7's roofline itself remains motionless until about Frame 46. "Even then," Chandler pointed out, "there isn't any progressive, ongoing movement of the roofline until about Frame 60,"[89] which shows the building 1.5 seconds later than the time at which NIST claimed the collapse had begun.

So why did NIST claim that the collapse began 1.5 seconds prior to the time at which this ongoing movement of the roofline occurred? Chandler said:

> The only rationale I can see… is to make the measurement come out to exactly 5.4 seconds, to agree with the prediction of NIST's collapse model.… [I]t's pretty clear that the whole idea there's any kind of real 5.4 second collapse interval is a fiction. It's a crude fabrication, and the 3-stage collapse sequence is pseudo-science in the service of an ongoing coverup.[90]

The purpose, in other words, was to obscure the fact that WTC 7, after being motionless, suddenly began to come down in free fall.

Did Chandler's use of the word "fabrication" mean that he was accusing NIST of scientific fraud? Yes. He even used the term "dry labbing,"[91] which, as mentioned in Chapter 2, is often used as a synonym for fabrication.

Chandler on the Significance of WTC 7's Free-Fall Descent: After exposing the fraudulent nature of NIST's claim that the descent of the upper 18 floors took 40 percent longer than free fall, Chandler discussed the significance of NIST's belated admission that WTC 7 came down in free fall for over two seconds. Explaining the basic physical principles involved, Chandler said:

> Anything at an elevated height has gravitational potential energy. If it falls, and none of the energy is used for other things along the way, all of that energy is converted into kinetic energy—the energy of motion, and we call it "free fall." If any of the energy is used for other purposes, there will be less kinetic energy, so the fall will be slower. In the case of a falling building, the only way it can go into free fall is if an external force removes the supporting structure. None of the gravitational potential energy of the building is available for this purpose, or it would slow the fall of the building. The fact of free fall by itself is strong evidence of explosive demolition.[92]

However, Chandler continued, the *way* in which WTC 7 came down provides even stronger evidence of its explosive demolition:

> What is particularly striking is the suddenness of onset of free fall. Acceleration doesn't build up gradually.… The building went from full support to zero support, instantly.… One moment, the building is holding; the next moment it lets go and is in complete free fall.[93]

Still further evidence is provided, Chandler said, by another fact about WTC 7's descent:

> The onset of free fall was not only sudden; it extended across the whole width of the building....The fact that the roof stayed level shows the building was in free fall across the entire width. The collapse we see cannot be due to a column failure, or a few column failures, or a sequence of column failures. All 24 interior columns and 58 perimeter columns had to have been removed... simultaneously, within a small fraction of a second.[94]

Having made that point—which is surely the clearest proof that explosives of some sort were used to remove the columns—Chandler emphasized the importance of recognizing the deceptiveness of NIST's three-stage analysis:

> We saw [earlier] that the 5.4 seconds depends on an artificially early start time which has no valid observational basis. Without the 5.4 second fig-leaf, we're left with freefall and nothing more.[95]

Finally, pointing out the contradiction between NIST's collapse model and the empirical fact that WTC 7 was in free fall for over two seconds—which NIST has reluctantly admitted—Chandler concluded:

> One fact we do know about NIST's model is: it does not allow for free fall.... There is nothing in the models we have been shown that even resembles a 3-stage collapse with a free-fall component. After all, as Shyam Sunder put it himself, "Free fall happens only when there are no structural components below the falling section of the building." Any natural scenario is going to involve a progression of failures, and these don't happen instantaneously.[96]

In other words, by admitting "a free-fall component," NIST has ended up with a self-contradictory position. On the one hand, its Final Report offers the same theory of WTC 7's collapse that was contained in its Draft Report, which was a theory of progressive collapse, in which the building's supports failed sequentially. On the other hand, NIST's Final Report concedes that the building came down part of the time in free fall, which means that all of the supports had to have failed simultaneously.

Given this contradiction at the very heart of the final version of NIST's theory, Shyam Sunder should be asked by the press whether he still stands by his confident assertion at the August 2008 press briefing that, thanks to NIST's analysis, "the reason for the collapse of World Trade Center 7 is no longer a mystery."[97] Far from solving the mystery of WTC 7's collapse, NIST has—by continuing to provide a non-demolition theory of this collapse while admitting that it involved over two seconds of complete free fall—built an absolute mystery into the official explanation.

Sunder also needs to be asked whether he still stands by his statement, made on that same occasion, that "science is really behind what we have said."[98] If he still believes this, why are all of NIST's previous claims that its analysis is "consistent with physical principles" missing in the final version of its report?

These claims had to be removed, of course, because Sunder and his fellow scientists at NIST know that the 2.25-second period of free fall they have admitted is *not* consistent with physical principles. Outdoing the cartoon mentioned in Chapter 2, these NIST scientists presented 606 pages of descriptions, testimonies, photographs, graphs, analyses, mathematical formulae, and explanations, after which they in effect said on page 607: "Then a miracle happens."

The Compact Debris Pile

Having shown that NIST's theory of progressive collapse cannot do justice to the actual collapse of WTC 7, as observed on videos, I will conclude this chapter by showing that this theory also cannot explain the result: a very compact debris pile, no more than two stories high, that was almost entirely within the building's footprint. (Photos showing this very tidy pile of rubble, situated cleanly between the neighboring buildings, are available on the internet.[99])

Phillip Tompkins, whose comment to NIST about its picture of the collapse was quoted above, also drew attention to this problem, writing: "I do not see how [NIST] explains the contents of the pile at the end of the collapse. Where and in what condition were all the long core columns?"[100]

I myself had raised this problem—about all of the columns, not only the core columns—in an earlier book. Having quoted the statement by *New York Times* writer James Glanz that, if the collapse of WTC 7 had not been overshadowed by that of the Twin Towers, it would have been "a mystery that... would probably have captured the attention of the city and the world,"[101] I wrote:

> One of the biggest elements of this mystery is how this 47-story building's 81 columns—24 core and 57 perimeter columns—could have collapsed into a very compact pile of rubble without being sliced by explosives.[102]

My statement contained two errors: First, although there were indeed 24 interior columns, only 21 of them were *core* columns (the other three—Columns 79, 80, and 81—were in the eastern region of the building); second, there were 58 perimeter (exterior) columns, not 57, hence a total of 82 columns.[103] Correcting these two errors does not, however, affect the problem raised by my statement: Given the existence of all those columns, how could virtually all of the debris from the collapse have ended up in the building's footprint?

Here is the problem: WTC 7 was 610 feet high, so each column was 610 feet long. According to NIST's theory, the columns all buckled between the 7th and 14th floors,[104] after which "the entire building above the buckled-column region moved downward as a single unit."[105] Even if all of the columns buckled exactly at the 14th floor, the unbroken sections from the upper 33 floors would have been 429 feet long (each floor was 13 feet high).

Could these 429-foot-long columns have all come down into WTC 7's footprint? The building, which had a trapezoidal shape, was 247 feet long on the south side, 329 feet long on the north side, and about 150 feet on the east and west sides.[106] So even if all the columns had been placed in the middle of the footprint with their ends pointing east and west, they would not have fit within the footprint.

The columns, moreover, would not have come down so neatly. Many would have fallen outside the footprint in various directions, blocking the streets and destroying numerous nearby buildings, especially the Federal Building and the New York Telephone Building, which were very close to WTC 7.[107] That, however, did not happen—which means that the columns must have been broken into smaller segments before they came down.

The compact pile of debris that resulted from the collapse of WTC 7 is what would be expected from the kind of controlled demolition known as "implosion," in which explosives are used to cut the steel columns in the right places and in the right order to make the building fold in on itself. During an interview in 1996, Stacey Loizeaux—daughter of Mark Loizeaux, the president of Controlled Demolition, Inc.—explained how it is done:

> Depending on the height of the structure, we'll work on a couple different floors—usually anywhere from two to six. The taller the building, the higher we work. We only really need to work on the first two floors, because you can make the building come down that way. But we work on several upper floors to help fragment debris for the contractor, so all the debris ends up in small, manageable pieces.[108]

There is, accordingly, an obvious explanation for the fact that WTC 7 collapsed into a relatively small pile of debris, with "small, manageable pieces" of steel. This is the same explanation that would account for the melted and sulfidized steel, the thermite residue in the dust, the reports of explosions in the building, and the rapid, straight-down collapse of the building, with over two seconds of absolute free fall. This is, in other words, the explanation that scientists guided by Occam's razor would have chosen.

NIST, however, refused to entertain this obvious explanation. As a result, it could not explain why the area surrounding the site of WTC 7 was not littered with 82 columns that were each at least 429 feet long. It simply ignores the problem, evidently hoping that no one—at least no one who matters, such as the press or the next administration's Department of Justice—would notice.

* * *

Every aspect of NIST's theory of a fire-induced global collapse of WTC 7, we have seen, depends on implausible claims and outright fabrications. Its theory of weakened floor beams depends on implausible steel temperatures, which in turn depend on implausible fire temperatures and durations. Its theory of thermally induced girder failure depends on two cases of fraud: denying the existence of shear studs and fabricating a "differential thermal expansion" in its computer simulation by heating the steel beams but not the floor slabs. Its theory of how thermally expanded beams wreaked havoc presupposes an implausible amount of elongation.

And yet, even with all of these fabrications and implausibilities, NIST ends up with a theory that cannot explain several obvious features of WTC 7's collapse: that the building's roofline remained essentially horizontal, that its upper floors came down in free fall for over two seconds, and that its debris ended up in a tidy pile, with most of it contained within the building's footprint.

CONCLUSION:
NIST'S WTC 7 REPORT AS
UNSCIENTIFIC AND FALSE

NIST's lead investigator, Shyam Sunder, announced with great bravado at his August 2008 press briefing that, although the reason for the collapse of WTC 7 had been a mystery, NIST had solved this mystery. Science, he added, was solidly behind NIST's explanation. We have seen, however, that there are abundant reasons to consider NIST's explanation both unscientific and false.

In this conclusion, I first summarize the major ways in which NIST's report on WTC 7 is unscientific. Next, pointing out that much of the evidence showing NIST's report to be unscientific also shows it to be false, I reflect on the importance of this fact.

1. NIST'S WTC 7 REPORT AS UNSCIENTIFIC: A SUMMARY

NIST's report on WTC 7 is not, as we have seen, merely "unscientific" in a loose sense of that term. Rather, its authors have committed *scientific fraud* in the strict sense by ignoring, falsifying, and fabricating evidence.

Ignoring Evidence
The amount of relevant evidence ignored by NIST is impressive. In Chapter 4, we saw, NIST ignores various kinds of physical evidence, including:

· Evidence of squibs in videos of the collapse;
· Video evidence that a vertical row of windows was blown out just as the building began to collapse;
· Various reports of molten steel or iron in the debris;
· The report by three professors from Worcester Polytechnic Institute

(WPI), contained in an appendix to the FEMA report, that a piece of steel recovered from WTC 7 had been sulfidized, vaporized, and oxidized;

· Professor Abolhassan Astaneh-Asl's report that a steel I-beam from WTC 7 had been partially vaporized;

· Evidence from inextinguishable and long-lasting fires that materials in the rubble pile were providing their own fuel and oxidant;

· Reports by Professor Thomas Cahill and the EPA of particles in the air that should not have been there (assuming the official account of the destruction of the WTC);

· Reports by three groups of scientists revealing particles in the WTC dust that could have been produced only by extremely high temperatures, including the temperatures needed to melt molybdenum (2,623°C [4,753°F]) and to vaporize steel (2,861°C [5,182°F]);

· Evidence in particular for thermitic material, including nanothermite, in uncontaminated samples of WTC dust.

In Chapter 5, moreover, we saw that NIST ignored still more evidence, including:

· Testimonial evidence of explosions going off before and during the collapse;

· Testimonial evidence from two city officials—Michael Hess and Barry Jennings—of a huge explosion in WTC 7 after the South Tower was struck but before it collapsed;

· Testimonial evidence from Michael Hess, Matthys Levy, and Barry Jennings that fires started burning in WTC 7 about 9:30AM;

· Testimonial evidence from Barry Jennings that people had been killed in WTC 7 before he was rescued;

· Testimonial evidence of people reporting foreknowledge of WTC 7's collapse.

This is an enormous amount of relevant evidence. That NIST ignored it deliberately, not inadvertently, is shown by the fact that each ignored item has a common characteristic: It provides evidence that explosives were used to bring down WTC 7.

Fabricating and Falsifying Evidence
As mentioned in Chapter 2, it is difficult in relation to NIST's WTC 7 report to draw a clear line between fabrication and falsification. In reports

that are based on physical experiments, by contrast, a clear distinction *can* be made. As Richard Lewontin was quoted there as saying:

> Fabrication is the creation of claimed observations and facts out of whole cloth.... Falsification is the trimming and adjustment of the results of genuine experiments so that they come to be in agreement with a desired conclusion.[1]

As we have seen, however, NIST did not do any physical experiments (eschewing any study of the WTC dust, for example, and also denying that it had any recovered steel to work with—in spite of the pieces reported by Professor Astaneh-Asl and the WPI professors). Insofar as it performed "experiments," these were carried out on its computers.

For this reason, combined with the fact that NIST has not made its data available to other researchers, making a clear distinction between falsification and outright fabrication is difficult. Also, the distinction is not really important, as these two kinds of fraud, insofar as they *can* be distinguished, are equally serious. They are, therefore, treated together here.

The previous chapters provided reasons to believe that many of the claims made in NIST's WTC 7 report involve the fabrication or falsification of evidence, including:

· The claim that all of the fires in WTC 7 began at 10:28, when the North Tower fell (as distinct from starting either earlier or later);
· The claim that fires on several floors lasted for seven hours;
· The claim that fires began to appear "shortly after" the North Tower collapsed (even though the first visual evidence for fire appeared over an hour and a half later);
· The claim that a WTC security officer spotted a fire on the 7th floor at 10:30AM;
· The claim that eyewitnesses reported an 8th floor fire sometime between 12:15 and 2:30PM;
· The claim that Floors 11, 12, and 13 had far more combustibles than other floors;
· The claim that Floor 12 had a raging fire in its northeast corner at 5:00PM (even though its 2004 *Interim Report on WTC 7* showed that fire had left that corner by 3:00 and had completely burned out on the entire floor by 4:45);

· The claim that NIST could reasonably model the 13th floor fire on that of the 12th floor because NIST had little information about the layout of the 13th floor (even though a schematic of Floor 13 provided by NIST itself shows that it had information indicating that the floor would have had relatively few combustibles);

· The claim that it was justifiable for NIST to use the Case B variables for its simulations, rather than the variables that, according to its own simulator, were the most accurate;

· The claim that fires caused the air temperatures on some floors to reach 1,000 to 1,100°C (1,832 to 2,012°F);

· The claim that some of the steel beams reached 600 to 675°C (1,100 to 1,250°F);

· The claim, made at least implicitly, that structural steel's thermal conductivity is zero;

· The claim that, although each cubicle or office would have provided only enough fuel for 20 to 30 minutes of burning, the steel in some areas would have been subjected to four hours of heating;

· The claim that the girders in WTC 7 were not connected to the floors by shear studs (even though NIST's 2004 *Interim Report on WTC 7* said otherwise);

· The claim that some steel beams, when heated to temperatures approaching 400°C (752°F), expanded (elongated) enough to cause their 28 shear studs to fail and also to force a girder off of its support;

· The claim that "differential thermal heating" would have caused the shear studs anchoring the floor beams to the floor slabs to fail (even though this happened in the computer simulation only because NIST did not heat the simulated floor slab);

· The claim that the top portion of Column 79 would have begun a rapid descent 0.2 seconds after it buckled at a lower floor (even though it would have still had its lateral supports from the upper floors);

· The claim that NIST's simulation-based graphic of WTC 7's collapse matches the video images of the collapse "reasonably well" (even though the contorted roofline in the graphic looks nothing like the essentially horizontal roofline seen in the videos);

· The claim that the collapse of WTC 7 began 5.4 seconds before the roofline reached the level of the 29th floor (even though the roofline was immobile during the first 1.5 seconds of this period);

· The claim in NIST's Draft Report, and hence at its August 2008 press briefing, that WTC 7 had not entered into free fall (even though simple measurements, using the video evidence, showed that it had);

· The implicit claim of NIST's Final Report that the now-acknowledged 2.25 seconds of free fall does not contradict its theory of a "fire-induced progressive collapse" (even though Shyam Sunder had explained in his August technical briefing why this theory would not allow for free fall);

· The implicit claim that the collapse of WTC 7 almost entirely into its own footprint, with no several-hundred-foot-long columns falling on other buildings and into the streets, is consistent with NIST's non-demolition theory of the collapse, according to which explosives did not cut the columns into short segments.

Whether we classify these claims as fabrications or falsifications, they add up to an enormous amount of fraud. The hypothesis that they might instead be due simply to incompetence can be ruled out by the fact that all of these claims share one obvious characteristic: They all support NIST's attempt to provide a non-demolition explanation of WTC 7's collapse.

Other Violations of Scientific Principles

The starting point of NIST's investigation, in which it *refused to begin with the most likely hypothesis*, was also the starting point for all of its other violations. Although there were many reasons to assume that WTC 7 was brought down by controlled demolition, NIST's lead investigator, Shyam Sunder, claimed that this hypothesis was "not credible enough to justify a careful investigation."[2] Instead, NIST declared: "The challenge was to determine if a fire-induced floor system failure could occur in WTC 7 under an ordinary building contents fire."[3] So although every collapse of steel-framed high-rise buildings that had occurred before or after September 11, 2001, had been brought about by explosives, which means that none of them had been induced by fire, NIST determined that, in this case, the fire hypothesis was the most credible one.

The claim that this is what NIST really determined is, of course, simply not believable. The only plausible explanation for NIST's behavior is that, as an agency of the Bush–Cheney administration's Commerce Department, it had to exclude, and even try to discredit, the view that WTC 7 was brought down by explosives. This means that NIST, in restricting itself to the fire hypothesis, was violating the most general formal principle of scientific work: *Extra-scientific considerations should not be allowed to determine conclusions.*

By rejecting the controlled demolition hypothesis, NIST was also violating *Occam's razor*, according to which, if there are two explanations that are equally adequate, the simplest one should be chosen. In this case, of course, the two competing hypotheses were not even close to being equally adequate, because NIST, to advocate its fire hypothesis, had to ignore much of the relevant evidence. But even if NIST had come up with explanations for all of the ignored evidence, it would have needed one explanation for the melted steel, another for the inextinguishable fires, another for the unusual particles in the air, another for the particles in the dust that appear to have required extremely high temperatures, another for the apparent nanothermite residue in the dust, and still others for the testimonial evidence about explosions. The result would have been an extremely complex hypothesis. But all of these phenomena can be explained by one and the same hypothesis, namely, that explosives, including nanothermite, were used to demolish WTC 7.

By rejecting and seeking to discredit this hypothesis, NIST was also led to violate the *prohibition against straw-man arguments*. The most obvious example is NIST's argument that, if explosive material had been used, it would have been RDX. But NIST also created a straw-man version of the argument that the sulfidized steel found at the site provides evidence of a sulfur-containing incendiary or explosive.

NIST's report also, especially in its claims about fire and steel temperatures, violates the principle that *prima facie implausible claims should not be made without good reasons*. Part of offering a good reason, we saw in Chapter 2, would be providing extraordinarily good evidence to back up such claims. The evidence presented by NIST for its prima facie implausible claims, however, is extraordinarily weak.

NIST's refusal of the demolition explanation also led it to an even more serious problem: its violation of the principle that scientists *should not affirm an unprecedented cause for a familiar occurrence without good reasons*. Sunder's vague claim that NIST did not find the demolition hypothesis credible does not constitute a "good reason."

NIST's refusal to begin with the most likely hypothesis led it, still more seriously, down a path that forced it, at the end, to make *a claim implying that fundamental laws of physics had been violated.* This is the claim that, although WTC 7's columns had not been simultaneously removed by explosives, the building came down vertically in free fall for over two seconds. After over 600 pages of explanations, simulations, and graphics, NIST resorted to saying, in effect, that a miracle had occurred.

Peer Review

Chapter 2 articulated one more principle: *scientific work should be reviewed by peers before it is published.* Because this principle is different in kind from the others—it concerns not the content of a report but the process of preparing one for publication—it is here discussed separately.

NIST's WTC team did not submit its report to peers in the scientific community to be reviewed before publication. In not doing this, NIST ignored the recommendation of Dr. James Quintiere, someone it should have taken seriously. A professor of Fire Protection Engineering at the University of Maryland, Quintiere was a member of the advisory committee for NIST's WTC project. This was a natural assignment, as he had previously been employed in NIST's fire program for nineteen years, the final years of which he served as Chief of the Fire Science Division.

In a lecture on the WTC investigations at the 2007 World Fire Safety Conference, Quintiere said:

> I wish that there would be a peer review of this.... I think all the records that NIST has assembled should be archived. I would really like to see someone else take a look at what they've done; both structurally and from a fire point of view.[4]

In an interview later that same year, Quintiere repeated his call, saying:

> I think there should be a full airing of the NIST analyses and results with questions raised by the public before an impartial panel judging the completeness and accuracy of their results. In other words, peer review with accountability to a national body. That should determine whether further investigation is needed.[5]

But NIST did not take the advice of the former head of its Fire Science Division. There was no peer-review process, and NIST certainly did not submit its results to an impartial panel empowered to judge their "completeness and accuracy" and to decide, on the basis of that judgment, whether "further investigation [was] needed."

The authors of the NIST report on WTC 7 were evidently not responsible to anyone—except to the agencies mentioned by the former NIST employee quoted above in Chapter 1: the Department of Commerce, the National Security Agency, and President Bush's Office of Management and Budget.

NIST did, to be sure, meet from time to time with an advisory committee. But it evidently did not take any advice from its members or even answer their questions. Speaking directly to a NIST representative, Quintiere said:

> I found that throughout your whole investigation it was very diffi-cult to get a clear answer. And when anyone went to your advisory panel meetings or hearings, where they were given five minutes to make a statement; they could never ask any questions. And with all the commentary that I put in, and I spent many hours writing things…, I never received one formal reply.[6]

There was, finally, one other way in which NIST, without having a formal review process, might have had a process that could have prevented the publication of a report replete with scientific fraud. As we have seen, NIST first published a Draft for Public Comment, invit-ing anyone from the general public—thereby any scientists—who wished to send in comments to do so.

There were three signs, however, that NIST did not take this process seriously as an opportunity to improve its report. First, after spending several years to compile an over 700-page report, plus a briefer version, it gave people only three weeks to send in their comments.[7] Second, NIST evidently did not reply to any of the people who sent in comments.[8]

The third and most important sign that NIST did not take this process seriously is that it simply ignored most of the comments, even if they pointed out contradictions—such as the observation by James Gourley that NIST's graphic showing a raging fire on Floor 12 at 5:00PM is contradicted by the statement, made in NIST's 2004 *Interim*

Report on WTC 7, that the fire on this floor had burned out by 4:45PM. As far as I know, the only major change made by NIST in response to a comment was its acceptance of David Chandler's insistence that WTC 7 did enter into free fall, and this was a special case: Chandler had put a very effective video presentation on the internet and he also made an impressive statement at NIST's technical briefing, which was broadcast live.

In short, besides not having a formal peer-review process, NIST showed contempt for those who offered advice (with the exception of David Chandler), including people such as James Quintiere and Frank Greening, who, not believing that NIST was engaged in a cover-up operation, really wanted to help it produce a better report.

2. NIST'S WTC 7 REPORT AS FALSE

This book's subtitle makes two claims: NIST's WTC 7 report is unscientific, and it is false. Although the focus of the book has been on the former claim, the latter one is more important.

To explain this point, it is first necessary to make clear that the two claims really are distinct. Some readers might think that to show a report to be unscientific is *ipso facto* to prove it to be false. But a report might be based on a very unscientific approach and yet just happen to reach conclusions that are close to the truth of the matter. Likewise, a report might be based on excellent scientific work and nevertheless reach a false conclusion, perhaps because of information unknowable to the researchers at the time. Answering the question of whether a report is scientific or unscientific does not, therefore, necessarily settle the question of whether its conclusions are basically true or false.

Although in some cases the former question is more important, the latter question—the question of truth—is far more important in relation to NIST's WTC 7 report. If this report were terribly unscientific and yet basically true—if WTC 7 did, in fact, come down because of a fire-induced collapse—not much would follow, except that NIST should hire better scientists. But if NIST's conclusion is false, because WTC 7 was demolished with explosives of some sort, this fact is of overwhelming importance, regardless of how good or bad NIST's scientific work was.

Why NIST's Conclusion about WTC 7 Can Be Called False

Postponing for a moment the question of why it would be so important, let us ask whether the conclusion of NIST's WTC 7 report—-that WTC 7 was brought down by fire—might conceivably be true even though NIST's report is, from a scientific point of view, a travesty. The answer is that this is *not* conceivable, because much of the evidence used to demonstrate the unscientific nature of NIST's report serves equally well to show the falsity of any fire-theory of WTC 7's collapse.

This is the case, for example, with Chapter 4's evidence of particles in the air, the rubble, and the dust that cannot be explained apart from the use of explosives. It was surely because NIST's scientists knew this that they had to ignore all of this evidence.

The same is true of Chapter 5's testimonial evidence about explosions in WTC 7, especially the explosions in the morning reported by Barry Jennings. There is simply no conceivable explanation of those explosions that would be consistent with the official line, according to which WTC 7 came down as a result of the North Tower's collapse at 10:28. This would explain why NIST and then the BBC went to such lengths to distort the timeline of Jennings' testimony.

A complete list of further reasons to call NIST's WTC 7 report false—as well as unscientific—would include:

· Evidence that, instead of all starting at 10:28, some fires in WTC 7 started before, and others started after, that time;

· Evidence that neither fires nor steel beams became nearly as hot as NIST claims;

· Evidence for the falsity of both of NIST's claims about shear stud failure—that the shear studs connecting beams to the floor slabs failed because of differential thermal heating, and that the girder shear studs simply failed to exist;

· The fact that a fire-based collapse, which if even possible would necessarily be a "progressive collapse," could not possibly mimic the collapse of WTC 7 as seen on videos, in which the building comes straight down with its roofline remaining essentially horizontal;

· The fact that, even if otherwise possible, the collapse of a steel-framed building that was not produced by using explosives could not possibly enter free fall, even for a second or two;

· The fact that, even if otherwise possible, the collapse of a steel-framed high-rise building, assuming that it did not result from the use of explosives to cut the steel columns into relatively short segments, could not possibly result in a short, compact debris pile essentially within the building's footprint;

· The fact that the demolition theory of WTC 7's collapse, which NIST rejects, can explain all of the phenomena that NIST either ignored or inadequately explained.

In the case of NIST's WTC 7 report, in other words, to show it to be unscientific is also to show it to be false. I turn next to the question of why this conclusion is of great importance.

Why the Falsity of NIST's WTC 7 Report Is Important

The fact that NIST's report on WTC 7 is false implies, in the first place, that Muslim terrorists were not responsible for the collapse of this building (by flying an airliner into the North Tower, the collapse of which started fires in WTC 7). Instead, WTC 7 must have been brought down by domestic terrorists with the ability to plant explosives in it and then to orchestrate a cover-up.

If WTC 7 was demolished by such well-connected domestic terrorists, moreover, then the Twin Towers, which—after the initial explosions at the top—also came straight down in virtual free fall, must also have been brought down by explosives planted by these same terrorists. Indeed, the evidence in the dust and rubble that WTC 7 was demolished by explosives is equally evidence that the same is true of the Twin Towers.

Furthermore, once we see that the Twin Towers came down because of explosives, not because of the airplane impacts and the resulting fires, we can also see that the whole story about the airliners is irrelevant to the destruction of the World Trade Center: This destruction could have been carried out equally well without the airplane impacts. The only difference would be that it would have been more obvious that the buildings were victims of controlled demolition.

Finally, once people see that Muslim hijackers played no essential role in the destruction of the World Trade Center, they are likely to become open to evidence that the entire official account of 9/11, according to which America was attacked by al-Qaeda terrorists, is false. And once people become open to examining such evidence, they will find that it shows every part of the official story to be false.

To support this claim, I am here reprinting most of a little article of mine entitled "21 Reasons to Question the Official Story about 9/11" (I have included only 15 of them, because the final 6 deal with points already made in the present book). Although the points are stated very briefly, they include the pages in my previous 9/11 book, *The New Pearl Harbor Revisited* (NPHR),[9] where the issues are discussed much more extensively.

(1) Although the official account of 9/11 claims that Osama bin Laden ordered the attacks, the FBI does not list 9/11 as one of the terrorist acts for which he is wanted and has admitted that it "has no hard evidence connecting Bin Laden to 9/11" (NPHR 206–11).

(2) Although the official story holds that the four airliners were hijacked by devout Muslims ready to die as martyrs to earn a heavenly reward, Mohamed Atta and the other alleged hijackers regularly drank heavily, went to strip clubs, and paid for sex (NPHR 153–55).

(3) Many people reported having received cell phone calls from loved ones or flight attendants on the airliners, during which they were told that Middle Eastern hijackers had taken over the planes. One recipient, Deena Burnett, was certain that her husband had called her several times on his cell phone because she had recognized his number on her Caller ID. But the calls to Burnett and most of the other reported calls were made when the planes were above 30,000 feet, and evidence presented by the 9/11 truth movement showed that, given the technology of the time, cell phone calls from high-altitude airliners had been impossible. By the time the FBI presented a report on phone calls from the planes at the trial of Zacarias Moussaoui in 2006, it had changed its story, saying that there were only two cell phone calls from the flights, both from United 93 after it had descended to 5,000 feet (NPHR 111–17).

(4) US Solicitor General Ted Olson's claim that his wife, Barbara Olson, phoned him twice from AA 77, reporting that hijackers had taken it over, was also contradicted by this FBI report, which

says that the only call attempted by her was "unconnected" and hence lasted "0 seconds" (NPRH 60–62).

(5) Although decisive evidence that al-Qaeda was responsible for the attacks was reportedly found in Mohamed Atta's luggage—which allegedly failed to get loaded onto Flight 11 from a commuter flight that Atta took to Boston from Portland, Maine, that morning—this story was made up after the FBI's previous story had collapsed. According to that story, the evidence had been found in a Mitsubishi that Atta had left in [Boston's] Logan Airport parking lot and the trip to Portland was taken by Adnan and Ameer Bukhari. After the FBI learned that neither of the Bukharis had died on September 11, it simply declared that the trip to Portland was made by Atta and another al-Qaeda operative (NPHR 155–62).

(6) The other types of reputed evidence for Muslim hijackers—such as videos of al-Qaeda operatives at airports, passports discovered at the crash sites, and a headband discovered at the crash site of United 93—also show clear signs of having been fabricated (NPHR 170–73).

(7) In addition to the absence of evidence for hijackers on the planes, there is also evidence of their absence: If hijackers had broken into the cockpits, the pilots would have "squawked" the universal hijack code, an act that takes only a couple of seconds. But not one of the eight pilots on the four airliners did this (NPHR 175–79).

(8) Given standard operating procedures between the FAA and the military, according to which planes showing signs of an in-flight emergency are normally intercepted within about 10 minutes, the military's failure to intercept any of the flights implies that something, such as a stand-down order, prevented standard procedures from being carried out (NPHR 1–10, 81–84).

(9) Secretary of Transportation Norman Mineta reported an episode in which Vice President Cheney, while in the bunker under the White House, apparently confirmed a stand-down order at about 9:25AM, which was prior to the strike on the Pentagon. Another man has reported hearing members of LAX Security learn that a stand-down order had come from the "highest level of the White House" (NPHR 94–96).

(10) The 9/11 Commission did not mention Mineta's report, removed it from the Commission's video record of its hearings, and claimed that Cheney did not enter the shelter conference room until almost 10:00, which was at least 40 minutes later than he was really there, according to Mineta and several other witnesses, including Cheney's photographer (NPHR 91–94).

(11) The 9/11 Commission's timeline for Cheney that morning even contradicted what Cheney himself had told Tim Russert on "Meet the Press" September 16, just five days after 9/11 (NPHR 93).

(12) Hani Hanjour, known as a terrible pilot who could not safely fly even a single-engine airplane, could not possibly have executed the amazing trajectory reportedly taken by American Flight 77 in order to hit Wedge 1 of the Pentagon (NPHR 78–80).

(13) Wedge 1 would have been the least likely part of the Pentagon to be targeted by foreign terrorists, for several reasons: It was as far as possible from the offices of Rumsfeld and the top brass, whom Muslim terrorists presumably would have wanted to kill; it was the only part of the Pentagon that had been reinforced; the reconstruction was not finished, so there were relatively few people there; and it was the only part of the Pentagon that would have presented obstacles to a plane's flight path (NPHR 76–78).

(14) Contrary to the claim of Pentagon officials that they did not have the Pentagon evacuated because they had no way of knowing that an aircraft was approaching, a military E-4B—the Air Force's most advanced communications, command, and control airplane—was flying over the White House at the time. Also, although there can be no doubt about the identity of the plane, which was captured on video by CNN and others, the military has denied that it belonged to them (NPHR 96–98).

(15) The Secret Service, after learning that a second World Trade Center building had been attacked—which would have meant that terrorists were going after high-value targets—and that still other planes had apparently been hijacked, allowed President Bush to remain at the school in Sarasota, Florida, for another 30 minutes. It thereby revealed its foreknowledge that Bush would not be a target: If these had really been surprise attacks, the agents, fearing that a hijacked airliner was bearing down on the school, would have hustled Bush away. On the first anniversary of 9/11, the White House started telling a new story, according to which Bush, rather

than remaining in the classroom several minutes after Andrew Card whispered in his ear that a second WTC building had been hit, immediately got up and left the room. This lie was told in major newspapers and on MSNBC and ABC television (NPHR 129–31).[10]

If the truth about WTC 7 opens large numbers of people up to such evidence about 9/11, the whole "war on terror" will come to be widely seen as a sham. The Obama administration has dropped this language, but as this book was being readied for publication, it was still arguing that we had to continue the war in Afghanistan "to make sure that al-Qaeda cannot attack us again." The implication of the truth about WTC 7, however, is that al-Qaeda never attacked us in the first place. If we want to find those who did attack us on 9/11, we will need to look much closer to home.

If the truth about WTC 7, made evident by the many flaws in NIST's report, does lead to a much more widespread realization of the complete falsity of the official account of 9/11, then the 9/11 truth movement's prediction about WTC 7's collapse—that it would prove to be the Achilles' heel of the official account—will be borne out.

This widespread realization, however, will not produce changes in policy unless it leads to political action. An organization called Political Leaders for 9/11 Truth has been formed precisely for the purpose of trying to bring about such action. It has a petition that "ask[s] President Barack Obama to authorize a new, truly independent, investigation to determine what happened on 9/11."[11] The emergence of this organization represents a further evolution of the 9/11 truth movement.

At one time, this movement was ridiculed for having few scientists and other professionals in the relevant fields. In recent years, however, many organizations of such professionals have emerged, including Firefighters for 9/11 Truth, Intelligence Officers for 9/11 Truth, Pilots for 9/11 Truth, Scholars for 9/11 Truth, Scholars for 9/11 Truth and Justice, Scientific Panel Investigating Nine-Eleven, Veterans for 9/11 Truth, and Architects and Engineers for 9/11 Truth (the membership of which now includes over 700 licensed architects and engineers).[12] These organizations have been formed to spread the truth about 9/11, with "the truth" understood primarily as simply the fact that the official account of 9/11 is false.

More recently, however, professional organizations have emerged that, persuaded that this truth has now been established beyond any reasonable doubt (among people who have studied the evidence), are seeking to bring about public policy changes. These organizations include, in addition to Political Leaders for 9/11 Truth, also Lawyers for 9/11 Truth, Medical Professionals for 9/11 Truth, Religious Leaders for 9/11 Truth, and, most recently, Actors and Artists for 9/11 Truth.[13]

The obvious falsity of the official account of WTC 7 has already played a major role in the growth of this worldwide movement. It is my hope that the present book, by demonstrating beyond any doubt that the official account could not possibly be true, will help strengthen this movement to the point where it can bring about a new, truly independent investigation, which will publicly reveal the big lie that is the official account of 9/11, and thereby bring about a change of all the policies that have been based on this lie.

Might the National Science Foundation Expose NIST's Scientific Fraud?

In Chapter 2, while discussing the seriousness of scientific fraud, I pointed out that the National Science Foundation (NSF) has urged anyone aware of scientific fraud to contact its inspector general. Does this mean that there is a good chance that NSF would expose the massive fraud perpetrated by NIST? It might, except for a set of facts reported in Chapter 6: The director of NIST from 2001 until 2004—during which time the approach to be taken by NIST in its reports on the Twin Towers and WTC 7 was established—was Arden Bement. Then in 2004, President Bush, who had appointed Bement to the NIST post, made him the director of the NSF, a position he still held as this book went to press. It seems likely that President Obama, if he is to fulfil his pledge to "restore science to its rightful place," will need to appoint a new NSF director.

APPENDIX A
WHY DID EXPLOSIONS IN WTC 7 BEGIN
BY 9:30AM?

As we have seen, there is strong evidence not only for the proposition that WTC 7 was brought down by explosives but also for the conclusion that explosions began going off in this building by 9:30 in the morning. Barry Jennings consistently testified to this effect. On 9/11, Michael Hess spoke of an early morning explosion, and his later retraction is not credible. The attempts by NIST and the BBC to undermine these men's reports are too riddled with problems to be convincing. And even engineer Matthys Levy, who supports the view that fire brought WTC 7 down, said that fires had begun in this building at about 9:30.

But why, in light of the fact that WTC 7 was not brought down until 5:21PM, would explosives have started going off by 9:30AM?

It is true, of course, that demolitions of large buildings with many support columns normally begin with the use of explosives to take out some of the core columns, so that they do not need to be removed all at once just before the collapse. Having preliminary removals would be especially important in a surreptitious operation, in which the perpetrators hoped to disguise the fact that the building was brought down with explosives.

A preliminary removal of some of the core columns evidently occurred in the North Tower. According to North Tower janitor William Rodriguez, as we saw in Chapter 5, a massive explosion occurred in the basement of the North Tower at 8:46AM, shortly before this building was hit by a plane.[1] (Rodriguez's account has been corroborated by other North Tower employees.[2]) The time of this explosion, 8:46, was almost an hour and 45 minutes before the North Tower came down (at 10:28).

These facts provide a possible answer as to why there were explosions in WTC 7 long before it came down. They do not, however, provide a possible explanation for why they occurred *so long*—over eight hours—before the collapse.

An answer to this question lies beyond the scope of the main body of this book, which is limited to a critique of NIST's report on WTC 7, showing it to be unscientific and false.

But one of the reasons for calling this report unscientific and false is the fact that it ignored much of the relevant evidence, and the ignored evidence to which the most space was devoted was Jennings' testimony about explosions that evidently began by 9:30AM. The evidence for such explosions, especially the big explosion reported by Hess as well as Jennings, is very strong. But unless we have a possible explanation as to why explosions began so early, their occurrence will remain an anomaly—a brute fact that plays no intelligible role in any conceivable narrative of what happened that day. Indeed, if the occurrence of these reported early morning explosions cannot be made intelligible, many people will likely suspect that, in spite of the strong evidence for them, they did not really happen.

These explosions would be intelligible, however, if those who brought down WTC 7 had originally intended to bring it down in the morning.

Doing so would have certainly been more sensible than bringing it down late in the day, especially if the perpetrators had brought it down shortly after one of the Twin Towers had collapsed, when WTC 7 was still hidden from view by the resulting dust cloud. As we saw in Chapter 8, the dust cloud resulting from the North Tower's 10:28 collapse did not dissipate sufficiently to allow videographers to begin capturing images again until about 11:00AM. Accordingly, if WTC 7 had come down at, say, 10:45, we would probably have no videos showing that the collapse of this building started suddenly and then came straight down in virtual free fall, with over two seconds of the collapse being in *absolute* free fall. The collapse of this building could have been dismissed as a mystery—as having resulted from the collapse of the Twin Towers for some unknown reason. WTC 7 would not have become the official account's Achilles' heel. This would have been, therefore, the sensible plan. There are, moreover, some pieces of evidence suggesting that this was, in fact, the original plan.

One such piece of evidence is the fact that a CNN correspondent, Alan Dodds Frank, filed the following report from Lower Manhattan at 11:07AM:

[A]t a quarter to 11, there was another collapse or explosion following the 10:30 collapse of the second tower. And a firefighter who rushed by us estimated that 50 stories went down. The street filled with smoke. It was like a forest fire roaring down a canyon.[3]

Note that, although Frank first said "collapse *or* explosion," his later statement—that a firefighter "estimated that 50 stories went down"— shows that he did believe that a collapse had occurred.

Matthew Everett, who in 2008 discovered this report by Frank, wrote:

> What could have led Frank to make his incorrect report? Surely, even in the chaos of that morning, it would have been quite difficult for a mistaken report of another massive skyscraper coming down to have emerged out of nothing. Could the reason be that WTC 7 had originally been scheduled to be brought down (with explosives) at 10:45am? The incorrect information Frank reported had therefore been put out, by persons unknown, on the assumption that this would be the case. However, something—as yet unknown to us— happened that meant the demolition had to be delayed, and so Building 7 was not ready to be brought down until late that afternoon.[4]

Everett's suggestion, as this statement shows, is that Frank falsely reported that WTC 7 came down at 10:45 because someone, perhaps a firefighter, had been told that it would come down at this time.

Another piece of information discovered in 2008 led another student of 9/11, Jeremy Baker, to offer another explanation. Prior to 2008, Baker had already decided on the basis of a consideration mentioned above—namely, that it would have made more sense for the perpetrators to have brought the building down shortly after the collapse of the North Tower—that this was indeed what they had intended, but that the explosives failed to go off. WTC 7 was, Baker suggested in 2005, "a dud."[5] In 2007, alluding to "Murphy's law" (that "whatever *can* go wrong, *will* go wrong"), Baker wrote:

> Murphy was working overtime that day. Incredibly, the demolition system in WTC 7 simply did not respond as intended and the building defiantly remained intact.[6]

In 2008, besides learning of the report by Alan Dodds Frank, Baker discovered a short ABC News video clip, which had been taken some time between the collapse of the Twin Towers and that of WTC

7 and which showed "an enormous gash that extends down the center of WTC 7's facade from its roofline all the way to the ground."[7] (This video is available on the internet.[8]) Pointing out the significance of this discovery, Baker wrote:

> The force required to gouge the straight, clean, cavernous gash in WTC 7 represents a source of destructive power far greater than anything that was [supposedly] present that day and simply could not have been caused by falling debris.[9]

Then, connecting this discovery with his previous hypothesis, Baker asked:

> Could the straight, clean gouge in WTC 7's south face be an indication that a line of explosives running up the center of the building detonated but then stalled? Buildings typically have their centers blown out first when they are being demolished and this kind of failure is certainly not without precedent. Though this theory is surely speculative, is it unreasonable to ask the question: *What else could have caused such a bizarre wound in the south face of WTC 7?*

An alternative cause *was* suggested, Baker pointed out, by Larry Silverstein. In the course of offering his own explanation of what caused WTC 7 to collapse, Silverstein said:

> [One cause was] the falling antenna from the roof of the North Tower. That antenna came crashing down and sliced through the façade in the front of 7. As it did so, it ruptured fuel lines in the building… [which] caught fire. That fire started to burn and burned intensively the rest of the day.[10]

Baker was unimpressed by this explanation for the gash, saying: "[T]his ridiculous claim… is easily refuted by video evidence." Another problem with Silverstein's explanation is that his claim about fires in WTC 7 being fed by ruptured fuel lines was not even supported by NIST's final report.

Silverstein's statement was, nevertheless, of utmost importance, because the existence of the vertical gash down the front of WTC 7 had not previously been publicly acknowledged. Silverstein's statement provided confirmation, by one of the central supporters of the official story, of the existence of this gash.

The existence of this gash, visible on an ABC video and confirmed by Silverstein, led Baker to offer a new possible explanation of the report by CNN reporter Allan Dodds Frank, who had said, to recall:

[A]t a quarter to 11, there was another collapse or explosion following the 10:30 collapse of the second tower. And a firefighter who rushed by us estimated that 50 stories went down. The street filled with smoke.

Baker wrote:

Could this uncanny description from a firefighter be a hasty reference to the botched attempt to demolish Building 7? The time frame is perfect. The few explosives that did detonate would certainly have sounded like a "collapse or explosion".... A vertical column of explosives blasting out the full height of the building could very well have given someone the impression that "fifty stories" were going down.[11]

If, as Everett and Baker have suggested, WTC 7 was intended to go down at 10:45 that morning, this would have been about an hour and a quarter to an hour and a half after the first explosion reported by Hess and Jennings. The interval would, therefore, have been roughly the same as that between the collapse of the North Tower (at 10:28) and the explosion in the basement of that building reported by William Rodriguez and others (at 8:46).

The idea that there was a good-sized explosion in WTC 7 at 10:45 is also consistent with the testimony of Barry Jennings. As we saw in Chapter 5, the big explosion that knocked the landing out from under him when he was on the sixth floor is not the only explosion he reported. While describing his experience of waiting to be rescued after the firefighters had run away a second time (after the 10:28 collapse of the North Tower), he said: "All this time, I'm hearing all type of explosions. All this time, I'm hearing explosions."[12]

If WTC 7 remained standing at 10:45 because explosives that were supposed to bring it down at that time failed to do so, can we form a reasonable hypothesis about what happened next? Baker suggested that the building could be brought down only after "the conspirators... scrambled to bring the demolition system in WTC 7 back online."[13] This is a reasonable suggestion.

But it surely would have taken considerable time to discover the problem with the demolition system and then repair it. And that would have created a problem as to how the subsequent collapse of WTC 7 could be explained. Besides not having been hit by a plane, this building apparently, according to the available photographs and videos (as we saw in Chapter 8), did not even have any fires in it prior to 12:08PM (except for fires on lower floors, started by the explosion reported by Hess and Jennings, that had evidently burned out quickly).

Therefore, perhaps the perpetrators, having decided that the building needed to have more fires to provide a plausible explanation for its collapse, sent agents into the building to set fires (as well as agents to repair the demolition system). This hypothesis could explain the tension between NIST's claim, according to which all the fires started at 10:28, and the empirical evidence, which suggests that fires were started on various floors at various times throughout the afternoon.

The complex hypothesis presented in this appendix is just that, a hypothesis, which could only be verified, if at all, by an independent investigation employing subpoena power. But this hypothesis can certainly do what a hypothesis is supposed to do, namely, account for the various types of relevant facts. Besides explaining several things already mentioned—why WTC 7 did not come down until late in the afternoon (even though this allowed for videos showing that it must have been brought down with explosives), why explosions nevertheless began by about 9:30 in the morning, why there was a gash down the middle of the south side of the building, and why fires apparently started on various floors at various times in the afternoon—this hypothesis can also explain why Barry Jennings, calling from WTC 7 shortly after 9:03 to ask what he and Michael Hess should do, was told that they should leave the building *immediately*. This is a hypothesis that, accordingly, should be investigated.

APPENDIX B
ANOTHER TOWERING INFERNO THAT DID NOT COLLAPSE

In Chapter 10, we saw that NIST acknowledged the fact that fires in previous high-rise steel-framed buildings—such as the 1988 fire in the First Interstate Bank building in Los Angeles, which burned for 3.5 hours, and the 1991 fire in One Meridian Plaza in Philadelphia, which burned for 18 hours—did not cause them to collapse.[1] (NIST could have also mentioned the 2004 fire in Caracas, Venezuela, which raged for 17 hours in a 50-story building, completely gutting its top 20 floors.[2])

NIST sought to rationalize this fact, as we saw in Chapter 10, in terms of differences in design. One of the crucial differences, NIST claimed in its Draft Report, was the fact that, in all of those other buildings, shear studs had secured the girders to the floor slabs, whereas in WTC 7 the girders were not secured with shear studs.

In its Final Report, however, NIST admitted that its former claim was not true: There were no girder shear studs in one of the buildings that had remained standing. NIST's attempt to blame WTC 7's collapse on the absence of girder shear studs was thereby significantly undermined.

This attempt was then completely destroyed by the discovery, reported in Chapter 10, that NIST's claim about WTC 7 was also not true: Its 2004 report on WTC 7 showed that shear studs *had* connected its girders to the floors.

Accordingly, although NIST tried to mitigate the evident absurdity of its claim that WTC 7 was brought down by fire—in spite of the fact that fires in steel-framed high-rise buildings prior to 9/11 had never caused any of them to collapse, even though some of those fires had been much larger and longer-lasting than the fires in WTC 7—the NIST report served only to show that the absurdity of this claim could *not* be mitigated.

On February 9, 2009—less than three months after NIST had issued its Final Report—the absurdity of this claim was made dramatically evident by a fire in Beijing's Television Cultural Center (TVCC), a 500-foot-high steel-framed structure. This building consisted of a main tower plus two wings. The main tower was to be occupied by a luxury hotel, the Mandarin Oriental, so some news reports about the fire referred to the building by that name. The headline for the Associated Press story, for example, was: "Fire Rages at Beijing Mandarin Hotel."[3]

The fire, which was started by fireworks, evidently began about 7:30PM, quickly spread throughout the entire structure, and was not put out until early the next morning.[4] "The entire hotel building was engulfed in flames," said the Associated Press. "Flames were visible from the ground floor to the top floor of the large building," reported another story.[5] "Flames 20–30 feet high shot out of the building," reported Reuters, adding that the fire did not begin to abate until about midnight.[6] The all-engulfing nature of this fire is shown in videos available on the internet.[7]

The building's structure, however, was unaffected. "For all the ferocity of the fire that reached the top of the brand new cultural centre and hotel complex," the *Guardian* observed, "the structure of the building looked to be remarkably unscathed." This newspaper even highlighted this fact with its headline: "Beijing's Newest Skyscraper Survives Blaze."[8] A report on the aftermath, which accompanies a video showing the surviving structure, states: "Local sources say the structure of the building remains sound."[9]

The fires in the TVCC tower and WTC 7 were alike in one respect, namely, that the buildings in which they occurred were similar, being steel-framed structures of roughly the same height (the TVCC tower was approximately 500 feet high, WTC 7 approximately 600 feet), in which no sprinkler system was working on the floors on which fires occurred (in WTC 7, these were the lower floors; in the TVCC tower, these were all the floors, as the system had not yet been installed).

Otherwise, however, the fires were completely different. Whereas the TVCC fire engulfed the entire building, from top to bottom, WTC 7 had what NIST called "sustained fires" on only six of its 47 floors, and even these six floors were never entirely engulfed by fire. Also, whereas the TVCC fire endured for a long time—at least eight hours; one report says fifteen[10]—the fires on the six floors of WTC 7 evidently lasted, as we saw in Chapter 8, for periods ranging from 40 minutes to slightly over three hours. As a result, the thermal expansion and weakening of steel in WTC 7 would have been insignificant compared with the expansion and weakening in the TVCC tower.

This would be true even if we accepted NIST's unsubstantiated claim that the fires on these floors lasted for seven hours.

And yet, NIST would have us believe that the fires on those six floors of WTC 7 brought it down, whereas the all-engulfing fire in the Beijing building left it structurally unaffected. One might be forgiven for suspecting that this fire in Beijing, coming so soon after the appearance of NIST's Final Report on WTC 7, was arranged by the gods in order to drive home the absurdity of this report.

NOTES

Introduction

1 See David Ray Griffin, *The New Pearl Harbor Revisited: 9/11, the Cover-Up, and the Exposé* (Northampton: Olive Branch Press, 2008), esp. Ch. 6, "Continuing Obstructions and New Doubts about Hijackers," and Ch. 8, "9/11 Commission Falsehoods about Bin Laden, al-Qaeda, Pakistanis, and Saudis."

2 See ibid., Ch. 7, "Motives of US Officials: The Silence of the 9/11 Commission."

3 See David Ray Griffin, "Was America Attacked by Muslims on 9/11?" OpEdNews, September 9, 2008 (www.opednews.com/articles/Was-America-Attacked-by-Mu-by-David-Ray-Griffin-080909-536.html).

4 See, for example, Paul Joseph Watson, "BBC's 9/11 Yellow Journalism Backfires: Building 7 Becomes the Achilles Heel of the Official Conspiracy Theory," Prison Planet, March 5, 2007 (infowars.wordpress.com/2007/03/05/bbcs-911-yellow-journalism-backfires), and "WTC 7: The Smoking Gun of 9/11" (www.youtube.com/watch?v=MwSc7NPn8Ok).

5 See Architects and Engineers for 9/11 Truth (www.ae911truth.org) and *Journal of 9/11 Studies* (www.journalof911studies.com).

6 James Glanz, "Engineers Suspect Diesel Fuel in Collapse of 7 World Trade Center," *New York Times*, November 29, 2001 (query.nytimes.com/gst/fullpage.html?res=9E02E3DE143DF93AA15752C1A9679C8B63&scp=1&sq=%20%22Engineers%20Suspect%20Diesel%20Fuel%22&st=cse).

7 As Australian scientist Frank Legge has written: "As no reports have come to light of any steel framed buildings collapsing due to fire, and as all steel framed buildings which had collapsed had done so due to explosive demolition, the logical way to have started the investigation of this surprising event would have been to question whether explosives had been used. This apparently did not occur. The organizations carrying out the investigations clearly selectively collected data and contrived arguments to support the fire theory and ignored contradictory evidence. This is in defiance of the scientific method." Frank Legge, "9/11: Proof of Explosive Demolition without Calculations," *Journal of 9/11 Studies* 15 (September 2007) (journalof911studies.com/volume/2007/LeggeVerticalCollapseWTC7_6.pdf).

8 After the collapse of WTC 7, CBS anchor Dan Rather said: "Amazing…. For the third time today, it's reminiscent of those pictures we've all seen too much on television before, where a building was deliberately destroyed by well-placed dynamite to knock it down" (www.youtube.com/watch?v=Nvx904dAw0o). Likewise, Al Jones, a reporter for WINS NYC News Radio, said: "I turned in time to see what looked like a skyscraper implosion—

looked like it had been done by a demolition crew.... So that's number one, number two, and now number seven that have come down from this explosion" (see *911 Eyewitness* [video.google.com/videoplay?docid= 654607577 34339444] at 28:25). Referring only to the Twin Towers, CNN's Lou Dobbs said: "[T]his was the result of something that was planned.... [I]t's not accidental that the first tower just happened to collapse and then the second tower just happened to collapse in exactly the same way. How they accomplished this, we don't know," CNN, September 11, 2001 (forum.nashuatelegraph.com/viewtopic.php?t=164&sid=afe1027e2c958e2ee72 2310cc126ddc1).

9 Glanz, "Engineers Suspect Diesel Fuel."

10 See "A Word about Our Poll of American Thinking Toward the 9/11 Terrorist Attacks," Zogby International, May 24, 2006 (www.zogby.com/features/features.dbm?ID=231).

11 Daniel Hofnung, Patriots Question 9/11 (patriotsquestion911.com/engineers.html#Dhofnung).

12 Chester W. Gearhart, Patriots Question 9/11 (patriotsquestion911.com/engineers.html#Gearhart).

13 "Danish Scientist Niels Harrit, on Nanothermite in the WTC Dust (English subtitles)," YouTube, April 6, 2009 (www.youtube.com/watch?v=8_tf25lx_3o).

14 This interview is in "Controlled Demolition Expert and WTC7" (www.youtube.com/watch?v=877gr6xtQIc). This video clip is an excerpt from a 2006 Dutch television program entitled "Zembla Investigates 9/11 Theories" (cgi.omroep.nl/cgi-bin/streams?/tv/vara/zembla/bb.20060911.asf). A portion of it is contained in *Loose Change Final Cut.*

15 Patriots Question 9/11 (patriotsquestion911.com/engineers.html#Jowenko).

16 Australian scientist Frank Legge, providing a graph showing that "from the moment [the corner of the roof line nearest the viewer] starts to move the collapse of this corner is uniform and close to vertical free fall," added: "There is no sign of the slow start that would be expected if collapse was caused by the gradual softening of the steel." See "9/11: Acceleration Study Proves Explosive Demolition," *Journal of 9/11 Studies* 5 (November 2006) (journalof911studies.com/volume/200611/911-Acceleration-Study-Proves-Explosive-Demolition.pdf).

17 "This is an Orange," a video by Anthony Lawson (www.youtube.com/watch?v=Zv7BimVvEyk). The point is that if viewers would not accept the claim, even if made by federal officials, that an orange is an apple, they should not accept the claim that WTC 7 was brought down by fire.

18 See FEMA, *World Trade Center Building Performance Study* (www.fema.gov/pdf/library/fema403_ch5.pdf), Ch. 5, Sect. 6.2, "Probable Collapse Sequence."

19 "Progress Report on the NIST Building and Fire Investigation into the World Trade Center Disaster," National Institute of Standards and Technology (henceforth NIST), December 9, 2002 (www.fire.nist.gov/bfrlpubs/build03/PDF/b03040.pdf); "Progress Report on the Federal Building and Fire Safety Investigation of the World Trade Center Disaster," NIST, May 2003 (wtc.nist.gov/pubs/MediaUpdate%20_FINAL_ProgressReport051303.pdf).

20 *Interim Report on WTC 7*, NIST, June 2004 (wtc.nist.gov/progress_report_june04/appendixl.pdf).

21 "Answers to Frequently Asked Questions," NIST, August 30, 2006 (wtc.nist.gov/pubs/factsheets/faqs_8_2006.htm), Question 14.

22 "WTC 7 Collapse," NIST, April 5, 2005 (wtc.nist.gov/pubs/ WTC%20Part%20IIC%20-%20WTC%207%20Collapse%20Final.pdf).

23 Ibid., 6.

24 "9/11: Debunking the Myths," *Popular Mechanics*, March 2005.

25 Ibid.

26 David Dunbar and Brad Reagan, eds., *Debunking 9/11 Myths: Why Conspiracy Theories Can't Stand Up to the Facts: An In-Depth Investigation by Popular Mechanics*, (New York: Hearst Books, 2006), 53, 56.

27 Ibid., 53–54.

28 Ibid., 29.

29 Ibid., 53.

30 Ibid., 56.

31 Ibid., 58, quoting NIST, "WTC 7 Collapse" (the preliminary report of April 5, 2005).

32 Marc Jacobsen, "The Ground Zero Grassy Knoll," *New York Magazine*, March 20, 2006 (nymag.com/news/features/16464 or infowars.net/articles/september2007/110907Knoll.htm).

33 As this sentence illustrates, the lowercase title "final report" is used to differentiate NIST's final report on WTC 7, which was issued in 2008, from its preliminary reports, which were issued in earlier years. The uppercase title "Final Report" is used to designate the final version of the 2008 final report, which was released in November 2008, in distinction from the first draft of this final report, which is referred to variously as the "Draft for Public Comment," the "Draft Report," or the "Draft version" of the final report.

34 NIST NCSTAR 1A, *Final Report on the Collapse of World Trade Center Building 7* (brief report), November 2008 (wtc.nist.gov/NCSTAR1/PDF/NCSTAR%201A.pdf), xxxii. This document is henceforth cited simply as NIST NCSTAR 1A, which will always refer, unless otherwise designated, to the final (November 2008) version (as distinct from the Draft for Public Comment, which was issued in August 2008).

35 Ibid., xxxvii.

36 "The Conspiracy Files: 9/11," BBC, February 18, 2007. It can be

viewed on 9/11 Blogger (www.911blogger.com) or YouTube (www.youtube.com/watch?v=vR3aNMLkahc).

37 Shyam Sunder, "Opening Statement," NIST Press Briefing, August 21, 2008 (wtc.nist.gov/media/opening_remarks_082108.html); henceforth cited simply as Sunder, "Opening Statement." For a C-SPAN video of this opening statement and the ensuing discussion, see "NIST WTC 7 Report—Press Briefing 8/21/08 pt 1" (www.youtube.com/watch?v=iSnjyZNYlW8); there are five more parts.

38 Ibid.

39 Quoted in "Report: Fire, Not Bombs, Leveled WTC 7 Building," *USA Today*, August 21, 2008 (www.usatoday.com/news/nation/2008-08-21-wtc-nist_N.htm).

40 Ordinary thermite, which is classified as an incendiary, is to be distinguished from nanothermite (sometimes called "superthermite"), which is qualitatively different, being classified as a "high explosive" (as well as an incendiary).

41 *Military Dictionary*, quoted at Answers.com (www.answers.com/topic/shaped-charge).

PART I
Chapter One

1 "A Word about Our Poll of American Thinking toward the 9/11 Terrorist Attacks," Zogby International, May 24, 2006 (www.zogby.com/features/features.dbm?ID=231).

2 Thomas Hargrove and Guido H. Stempel III, "Anti-Government Anger Spurs 9/11 Conspiracy Belief," NewsPolls.org, Scripps Survey Research Center at Ohio University, August 2, 2006 (newspolls.org/story.php?story_id=55). The title of the story, incidentally, is the pollster's inference, not a conclusion supported by the answers.

3 Lev Grossman, "Why the 9/11 Conspiracies Won't Go Away," *Time*, September 3, 2006 (www.time.com/time/magazine/printout/0,8816,1531304,00.html).

4 WorldPublicOpinion.org, "International Poll: No Consensus On Who Was Behind 9/11," September 10, 2008 (www.worldpublicopinion.org/pipa/pdf/sep08/WPO_911_Sep08_pr.pdf).

5 Ibid.

6 Ibid.

7 Architects and Engineers for 9/11 Truth (www.ae911truth.org).

8 Firefighters for 9/11 Truth (firefightersfor911truth.org).

9 Lawyers for 9/11 Truth (l911t.com).

10 Intelligence Officers for 9/11 Truth (IO911Truth.org).

11 Medical Professionals for 9/11 Truth (mp911truth.org).

12 Pilots for 9/11 Truth (pilotsfor911truth.org).

13 Political Leaders for 9/11 Truth (pl911truth.com).

14 Religious Leaders for 9/11 Truth (rl911truth.org).

15 Scholars for 9/11 Truth (911scholars.org).

16 Scholars for 9/11 Truth and Justice (stj911.org).

17 Veterans for 9/11 Truth (v911t.org).

18 Scientific Panel Investigating Nine-Eleven: Physics 911 (physics911.net).

19 Patriots Question 9/11 (patriotsquestion911.com).

20 The official report on the Pentagon attack, which was issued by the American Society of Civil Engineers in January 2003, is titled *Pentagon Building Performance Report* (fire.nist.gov/bfrlpubs/build03/PDF/b03017.pdf_). Although I do not discuss it here, the point at hand—that none of the 9/11 investigations were independent from the Bush–Cheney administration— applies equally to it. For a good critique, see Sami Yli-Karjanmaa, "The ASCE's Pentagon Building Performance Report: Arrogant Deception—Or an Attempt to Expose a Cover-up?" (www.kolumbus.fi/sy-k/pentagon/asce_en.htm). I have discussed problems with the official view of the Pentagon, which is supported by the ASCE's building performance report, in *Debunking 9/11 Debunking: An Answer to Popular Mechanics and Other Defenders of the Official Conspiracy Theory* (Northampton: Olive Branch Press, 2007), 261–88, and *The New Pearl Harbor Revisited: 9/11, the Cover-Up, and the Exposé* (Northampton: Olive Branch Press, 2008), 59–109.

21 See "Learning from 9/11: Understanding the Collapse of the World Trade Center," House of Representatives' Committee on Science, Hearing, March 6, 2002, under "Background" (web.archive.org/web/20021128021952/ http://commdocs.house.gov/committees/science/hsy77747.000/hsy77747_0.htm).

22 Bill Manning, "Selling Out the Investigation," *Fire Engineering*, January 2002 (www.globalresearch.ca/articles/MAN309A.html).

23 Philip Shenon, *The Commission: The Uncensored History of the 9/11 Investigation* (New York: Twelve, 2008), 69, 83.

24 Ibid., 389–90.

25 James Mann, *Rise of the Vulcans: The History of Bush's War Cabinet* (New York: Viking, 2004), 316, 331.

26 I have called this a doctrine of "preemptive-preventive war" in "The Bush Doctrine & *The 9/11 Commission Report*: Both Authored by Philip Zelikow," Information Clearing House, October 4, 2008 (www.information-clearinghouse.info/article20947.htm).

27 Shenon, *The Commission*, 170.

28 Ibid., 106–07, 175–76.

29 Thomas H. Kean and Lee H. Hamilton (with Benjamin Rhodes), *Without Precedent: The Inside Story of the 9/11 Commission* (New York: Alfred A. Knopf, 2006), 269–70.

30 Ibid., 116.

31 Shenon, *The Commission*, 388–89.

32 Ibid.

33 See Margie Burns, "Secrecy Surrounds a Bush Brother's Role in 9/11 Security," *American Reporter* 9/2021 (January 20, 2003), which reported that the company's present CEO, Barry McDaniel, said that the company had had an ongoing contract to provide security at the World Trade Center "up to the day the buildings fell down." Marvin Bush's role in the company is mentioned in Craig Unger, *House of Bush, House of Saud: The Secret Relationship between the World's Two Most Powerful Dynasties* (New York: Scribner, 2004), 249.

34 *Politics and Science in the Bush Administration*, US House of Representatives Committee on Government Reform—Minority Staff, Special Investigation Division, prepared for Henry A. Waxman, August 2003, updated November 13, 2003 (www.democrats.reform.house.gov/features/politics_and_science/pdfs/pdf_poli tics_and_science_rep.pdf), Executive Summary, 3.

35 In July 2004, the Union of Concerned Scientists published an updated version of this document, with a slightly different title, *Scientific Integrity in Policy Making: Further Investigation of the Bush Administration's Misuse of Science* (www.ucsusa.org/assets/documents/scientific_integrity/scientific_integrity_in_ policy_making_july_2004_1.pdf). For a review of the original version of this document by one of our leading scientists, see the first half of Richard C. Lewontin, "Dishonesty in Science," *New York Review of Books*, November 18, 2004 (www.nybooks.com/articles/17563).

36 Originally called "Restoring Scientific Integrity in Policymaking: Scientists Sign-on Statement," this document by the Union of Concerned Scientists is now titled "2004 Scientist Statement on Restoring Scientific Integrity to Federal Policy Making" (www.ucsusa.org/scientific_integrity/abuses_of_science/scientists-sign-on-statement.html).

37 Gareth Cook and Tatsha Robertson, "Another Worry: Asbestos Dust Poses Threat to Rescue Crews," *Boston Globe*, September 14, 2001 (www.boston.com/news/packages/underattack/globe_stories/0914/Asbestos_du st_poses_threat_to_rescue_crews+.shtml).

38 EPA, Press Release, September 18, 2001 (www.cpa.gov/wtc/stories/headline_091801.htm).

39 "Insider: EPA Lied About WTC Air," CBS News, September 8, 2006 (www.cbsnews.com/stories/2006/09/08/earlyshow/main1985804.shtml).

40 John Heilprin, Associated Press, "White House Edited EPA's 9/11 Reports," *Seattle Post-Intelligencer*, August 23, 2003 (seattlepi.nwsource.com/national/136350_epa23.html), citing "EPA's Response to the World Trade Center Collapse," EPA Office of Inspector General, August 21, 2003, Executive Summary and Chapter 2 (www.mindfully.org/Air/2003/EPA-WTC-OIG-Evaluation21aug03.htm).

41 The figure of 60 percent was given in "Dust and Disease," *News Hour with Jim Lehrer*, PBS, November 21, 2006; the discussion is available as "60 Percent of Ground Zero Workers Sick" (www.youtube.com/watch?v= qdS4X4r28Og). The 70 percent figure was given in Anthony DePalma, "Illness Persisting in 9/11 Workers, Big Study Finds," *New York Times*, September 6, 2006 (www.nytimes.com/2006/09/06/nyregion/06health.html?ex= 1315195200&en=aaf1bba2e01bc497&ei=5088&partner=rssnyt&emc=rss), which said: "Roughly 70 percent of nearly 10,000 workers tested at Mount Sinai from 2002 to 2004 reported that they had new or substantially worsened respiratory problems while or after working at ground zero."

42 "Dust and Disease."

43 Kristen Lombardi, "Death by Dust: The Frightening Link between the 9-11 Toxic Cloud and Cancer," *Village Voice*, November 28, 2006 (villagevoice.com/news/0648%2Clombardi%2C75156%2C2.html; also at www.911truth.org/article.php?story=20061204132809573); "Dust and Disease"(see note 41); *Dust to Dust: The Health Effects of 9/11*, a documentary film (www.informationliberation.com/index.php?id=21627; also at video.google.com/videoplay?docid=9137295628446919478&ei=ll7 pSMnmDYz-qAO54OGYCw&q=%22dust+to+dust%22).

44 Jerry Mazza, "9/11's Second Round of Slaughter," Online Journal, January 16, 2008 (onlinejournal.com/artman/publish/article_2845.shtml), a review of the documentary film, *Dust to Dust* (see previous note).

45 "NIST Whistleblower," October 1, 2007 (georgewashington.blogspot.com/2007/10/former-nist-employee-blows-whistle.html).

46 Email letter from Steven Jones, December 3, 2007.

47 "NIST Whistleblower."

48 Ibid.

49 Shenon, *The Commission*, 15, 19, 29, 175–76. I discuss this issue in *The New Pearl Harbor Revisited*, 249–51.

50 Sunder, "Opening Statement."

51 See especially my *Debunking 9/11 Debunking*, Chs. 3 and 4.

Chapter Two

1 "Barack Obama's Inaugural Address," *New York Times*, January 20, 2009 (www.nytimes.com/2009/01/20/us/politics/20text-obama.html).

2 Richard Jones, "Obama Signs Presidential Memorandum on Scientific Integrity," AIP Bulletin of Science Policy News, American Institute of Physics, March 9, 2009 (www.aip.org/fyi/2009/028.html).

3 Saswato R. Das, "Scientific Fraud: There's More of It Than You Think," *International Herald Tribune*, June 30, 2008 (www.iht.com/articles/2008/06/30/opinion/eddas.php?page=1).

4 William Broad and Nicholas Wade, *Betrayers of the Truth: Fraud and*

Deceit in the Halls of Science (Oxford: Oxford University Press, 1985).

5 Horace Freeland Judson, *The Great Betrayal: Fraud in Science* (New York: Harcourt, 2004).

6 "What is Research Misconduct?" National Science Foundation, Office of Inspector General, *New Research Misconduct Policies* (www.nsf.gov/oig/session.pdf). Although this document is undated, internal evidence suggests that it was published in 2001.

7 Ibid.

8 Richard C. Lewontin, "Dishonesty in Science," *New York Review of Books*, November 18, 2004 (www.nybooks.com/articles/17563).

9 Ibid.

10 Eric Douglass, "The NIST WTC Investigation: How Real Was The Simulation?" *Journal of 9/11 Studies* 6 (December 2006) (www.journalof911studies.com/volume/200612/NIST-WTC-Investigation.pdf): 1–28, at 8.

11 NIST NCSTAR 1-9, *Structural Fire Response and Probable Collapse Sequence of World Trade Center Building 7*, November 2008: 378. (This is the long version of NIST's Final Report on WTC 7 and consists of two volumes. For the URLs, see under Frequently Cited Works.) Henceforth cited simply as NIST NCSTAR 1-9.

12 "What is Research Misconduct?"

13 Judson, *The Great Betrayal*, 172.

14 See Peter Lipton, *Inference to the Best Explanation*, 2nd ed. (New York: Routledge, 2004).

15 Alfred North Whitehead, *Science and the Modern World* (1925; New York: Free Press, 1967), 187.

16 Quoted in "Report: Fire, Not Bombs, Leveled WTC 7 Building," *USA Today*, August 21, 2008.

17 Former NIST employee, letter to Steven Jones, November 30, 2007.

18 Quoted in William Kneale and Martha Kneale, *The Development of Logic* (London: Oxford University Press, 1962), 243.

19 "Occam's Razor," Principia Cybernetica Web (pespmc1.vub.ac.be/occamraz.html).

20 See David Ray Griffin, *Religion and Scientific Naturalism: Overcoming the Conflicts* (Albany: State University of New York Press, 2000), and *Two Great Truths: A New Synthesis of Scientific Naturalism and Christian Faith* (Louisville: Westminster John Knox Press, 2004).

21 This cartoon can be seen on the internet at www.sciencecartoonsplus.com/pages/gallery.php.

22 I refer to philosopher Daniel E. Dennett's discussion in his *Consciousness Explained* (Boston: Little, Brown & Co., 1991), which I examine in my *Unsnarling the World-Knot: Consciousness, Freedom, and the Mind-Body Problem* (Berkeley & Los Angeles: University of California Press, 1998; reprint, Eugene:

Wipf and Stock, 2008), 69–70.

23 See Judson, *The Great Betrayal*, and also Lawrence K. Altman, M.D., "For Science's Gatekeepers, a Credibility Gap," *New York Times*, May 2, 2006 (www.nytimes.com/2006/05/02/health/02docs.htm).

Chapter Three

1 Sunder, "Opening Statement."

2 Most of these features are brought out in a video entitled "This is an Orange" (www.youtube.com/watch?v=Zv7BimVvEyk).

3 National Fire Protection Association, *921 Guide for Fire and Explosion Investigations*, 2001 edition, Section 18.3.2.

4 NIST NCSTAR 1A: xxxi.

5 NCSTAR 1-9: 330.

6 Email from Steven Jones, October 10, 2005.

7 Obeid made this statement on a BBC program entitled *The Conspiracy Files: 9/11—The Third Tower*, BBC News, July 6, 2008 (www.911blogger.com/node/16541).

8 John D. Wyndham, Letter to NIST, September 7, 2008 (wtc.nist.gov/comments08/johnWyndhamwtc7comments.pdf).

9 Ibid.

10 Sunder, "Opening Statement."

11 Eric Lipton, "Fire, Not Explosives, Felled 3rd Tower on 9/11, Report Says," *New York Times*, August 22, 2008 (www.nytimes.com/2008/08/22/nyregion/22wtccnd.html?_r=1&ei=5070&emc=eta1&oref=slogin).

Chapter Four

1 See "WTC 7 Collapse" (www.youtube.com/watch?v=LD06SAf0p9A); "9/11: Dan Rather Says WTC Collapses Look like Demolitions" (www.youtube.com/watch?v=Nvx904dAw0o&feature=PlayList&p=3D30132C 75A35683&index=0&playnext=1); and "Footage of Buildings Getting Demolished" (www.youtube.com/watch?v=PtHl3c7E9RY).

2 "Second Tallest Building Ever Imploded" (www.youtube.com/watch?v=8U4erFzhC-U); "Wachovia Building Implosion" (www.youtube.com/watch?v=tx1UiFZ6rWY).

3 Kevin Ryan, "High Velocity Bursts of Debris From Point-Like Sources in the WTC Towers," *Journal of 9/11 Studies* 13 (July 2007) (www.journalof911studies.com/volume/2007/Ryan_HVBD.pdf), 1.

4 Jones referred to "the three photos at the top of http://911research.wtc7.net/talks/wtc/videos.html"; he also mentioned "a video close-up of the southwest corner of WTC 7 as this corner begins its steady drop to the ground: http://st12.startlogic.com/~xenonpup/

Flashes/squibs_along_southwest_corner.htm," but this second URL no longer works. For similar footage, see "WTC-7 Collapse Footage Shows Unmistakable Demolition Charges" (www.youtube.com/watch?v=2EadoxWXpgY).

5 Steven E. Jones, "Why Indeed Did the WTC Buildings Collapse?" David Ray Griffin and Peter Dale Scott, eds., *9/11 and American Empire: Intellectuals Speak Out* (Northampton: Olive Branch Press, 2006), 33–62. For visual evidence of his points, Jones referred readers to the online version of his paper, which had been posted on his BYU website. But Jones was later forced to remove the paper from that site. The online version can now be read—under the title "Why Indeed Did the World Trade Center Buildings Completely Collapse?" in the *Journal of 9/11 Studies* 3 (September 2006) (www.journalof911studies.com/volume/200609/WhyIndeedDidtheWorldTrad eCenterBuildingsCompletelyCollapse.pdf): 1–48. The quotation is from page 43 of the original article.

6 "Answers to Frequently Asked Questions," NIST, August 2006 (wtc.nist.gov/pubs/factsheets/faqs_8_2006.htm), Question 4.

7 9/11 oral history of James Curran, December 30, 2001 (graphics8.nytimes.com/packages/pdf/nyregion/20050812_WTC_GRAPHIC/ 9110412.PDF), 10–11.

8 Ryan, "High Velocity Bursts of Debris," 6.

9 Jones, "Why Indeed Did the WTC Buildings Collapse?"

10 For a video showing squibs moving up near the top of WTC 7, see www.911hardfacts.com/video/video_10_wtc_7_squibs.mov.

11 NIST's document entitled "Questions and Answers about the NIST WTC 7 Investigation" (www.nist.gov/public_affairs/factsheet/ wtc_qa_082108.html) first appeared in August 2008; an updated version appeared December 18, 2008; then another updated version appeared April 21, 2009 (www.nist.gov/public_affairs/factsheet/wtc_qa_082108.html).

12 This video can be seen at YouTube (www.youtube.com/ watch?v=G5UM9q7cj7I), at VodPod (vodpod.com/watch/1134985-new-911-building-7-collapse-clearly-shows-demolition), and at Disclose.tv (www.disclose.tv/action/viewvideo/11576/New_911_Building_7_Collapse_Cl early_Shows_Demoliti). It is also available as "New Building 7 Collapse Video Clearly Shows Demolition" (justgetthere.us/blog/archives/New-Building-7-Collapse-Video-Clearly-Shows-Demolition.html).

13 James Williams, "WTC a Structural Success," *SEAU News: The Newsletter of the Structural Engineers Association of Utah*, October 2001 (www.seau.org/SEAUNews-2001-10.pdf).

14 The quotations from Loizeaux and Tully are in "Molten Steel Flowed Under Ground Zero for Months after 9/11," George Washington's Blog, April 28, 2008 (www.nogw.com/download2/%5E8_molten_steel.pdf).

15 Lou Lumenick, "Unflinching Look Among the Ruins," *New York Post*, March 3, 2004.

16 Ruvolo is quoted in the DVD "Collateral Damages" (www.allhands-fire.com/page/AHF/PROD/ISIS-COLL). For just this segment plus discussion, see Steve Watson, "Firefighter Describes 'Molten Metal' at Ground Zero, Like a 'Foundry,'" Inforwars.net, November 17, 2006 (www.infowars.com/articles/sept11/firefighter_describes_molten_metal_ground_zero_like_foundry.htm). Most helpful is a seven-minute clip from *Loose Change Final Cut*, entitled "911stealth Bush's Legacy: Meteorites From Molten Iron. NIST Denial" (www.youtube.com/watch?v=U9nE372Ymc4).

17 Jennifer Lin, "Recovery Worker Reflects on Months Spent at Ground Zero," Knight Ridder, May 29, 2002 (www.whatreallyhappened.com/ground_zero_fires.html).

18 Trudy Walsh, "Handheld APP Eased Recovery Tasks," *Government Computer News* 21.27a, September 11, 2002 (www.gcn.com/21_27a/news/19930-1.html).

19 Tom Arterburn, "D-Day: NY Sanitation Workers' Challenge of a Lifetime," *Waste Age*, April 1, 2002 (wasteage.com/mag/waste_dday_ny_sanitation).

20 Quoted in Francesca Lyman, "Messages in the Dust: What Are the Lessons of the Environmental Health Response to the Terrorist Attacks of September 11?" National Environmental Health Association, September 2003 (www.neha.org/9-11%20report/index-The.html).

21 "Mobilizing Public Health: Turning Terror's Tide with Science," *Magazine of Johns Hopkins Public Health,* Late Fall 2001 (www.jhsph.edu/Publications/Special/Welch.htm).

22 The melting point of iron is 1,538°C (2,800°F). Steel, as an alloy, comes in different grades, with a range of melting points, depending on the percent of carbon (which lowers the melting point), from 1,371°C (2,500°F) to 1,482°C (2,700° F); see "Melting Points of Metals" (www.uniweld.com/catalog/alloys/alloys_melting.htm).

23 NIST NCSTAR 1-9: 395.

24 Thomas Eagar, "The Collapse: An Engineer's Perspective," which is part of "Why the Towers Fell," NOVA, April 30, 2002 (eagar.mit.edu/EagarPapers/Eagar185supplement1.pdf).

25 NIST NCSTAR 1, *Final Report of the Collapse of the World Trade Center Towers*, September 2005 (wtc.nist.gov/NCSTAR1/PDF/NCSTAR%201.pdf), 90.

26 "Answers to Frequently Asked Questions," NIST, August 30, 2006 (wtc.nist.gov/pubs/factsheets/faqs_8_2006.htm), Question 13.

27 Jones, "Why Indeed Did the WTC Buildings Collapse?" 37.

28 "NIST Engineer, John Gross, Denies the Existance [*sic*] of Molten Steel" (video.google.com/videoplay?docid=-7180303712325092501&hl=en). For a more extensive treatment, complete with evidence, see a clip from *Loose Change Final Cut* entitled "911stealth Bush's Legacy: Meteorites From Molten Iron. NIST Denial" (www.youtube.com/watch?v=U9nE372Ymc4).

29 Answers to Frequently Asked Questions," NIST, August 30, 2006 (wtc.nist.gov/pubs/factsheets/faqs_8_2006.htm), Question 13.

30 Jones, "Why Indeed Did the WTC Buildings Collapse?"39.

31 "Answers to Frequently Asked Questions," NIST, August 30, 2006.

32 James Fetzer, "Why NIST Hasn't Answered Its Own Questions," Scholars for 9/11 Truth, October 5, 2006 (www.scholarsfor911truth.org/Why-NIST-hasn%27t-Answered-its-own-Questions.html).

33 RJ Lee Group, "WTC Dust Signature," Expert Report, May 2004 (www.nyenvirolaw.org/WTC/130%20Liberty%20Street/Mike%20Davis%20L MDC%20130%20Liberty%20Documents/Signature%20of%20WTC%20du st/WTCDustSignature_ExpertReport.051304.1646.mp.pdf), 5.

34 RJ Lee Group, "WTC Dust Signature Study: Composition and Morphology," December 2003 (www.nyenvirolaw.org/ WTC/130%20Liberty%20Street/Mike%20Davis%20LMDC%20130%20Lib erty%20Documents/Signature%20of%20WTC%20dust/WTC%20Dust%20 Signature.Composition%20and%20Morphology.Final.pdf).

35 RJ Lee Group, "WTC Dust Signature" (2004), 2, 4.

36 Ibid., 11.

37 RJ Lee Group, "WTC Dust Signature Study" (2003), 5. This report suggested that these particles were common in the WTC dust "because of the fire that accompanied the WTC Event." It did not discuss the issue, however, of how the fire could have melted iron.

38 Ibid., 24, 17.

39 RJ Lee Group, "WTC Dust Signature" (2004), 11.

40 RJ Lee Group, "WTC Dust Signature Study" (2003), 5.

41 WebElements: The Periodic Table on the Web (www.webelements.com/iron/physics.html).

42 RJ Lee Group, "WTC Dust Signature" (2004), 12.

43 RJ Lee Group, "WTC Dust Signature Study" (2003), 21.

44 WebElements: The Periodic Table on the Web (www.webelements.com/lead/physics.html).

45 This is one respect in which the final RJ Lee report made a stronger statement than the 2003 version: The earlier report had not spoken of *extremely* high temperatures.

46 Heather A. Lowers and Gregory P. Meeker, US Geological Survey, US Department of the Interior, "Particle Atlas of World Trade Center Dust," 2005 (pubs.usgs.gov/of/2005/1165/508OF05-1165.html).

47 To see enlarged photos of the iron-rich particles, go to pubs.usgs.gov/ of/2005/1165/table_1.html, then click on "Yes" at the far right of the lines for "Iron-03" and "Iron-04."

48 Steven E. Jones et al., "Extremely High Temperatures during the World Trade Center Destruction," *Journal of 9/11 Studies* 19 (January 2008) (journalof911studies.com/articles/WTCHighTemp2.pdf), 8.

49 The question was sent to NIST by Shane Geiger. NIST's email reply, dated August 29, 2008, was sent by Gail Porter. My thanks to Geiger for sharing this email exchange.

50 Jones et al., 1–2.

51 WebElements: The Periodic Table on the Web (www.webelements.com/molybdenum/physics.html).

52 Jones et al., "Extremely High Temperatures," 4.

53 James Glanz and Eric Lipton, "A Search for Clues in Towers' Collapse," *New York Times*, February 2, 2002 (*query*.nytimes.com/gst/ fullpage.html?res=9C04E0DE153DF931A35751C0A9649C8B63).

54 Steven E. Jones, "Revisiting 9/11/2001: Applying the Scientific Method," *Journal of 9/11 Studies* 11, May 2007 (www.journalof911 studies.com/volume/200704/JonesWTC911SciMethod.pdf), 73.

55 They provided a brief analysis of a section of a steel beam from WTC 7 in "An Initial Microstructural Analysis of A36 Steel from WTC Building 7," *JOM: Journal of the Minerals, Metals, and Materials* 53.12 (2001), 18 (www.tms.org/pubs/journals/JOM/0112/Biederman/Biederman-0112.html).

56 Joan Killough-Miller, "The 'Deep Mystery' of Melted Steel," *WPI Transformations*, Spring 2002 (www.wpi.edu/News/Transformations/2002Spring/steel.html).

57 NIST NCSTAR 1-9: 324.

58 Killough-Miller, "The 'Deep Mystery' of Melted Steel."

59 James Glanz, "Engineers Suspect Diesel Fuel in Collapse of 7 World Trade Center," *New York Times*, November 29, 2001 (www.nytimes.com/ 2001/11/29/nyregion/29TOWE.html). I have here quoted Glanz's paraphrase of Barnett's statement.

60 See Kenneth Change, "Scarred Steel Holds Clues, and Remedies," *New York Times*, October 2, 2001 (query.nytimes.com/gst/ fullpage.html?res=9B05E6DC123DF931A35753C1A9679C8B63).

61 Jonathan Barnett, Ronald R. Biederman, and Richard D. Sisson, Jr., "Limited Metallurgical Examination," FEMA, *World Trade Center Building Performance Study*, May 2002, Appendix C (wtc.nist.gov/media/AppendixC-fema403_apc.pdf).

62 Ibid.

63 Email letter from Kevin Ryan, October 16, 2008.

64 Email letter from Steven Jones, October 17, 2008.

65 Personal communication from Niels Harrit, May 8, 2009.

66 "Eutectic" is a word of Greek origin meaning "easily melted." A eutectic mixture is one in which the proportions are such that "the melting point is as low as possible" and in which, at the melting point, "all the constituents crystallize simultaneously." This "simultaneous crystallization of a eutectic mixture" is called a eutectic reaction ("Eutectic Point," Wikipedia [en.wikipedia.org/wiki/Eutectic]).

67 Jones, "Revisiting 9/11/2001," 81.

68 Ibid.

69 Barnett, Biederman, and Sisson, "Limited Metallurgical Examination," C-13.

70 Dr. Arden L. Bement, Jr., Testimony before the House Science Committee Hearing on "The Investigation of the World Trade Center Collapse," May 1, 2002 (911research.wtc7.net/cache/wtc/official/nist/bement.htm). In the quoted statement, the name "FEMA" replaces "BPAT," which is the abbreviation for "Building Performance Assessment Team," the name of the ASCE team that prepared this report for FEMA.

71 NIST, "WTC 7 Collapse," April 5, 2005 (wtc.nist.gov/pubs/WTC%20Part%20IIC%20-%20WTC%207%20Collapse%20Final.pdf), 6.

72 NIST NCSTAR 1-9: 324.

73 NIST NCSTAR 1A: xxxii.

74 See Kenneth Change, "Scarred Steel Holds Clues, and Remedies."

75 Kevin R. Ryan, "The NIST WTC 7 Report: Bush Science Reaches Its Peak," 911Truth.org, September 11, 2008 (www.911truth.org/article.php?story=20080911073516447). Ryan referred to Steven E. Jones et al., "Extremely High Temperatures during the World Trade Center Destruction."

76 "Questions and Answers about the NIST WTC 7 Investigation," updated April 21, 2009 (www.nist.gov/public_affairs/factsheet/wtc_qa_082108.html).

77 NIST NCSTAR 1-3, "Mechanical and Metallurgical Analysis of Structural Steel," by Frank W. Gayle, et al., September 2005 (fire.nist.gov/bfrlpubs/fire05/PDF/f05130.pdf), iii.

78 Skeptosis (pseudonym), Letter to NIST, September 15, 2008 (wtc.nist.gov/comments08/skeptosiswtc7comments.pdf). This comment can also be read in "Two Comments re: NIST's draft of NCSTAR 1A," which is posted at a blog by Skeptosis, "Missing Steel" (missingsteel.blogspot.com). The quoted passage is from NIST NCSTAR 1-3 (2005): 113.

79 Sunder here referred to *The Conspiracy Files: 9/11—The Third Tower*, July 6, 2008 (available at www.911blogger.com/node/16541), which is discussed in the following chapter in relation to the testimony of Michael Hess and Barry Jennings.

80 "WTC 7 Technical Briefing," NIST, August 26, 2008 (event.on24.com/eventRegistration/EventLobbyServlet?target=lobby.jsp&eventid=118145), at 2:09:15. Henceforth cited as "WTC 7 Technical Briefing."

81 "Questions and Answers about the NIST WTC 7 Investigation," NIST, updated April 21, 2009 (www.nist.gov/public_affairs/factsheet/wtc_qa_082108.html).

82 Roger K. Fulmer, "New York City World Trade Center Disaster

Deployment," *The Prospector* (US Army Corps of Engineers, Sacramento District), January 2002 (web.archive.org/web/20040405130825/ www.911research.wtc7.net/cache/wtc/groundzero/usace_deployment.html).

83 Jonathan Beard, "Ground Zero's Fires Still Burning," *New Scientist*, December 3, 2001 (www.newscientist.com/article.ns?id=dn1634).

84 Trimpe's account, titled "The Chaplain's Tale," was originally published in 2002 in the *Times-Herald Record*; it is now cited in "Molten Metal Workers Reported Molten Metal in Ground Zero Rubble" (911research.wtc7.net/wtc/evidence/moltensteel.html#ref5).

85 Trudy Walsh, "Handheld APP Eased Recovery Tasks," *Government Computer News* 21.27a, September 11, 2002 (911research.wtc7.net/cache/wtc/evidence/gcn_handheldapp.html).

86 Beard, "Ground Zero's Fires Still Burning"; Eric Lipton and Andrew C. Revkin, "The Firefighters: With Water and Sweat, Fighting the Most Stubborn Fire," *New York Times*, November 19, 2001 (911research.wtc7.net/cache/wtc/evidence/gcn_handheldapp.html).

87 Quoted in Sylvia Wright, "Air Quality Scientists Release WTC Study," Dateline UC Davis, February 15, 2002 (www-dateline.ucdavis.edu/ 021502/DL_wtc.html).

88 Thomas A. Cahill et al., "Very Fine Aerosols from the World Trade Center Collapse Piles: Anaerobic Incineration?" September 12, 2003 (209.85.173.132/search?q=cache:aWx4Gz8EkzIJ:delta.ucdavis.edu/WTC%25 20aersols%2520ACS%25202003.ppt+%E2%80%9CWe+see+very+fine+aeros ols+typical+of+combustion+temperatures+far+higher%22%22&cd=1&hl=en &ct=clnk&gl=ca). I am indebted to Ryan et al., "Environmental Anomalies" (see note 93 below), for these references to Cahill's work.

89 Sylvia Wright, "Air Quality Scientists Release WTC Study"; the wording is her paraphrase.

90 Thomas A. Cahill et al., "Analysis of Aerosols from the World Trade Center Collapse Site, New York, October 2 to October 30, 2001," *Aerosol Science and Technology* 38/2 (February 2004):165–83 (www.informaworld.com/smpp/section?content=a714044206&fulltext=71324 0928).

91 Wright, "Air Quality Scientists Release WTC Study."

92 Laurie Garrett, "Full Effects of WTC Pollution May Never Be Known," *Newsday*, September 14, 2003 (www.newsday.com/news/health/ny-hsair0911,0,471193.story?coll=ny-homepageright-Area).

93 Kevin R. Ryan, James R. Gourley, and Steven E. Jones, "Environmental Anomalies at the World Trade Center: Evidence for Energetic Materials," *Environmentalist* 29 (2009): 56–63, at 57. (This paper had been published online [www.springerlink.com/content/f67q6272583h86n4/fulltext.html] by the *Environmentalist* on August 4, 2008.)

94 Ibid., 58.

95 Ibid., 58, 56; emphasis added.

96 John Gartner, "Military Reloads with Nanotech," *Technology Review*, January 21, 2005 (www.technologyreview.com/nanotech/14105).

97 For an explanation for laypeople, see "A Basic Chemistry Lesson with Dr. Niels Harrit: Transcript from Visibility 9-11," April 15, 2009 (www.911truth.org/article.php?story=20090415231352441).

98 Gartner, "Military Reloads with Nanotech."

99 Kevin Ryan, "The Top Ten Connections between NIST and Nano-Thermites," *Journal of 9/11 Studies* 22 (July 2008) (www.journalof911studies.com/volume/2008/Ryan_NIST_and_Nano-1.pdf), citing T. M. Tillotson, R. L. Simpson, and L.W. Hrubesh, "Nanostructure High Explosives Using Sol-gel Chemistry," Lawrence Livermore National Laboratory, 1999 (https://e-reports-ext.llnl.gov/pdf/238334.pdf).

100 Jim Hoffman, "Explosives Found in World Trade Center Dust: Scientists Discover Both Residues and Unignited Fragments of Nano-Engineered Thermitic Pyrotechnics in Debris from the Twin Towers" (911research.wtc7.net/essays/thermite/explosive_residues.html).

101 Ryan, Gourley, and Jones, "Environmental Anomalies," 62; Steven Jones, "Revisiting 9/11/2001," 73; Ryan, "The Top Ten Connections."

102 Lawrence Livermore National Laboratory, "Nanoscale Chemistry Yields Better Explosives," *Science and Technology Review*, October 2000 (www.llnl.gov/str/RSimpson.html).

103 Ryan, "The Top Ten Connections."

104 A. E. Gash et al., "Energetic Nanocomposites with Sol-gel Chemistry: Synthesis, Safety, and Characterization," Proceedings of the 29th International Pyrotechnics Seminar, Westminster, CO, July 14–19, 2002: 227–28. Although this paper is not online, the quoted statement is in "US Patent 6818081—Inorganic metal oxide/organic polymer nanocomposites and method thereof," November 16, 2004 (www.patentstorm.us/patents/6818081/fulltext.html).

105 Ryan, "The Top Ten Connections."

106 Kevin Ryan, "Another Amazing Coincidence Related to the WTC," 911Blogger.com, January 6, 2008 (www.911blogger.com/node/13272). Some of the evidence for this correlation is laid out by Ryan in this article.

107 Ryan, Gourley, and Jones, "Environmental Anomalies," 56.

108 Ibid., 61.

109 Ibid., 60, referring to M. Kidder et al., "Pore Size Effects in the Pyrolysis of 1,3-Diphenylpropane Confined in Mesoporous Silicas," Chemical Communications (Cambridge), November 21, 2003: 2804–05.

110 Ibid., 61.

111 Ibid., 59.

112 Jones et al., "Extremely High Temperatures during the World Trade Center Destruction," 4–5.

113 Ryan, Gourley, and Jones, "Environmental Anomalies," 62.

114 See "Zero: An Investigation Into 9/11—Part 3 of 10" (www.youtube.com/watch?v=eZLeDb9dJs0&feature=related), at 3:30.

115 Ryan, Gourley, and Jones, "Environmental Anomalies," 62.

116 Ibid.

117 Ibid., 58–59.

118 Niels H. Harrit, Jeffrey Farrer, Steven E. Jones, Kevin R. Ryan, Frank M. Legge, Daniel Farnsworth, Gregg Roberts, James R. Gourley, and Bradley R. Larsen, "Active Thermitic Material Observed in Dust from the 9/11 World Trade Center Catastrophe," *Open Chemical Physics Journal* 2 (2009): 7–31 (www.bentham.org/open/tocpj/openaccess2.htm). Immediately after the publication of this article, incidentally, the journal's editor-in-chief, Professor Marie-Paule Pileni of France, resigned. In response to critics who suggested that this resignation cast doubt on the scientific soundness of the paper, Professor Harrit prepared a statement explaining why it did not. It is posted as "Professor Pileni's Resignation" on a Danish website (videnskab.dk/content/dk/debat?personguid=8C55E167-347B-4AD1-8BF7-F50BA5754FAC&link=ShowProfile) and as "Niels Harrit: Professor Pileni's Resignation as Editor-in-Chief of the Open Chemical Physics Journal" on 9/11 Blogger, July 12, 2009 (911blogger.com/node/20614).

119 Harrit et al., "Active Thermitic Material," 17.

120 Ibid., 22.

121 Ibid., 12.

122 Ibid., 26, 29.

123 Ibid., 29.

124 Ibid., 10.

125 Ibid., 19.

126 Ibid., 29.

127 Ibid., 22, 29. Some critics, nevertheless, have claimed that the red side of the chips might simply be primer paint—even though this hypothesis has been ruled out still more decisively in the meantime by the discovery that, according to NIST, the primer paint used in the buildings contained a high percentage of zinc (NIST NCSTAR 1-3C (2005), Appendix D (wtc.nist.gov/NCSTAR1/PDF/NCSTAR%201-3C%20Appxs.pdf), which is not present in the red/gray chips. In response to these ongoing claims, Niels Harrit wrote a paper, "Why the Red/Gray Chips Are Not Primer Paint," posted at "Norwegian State Radio Initiates Public Debate on 9/11 Truth," From the Top of the World at the End of Time Blog, updated June 20, 2009 (zelikow.wordpress.com/2009/05/22/norwegian-state-radio-initiates-public-debate-on-911-truth/), scroll halfway down (Harrit's paper is also posted at Scholars for 9/11 Truth & Justice Blog, June 20, 2009 [stj911.org/blog/?p=325].) This Norwegian site also contains a response from Steven Jones to Professor Ola Nilsen of the University of Oslo, who had suggested the paint hypothesis. Jones's reply includes the following four points:

"(1) We have learned the composition of the 'corrosion inhibition' or primer paint actually used on the WTC towers from a NIST document; see attached paper by Prof. Niels Harrit…. We find that zinc, chromium and magnesium are significant components of the paint used—yet these elements are absent from the red material, as demonstrated in Figure 7 of our paper. Thus, the red chips cannot be the primer paint used. (2) On the other hand, the elements which are present in the red chips—namely aluminum, iron, oxygen, silicon, and carbon (Fig. 7)—are precisely those expected in formulations of nano-thermite as described in the literature and delineated in the paper. (3) Furthermore, iron oxide is found in grains approximately 100 nm across and aluminum in plate like structures about 40 nm thick—and these particles appear quite uniform and intimately mixed across the four separate samples. It is this ultra-fine, nano-scale structure of the Al and iron oxide in the red material that is emphasized in the paper, which we expect for nanothermite…. (4) The composition of any other paint used in the WTC must address the absence of common paint ingredients as well as the presence of those elements observed, and the nano-scale structure of the ingredients observed."

128 Harrit et al., "Active Thermitic Material," 29.

129 Ibid., 25.

130 Ibid., 29.

131 Ibid., 19.

132 Ibid., 26.

133 Ibid., 9.

134 "Interview with Dr. Harrit: Questions to Niels Harrit concerning the Study 'Active Thermitic Material Discovered in Dust from the 9/11 World Trade Center Catastrophe,'" gulli.news, May 24, 2009 (www.gulli.com/news/world-trade-center-destruction-2009-05-24).

135 Harrit et al., "Active Thermitic Material Observed," 29.

136 For an excellent explanation and analysis of the paper by Harrit and his colleagues, see Jim Hoffman, "Explosives Found in World Trade Center Dust: Scientists Discover Both Residues and Unignited Fragments of Nano-Engineered Thermitic Pyrotechnics in Debris from the Twin Towers" (911research.wtc7.net/essays/thermite/explosive_residues.html). Intelligible to readers who are neither physicists nor chemists, it begins with a section entitled "Aluminothermics 101."

137 "Danish Scientist Niels Harrit, on Nanothermite in the WTC Dust (English Subtitles)," April 6, 2009 (www.youtube.com/watch?v=8_tf25lx_3o).

138 Ibid.

139 "Interview with Dr. Harrit."

140 "Danish Scientist Niels Harrit."

141 Ibid.

142 "Answers to Frequently Asked Questions," NIST, Question 12.

143 "Questions and Answers about the NIST WTC 7 Investigation,"

NIST (www.nist.gov/public_affairs/factsheet/wtc_qa_082108.html).

144 "Request for Correction Submitted to NIST," *Journal of 9/11 Studies* 12 (June 2007) (www.journalof911studies.com/ volume/200704/RFCtoNIST-byMcIlvaineDoyleJonesRyanGageSTJ.pdf), 23. This letter was signed by Bob McIlvaine, Bill Doyle, Steven Jones, Kevin Ryan, Richard Gage, and Scholars for 9/11 Truth and Justice.

145 "Appeal Filed with NIST, Pursuant to Earlier Request for Correction," by James Gourley, Bob McIlvaine, Bill Doyle, Steven Jones, Kevin Ryan, Richard Gage, and Scholars for 9/11 Truth and Justice, *Journal of 9/11 Studies* 17 (November 2007) (www.journalof911studies.com/volume/ 2007/Appeal-LetterToNISTGourleyEtAl.pdf), 17.

146 Newsletter, Materials Engineering, Inc., Spring 1996 (www.materials-engr.com/ns96.html).

147 Ibid., quoted in "Appeal Filed with NIST," emphasis added by Gourley et al.

148 Ibid.

149 A C-SPAN video of this press briefing is available on YouTube in 6 parts, the first of which is "NIST WTC 7 Report—Press Briefing 8/21/08 pt 1" (www.youtube.com/watch?v=iSnjyZNYlW8). The exchange between Geiger and Sunder is in Part 6 (www.youtube.com/ watch?v=AgmAMr1NGak&NR=1). A transcription of most of this exchange (with slightly different wording) is available in Jim Hoffman's helpful essay, "Wake Up and Smell the Aluminothermic Nanocomposite Explosives: As Documentation of Thermitic Materials in the WTC Twin Towers Grows, Official Story Backers Ignore, Deny, Evade, and Dissemble," April 3, 2009 (Version 1.0), 9-11 Research (911research.wtc7.net/essays/thermite/explosives_evidence_timeline.html#wtc7_press_conference).

150 "NIST WTC 7 Report—Press Briefing 8/21/08 pt.1"

151 "WTC 7 Technical Briefing," at 2:10:35.

152 Ibid., at 2:08.

153 Barnett, Biederman, and Sisson, "Limited Metallurgical Examination."

154 Jones et al., "Extremely High Temperatures during the World Trade Center Destruction," 3.

155 Jones wrote: "Note that the iron-aluminum-sulfur spheres from MacKinlay's apartment contained very low calcium, so the sulfur is evidently not from gypsum" ("Revisiting 9/11/2001," 79).

156 See wtc.nist.gov/media/JonesWTC911SciMethod.pdf.

157 Email letter from Steven Jones, October 17, 2008.

158 Sunder, "Opening Statement."

159 "Appeal Filed with NIST," 14.

160 Jennifer Abel, "Theories of 9/11," *Hartford Advocate*, January 29, 2008 (www.hartfordadvocate.com/article.cfm?aid=5546).

161 National Fire Protection Association, *921 Guide for Fire and Explosion*

Investigations, 1998 edition, Section 12-2.4. To read this online, see Section 12-2.4 of "NFPA 921, Sections 12-2.1 through 12-6" (www.interfire.org/res_file/92112m.asp).

162 See ibid., Section 19.2.4, "Exotic Accelerants" and "Thermite Mixtures." Niels Harrit, explaining in an interview why the authorities should have looked for residue of thermitic material, said: "[W]hen there is a fire in the United States, which is suspicious or which is violent or which is unexpected, according to [an NPFA] regulation you should look for thermite—because you can use it for arson, and if you want to burn your house, this is the way to do it: You put in a thermitic reaction and you go on vacation and you can trigger it with your cell phone from long distance, if you wish. So this is routine for [the] FBI to look for remains of thermite. They do this very frequently, actually, but they didn't do it this time." This interview is available as "Nano-thermite Took Down the WTC?" posted at YouTube on July 9, 2009 (www.youtube.com/watch?v=4RNyaoYR3y0). The quoted statement is at 10:14–10:50.

163 Alfred North Whitehead, *Science and the Modern World* (1925; New York: Free Press, 1967), 187.

Chapter Five

1 NIST NCSTAR 1-9: 324.

2 NIST NCSTAR 1, *Final Report on the Collapse of the World Trade Center Towers*, September 2005 (wtc.nist.gov/NCSTAR1/PDF/NCSTAR%201.pdf), xxxviii, 146, 176.

3 These oral testimonies are available at a *New York Times* website (graphics8.nytimes.com/packages/html/nyregion/20050812_WTC_GRAPHIC/met_WTC_histories_full_01.html).

4 David Ray Griffin, "Explosive Testimony: Revelations about the Twin Towers in the 9/11 Oral Histories," 911Truth.org, January 18, 2006 (www.911truth.org/article.php?story=20060118104223192); reprinted as Chap. 2 of Griffin, *Christian Faith and the Truth behind 9/11* (Louisville: Westminster John Knox, 2006).

5 "We Will Not Forget: A Day of Terror," *Chief Engineer*, August 1, 2002 (www.chiefengineer.org/article.cfm?seqnum1=1029).

6 Quoted in Susan Hagen and Mary Carouba, *Women at Ground Zero: Stories of Courage and Compassion* (Indianapolis: Alpha Books, 2002), 65–66, 68.

7 John Bussey, "Eye of the Storm: One Journey Through Desperation and Chaos," *Wall Street Journal*, September 12, 2001 (online.wsj.com/public/resources/documents/040802pulitzer5.htm).

8 Quoted in Alicia Shepard, Cathy Trost, and Newseum, *Running Toward Danger: Stories Behind the Breaking News of 9/11*, foreword by Tom Brokaw (Lanham, Md.: Rowman & Littlefield, 2002), 87.

9 Graeme MacQueen, "118 Witnesses: The Firefighters' Testimony to Explosions in the Twin Towers," *Journal of 9/11 Studies* 2 (August 2006) (www.journalof911studies.com/articles/Article_5_118Witnesses_WorldTradeCenter.pdf): 49–123.

10 Oral History: Chief Frank Cruthers (graphics8.nytimes.com/packages/pdf/nyregion/20050812_WTC_GRAPHIC/9110179.PDF), 4.

11 Oral History: Firefighter Richard Banaciski (graphics8.nytimes.com/packages/pdf/nyregion/20050812_WTC_GRAPHIC/9110253.PDF), 3.

12 NIST NCSTAR 1, *Final Report on the Collapse of the World Trade Center Towers* (2005), 163.

13 NIST, "Answers to Frequently Asked Questions," 2006 (wtc.nist.gov/pubs/factsheets/faqs_8_2006.htm), Q. 2.

14 NIST NCSTAR 1, *Final Report on the Collapse of the World Trade Center Towers* (2005), 179.

15 Oral History: Firefighter Timothy Burke, 8–9.

16 Oral History: Firefighter Edward Cachia (graphics8.nytimes.com/packages/pdf/nyregion/20050812_WTC_GRAPHIC/9110251.PDF), 5.

17 Oral History: Assistant Fire Commissioner Stephen Gregory (graphics8.nytimes.com/packages/pdf/nyregion/20050812_WTC_GRAPHIC/9110008.PDF), 14–16.

18 Oral History: Firefighter Kenneth Rogers (graphics8.nytimes.com/packages/pdf/nyregion/20050812_WTC_GRAPHIC/9110290.PDF), 3–4.

19 Oral History: Firefighter Howie Scott (graphics8.nytimes.com/packages/pdf/nyregion/20050812_WTC_GRAPHIC/9110365.PDF), 6.

20 "Request for Correction Submitted to NIST," *Journal of 9/11 Studies* 12 (June 2007) (www.journalof911studies.com/volume/ 200704/RFCtoNIST-byMcIlvaineDoyleJonesRyanGageSTJ.pdf), 23. This letter was signed by Bob McIlvaine, Bill Doyle, Steven Jones, Kevin Ryan, Richard Gage, and Scholars for 9/11 Truth and Justice.

21 NIST, "Letter of Response to Request," September 27, 2007; published in *Journal of 9/11 Studies* 17 (November 2007) (www.journalof911studies.com/volume/2007/NISTresponseToRequestForCorrectionGourleyEtal2.pdf).

22 "William Rodriguez: 9/11 Survivor to Speak in London" (www.indymedia.org.uk/en/2006/11/356684.htm).

23 Greg Szymanski, "WTC Basement Blast and Injured Burn Victim Blows 'Official 9/11 Story' Sky High; Eye Witness Testimony Is Conclusive that North Tower Collapsed from Controlled Demolition," June 24, 2005 (web.archive.org/web/20060518021614/www.whale.to/b/szy6.html).

24 See "Uncut BBC News Report of 9-11 Explosion of the 1st Tower," YouTube (www.youtube.com/watch?v=66PR0z1n9HA). This video also contains footage of the BBC's Stephen Evans reporting that, about an hour after the plane hit the North Tower, a huge explosion occurred "much, much lower."

25 Szymanski, "WTC Basement Blast and Injured Burn Victim Blows 'Official 9/11 Story' Sky High."

26 Ibid.

27 Demarco's statement is quoted in Chris Bull and Sam Erman, eds., *At Ground Zero: Young Reporters Who Were There Tell Their Stories* (New York: Thunder's Mouth Press, 2002), 97.

28 Bartmer's statement is quoted in Paul Joseph Watson, "NYPD Officer Heard Building 7 Bombs," Prison Planet, February 10, 2007 (www.prison-planet.com/articles/february2007/100207heardbombs.htm). Part of Bartmer's statement can be seen in the documentary *Loose Change Final Cut*.

29 This unnamed medical student can be seen making this statement in the film *911 Eyewitness*, number 2 of 3 (video.google.com/videosearch?q=911+eyewitness&emb=0&aq=0&oq=911+eyew#q=911+eyewitness+2+of+3&emb=0), at 31:30.

30 NIST NCSTAR 1-9: 324.

31 David Firestone, "Mayor Picks Ex-Prosecutor To Take Job of Top Lawyer," *New York Times*, November 21, 1997 (www.nytimes.com/1997/11/21/nyregion/mayor-picks-ex-prosecutor-to-take-job-of-top-lawyer.html).

32 Rudolph W. Giuliani with Ken Kurson, *Leadership* (New York: Hyperion, 2002), 20.

33 See David Ray Griffin, "The 9/11 Interview with Michael Hess: Evidence that NIST Lied about When He and Barry Jennings Were Rescued," WantToKnow.Info (www.wanttoknow.info/008/hessjenningswtc7explosiontvbroadcast). According to writing on a DVD containing UPN 9 programs from that morning, the video began at 10:37AM. The Hess interview begins at the 57-minute mark. At one time, accordingly, it was believed that the Hess interview began at 11:34. Further research, however, showed that the video actually started at 11:00 (see web.archive.org/web/20050111201245/http://transcripts.cnn.com/TRANSCRIPTS/0109/11/bn.25.html). The crucial evidence is that, at the 111-minute mark, the UPN 9 program switched to live CNN coverage of a Taliban news conference, which began at 12:50 (see findarticles.com/p/articles/mi_m0DIZ/is_/ai_78963666; for further evidence, see Michael Ventura, "9/11: American Ungoverned" [www.austinchronicle.com/gyrobase/Issue/column?oid=oid%3A83213]).

34 "Michael Hess, WTC7 Explosion Witness," YouTube (www.youtube.com/watch?v=BUfiLbXMa64). Hess should have said "down to the sixth floor." As we will see later, Jennings also once said that the explosion occurred on the eighth floor, but he quickly corrected this, clarifying that, after

experiencing the explosion when they got down to the sixth floor, they walked back up to the eighth floor, where they waited to be rescued.

35 Giuliani, *Leadership*, 20.

36 There were two videos—"Barry Jennings," YouTube (www.youtube.com/watch?v=NttM3oUrNmE), and Paul Joseph Watson, "Emergency Official Witnessed Dead Bodies In WTC 7," Prison Planet, June 23, 2008 (www.prisonplanet.com/articles/june2008/ 062308_dead_bodies.htm)—plus a transcript in "NIST Exploring 9/11 Conspiracy Theory for WTC-7: New Witness Confirms Scholars Previous Findings," Scholars for 9/11 Truth, July 1, 2007 (twilightpines.com// index.php?option=com_ content&task=view&id=113&Itemid=67).

37 *The Conspiracy Files: 9/11—The Third Tower*, BBC, July 6, 2008 (available at www.911blogger.com/node/16541).

38 "Barry Jennings Uncut" is now available on YouTube in two parts as "Barry Jennings—9/11 WTC7 Full Uncut Interview," Part 1 (www.youtube.com/watch?v=VQY-ksiuwKU) and Part 2 (www.youtube.com/ watch?v=kxUj6UgPODo). Both parts are also available at Hidden History (hidhist.wordpress.com/2008/07/12/barry-jennings-uncut). These two parts are henceforth referred to as "Barry Jennings Uncut, Part 1," and "Barry Jennings Uncut, Part 2." The times cited refer to this version of the interview (which are different from the times given on the original version, which can be found at 9/11 Blogger [www.911blogger.com/node/16573] and other places on the internet).

39 In explaining why he put the entire interview online, Avery gave three reasons: "(1) To see the difference between the interview he gave us, and the interview he gave the BBC. (2) To establish Barry's timeline in his own words. (3) To preserve his testimony, in his own words, for the historical record." This statement, which was originally posted at the Loose Change website, is now more readily available at 9/11 Blogger (www.911blogger.com/node/16573). Jennings also claimed in his BBC interview that it was because he was upset by this (alleged) distortion that he asked for his interview not to be included in Avery's film. According to Avery, however, the only reason Jennings had given at the time was his fear that, if his interview was included in the film, he would lose his job. (I learned this in my capacity as the script consultant for *Loose Change Final Cut*.)

40 Jennings himself was uncertain whether he had spoken to NIST or the 9/11 Commission, and evidently thought that it was probably the latter ("Barry Jennings Uncut," Part 2, at 2:36–3:36). However, NIST's documents show that it interviewed Jennings. Interviews of both Michael Hess and Barry Jennings, which are stated as having taken place during "spring 2004," are cited in NIST NCSTAR 1-8, *The Emergency Response Operations*, September 2005 (wtc.nist.gov/NCSTAR1/PDF/NCSTAR%201-8.pdf), 109n380. This document was written by J. Randall Lawson and Robert L. Vettori. Although

the interviews are referred to with numbers ("WTC 7 Interviews 2041604 and 1041704"), not with the names of Hess and Jennings, the content of the text clearly shows that it is their experiences that are being described.

41 "Barry Jennings Uncut," Part 2, at 3:00–3:10 and 7:35–7:44.

42 Hess stated this in an interview with the BBC that was recorded for the second version of its program on WTC 7, which will be discussed later. To view the Hess interview, see Mike Rudin, "Caught Up in a Conspiracy Theory," BBC, October 21, 2008 (www.bbc.co.uk/blogs/theeditors/2008/10/caught_up_in_a_conspiracy_theo.html).

43 "Barry Jennings Uncut," Part 2, at 5:34–5:40.

44 Ibid., at 0:20 0:32.

45 Paul Vallely, "Terror in America: The Survivors—Inside the Towers, They Scrambled," *Independent*, September 13, 2001 (www.independent.co.uk/news/world/americas/inside-the-towers-they-scrambled-for-their-lives-751928.html).

46 "Barry Jennings Uncut," Part 1, at 1:18–1:48.

47 *The Conspiracy Files: 9/11—The Third Tower*, BBC, July 6, 2008 (available at www.911blogger.com/node/16541), at 12:06–12:26.

48 "Barry Jennings Uncut," Part 1, at 2:04–2:15.

49 Ibid., at 6:18–6:29.

50 Ibid., at 6:49–6:51.

51 BBC interview with Michael Hess, in Rudin, "Caught Up in a Conspiracy Theory."

52 ABC 7 News interview of Barry Jennings (www.youtube.com/watch?v=5LO5V2CJpzI). This was a brief on-the-street interview conducted on 9/11 by a reporter from ABC 7 News, a portion of which was placed at the beginning of the original version of "Barry Jennings Uncut." During the interview with Avery, however, Jennings started to say "the eighth floor" but then corrected himself and said "the sixth floor" ("Barry Jennings Uncut," Part 1, at 2:00–2:02). Then, under questioning from Avery, Jennings clarified that the explosion occurred when he and Hess were on the sixth floor, after which they went back up to the eighth floor (Part 1, at 5:56–6:18).

53 "Barry Jennings Uncut," Part 2, at 4:52–5:17.

54 ABC 7 News Interview of Barry Jennings (www.youtube.com/watch?v=5LO5V2CJpzI).

55 "Barry Jennings Uncut," Part 1, at 2:49–3:44.

56 "Barry Jennings Uncut," Part 2, at 5:08–5:33.

57 "Barry Jennings Uncut," Part 1, at 3:57–4:05.

58 Ibid., at 4:19–4:45.

59 "Barry Jennings Uncut," Part 2, at 2:15–2:30.

60 NIST NCSTAR 1-9 (2008 on WTC 7), Vol. 1 (wtc.nist.gov/NCSTAR1/PDF/NCSTAR%201-9%20Vol%201.pdf): 78. The

BBC, as we will see later in the text, repeated this claim.

61 "Barry Jennings Uncut," Part 1, at 4:45-4:56.

62 Vallely, "Terror in America: The Survivors: Inside the Towers, They Scrambled."

63 "Barry Jennings Uncut," Part 1, at 4:57-5:26.

64 NIST-SP 1000-5: *June 2004: Progress Report on the Federal Building and Fire Safety Investigation of the World Trade Center* (wtc.nist.gov/progress_report_june04/progress_report_june04.htm).

65 *Interim Report on WTC 7*, which is Appendix L of the June 2004 progress report mentioned in the previous note (wtc.nist.gov/progress_report_june04/appendixl.pdf). When a NIST spokesman, Benjamin Stein, was asked who wrote this interim report, he replied that he did not know, but he did supply the names of all the people who worked on the 2004 progress report as a whole, the first named of whom was Therese McAllister. Stein also added: "The work presented in Appendix L was conducted under Project 6 of the NIST WTC Investigation, Structural Fire Response and Collapse Analysis" (letter from Benjamin Stein, January 22, 2009). Given the fact that Therese McAllister was not only a co-leader of Project 6 (NC NCSTAR 1A [2008]: iii]), but was also the only co-leader to be listed among the contributors to the 2004 progress report, one can infer that she had primary responsibility for Appendix L, the *Interim Report on WTC 7*.

66 *Interim Report on WTC 7* (2004), L-18 (each page number is preceded by "L" because this is Appendix L of the 2004 progress report).

67 The conclusion that Hess and Jennings were rescued no later than 11:30 might seem to be ruled out by the fact that Jennings, near the end of the interview with Dylan Avery posted as "Barry Jennings Uncut," said that he and Hess "didn't get out of there until like 1:00" (Part 2, at 5:49–5:53), after which Avery made a supporting statement, saying that the interview with Hess took place at about 1:00. But there are many reasons to conclude that they both misspoke. First, Avery, who supplied the tape of the UPN 9 News interview of Hess (which shows that Hess was being interviewed before noon), has confirmed that he misspoke (email July 9, 2008). Second, if Hess and Jennings had not gotten out of the building until 1:00, they would have been trapped for three-and-a-half hours, and Hess surely would not have described such a long period as "an hour and a half." Third, Jennings said that the firemen came back to rescue them after the collapse of the North Tower, which occurred at 10:28, and the rescue certainly would not have taken another two-and-a-half hours after that. Fourth, 1:00 would be about 45 minutes later than even NIST claimed that the men had been rescued.

68 NIST's main report on the Twin Towers, which has 247 pages, is NIST NCSTAR 1, *Final Report on the Collapse of the World Trade Center Towers*, September 2005 (wtc.nist.gov/NISTNCSTAR1CollapseofTowers.pdf). "NCSTAR" stands for the National Construction Safety Team Act Report. The

entire report, which consists of some 10,000 pages, includes the main report plus 42 companion volumes, which contain the results of eight investigations. They are abbreviated NIST NCSTAR 1-1, NIST NCSTAR 1-2, on up to NIST NCSTAR 1-8. (The brief report on WTC 7 is numbered NIST NCSTAR 1A; the long version is NCSTAR 1-9, which is divided into Volume 1 and Volume 2.) For the entire set of documents, see Final Reports of the Federal Building and Fire Investigation of the World Trade Center Disaster (http://wtc.nist.gov/NCSTAR1/).

69 NIST NCSTAR 1-8, *The Emergency Response Operations*, by J. Randall Lawson and Robert L. Vettori, September 2005 (wtc.nist.gov/NCSTAR1/PDF/NCSTAR%201-8.pdf), 109–10. Henceforth cited simply as NIST NCSTAR 1-8.

70 Ibid., 109n380. NIST also ignored Jennings' statement that, before he and Hess were finally rescued, the firefighters had come twice but then had run away twice when the two towers came down. NIST simply said: "The two men went back to the 8th floor [and] broke out a window and called for help. Firefighters on the ground saw them and went up the stairs." NIST thereby portrayed Jennings as having broken the window after 10:30, rather than, as Jennings indicated, an hour or more earlier.

71 "Death of Key Witness Barry Jennings: New Info Points to Foul Play," Dylan Avery interviewed by Jack Blood on *Deadline Live*, April 16, 2009: Part II (www.videosurf.com/video/death-of-911-key-witness-barry-jennings-new-info-points-to-foul-play-2-of-4-65323174), at 8:00.

72 *The Conspiracy Files: 9/11—The Third Tower*, July 6, 2008 (available at www.911blogger.com/node/16541).

73 Ibid., at 10:36–10:39.

74 Ibid., at 12:06–12:40.

75 Ibid., at 13:29–13:40.

76 Ibid., at 13:45–13:55.

77 Ibid., at 14:20–14:31.

78 Ibid., at 18:55–19:10.

79 Ibid., at 13:45–14:10.

80 Ibid., at 46:47–47:40.

81 Ibid., at 47:14–47:35.

82 Aaron Dykes, "Key Witness to WTC 7 Explosions Dead at 53," Infowars.com, updated September 17, 2008 (www.infowars.com/?p=4602); "Passing of Barry Jennings," NYCHA [New York City Housing Authority] Bulletin, October 2008 (www.nyc.gov/html/nycha/downloads/pdf/emp_bulletin_oct_2008.pdf). This NYCHA obituary, incidentally, says the following about Jennings: "In 2002 Mr. Jennings was promoted to the highly demanding position of Emergency Coordinator/Deputy Director in ESD. The dedication and proficiency with which he discharged his duties were widely recognized within and beyond his department.... Mr. Jennings's ability to face

and survive disaster had earlier been tested during the tragic events of 9/11, when he was credited with saving the life of Corporation Counsel Michael Hess."

83 "Death of Key Witness Barry Jennings: New Info Points to Foul Play," Dylan Avery interviewed by Jack Blood on *Deadline Live*, April 16, 2009, Part III (www.videosurf.com/video/death-of-911-key-witness-barry-jennings-new-info-points-to-foul-play-3-of-4-65225203), at 1:35–2:45. He had paid this private investigator, Avery added, "a decent sum of money. It was definitely not a sum that would be turned down unless there was something at stake."

84 *The Conspiracy Files: 9/11—The Truth behind the Third Tower*, BBC, October 26, 2008 (available at video.google.com/videoplay?docid=5313004818217244745 or bestdocumentaries.blogspot.com/2009/01/conspiracy-files-truth-behind-third.html).

85 Ibid., at 30:17–30:24.

86 Mike Rudin, "Caught Up in a Conspiracy Theory," BBC, October 21, 2008 (www.bbc.co.uk/blogs/theeditors/ 2008/10/caught_up_in_a_conspiracy_theo.html). A video of the BBC interview with Hess is available at this blog. This interview, henceforth called "Michael Hess BBC interview," is the source for most of the footage of Hess contained in the second version of the BBC's show.

87 Rudin, "Caught Up in a Conspiracy Theory."

88 *The Conspiracy Files: 9/11—The Truth behind the Third Tower*, at 30:24–30:40; see also Michael Hess BBC interview (see note 86).

89 *The Conspiracy Files: 9/11—The Truth behind the Third Tower*, at 30:09–30:16.

90 Much of this interview is included in *Loose Change 9/11: An American Coup*, scheduled to appear in September 2009.

91 "Michael D. Hess, Vice Chairman," Giuliani Partners (www.giuliani-partners.com/mhess.aspx).

92 Michael Hess BBC interview; *The Conspiracy Files: 9/11—The Truth behind the Third Tower*, at 58:39.

93 Michael Hess BBC interview.

94 Ibid.; *The Conspiracy Files: 9/11—The Third Tower*, at 14:57–15:01.

95 Michael Hess BBC interview; *The Conspiracy Files: 9/11—The Truth behind the Third Tower*, at 30:17–30:24.9.

96 Paul Vallely, "Terror in America: The Survivors—Inside the Towers, They Scrambled."

97 *The Conspiracy Files: 9/11—The Truth behind the Third Tower*, 9:12–9:25; also in Michael Hess BBC interview.

98 Ibid.

99 NIST NCSTAR 1-9 (2008): 298–99. The note cites "WTC 7 Interviews 2041604 and 1041704, spring 2004," which designate the interviews with Hess and Jennings (as can be seen at NIST NCSTAR 1-8: 109, n. 380).

100 NIST NCSTAR 1-9: 299.

101 The 2005 rescue account is contained in NIST NCSTAR 1-8, Chapter 6, which was written by J. Randall Lawson and Robert Vettori. The primary author of NIST's 2004 *Interim Report on WTC 7*, as pointed out in note 65, was likely Therese McAllister.

102 On the cover page of NIST NCSTAR 1-8, *The Emergency Response Operations* (2005), J. Randall Lawson is the first of two authors listed, the other being Robert L. Vettori. In NIST's 2008 report on WTC 7, Lawson was the first-mentioned author of Chapter 6, entitled "Emergency Response," which includes the rescue account. (The other author was Richard G. Gann.) Lawson was the Project Leader for the project dealing with Emergency Response Technologies and Guidelines, which had the task of documenting the activities of the emergency responders; see NC NSTAR 1A [2008]: xxviii).

103 NIST NCSTAR 1-8: 110.

104 As we saw earlier, the BBC suggested that Jennings got out of the building at 12:03.

105 NIST NCSTAR 1-9: 197.

106 Ibid., 298–99.

107 Oral History: Captain Karin Deshore of the FDNY Emergency Medical Services (graphics8.nytimes.com/packages/pdf/nyregion/20050812_WTC_GRAPHIC/9110192.PDF), 10–12.

108 Oral History: Paramedic Louis Cook (graphics8.nytimes.com/packages/pdf/nyregion/20050812_WTC_GRAPHIC/9110103.PDF), 14–17.

109 "Barry Jennings Uncut," Part 2, at 5:17.

110 Jennings certainly would have said this, and Hess at that time probably would have had no reason to give a false account.

111 See NIST NCSTAR 1-8: iii.

112 "WTC 7 Technical Briefing," NIST, August 26, 2008 (event.on24.com/eventRegistration/EventLobbyServlet?target=lobby.jsp&eventid=118145), at 2:02:30.

113 Ibid., at 2:10:10.

114 NIST NCSTAR 1-8: 110.

115 Oral History: Captain Ray Goldbach (graphics8.nytimes.com/packages/pdf/nyregion/20050812_WTC_GRAPHIC/9110150.PDF), 14.

116 Oral History: Firefighter Vincent Massa (graphics8.nytimes.com/packages/pdf/nyregion/20050812_WTC_GRAPHIC/9110222.PDF), 17.

117 Oral History: EMT Decosta Wright (graphics8.nytimes.com/packages/pdf/nyregion/20050812_WTC_GRAPHIC/9110054.PDF), 12.

118 Oral History: Chief Daniel Nigro (graphics8.nytimes.com/packages/pdf/nyregion/20050812_WTC_GRAPHIC/9110154.PDF), 10.

119 Oral History: Firefighter Kevin McGovern (graphics8.nytimes.com/packages/pdf/nyregion/20050812_WTC_GRAPHIC/9110301.PDF), 12.

120 Oral History: Captain Robert Sohmer (graphics8.nytimes.com/packages/pdf/nyregion/20050812_WTC_GRAPHIC/9110472.PDF), 5.

121 Oral History: Chief Frank Fellini (graphics8.nytimes.com/packages/pdf/nyregion/20050812_WTC_GRAPHIC/9110217.PDF), 3.

122 Oral History: Chief Thomas McCarthy (graphics8.nytimes.com/packages/pdf/nyregion/20050812_WTC_GRAPHIC/9110055.PDF), 10–11.

123 Oral History: EMT Decosta Wright (graphics8.nytimes.com/packages/pdf/nyregion/20050812_WTC_GRAPHIC/9110054.PDF), 11.

124 "WTC: This Is Their Story: Deputy Chief Nick Visconti," *Firehouse Magazine*, August 2002 (www.firehouse.com/terrorist/911/magazine/gz/visconti.html).

125 Thomas von Essen, *Strong of Heart: Life and Death in the Fire Department of New York* (New York: William Morrow, 2002), 45.

126 Dean E. Murphy, *September 11: An Oral History* (New York: Doubleday, 2002), 175–76.

127 David Ray Griffin, *9/11 Contradictions: An Open Letter to Congress and the Press* (Northampton: Olive Branch Press, 2008), 226–29.

128 Ibid., Chap. 7, "How Did Rudy Giuliani Know the Towers Were Going to Collapse?"

129 "Another Smoking Gun? Now CNN Jumps the Gun," Information Liberation, February 27, 2007 (www.informationliberation.com/?id=20521).

130 See Paul Joseph Watson and Alex Jones, "BBC Reported Building 7 Had Collapsed 20 Minutes Before It Fell," Prison Planet.com, February 27, 2007 (www.prisonplanet.com/articles/february2007/260207building7.htm); "BBC's 'WTC 7 Collapsed at 4:45 p.m.' Videos," What Really Happened (www.whatreallyhappened.com/bbc_wtc7_videos.html).

131 Richard Porter, "Part of the Conspiracy?" February 27, 2007 (www.bbc.co.uk/blogs/theeditors/2007/02/part_of_the_conspiracy.html).

132 Sheila Barter, "How the World Trade Center Fell," BBC News, September 13, 2001 (news.bbc.co.uk/1/hi/world/americas/1540044.stm).

133 "The Conspiracy Files: 9/11," produced by Guy Smith, was broadcast February 18, 2007, by BBC 2. The documentary can be viewed on Live Video (www.livevideo.com/video/094F3DD8A30B485ABEA1313A9D50CACF/the-conspiracy-files-9-11-p1.aspx?lastvcid=78869). I pointed out some of the failings of this show in my *Debunking 9/11 Debunking: An Answer to Popular Mechanics and Other Defenders of the Official Conspiracy Theory* (Northampton: Olive Branch Press, 2007). A more extensive, truly devastating, critique has been provided in a documentary, "911 and the British Broadcasting Conspiracy," produced by Adrian Connock (video.google.com/videoplay?docid=-1882365905982811133). Still another devastating critique

has charged that this program egregiously violates the BBC's charter, which stipulates: "The BBC must do all it can to ensure that controversial subjects are treated with due accuracy and impartiality in all relevant output." Pointing out that there are over 230 survivors of 9/11 and family members of victims who have publicly questioned the official story, this critique asks: "How could the BBC make a documentary without including even one 'questioning' survivor, eye witness or relative of a victim?" Moreover, the critique adds: "Neither is any mention made of the many politicians, military personnel, scientists, engineers and pilots who question the accuracy of the government's account." Still more: "The BBC omits the all-important question of physics, with the Twin Towers and Building 7 disintegrating at near free-fall speed—yet no account made for conservation of energy momentum, nor of the source of energy needed to turn most of the towers into dust, fragmented rubble and pockets of molten iron. *How were the immutable laws of physics suspended?"* ("Reviewing the BBC's Coverage of the 2001 Attack on the World Trade Center & the Pentagon," which is on a blog called Monitoring Authority: BBC Charter Compliance [www.bbcmot.blogspot.com]).

134 Richard Porter, "Part of the Conspiracy? (2)," BBC World, March 2, 2007 (www.bbc.co.uk/blogs/theeditors/2007/03/part_of_the_conspiracy_2.html).

135 *Guns and Butter*, KPFA, April 27, 2005 (kpfa.org/archives/index.php?arch=781), quoted in Paul Joseph Watson and Alex Jones, "More Ground Zero Heroes on the Record: Building 7 Was Deliberately Brought Down," Prison Planet (www.prisonplanet.com/articles/february2007/090207broughtdown.htm).

136 "Seven Is Exploding" (www.youtube.com/watch?v=58h0LjdMry0).

137 Paul Joseph Watson and Alex Jones, "More Ground Zero Heroes on the Record."

138 *America Rebuilds*, PBS documentary, September 2002. This portion of the program can now be seen on YouTube (www.youtube.com/watch?v=CahEva8zQas).

139 NIST NCSTAR 1-9: 301–02. NIST's footnote says: "Letter from Silverstein Properties to NIST, March 24, 2006."

140 See "We Are Change Confronts Larry Silverstein 3/13/03," 911Blogger.com (www.911blogger.com/node/14361).

141 NIST NCSTAR 1-9: 303.

142 David Dunbar and Brad Reagan, eds., *Debunking 9/11 Myths: Why Conspiracy Theories Can't Stand Up to the Facts: An In-Depth Investigation by Popular Mechanics* (New York: Hearst Books, 2006), 58.

143 This endorsement was given in a critique of *9/11 Revealed: The Unanswered Questions*, by Rowland Morgan and Ian Henshall (New York: Carroll & Graf, 2005). This critique, entitled "9/11 Revealed? New Book Repeats False Conspiracy Theories," was published on a US Department of State webpage called "Identifying Misinformation" in 2005, the year that

Condoleezza Rice became secretary of state. It remained there throughout Rice's tenure but has since been removed. It can still be read, however, on the Internet Archive (web.archive.org/web/20080214143807re_/ usinfo.state.gov/media/Archive/2005/Sep/16-241966.html).

144 "WTC 7 Technical Briefing," at 2:19:50.

145 Ibid., at 2:22:05.

146 Ibid., at 2:27:50.

147 Rather's statement is available on YouTube (www.youtube.com/watch?v=Nvx904dAw0o).

148 See Patriots Question 9/11: Hugo Bachmann (www.patriotsques-tion911.com/engineers.html#Bachmann) and Jörg Schneider (patriotsquestion911.com/engineers.html#Schneider). These quotations were drawn from Daniele Ganser, "Swiss Professors: WTC 7 Most Likely Controlled Demolition," trans. Jesse Goplen, *Journal of 9/11 Studies*, Letters, February 29, 2008. This letter can be accessed directly (journalof911studies.com/ letters/d/GanserSwissProfs.pdf) or by scrolling down to "Prof. Ganser article in English (February 29, 2008)" under "Letters" (journalof911studies.com/ letters.html).

149 Architects and Engineers for 9/11 Truth (www.ae911truth.org/supporters.php?g=ENG#998929).

150 Jowenko Explosieve Demolitie B.V.

151 See "Danny Jowenko on WTC 7 Controlled Demolition," YouTube (www.youtube.com/watch?v=877gr6xtQIc), or, for more of the interview, "Jowenko WTC 7 Demolition Interviews," in three parts (www.youtube.com/ watch?v=k3DRhwRN06I&feature=related). These videos are taken from a Dutch television program entitled *Zembla Investigates 9/11 Theories* (cgi.omroep.nl/cgi-bin/streams?/tv/vara/zembla/bb.20060911.asf). A portion of this interview is contained in *Loose Change Final Cut.*

152 Patriots Question 9/11 (patriotsquestion911.com/engineers.html# Jowenko).

153 Interview of Danny Jowenko by Jeff Hill, Patriots Question 9/11 (patriotsquestion911.com/engineers.html#Jowenko).

154 "Questions and Answers about the NIST WTC 7 Investigation (Updated 04/21/2009)" (www.nist.gov/public_affairs/ factsheet/ wtc_qa_082108.html).

Chapter Six

1 NIST NCSTAR 1-9: 693

2 Ibid., 709.

3 Ibid., 694

4 Ibid., 357.

5 This video can be seen at Daily Newscaster (www.dailynewscaster.com/2008/11/03/newly-discovered-footage-of-building-

seven-and-north-tower-collapse) and YouTube (www.youtube.com/watch?v=G5UM9q7cj7I).

6 Demarco's statement is quoted in Chris Bull and Sam Erman, eds., *At Ground Zero: Young Reporters Who Were There Tell Their Stories* (New York: Thunder's Mouth Press, 2002), 97.

7 This unnamed medical student can be seen making this statement in the film *911 Eyewitness* (video.google.com/videosearch?q=911+eyewitness&emb=0&aq=0&oq=911+eyew#), #2 of 3, at 31:30.

8 NIST NCSTAR 1-9: 614.

9 James Gourley, "Public Comments on WTC 7 Draft Reports," September 15, 2008 (wtc.nist.gov/comments08/jamesGourleywtc7comments.pdf).

10 Bartmer's statement is quoted in Paul Joseph Watson, "NYPD Officer Heard Building 7 Bombs," Prison Planet, February 10, 2007 (www.prison-planet.com/articles/february2007/100207heardbombs.htm). Part of Bartmer's statement can be seen in the documentary *Loose Change Final Cut.*

11 This statement can be seen in the film *911 Eyewitness* at 31:30.

12 "Seven Is Exploding" (www.youtube.com/watch?v=58h0LjdMry0).

13 NIST NCSTAR 1A: 28.

14 Letter to NIST from Michael Smith (wtc.nist.gov/comments08/michaelSmithwtc7comments.pdf).

15 Ibid. (quoting NIST NCSTAR 1-9: 615).

16 Ibid.

17 NIST NCSTAR 1-9: 694.

18 Ibid., 614–15.

19 Earl Staelin, Comments on NIST Draft Report on WTC 7, September 11, 2008 (wtc.nist.gov/comments08/earlStaelinwtc7comments.pdf).

20 This incident is pointed out by Jim Hoffman in "Frequently Asked Questions: Controlled Demolition," 9-11 Research (911research.wtc7.net/faq/demolition.html#ref1).

21 Ibid.

22 NIST NCSTAR 1-9: 614.

23 "Questions and Answers about the NIST WTC 7 Investigation," NIST, updated April 21, 2009 (www.nist.gov/public_affairs/factsheet/wtc_qa_082108.html). Sunder had given a longer version of this argument in "WTC 7 Technical Briefing," NIST, August 26, 2008 (event.on24.com/eventRegistration/EventLobbyServlet?target=lobby.jsp&eventid=118145), at 2:28.

24 "Complex Question" (www.lich-mc.com/vietnam/complexquestion.htm).

25 Skeptosis (pseudonym), Letter to NIST, September 15, 2008 (wtc.nist.gov/comments08/skeptosiswtc7comments.pdf). This comment can also be read in "Two Comments re: NIST's draft of NCSTAR 1A," which is posted at a blog by Skeptosis, "Missing Steel" (missingsteel.blogspot.com).

26 Ibid.

27 "Questions and Answers about the NIST WTC 7 Investigation," updated April 21, 2009.

28 "Answers to Frequently Asked Questions," NIST, August 30, 2006 (wtc.nist.gov/pubs/factsheets/faqs_8_2006.htm).

29 Email letter, December 30, 2008.

30 Ibid.

31 See Jan A. Puszynski, Christopher J. Bulian, and Jacek J. Swiatkiewicz, "Processing and Ignition Characteristics of Aluminum–Bismuth Trioxide Nanothermite System," *Journal of Propulsion and Power* 23.4 (July–August 2007) (pdf.aiaa.org/jaPreview/JPP/2007/PVJA24915.pdf), the abstract for which says: "During the past few years, significant progress has been made in the development of new nanoenergetic materials consisting of mixtures of metal and oxidizer nanopowders. It has been found that such reacting mixtures release energy by 2 to 3 orders of magnitude faster than similar systems consisting of micron-size reactants. In some cases, combustion-front velocities reach hundreds of meters per second."

32 For this section, I am heavily indebted to Kevin Ryan, "The Top Ten Connections between NIST and Nano-Thermites," *Journal of 9/11 Studies* 22 (July 2008) (www.journalof911studies.com/volume/2008/ Ryan_NIST_and_Nano-1.pdf).

33 Battelle web page for Nanomaterials/Nanotechnology (under "Advanced Materials" under "Solutions") says: "Battelle specializes in nanocomposites solutions for every application—from electronics to health sciences, coatings to telecommunications, transportation to energy" (www.battelle.org/solutions/?Nav_Area=Solution&Nav_SectionID=1&Nav_C atID=1_NanomaterialsNanotechnology).

34 "Special Issue: Nanotechnology," *Amptiac Quarterly* 6.1 (2002) (www.p2pays.org/ref/15/14610.pdf). *Amptiac* is published by the DOD Information Analysis Center. The ten essays in this special issue were intended to provide "a snapshot of what the DOD is doing to utilize nanotechnology and nanomaterials in practical terms."

35 "Biography: Dr. Arden L. Bement, Jr.," National Science Foundation (www.nsf.gov/news/speeches/bement/bement_bio.jsp).

36 "Speech by Dr. Arden Bement, Director, National Institute of Standards & Technology, Technologies for the Warfighter and Industry," March 18, 2002 (www.nist.gov/speeches/bement_031802.htm).

37 A list of Michael Zachariah's scientific publications, including the papers co-authored with Hratch Semerjian, is available on the internet (www.enme.umd.edu/facstaff/fac-profiles/zachariah.html).

38 "Hratch G. Semerjian, Chief Scientist," NIST, Office of the Director (www.nist.gov/director/bios/semerjian.htm).

39 See "Remarks by Dr. Hratch Semerjian, Acting Director, National Institute of Standards and Technology, Technology Administration, U.S.

Department of Commerce, World Trade Center Investigation Report Press Briefing, June 23, 2005 (wtc.nist.gov/pubs/semerjian_remarks_62305.htm).

40 "The Journal Talks with NIST Director William Jeffrey," *JOM: Journal of the Minerals, Metals, and Materials Society* 57.10 (October 2005) (findarticles.com/p/articles/mi_qa5348/is_/ai_n21380892?tag=artBody;col1).

41 "William Jeffrey Leads Cutting-Edge Technologies at NIST, Garners ISA's Highest Honor," InTech, August 2006 (www.isa.org/InTechTemplate.cfm?Section=article_index1&template=/ContentManagement/ContentDisplay.cfm&ContentID=63200).

42 "Testimony of Dr. James M. Turner, Acting Director, NIST, Before the Committee on Commerce, Science and Transportation, Subcommittee on Science, Technology and Innovation, United States Senate," March 11, 2008 (74.125.95.132/search?q=cache:JZTnjF.CdoAAJ:www.nist.gov/director/ocla/jturner%2520senate%2520cst%2520subc%2520sti%2520nist%2520fy09.pdf+James+Turner,+NIST&hl=en&ct=clnk&cd=2&gl=us&client=safari).

43 "NIST's Investigation of the Sept. 11 World Trade Center Disaster," NIST and the World Trade Center Fact Sheet (wtc.nist.gov/pubs/factsheets/faqs.htm).

44 See Alexander M. Telengator, Stephen B. Margolis, and Forman A. Williams, "Ignition Analysis of a Porous Energetic Material," Sandia National Laboratories, April 1998 (http://74.125.95.132/search?q=cache:xxvQUpXH-PrwJ:www.osti.gov/bridge/servlets/purl/325728-w2gJX0/webviewable/325728.pdf+Ignition+Analysis+of+a+Porous+Energetic+Material+—II.+Ignition+at+a+Closed+Heated+End,&hl=en&ct=clnk&cd=1&gl=us&client=safari); S. B. Margolis and F. A. Williams, "Effect of Gas-phase Thermal Expansion on Stability of Deflagrations in Porous Energetic Materials," *International Journal of Multiphase Flow* 22 (1996): 69-91; Stephen B. Margolis and Forman A. Williams, "Structure and Stability of Deflagrations in Porous Energetic Materials," Sandia National Laboratories, March 1999 (www.osti.gov/bridge/servlets/purl/751013-HyqMT7/webviewable/751013.pdf).

45 T. M. Tillotson et al., "Sol-Gel Processing of Energetic Materials," *Journal of Non-Crystalline Solids* 225.1 (1998), 358–63; preprint available at www.osti.gov/bridge/servlets/purl/653598-voS3Zd/webviewable/653598.pdf (the acknowledgment says: "This work was performed under the auspices of the U.S. Department of Energy by the Lawrence Livermore National Laboratory"); A. E. Gash et al., "Making Nanostructured Pyrotechnics in a Beaker," Lawrence Livermore National Laboratory (LLNL), preprint, April 10, 2000 (nsdl.org/resource/2200/20061005073045187T); A. E. Gash et al., "Energetic Nanocomposites with Sol-Gel Chemistry: Synthesis, Safety, and Characterization," LLNL, June 5, 2002 (https://e-reports-ext.llnl.gov/pdf/244137.pdf).

46 T. M. Tillotson et al., "Nanostructure High Explosives Using Sol-gel Chemistry," *Laboratory Directed Research and Development*, Annual Report, LLNL, 1999 (https://e-reports-ext.llnl.gov/pdf/238334.pdf), 8-11 (meaning

page 11 of section 8).

47 "Nanotechnology How To Guide from NIST and NASA Shows Technique for Measuring Carbon Nanotubes," Azonanotechology (www.azonano.com/News.asp?NewsID=6264O).

48 "Memorandum of Understanding between the National Institute of Standards and Technology and the University of Maryland, College Park for the Development of a Cooperative Program in Nano-Metrology and Nano-Manufacturing," NIST, 2003 (www.nist.gov/public_affairs/ releases/univmdnanomou.htm).

49 Co-Laboratory for Nanoparticle Based Manufacturing and Metrology, between the University of Maryland, College Park, and NIST (www.nanow-erk.com/nanotechnology/labs/Co-Laboratory_for_NanoParticle_Based_Manuf acturing_and_Metrology.html).

50 "Center for Nano Manufacturing and Metrology," University of Maryland, 2005 (www.enme.umd.edu/cnmm).

51 "Nano at NIST: Recent Nanotechnology Accomplishments," NIST, 2008 (www.nist.gov/public_affairs/factsheet/ nano_at_nistaccomplish-ment0708.htm).

52 NIST Center for Nanoscale Science and Technology (cnst.nist.gov).

53 "Introducing the NIST Center for Nanoscale Science and Technology" (www.nist.gov/public_affairs/factsheet/CNST_factsheet.htm).

54 See "911 Eyewitness: Huge Steel Sections Ejected More than 600 Feet" (video.google.com/videoplay?docid=1807467434260776490) and the photo at www.reservoir.com/extra/wtc/wtc-small.1057.jpg. The images are also contained in *9/11 Mysteries: Demolitions* and *Loose Change Final Cut* (www.loosechange911.com).

55 Stated at Architects and Engineers for 9/11 Truth (www.ae911truth.org/profile.php?uid=998819).

56 Dunbar and Reagan, eds., *Debunking 9/11 Myths*, 53.

57 *Interim Report on WTC 7*: L-18.

58 NIST NCSTAR IA: 16.

PART II
Chapter Seven

1 NIST NCSTAR 1A: xxxv (also at NIST NCSTAR 1-9: 617).

2 Sunder, "Opening Statement"; "WTC 7 Technical Briefing," at 1:18:20-1:18:25, and 1:23:41-1:23:48.

3 NIST NCSTAR 1A: xxxvii.

4 Ibid., 25, 63.

5 Sunder, "Opening Statement."

6 Ibid.

7 John D. Wyndham, Letter to NIST, September 7, 2008

(wtc.nist.gov/comments08/johnWyndhamwtc7comments.pdf).

8 Richard Gage, "Undisputed Facts Point to the Controlled Demolition of WTC 7: Response to NIST's Invitation for Written Comments," December 18, 2007 (wtc.nist.gov/media/AE911Truth-NIST-Written-Submission12-18-07.pdf).

9 "WTC 7 Technical Briefing," NIST, August 26, 2008 (event.on24.com/eventRegistration/EventLobbyServlet?target=lobby.jsp&event id=118145), at 1:25:34.

10 NIST NCSTAR 1A: xxxvi.

11 Sunder, "Opening Statement."

12 NIST NCSTAR 1A: 51.

13 Sunder, "Opening Statement."

14 NIST NCSTAR 1A: xxxvi.

15 NIST NCSTAR 1-9: 341.

16 NIST NCSTAR 1A: xxxvi.

17 Ibid., 11.

Chapter Eight

1 Sunder, "Opening Statement."

2 NIST NCSTAR 1-9: 377.

3 NIST NCSTAR 1A: 51.

4 Eric Lipton, "Fire, Not Explosives, Felled 3rd Tower on 9/11, Report Says," *New York Times*, August 22, 2008 (www.nytimes.com/2008/08/22/nyregion/22wtccnd.htm).

5 "Report: Fire, Not Bombs, Leveled WTC 7 Building," Associated Press, August 21, 2008 (www.usatoday.com/news/nation/2008-08-21-wtc-nist_N.htm).

6 NIST NCSTAR 1-9: 125.

7 Ibid., 47.

8 Ibid., 341.

9 NIST NCSTAR 1A: 16.

10 F.R. Greening, "Comments on the Draft Report NIST NCSTAR 1-9: '*Structural Fire Response and Probable Collapse Sequence of World Trade Center Building 7*,' issued by NIST August 21st, 2008," revised and extended version of comments issued September 11, 2008 (www.cool-places.0catch.com/911/GreeningCommentsNCSTAR1-9.pdf). Although Greening submitted this revised version of his comments to NIST, his original version, which was submitted September 4, 2008, was still, at the time this book went to press, the one posted at NIST's website (wtc.nist.gov/comments08/frGreeningwtc7comments.pdf).

11 NIST NCSTAR 1-9: 87.

12 Ibid., 194.

13 Ibid., 196.

14 Ibid., 194. NIST states that an "early" fire was also observed on Floor 19, but that this fire was only "indirectly observed": there was "a single photograph showing smoke marks above two windows" (ibid., 78).

15 Ibid., 199–200, 244, 245.

16 Ibid., 243, 245.

17 Ibid., 204, 205.

18 Ibid., 243, 244, 247.

19 Ibid., 237.

20 NIST NCSTAR 1-9: 298–99. The note cites "WTC 7 Interviews 2041604 and 1041704, spring 2004." These were the interviews with Hess and Jennings, as can be seen at NIST NCSTAR 1-8: 109n380.

21 NIST NCSTAR 1-9: 299n17. WTC 7 was also known as the Salomon Smith Barney building. On the question of the reality of this interview, see note 30, below.

22 NIST NCSTAR 1-8: 110n381.

23 NIST NCSTAR 1A: 51.

24 NIST NCSTAR 1-9: 119.

25 "Barry Jennings Uncut," Part 2, at 5:18–5:26.

26 NIST NCSTAR 1-9: 197.

27 NIST NCSTAR 1-9: 377, 378. These statements occur in Chapter 9, "Fire Simulations," written by Kevin B. McGrattan, William L. Grosshandler, and Richard G. Gann.

28 Ibid., v.

29 Ibid., 304.

30 On February 20, 2009, a FOIA request was sent to NIST requesting "[t]he complete text of the interview referenced as 'SSB [Salomon Smith Barney] Interview 5, April, 2004' in NIST's November, 2008 'Final Report' on the collapse of World Trade Center 7 (NIST Final Report, Vol. 1, Nov. 2008, p. 299n17 [http://wtc.nist.gov/NCSTAR1/PDF/NCSTAR%201-9%20Vol%201.pdf])." On April 16, 2009, the following answer was received: "While NIST has in its possession records which are responsive to your request, these records are currently exempt from disclosure.... [A cited statute prohibits] the disclosure of any information received by NIST that is 'voluntarily provided safety information if that information is not directly related to the building failure being investigated and the Director finds that the disclosure of the information would inhibit the voluntary provision of that type of information.' The NIST Director has [so] determined.... Therefore, the information is exempt from disclosure under FOIA, and your request has been denied." NIST's claim, in other words, was that although NIST does have the text of the [alleged] interview, NIST's current director fears that revealing its content might prevent NIST from obtaining such information in the future—a completely implausible claim.

31 NIST NCSTAR 1-9: 380.

32 Ibid., 361.

33 Ibid., 242.

34 "Barry Jennings—9/11 WTC7 Full Uncut Interview," Part 1 (www.youtube.com/watch?v=VQY-ksiuwKU), at 2:19–2:23.

35 Matthys Levy and Mario Salvadori, *Why Buildings Fall Down: How Structures Fail* (New York: Norton, 2002).

36 James Glanz and Eric Lipton, "Vast Detail on Towers' Collapse May Be Sealed in Court Filings," *New York Times*, September 30, 2002 (query.nytimes.com/gst/fullpage.html?res=9D0DE4DD1538F933A0575AC0A9649C8B63).

37 Quoted in Aidan Monaghan, "History Channel 'Expert' Claims WTC 7 Fires Began Before Either WTC Tower Collapsed" (www.911blogger.com/node/11937). Monaghan actually quoted only the first half of this sentence, but the entire statement is in the video to which he refers the reader (www.youtube.com/watch?v=sc1PJq8ESIA).

38 NIST NCSTAR 1A: 51.

39 NIST NCSTAR 1-9: 242.

40 Ibid., 197.

41 Ibid., 80.

42 Ibid., 78, 194, 197, 242; NIST NCSTAR 1A: 51.

43 Ibid., 78.

44 NIST NCSTAR 1A: 51.

45 NIST NCSTAR 1-9: 245.

46 Ibid., 245.

47 Ibid., 244.

48 Ibid., 244.

49 Ibid., 213.

50 Ibid., 380.

51 Ibid., 377.

52 "MW" stands for megawatt, which is a million watts (and a watt is one joule of energy per second).

53 NIST NCSTAR 1-9: 380.

54 Ibid.

55 "WTC 7 Technical Briefing," NIST, August 26, 2008 (event.on24.com/eventRegistration/EventLobbyServlet?target=lobby.jsp&event id=118145), at 1:24:55.

56 NIST NCSTAR 1-9: 47. This is the only mention of this possibility in the long (two-volume) version of NIST's WTC 7 report.

57 NIST NCSTAR 1-9: 380.

58 NIST NCSTAR 1-9: 378.

59 NIST NCSTAR 1A: 51.

60 NIST NCSTAR 1-9: 361. This statement occurred on the first page of Chapter 9, "Fire Simulations," by McGrattan, Grosshandler, and Gann.

61 Ibid., 617.

Chapter Nine

1 NIST NCSTAR 1A: 36.

2 Ibid., 39.

3 NIST NCSTAR 1-9: 59. I made a correction in this passage, which occurs in Chapter 3 of NIST's long report on WTC 7. For some reason, this chapter, written by Richard Gann, has 20 kg/m³ and 32 kg/m³ (with meters cubed instead of squared), although other chapters have it written correctly (kg/m²). I brought this passage into line with the others.

4 NIST NCSTAR 1-9, Draft for Public Comment (August 2008): 56.

5 James Gourley, Letter to NIST ("Re: Public Comments on WTC 7 Draft Reports"), September 15, 2008 (wtc.nist.gov/comments08/jamesGourleywtc7comments.pdf). The other signatories of this letter included architect Richard Gage, chemists Kevin Ryan and Niels Harrit, engineers Tony Szamboti, Ron Brookman, Kamal Obeid, and Scott Grainger, and physicist Steven Jones.

6 NIST NCSTAR 1-9: 56. This issue is discussed in a video, "NIST Report on WTC7 Debunked and Exposed!" YouTube, December 28, 2008 (www.youtube.com/watch?v=qFpbZ-aLDLY), at 2:00–3:45; also available at Infowars.com, December 30, 2008 (www.infowars.com/?p=6917).

7 NIST NCSTAR 1-9: 52.

8 Ibid., 376.

9 Ibid., 55.

10 Ibid., 386.

11 Ibid., 56, 53. My thanks to Elizabeth Woodworth for this observation.

12 Ibid., 376.

13 Ibid., 56, 57. Although the letter by James Gourley (see note 5, above), which was written in response to NIST's Draft for Public Comment, pointed out this problem, NIST left the passages unchanged, except for adding the phrase "the central section of" and changing "east and west sides" to "east side." These modifications allow for only slightly more room where the density of combustibles might have been greater.

14 Gourley, Letter to NIST.

15 Ibid.

16 NIST NCSTAR 1-9: 382.

17 Ibid., 383.

18 Ibid., 382.

19 Ibid., 383.

20 Ibid., 382.

21 This contradiction was pointed out in James Gourley's letter. NIST did nothing in its Final Report, however, to overcome the problem, apparently being confident that it could get away with outright contradictions.

22 NIST NCSTAR 1-9: 384, Figure 9-11.

23 *Interim Report on WTC 7*: L-26. This contradiction is pointed out in

the video, "NIST Report on WTC7 Debunked and Exposed!" at 0:45–1:57.

24 Richard Gage, "Re: Public Comments of NIST Report NCSTAR 1-9 Volume 2," September 15, 2008 (wtc.nist.gov/comments08/richardGage AE911Truthwtc7comments.pdf).

25 Gourley, Letter to NIST. This comment by Gourley, like that by Gage in the previous note, was based on documents prepared by Chris Sarns, who had discovered this contradiction between the 2004 and 2008 reports.

26 NIST NCSTAR 1-9: 384, Figure 9-11.

27 Ibid., 206, Figure 5-119.

28 Ibid., 212, Figure 127.

29 Ibid., 225, Figure 139. Although I refer to different photographs than he did, I am indebted to Chris Sarns, whose evidence contained in Gage's letter to NIST first alerted me to these discrepancies.

30 "WTC 7 Technical Briefing," NIST, August 26, 2008 (event.on24.com/eventRegistration/EventLobbyServlet?target=lobby.jsp&event id=118145), at 22:12.

31 NIST NCSTAR 1-9: 383.

32 Ibid., 387.

33 Ibid., 378.

34 Ibid., 387.

35 Gourley, Letter to NIST.

36 NIST NCSTAR 1-9: 383.

37 In the letter he wrote to NIST on behalf of a group of sixteen critics of NIST's Draft for Public Comment, Gourley pointed out this discrepancy, writing: "NIST must explain why the visual evidence was not relied upon for inputs on the 11th floor…. The computer models should be re-run with the 11th floor fire delayed by 1.5 hours, not 1.0 hour." NIST, however, has done nothing to overcome or explain this discrepancy in its Final Report.

38 NIST NCSTAR 1-9: 384.

39 NIST NCSTAR 1-9: 383.

40 Ibid., 57, Figure 3-8.

41 Ibid., 384, Figure 9-11.

42 NIST NCSTAR 1-9: 383.

43 *Interim Report on WTC 7*: L-26.

44 My thanks to Elizabeth Woodworth for this observation.

45 This report even provided reason to doubt whether there were any significant fires on Floor 13 at all. It did have a sentence saying: "Some time later [after 3:00], fires were observed on Floors 8 and 13, with the fire on Floor 8 moving from west to east and the fire on Floor 13 moving from east to west" (L-24). But the photographs provided by NIST do not show any fire on the 13th floor (*Interim Report on WTC 7*: L-25, L-26). In fact, although there is a photograph showing the fire on Floor 8 moving from west to east on the north face (L-26), this photograph shows that there was no fire whatsoever visible on the 13th floor.

46 See Figures 9-11 and 9-12 of NIST NCSTAR 1-9: 384-85, in which the temperatures of various parts of Floor 12 are indicated with different colors. A scale shows that various shades of blue indicate temperatures up to 300°C, shades of green indicate temperatures from 350°C to 700°C, yellow and orange indicate 700°C to 900°C, and red indicates temperatures from 900°C to 1,000°C. The graphics for 3:00, 4:00, and 5:00PM have big areas colored red, indicating fires that were somewhere between 900°C (1,650°F) and 1,000°C (1,832°F). In fact, Shyam Sunder said that "red is about 900 to 1,000 [degrees Celsius] and more" ("WTC 7 Technical Briefing," at 0:21:44).

47 See the previous note, in which Sunder is quoted as saying that the red in NIST's graphics indicates temperatures of 900°C (1,650°F) to 1,000°C (1,832°F) "and more."

48 NIST NCSTAR 1-9: 455.

49 Thomas Eagar and Christopher Musso, "Why Did the World Trade Center Collapse? Science, Engineering, and Speculation," *JOM: Journal of the Minerals, Metals & Materials Society* 53.12 (2001): 8–11 (www.tms.org/pubs/journals/JOM/0112/Eagar/Eagar-0112.html).

50 "The Collapse: An Engineer's Perspective," Interview with Thomas Eagar, PBS Nova Online, May 2002 (911research.wtc7.net/cache/nova/nova_collapse_p1.html and 911research.wtc7.net/cache/nova/nova_collapse_p2.html). My thanks to Jim Hoffman for posting this document, which had otherwise disappeared from the internet.

51 NIST NCSTAR 1-9: 81–85, 329, 340–41, 367, 391, 532–34.

52 For descriptions of the FDS, see "Fire Dynamics Simulator and Smokeview" (fire.nist.gov/fds), and Michael J. Ferreira, "Fire Dynamics Simulator," *NFPA Journal* (January–February 2008) (findarticles.com/p/articles/mi_qa3737/is_200801/ai_n21279893).

53 NIST NCSTAR 1-9: 4.

54 See "ANSYS," Wikipedia (en.wikipedia.org/wiki/ANSYS) and ANSYS, Inc. Software Products (www.ansys.com/products/default.asp).

55 NIST NCSTAR 1-9: 6.

56 Ibid., 415, 489.

57 NIST NCSTAR 1A: 53.

58 Ibid., 25–26.

59 Sunder, "Opening Statement."

60 NIST NCSTAR 1-9: 323.

61 Ibid., 629.

62 Ibid., 630.

63 Eagar and Musso, "Why Did the World Trade Center Collapse?"

64 NIST NCSTAR 1-9: 629.

65 "WTC 7 Technical Briefing," at 1:49:51.

66 NCSTAR 1A: 53.

67 NIST NCSTAR 1-9: 396.

68 Ibid., 395.

69 Ibid., 353.

70 Greening, "Comments on the Draft Report NIST NCSTAR 1-9."

71 Kevin R. Ryan, "The NIST WTC 7 Report: Bush Science Reaches Its Peak," 911Truth.org, September 10, 2008 (www.911truth.org/article.php?story=20080911073516447); reprinted (in slightly revised form) in *Global Outlook*, Issue 13 (Fall 2008).

72 Greening, "Comments on the Draft Report NIST NCSTAR 1-9."

73 Steel has somewhat low conductivity compared with many other metals. Compared with non-metallic substances, however, its conductivity is high: 46 W/m/K (see cFunda [www.cfunda.com/materials/alloys/carbon_steels/show_carbon.cfm?ID=AISI_1524&prop=all&Page_Title=AISI%201524]).

74 Dr. Vytenis Babrauskas, "Temperatures in Flames and Fires," *Fire Science and Technology Inc.*, February 25, 2006 (www.doctorfire.com/flametmp.html).

75 NIST NCSTAR 1A: 39.

76 NIST NCSTAR 1-9: 493.

77 Ibid., 589, 597.

78 Ibid., 617.

79 Ibid., 233.

80 "Minutes: Meeting of the National Construction Safety Team Advisory Committee," NIST, December 18, 2007 (wtc.nist.gov/media/NCSTACMeetingMinutes121807.pdf), 5.

81 Although the transcript says only that the responses to the various questions were made by "members of the Investigative Team," Kevin Ryan, who heard the discussion, reported that this response—like most of the others—was made by Sunder (email letter, February 15, 2009).

82 "Minutes: Meeting of the National Construction Safety Team Advisory Committee," 5.

83 NIST NCSTAR 1-9: 98.

84 NIST NCSTAR 1-9: 362.

85 Ibid., 363, 601.

86 Ibid., 55, 174–75, 177, 377, 378, 380, 493.

87 Ibid., 380.

88 "WTC 7 Technical Briefing," at 2:11:20–2:11:42

89 Ibid, at 2:11:43–2:12:26

90 NIST NCSTAR 1-9: 617 (in the Draft version of NIST NCSTAR 1-9, this passage was on page 609).

91 Ibid., 378 (in the Draft version, page 377).

92 "WTC 7 Technical Briefing," at 2:12:26–2:12:51

93 NIST NCSTAR 1-9: 330.

94 "Answers to Frequently Asked Questions," NIST, August 30, 2006

(wtc.nist.gov/pubs/factsheets/faqs_8_2006.htm), Question 7.

95 *Final Report on the Collapse of the World Trade Center Towers*, NIST, September 2005 (wtc.nist.gov/NCSTAR1/PDF/NCSTAR%201.pdf), 90.

Chapter Ten

1 NIST NCSTAR 1A: 22–23.

2 NIST NCSTAR 1-9: 629. In his technical briefing of August 26, 2008, Shyam Sunder, after saying that temperatures at some places had gone "up to 600 and 700 degrees," added: "But the primary initial effects that caused damage, as we will show later, were really happening at much lower temperatures, on the order of less than 400."

3 *Final Report on the Collapse of the World Trade Center Towers*, NIST, September 2005 (wtc.nist.gov/NCSTAR1/PDF/NCSTAR%201.pdf), 90.

4 "Questions and Answers about the NIST WTC 7 Investigation," updated April 21, 2009 (www.nist.gov/public_affairs/factsheet/wtc_qa_082108.html).

5 NIST NCSTAR 1-9: 462.

6 Ibid., 346.

7 Ibid., 347–48.

8 "Questions and Answers about the NIST WTC 7 Investigation."

9 NIST NCSTAR 1-9, Draft for Public Comment (August 2008), 341.

10 Ibid.

11 Ibid., 525.

12 Ibid., 535 and 603.

13 Ibid., 615.

14 NIST NCSTAR 1-9 (November 2008): 341.

15 *Interim Report on WTC 7*, L-6-7.

16 NIST NCSTAR 1-9: 346, Figure 8-19.

17 This fact was highlighted in Kevin Ryan, "The NIST WTC 7 Report: Bush Science Reaches Its Peak," 911Truth.org, September 11, 2008 (www.911truth.org/article.php?story=20080911073516447). A slightly revised version of Ryan's article has appeared in *Global Outlook*, Issue 13 (Fall 2008).

18 NIST NCSTAR 1-9, Draft for Public Comment, 15.

19 I first learned of this contradiction from Kevin Ryan, "The NIST WTC 7 Report: Bush Science Reaches Its Peak." When I asked Ryan about the shear studs, he referred me to Chris Sarns as the person who had documented the contradiction. This documentation first appeared in Chris Sarns, "NIST Final Draft—Evidence of Fraud," 911Blogger.com, October 24, 2008 (www.911blogger.com/node/18272); see also Judy Shelton and Chris Sarns's, "NIST Fraud—WTC 7 Shear Studs," OpEdNews, November 9, 2008 (www.opednews.com/populum/diarypage.php?did=10699). This is Sarns' second discovery involving a discrepancy between NIST's 2004 *Interim Report on WTC 7* and its 2008 report: My previous chapter referred to his discovery

that, whereas NIST's 2008 report has a raging fire on Floor 12 at 5:00PM, the 2004 report had said that the fire on that floor was burned out by 4:45.

20 NIST NCSTAR 1-9, Draft for Public Comment, 346. (The Final Report has the same statement, on the same page.)

21 NIST NCSTAR 1-9 (Final Report): 15.

22 Ibid., 347–48.

23 Kevin Ryan, "The NIST WTC 7 Report: Bush Science Reaches Its Peak." (I spelled out "inches" and "feet," which Ryan had abbreviated.) As the basis for his statement about the 28 studs per beam, Ryan referred to NIST's 2004 *Interim Report on WTC 7*, which said on page L-5: "On the north and east sides, the typical beam was a W24X55 with 28 shear studs, spanning 53 ft."

24 Ibid. The media presentation to which Ryan referred can be seen at NIST's website (www.nist.gov/public_affairs/images/WTC7_ThermalExpansionPoster.jpg).

25 David Proe and Ian Thomas, Comments on NIST WTC7 Report (wtc.nist.gov/comments08/davidProeandIanThomaswtc7comments.pdf).

26 NIST NCSTAR 1-9: 473.

27 Ibid., 347–48.

28 See "223 Physics Lab: Linear Thermal Expansion," Clemson University, January 27, 2006 (phoenix.phys.clemson.edu/labs/223/expansion), which shows the linear expansion coefficient of concrete to be (in the system of measurement used at this website) 1.20 and that of steel to be 1.24 (compared with, say, lead, at one extreme, which is 2.90, and glass, at the other, which is 0.09). My thanks to engineer Ron Brookman for help with this issue.

29 NIST NCSTAR 1-9: 490.

30 Ibid., 490.

31 Ibid., 525.

32 Ibid., 352.

33 David Proe, Comment on NIST WTC7 Report (wtc.nist.gov/comments08/davidProeCESAREwtc7comments.pdf).

34 NIST NCSTAR 1-9: 352.

35 Ibid., 490.

36 Ibid., 396.

37 Proe and Thomas, Comments on NIST WTC7 Report.

38 NIST NCSTAR 1A: 22.

39 Ryan, "The NIST WTC 7 Report."

40 Email letter from Kevin Ryan of March 28, 2008, referring to a diagram showing a beam at NIST NCSTAR 1-9: 346.

41 NIST NCSTAR 1-9: 482.

42 Ryan, "The NIST WTC 7 Report" (emphasis his).

43 Ibid. Ryan quoted NIST's brief report on WTC 7, which says: "The temperatures of some sections of the beams supporting Floors 8, 12, 13, and 14 exceeded 600°C" (NIST NCSTAR 1A: 53). He could also have quoted its

long report, which says: "The temperatures of some sections of the floor beams supporting the 8th, 12th, 13th, and 14th floor exceeded 600°C" (NIST NCSTAR 1-9: 455).

44 Ibid.

45 NIST NCSTAR 1-9, Draft for Public Comment, 597. (The statement in the Final Report [on page 605] is only slightly different.)

46 F.R. Greening, "Comments on the Draft Report NIST NCSTAR 1-9: '*Structural Fire Response and Probable Collapse Sequence of World Trade Center Building 7*,' issued by NIST August 21st, 2008 (Revised and Extended Version of Comments Issued September 11th 2008)," Cool Places.com (www.cool-places.0catch.com/911/GreeningCommentsNCSTAR1-9.pdf). This is *not* the version of Greenings' comments that is posted at NIST's website (wtc.nist.gov/comments08). NIST instead has a combination of the first and third versions of Greening's comments. Here is what happened. On August 28, 2008, Greening sent his first version, entitled "Comments on the Draft Report NIST NCSTAR 1-9: '*Structural Fire Response and Probable Collapse Sequence of World Trade Center Building 7*,' issued by NIST August 21st, 2008." NIST posted it (wtc.nist.gov/comments08/frGreeningwtc7comments.pdf), but without indicating its date (August 28). Then on September 11, Greening sent his "Revised and Extended Version," which included two new sections (6.0 & 7.0), asking NIST to replace the first version with it. But NIST did not. On September 14, Greening sent an Addendum, asking NIST to add it, assuming that NIST would add it to the Revised and Extended Version. NIST did add this Addendum. But, having not replaced the first version with the Revised and Extended Version, NIST added the Addendum to the first version—on which it inserted the wrong date "September 11, 2008" (which was the date of the Revised and Extended Version). So, Greening's earliest and latest comments can be read at the NIST website, but his second version, which has some of his most important points, can only be read elsewhere, such as the site mentioned at the outset of this note.

47 NIST NCSTAR 1-9: 598.

48 Ibid., 599–600.

49 NIST NCSTAR 1A: 44. This statement in the brief version of the report is virtually identical to the statement in the long version (NIST NCSTAR 1-9: 600), except for the final sentence, which is not present in the long version.

50 Ibid.

51 Greening, "Comments on the Draft Report NIST NCSTAR 1-9," Revised and Extended Version (see note 46, above).

52 Greening was referring to Figures 12-66, 12-67, and 12-69 in NIST's Draft, which were identical to Figures 12-67, 12-68, and 12-70, respectively, in its Final Report (NIST NCSTAR 1-9: 592–94).

53 F.R. Greening, "Comments on the Draft Report NIST NCSTAR 1-9:

'*Structural Fire Response and Probable Collapse Sequence of World Trade Center Building 7,*' issued by NIST August 21st, 2008"
(wtc.nist.gov/comments08/frGreeningwtc7comments.pdf), Addendum, September 14, 2008 (see note 46, above).

54 NIST NCSTAR 1A: xxxvi.

55 Ibid., 23.

56 "WTC 7 Technical Briefing," NIST, August 26, 2008
(event.on24.com/eventRegistration/EventLobbyServlet?target=lobby.jsp&event id=118145), at 2:14:00–2:15:44.

57 "Questions and Answers about the NIST WTC 7 Investigation."

58 Greening, "Comments on the Draft Report NIST NCSTAR 1-9," Addendum (see note 46, above).

59 Ibid.

60 Greening, "Comments on the Draft Report NIST NCSTAR 1-9," Revised and Extended Version (see note 46, above). The kink can be seen in "WTC 7 Collapse" (www.youtube.com/watch?v=LD06SAf0p9A).

61 Ibid. The images cited as showing the extensive buckling of the exterior columns are at NIST NCSTAR 1-9, Figure 12-70 (which was Figure 12-69 in the Draft, to which Greening was referring), and NIST NCSTAR 1-9A, "Global Structural Analysis of the Response of World Trade Center Building 7 to Fires and Debris Impact Damage" (wtc.nist.gov/NCSTAR1/PDF/NCSTAR%201-9A.pdf), Figure E-4 (page xlii) and Figure 4-46 (page 99).

62 Ibid., referring to NIST NCSTAR 1-9A, Figures 4-53 and 4-54 (pages 103 and 104).

63 Ibid., quoting NIST NCSTAR 1-9: 600.

64 Philip J. Tompkins, Letter to NIST, September 7, 2008 (wtc.nist.gov/comments08/phillipTompkinswtc7comments.pdf). I changed his "12-69" to "12-70" because, as I explained three notes above, Figure 12-69 in the Draft version of NIST NCSTAR 1-9, to which Tompkins referred, is Figure 12-70 in the Final Report.

65 NIST NCSTAR 1-9, Draft for Public Comment, 595–96.

66 "Questions and Answers about the NIST WTC 7 Investigation," NIST, August 2008 (originally at www.nist.gov/public_affairs/ factsheet/ wtc_qa_082108.html). This version of this document, which was posted at NIST's website at the time its Draft version of its WTC 7 report was published, has been replaced by a version that was updated December 18, 2008, and then by a version updated April 21, 2009, in which NIST acknowl-edges a 2.25-second stage of "gravitational acceleration (free fall)" (www.nist.gov/public_affairs/ factsheet/wtc_qa_082108.html). The original version, however, can still be found in a few places on the internet (e.g., postmanpatel.blogspot.com/ 2008/08/wtc-7-nist-report-says-it-burned-down.html).

67 See David Chandler, "WTC7 in Freefall—No Longer Controversial," September 4, 2008 (www.youtube.com/watch?v=gC44L0-2zL8), 4:40–5:08.

68 "WTC 7 Technical Briefing," at 1:03:17–1:04:19

69 Ibid., at 1:01:45.

70 Chandler, "WTC7 in Freefall—No Longer Controversial," at 2:45.

71 Ibid., at 3:27.

72 Ibid., at 7:10.

73 Ibid., at 8:10.

74 Ibid., at 8:55.

75 David Chandler, "Comment" (to NIST's Draft for Public Comment), September 13, 2008 (wtc.nist.gov/comments08/davidChandlerwtc7comments.pdf).

76 NIST NCSTAR 1A: 44–45.

77 NIST NCSTAR 1-9: 607.

78 David Chandler, "WTC7: NIST Finally Admits Freefall," Part I, December 7, 2008 (www.youtube.com/watch?v=V0GHVEKrhng), at 9:07. My thanks to Elizabeth Woodworth for transcribing this and the other two parts of this video series.

79 "Questions and Answers about the NIST WTC 7 Investigation," NIST, updated April 21, 2009 (see note 66).

80 NIST NCSTAR 1-9, Draft for Public Comment, 596.

81 Ibid., 610.

82 NIST NCSTAR 1-9 (Final Report): 607.

83 Ibid., 603.

84 "Questions and Answers about the NIST WTC 7 Investigation," updated April 21, 2009.

85 Chandler, "WTC7in Freefall—No Longer Controversial," at 3:00.

86 "Questions and Answers about the NIST WTC 7 Investigation," updated April 21, 2009.

87 NIST NCSTAR 1-9: 602–03.

88 Chandler, "WTC7: NIST Finally Admits Freefall," Part II, December 31, 2008 (www.youtube.com/watch?v=XtKLtUiww80), at 3:20.

89 Ibid., at 4:15.

90 Ibid., at 4:27.

91 Ibid., at 8:37. Chandler said: "Don't you find it interesting that the 5.4 seconds he [John Gross] measured for the collapse time just happens to exactly match the theoretical prediction of their model? That kind of precision is incredibly rare when modeling real world events. 'Incredible' is the right word. It's not credible. This measurement has all the characteristics of what we call 'dry labbing': manipulating the data to fit the predetermined outcome. It's an ethics violation in science on a par with plagiarism. Any engineers engaging in this kind of sleight of hand should lose their licenses. The larger implication of course is: Dry labbing in this kind of investigation would constitute a criminal coverup."

92 Chandler, "WTC7: NIST Finally Admits Freefall," Part III, January 2, 2009 (www.youtube.com/watch?v=Vz43hcKYBm4), at 1:19.

93 Ibid., at 2:20.

94 Ibid., at 3:15.

95 Ibid., at 4:30.

96 Ibid., at 8:17.

97 Sunder, "Opening Statement."

98 Quoted in "Report: Fire, Not Bombs, Leveled WTC 7 Building," Associated Press, August 21, 2008 (www.usatoday.com/news/nation/2008-08-21-wtc-nist_N.htm).

99 For an aerial photograph, see wtc7.net/rubblepile.html; for an even more revealing side-view photograph, see blog.nj.com/ledgerupdates_impact/2008/08/large_WTC7XX.jpg.

100 Philip J. Tompkins, Letter to NIST, September 7, 2008 (wtc.nist.gov/comments08/phillipTompkinswtc7comments.pdf).

101 James Glanz, "Engineers Suspect Diesel Fuel in Collapse of 7 World Trade Center," *New York Times*, November 29, 2001 (www.nytimes.com/2001/11/29/nyregion/29TOWE.html).

102 David Ray Griffin, *Debunking 9/11 Debunking: An Answer to Popular Mechanics and Other Defenders of the Official Conspiracy Theory* (Northampton: Olive Branch Press, 2007), 198.

103 NIST NCSTAR 1-9: 98.

104 Ibid., 581, 586, 588, 607.

105 Ibid., 588; see similar statements on 606, 607, 609, 612, 618, 625, and 675.

106 Ibid., 98.

107 For the locations, see "WTC Site Map—from September 2001," Wired New York—World Trade Center Map (wirednewyork.com/wtc/wtc_map.htm).

108 "Interview with Stacey Loizeaux," PBS, NOVA Online, December 1996 (www.pbs.org/wgbh/nova/kaboom/loizeaux.html).

Conclusion

1 Richard C. Lewontin, "Dishonesty in Science," *New York Review of Books*, November 18, 2004 (www.nybooks.com/articles/17563).

2 "WTC 7 Technical Briefing," NIST, August 26, 2008 (event.on24.com/eventRegistration/EventLobbyServlet?target=lobby.jsp&eventid=118145), 2:10:35.

3 NCSTAR 1-9: 330.

4 Dr. James Quintiere, "Questions on the WTC Investigations," Spotlight Session, June 5, 2007, National Fire Protection Association (www.fleetwoodonsite.com/product_info.php?cPath=21_22&products_id=1634), quoted in Alan Miller, "Former Chief of NIST Fire Science Division Calls for Independent

Review of World Trade Center Investigation," OpEdNews, August 21, 2007 (www.opednews.com/articles/genera_alan_mil_070820_former_chief_of_nist. htm).

5 "Facts against Facts/Theory against Theory: Five Years Later" (translation from the Norwegian of interviews with Dr. Steven Jones and Dr. James Quintiere), September 7, 2006 (s15.invisionfrec.com/Loose_Change_Forum/ ar/t12263.htm).

6 Quoted in Miller, "Former Chief of NIST."

7 NIST's Draft for Public Comment was issued August 21; as a statement on its website reports, the "Comment Period Closed on September 15, 2008" (wtc.nist.gov/media/comments2008.html).

8 Of the ten people with whom I checked, not one reported receiving a response.

9 David Ray Griffin, *The New Pearl Harbor Revisited: 9/11, the Cover-Up, and the Exposé* (Northampton: Olive Branch, 2008).

10 David Ray Griffin, "21 Reasons to Question the Official Story about 9/11," Global Research, September 11, 2008 (www.globalresearch.ca/ index.php?context=va&aid=10145).

11 Political Leaders for 9/11 Truth (pl911truth.com).

12 Firefighters for 9/11 Truth (firefightersfor911truth.org); Intelligence Officers for 9/11 Truth (IO911Truth.org), Pilots for 9/11 Truth (pilotsfor911truth.org); Scholars for 9/11 Truth (911scholars.org); Scholars for 9/11 Truth and Justice (stj911.org); Scientific Panel Investigation Nine-Eleven (physics911.net); Veterans for 9/11 Truth (v911t.org); Architects and Engineers for 9/11 Truth (www.ae911truth.org).

13 Lawyers for 9/11 Truth (l911t.com), Medical Professionals for 9/11 Truth (mp911truth.org); Religious Leaders for 9/11 Truth (rl911truth.org); Actors and Artists for 9/11 Truth (AA911truth.com).

Appendix A

1 For Rodriguez's account of what happened, see "William Rodriguez's Story" (www.youtube.com/watch?v=wIZtqKiidlo) and "9/11 Survivor Questions Official Story on Local Fox News" (www.youtube.com/watch?v=DIC0Kl4TKoU&feature=related).

2 As we saw in Chapter 5, Rodriguez reported that Felipe David, a coworker, was severely burned by fire coming out of a freight elevator on the first sub-level floor. A similar report was given by another North Tower janitor, Kenny Johannnemann. After going to the first sub-basement, he said, "I put my cart in front of the elevator.... [A]ll of a sudden, Boom! There was a big explosion, the whole building shook.... [A]ll of a sudden, the whole elevator blew out.... [A]t my feet there was one of the delivery guys.... I grabbed him.... [H]e was all burnt up.... [S]kin ended up in my hand." This account by Johannemann is in a film, "From the Rubble," which, as this book went to

press, Rodriguez and his co-producer, J. Kerr-Smith, were hoping to release late in 2009. This film also contains testimony of Anthony Saltalamacchia, who was Rodriguez's supervisor that day. Saltalamacchia's testimony is also available in "New William Rodriguez Support Story" (www.youtube.com/watch?v=rzpaZE5Xsfg). Speaking of the explosion reported by Rodriguez, Saltalamacchia said: "I felt it also. It came from the mechanical room [right below us].... [W]e felt that it was underneath us.... [M]y gut reaction: it was definitely a bomb." Also, just as Barry Jennings reported that the massive explosion in WTC 7 was followed by other explosions, Saltalamacchia reported that, after the major explosion in the North Tower, there was a series of smaller ones—perhaps ten explosions. Additional testimony has been provided by José Sanchez, one of Rodriguez's coworkers. Sanchez reported that while he and another man were in the workshop on the fourth sub-level, they heard a big blast that "sounded like a bomb," after which "a huge ball of fire went through the freight elevator" (patriotsquestion911.com/survivors.html#Search). Still another coworker, Salvatore Giambanco, said: "We heard the explosion and the smoke all of a sudden came from all over. There was an incredible force of wind that also swept everything away.... [I]t had to be a bomb. Later they told me it was an airplane that hit the towers, ... but it was just too incredible to believe if you heard and experienced what I did. It had to be a bomb" (patriot-squestion911.com/survivors.html#Giambanco).

3 "America Under Attack," *CNN Breaking News*, 11:00AM (transcripts.cnn.com/TRANSCRIPTS/0109/11/bn.11.html). This statement by Frank was quoted in Shoestring, "Was 10:45AM the Originally Planned Demolition Time of WTC 7?" 9/11 Blogger, May 1, 2008 (911blogger.com/node/15318). "Shoestring" is the alias under which Matthew Everett wrote this article (a fact he gave me permission to reveal).

4 Shoestring (Matthew Everett—see previous note), "Was 10:45AM the Originally Planned Demolition Time of WTC 7?"

5 Jeremy Baker, "Was WTC 7 a Dud?" Serendipity, July 2005 (www.serendipity.li/wot/wtc7_dud.htm).

6 Jeremy Baker, "Last Building Standing," Serendipity, 2007 (www.serendipity.li/wot/last_building_standing.pdf). This is a revised and updated version of "Was WTC 7 a Dud?"

7 Jeremy Baker, "Stunning Video of WTC 7's Damaged South Face Discovered on a 9/11 Truth Debunking Website," Darkprints, July 15, 2008 (drkprnts.files.wordpress.com/2008/07/stunningvideowtc7ssouthface.pdf).

8 For this ABC footage (in which the gash can be seen through the smoke), see "ABC 13:45 WTC7 Damage" (www.youtube.com/watch?v=pAVHbI9CKpU&NR=1) and "ABC 13:54 WTV 7 Damage," YouTube (www.youtube.com/watch?v=5GEEzHn4tqo).

9 Baker, "Stunning Video."

10 Quoted in ibid. Silverstein can be seen making this statement in "We

Are Change Confronts Larry Silverstein," YouTube (www.youtube.com/
watch?v=EtPC0W4HII8).

11 Baker, "Stunning Video."

12 "Barry Jennings Uncut," Part 1, at 3:38.

13 Baker, "Last Building Standing."

Appendix B

1 See FEMA, "Interstate Bank Building Fire, Los Angeles, California,"
1988 (www.lafire.com//famous_fires/880504_1stInterstateFire/FEMA-TecRe-
port/FEMA-report.htm), and FEMA, "High-Rise Office Building Fire, One
Meridian Plaza, Philadelphia, Pennsylvania" (www.interfire.org/res_file/pdf/Tr-
049.pdf).

2 "Fire Practically Destroys Venezuela's Tallest Building," VenezuelaAnaly-
sis.com, October 18, 2004 (www.venezuelanalysis.com/news/741).

3 "Fire Rages at Beijing Mandarin Hotel," Associated Press, February 9,
2009 (www.washingtontimes.com/news/2009/feb/09/fire-rages-beijing-
mandarin-hotel).

4 Andrew Jacobs, "Fire Ravages Renowned Building in Beijing," *New York
Times*, February 9, 2009
(www.nytimes.com/2009/02/10/world/asia/10beijing.html?_r=1&hp).

5 "Koolhaas Building in CCTV Complex Engulfed by Fire," NY Arts:
New Media & Net-Art, February 11, 2009
(nyartsnewmedia.wordpress.com/2009/02/11/koolhaas-building-in-cctv-
complex-engulfed-by-fire). Andrew Jacobs, "Fire Engulfs Beijing Hotel
Complex," *New York Times*, February 9, 2009
(www.nytimes.com/2009/02/10/world/asia/10beijing.html?_r=1&hp).

6 Ben Blanchard, "Fire Claims Building at CCTV Beijing Headquarters,"
Reuters, February 9, 2009
(www.reuters.com/article/newsOne/idUSPEK19411020090209).

7 "CCTV/TVCC Fire in Beijing (HD version)," YouTube, February 9,
2009 (www.youtube.com/watch?v=6hSPFL2Zlpg); "Beijing CCTV Annex
Fire—Mandarin Oriental Hotel," YouTube, February 9, 2009
(www.youtube.com/ watch?v=3B1OnhSucP8).

8 Jonathan Glancey, "Beijing's Newest Skyscraper Survives Blaze," February 11, 2009 (www.guardian.co.uk/world/2009/feb/11/
television-cultural-centre-tower-beijing-fire).

9 "Aftermath—Beijing CCTV Annex Fire—Mandarin Oriental Hotel,"
iReport, February 2009 (www.ireport.com/docs/DOC-210759).

10 "2009 Beijing China Mandarin Luxury Hotel Fire Before & After
Video Compared to WTC 7," February 20, 2009 (www.youtube.com/
watch?v=mHqRw7lEK5A&NR=1).

INDEX

A

Abel, Jennifer, 73
Actors and Artists for 9/11 Truth, 260
Afghanistan war, xi, 7, 259
Al-Qaeda, xi, 3, 4, 5, 8, 255–56, 257, 259
Altman, Lawrence, 278n23
Architects and Engineers for 9/11 Truth,
    5, 8, 259
Arterburn, Tom, 36
Astaneh-Asl, Abolhassan, 47–48, 50, 51,
    199, 246, 247
Atta, Mohamed, 256, 257
Avery, Dylan, 86–87, 89, 91, 94–95, 97–
    99, 102, 110, 168, 292–93n39, 293–
    94n52, 295nn67,71, 296n83

B

Babrauskas, Vytenis, 193, 201
Bachmann, Hugo, 122
Baker, Jeremy, 263–65
Banaciski, Richard, 77
Barnett, Jonathan, 47–50, 51. *See also*
    WPI professors.
Barnett-Biederman-Sisson Appendix to
    FEMA Report, 48–54
"Barry Jennings Uncut," 87, 292n38
Bartmer, Craig, 83, 130
"BBC Charter Compliance," 299n133
BBC's premature announcement of WTC
    7's collapse, 115–16
BBC's prior 9/11 documentary, 115–16
    (*The Conspiracy Files: 9/11*: xix, 299n133)
BBC's WTC 7 documentary: first version,
    87, 95–99, 293n47 (*The Conspiracy
    Files: 9/11—The Third Tower.*
    284n79, 293n47); second version,
    99–104, 296n84 (*The Conspiracy
    Files: 9/11—The Truth behind the
    Third Tower.* 99, 196n84); its treat-
    ment of the Hess-Jennings testimony,
    95–104; its timeline distortion, 95–
    96, 99–100, 123, 254
Bement, Arden, 50, 139, 260

Biederman, Ronald, 46
Bin Laden, Osama, xi, 3, 8, 256
Broad, William, 14, 277n4
Brookman, Ron, 314n28
Brown, Aaron, 115
Bukhari, Adnan and Ameer, 257
Burger, Dr. Ronald, 37
Burke, Timothy, 78
Burnett, Deena, 256
Burns, Margie, 275n33
Bush (Bush-Cheney) administration, xi,
    3; its distortions of science, 9–10; its
    order to EPA to lie about Ground
    Zero air, 10
Bush, Marvin, 9, 133, 275n33
Bush, President George H. W., 7
Bush, President George W., 7, 133, 259,
    260
Bussey, John, 290n7

C

Cachia, Edward, 78
Cahill, Thomas, 55, 61, 284n88
Cantor, Irwin G., 216
Case B Variables, 194–96
Cell phone calls from airliners, 256
Chandler, David, 232–34, 235, 236,
    237–41, 253, 317n91
Cheney, Vice President Dick, 7, 257–58.
    See also Bush-Cheney administration.
Citicorp Tower, 133, 134
Clinton, President Bill, 11
Coburn, Davin, xix
Coefficient of linear (thermal) expansion,
    218–19, 221, 314n28
Collapse of WTC 7: as Achilles' heel of
    official 9/11 theory, xi–xii, xv, 259,
    262; as caused by fire alone, xi–xii,
    xvii, xix, 147–49, 213–22, 267; as
    caused by thermal expansion, 24,
    148–49, 151, 152, 153, 197–98,
    209, 210, 211, 212–13, 217, 218,
    220, 222, 223, 224; as mystery, xi–xx,

33, 45–46, 47, 50, 54, 241, 242, 245; as (not) involving free fall, 231–41; as progressive, 148, 149, 150, 154, 228–32, 240–41, 249, 254; as unprecedented, xi–xii, 24, 29, 250; compared with collapse of Twin Towers, xi; compared with implosions, xiv, 27–28; foreknowledge of, 111–21; kink in, 209, 210, 226, 315n60; media coverage of, xii, 114–16; most likely explanation for, xii, xx, 20, 27–31, 125; resulted in compact debris pile, 241–43; role of debris damage in, xvi–xix, 143, 147–48; role of diesel fuel in, xv, xvii–xix, 151; roofline: simulated vs. real, 225–31, 254; why it was not symmetrical (Sunder), 228. *See also* Global collapse.

Column 79: and east penthouse kink, 209, 210; as crucial, 126–27, 198; buckling of, 154, 209, 210, 224, 225, 227; disconnected from girder, 153, 209, 210, 213, 222, 223; failure in floor system near, 202, 209, 210; hot, long–lasting fires near, 153, 188, 206, 209; rapid descent of, 154, 210, 224–25, 248

Concrete: its coefficient of linear expansion, 218–19, 221; reinforced, 219
Connock, Adrian, 299n133
Cook, Louis, 118
Cruthers, Chief Frank, 76, 77
Curran, James, 34–35
Currid, Michael, 114

D

David, Felipe, 82, 319n2
Deets, Dwain, 142
Demarco, Peter, 83, 127
Demolition squibs, 34–35
Dennett, Daniel, 278n22
Dobbs, Lou, 271n8
Douglas, Eric, 16
Draft for Public Comment (Draft Report, Draft version), xvi, xviii, xix, xxi, 25, 43, 51, 52, 53, 98, 129–31, 154–55, 180, 187, 190, 205, 214, 215, 220, 225, 229, 230, 231–34, 236, 237,

240, 248–49, 252, 267, 272n33, 309n13, 310n37, 318n7
Dry labbing, 16, 317n91
Dust cloud from North Tower collapse, 107–08, 164, 262

E

Eagar, Thomas, 37, 193–94
E-4B airplane, 258
Empirical dimension of science, 17–18, 43, 49, 73
Environmental Protection Agency (EPA): lied about Ground Zero air, 10; on particles in Ground Zero air, 55–56, 61–62
Eutectic reaction, 46–47, 66, 283n66
Evans, Stephen, 291n24
Everett, Matthew, 263, 265, 320n3
Explosions: Barry Jennings on, 88–93, 104, 132, 150, 169, 261, 262, 292nn34,38,39; Michael Hess on, 84–85, 100, 102, 132, 261, 262; in Twin Towers, 75–82; testimonies from witnesses outside the building, 83
Explosives, xx–xxi; as cause of all prior collapses of steel-framed high-rises, 23–25, 29–30; NIST's implicit acknowledgment of their use in Twin Towers, 142–43; physical evidence for, 33–74; ruled out by NIST, xvi, xviii, xix, 30; testimonial evidence for, 75–124

F

Fabrication, 14–17, 25, 166, 189, 223, 239, 243, 244, 245, 246–49, 257
False-flag operation, xi
Falsification, 14–18, 111, 246–49
Faulkner, Bonnie, 117
FDNY (Fire Department of New York): its alleged 7th floor fire observation, 165; its advance knowledge of WTC 7's collapse, 112–14, 123; its test monies about explosions in Twin Towers, 75–81; its testimonies about WTC 7 safety zone, 112–14; when it evacuated the building, 119

I

Implosions, xiii, 24, 243; seven features of, xiv, 28, 33–34
Intelligence Officers for 9/11 Truth, 259
Interim Report on WTC 7, xvi, 299n65; authorship of, 294n65, 297n101; on beam shear studs, 313n23; on burned-out floors, 187–89, 193, 252–53; on debris damage from North Tower collapse, 143; on girder shear studs, 153–54, 215–16; its contradictions of NIST's 2008 report, 313n19
Iron-rich particles, 41, 42–43, 44, 60, 282n47

J

Jeffrey, William Alan, 140
Jenkins, Dr. Cate, 10
Jennings, Barry, 82, 86–110; death of, 82, 86–110; interview by ABC News, 295–96n52; interview by BBC, 87; interview by Dylan Avery (*Loose Change*), 86–87, 89, 292n38, 294n52 (*see also* "Barry Jennings Uncut"); interview by NIST, 87, 293n40, 297n101; NIST's straw-man argument about, 134; on destruction of lobby, 90–92, 94, 97; on explosions, 88–93, 104, 132, 158, 169, 261, 262, 265, 319n2; on extensive damage to 8th floor, 96, 110; rescue of, 90, 92, 104–10, 294–95n67
Jennings, Peter, 114
Johannemann, Kenny, 319n2
Jones, Al, 270n8
Jones, Steven: knows former NIST employee, 11; on demolition squibs, 34, 35, 279nn4,5; on Draft Report, 181; on energetic materials in WTC dust, 56–61; on impossibility of fire-induced symmetrical collapse, 30; on iron-rich spherules, 43; on long-lasting fires and chemical emissions at Ground Zero, 56, 60–62; on molten metal, 37, 38–39; on red-gray chips, 62–65, 287n127; on sulfur and gypsum, 46, 72, 289n155; on thermate reaction, 49–50

K

Kean, Thomas, 6, 8, 12, 275n29
Keane, Sue, 76
Keller, Jack, 122
Killough-Miller, Joan, 46–47
Kleinberg, Mindy, 228

L

Lawrence Livermore National Laboratories, 141
Laws of nature (laws of physics, physical principles), 24, 25, 231, 236–37, 239, 241, 251, 299n133. *See also* Miracles.
Lawson, Anthony, 271n17
Lawson-Gann rescue account, 105–07, 108–09, 163–65
Lawson, J. Randall, 92–93, 105–09, 162–65, 293n40, 297nn101,102
Lawyers for 9/11 Truth, 260
Legge, Frank, 270n7, 271n16
Levy, Matthys, 168–69, 261
Lewontin, Richard, 15, 16, 18, 275n35, 277n8
Lipton, Eric, 45–46, 48, 157
Lipton, Peter, 277n4
Loizeaux, Mark, 26, 243
Loizeaux, Stacey, 243
Loose Change Final Cut, 86–87, 97–98, 100, 271n14, 280n16, 292n38, 293n39, 294n52, 301n151, 305n54
Loose Change 9/11: An American Coup, 297n90
Lowers, Heather, 42

M

MacKinlay, Janette, 289n155
MacQueen, Graham, 76
McAllister, Therese, 92, 111, 177, 294n65, 297n101
McCarthy, Chief Thomas, 113
McGovern, Kevin, 113
McGrattan, William, 165, 166, 173–77
McPadden, Kevin, 117–18

Medical Professionals for 9/11 Truth, 260

Meeker, Gregory, 42

Mineta, Norman, 257–58

Miracle: affirmed by NIST, xx, 25, 241, 251; not to be affirmed in scientific reports, xx, 24–25

Molten metal (iron, steel), 36–39, 62, 66, 245, 280n16, 281n28, 299n133

Molybdenum, 44–45, 48, 58, 60, 246

Monaghan, Aidan, 307n37

Moussaoui, Zacarias, 256

Muslim (al-Qaeda) hijackers (terrorists), xi, 3, 4, 8, 255–56, 257, 258, 259, 270n3

Mystery: collapse of WTC 7 as, xi–xx, 33, 45–46, 47, 50, 54, 241, 242, 245; "deepest," 45–47, 50

N

Nanotechnology, 57–58, 64, 134, 303n34; NIST and, 138–42

Nanothermite(s), superthermite(s), xii, 57–59, 60, 61, 62–66, 70–71, 74, 128–29, 132, 134, 136–38, 246, 250, 287n127; as high explosive, 58, 137, 273n4; compared with ordinary (macro-) thermite, 57–58, 63–64, 137–38, 273n40; compared with RDX, 132, 137; NIST's knowledge of, 138–42; sol-gel, 58–59, 60

National Fire Protection Association (NPFA) *Guide*, 28–29, 73, 142, 278n3, 289n161

National Institute of Standards and Technology. *See* NIST.

National Science Foundation (NSF), 14, 15, 16, 17, 139, 260

Newman, Michael, 73–74

New York University medical student, 83, 128, 130

Nigro, Chief Daniel, 112, 113

Nilsen, Ola, 286n127

9/11 attacks: official reports about, 3–8; two main theories about, xi, 3

9/11 Commission Report, xiii, 6–8

9/11 Mysteries, 305n54

9/11 truth movement, xi, xiii, xv, 4–5, 9, 43, 68, 256, 259; its scientific and

professional organizations, 5

NIST (National Institute of Standards and Technology), xvi; and National Security Agency, 11, 252; and Office of Management and Budget, 11, 252; as agency of Bush-Cheney adminis-tration (Commerce Department), 8–12, 26, 27, 30, 31, 51, 149; as politi-cal, not scientific, agency, 3–12, 13, 19, 26, 27, 30–31, 82, 121, 122, 149; avoided peer review, 25–26, 251 53; employs straw-man arguments, 22, 29, 72, 125–44, 250; failed to test for thermitic residue, 66–74; former employee of, 10–12, 19–20; ignores physical evidence for explosives, 33–74; ignores question about internal damage, 110–11; ignores testimonial evidence for explosives, 75–124; its "hired guns," 11; its knowledge of nanotechnology, 138–42; its "mild overestimates," 88–89; its reports on Twin Towers, xv, 9, 12, 16, 24, 34, 37, 39, 42, 50, 55, 66–67, 75–82, 138, 148, 152, 180, 197, 206–07, 212, 295n68; on the Hess-Jennings testimonies, 92–95, 123; on the rescue of Hess, Jennings, and the security officer, 104–10; rejects most likely hypothesis, xii, xx, 20, 25, 27–31, 71, 125, 249, 251. *See also* Collapse of WTC 7; NIST's WTC 7 report; "WTC 7 Technical Briefing."

NIST's WTC 7 report: absurdity of, 39, 121, 135, 267–69; as based on sound science (Sunder), xx, 18, 30–31, 70, 121, 241, 245; as false, xx, 28, 51–52, 109, 127, 132, 155, 183–84, 211, 212, 216, 223, 231, 245, 253–60, 262; as solving the WTC 7 mystery (Sunder), xix–xx, 50, 245; as unscientific, xx, 15, 18, 19, 22, 23, 24, 25–26, 29, 30–31, 33, 38–39, 43, 49, 53, 54, 62, 66, 68, 70–71, 72, 73, 78, 79–81, 82, 120–21, 122, 129, 134–35, 149–50, 155, 189, 196, 201, 212, 216, 219–20, 234,

239, 241, 243, 245–53, 254, 261–
62, 270n7, 317n91; its theory of
progressive collapse, 148–50, 154,
228–32, 240–41, 254; scientific fraud
in, 15, 17, 43, 53, 78, 80, 153–54,
189, 216, 220–22, 237, 239, 245–
49, 252, 313n19, 317n91

O

Obama, President Barack, 13, 54, 259,
260
Obeid, Kamal, 30
Occam's razor, 21, 243, 250
Office of Emergency Management
(Giuliani's), 84, 87, 102–03, 105,
114, 116, 123
Official account (theory) of 9/11: xi, xv,
xvi, 3–5, 30, 34, 35, 37, 43, 46, 53–
54, 55, 86, 89, 91, 92, 95, 101, 102,
104, 119, 127, 138, 142, 158–59,
168–69, 193, 231, 234, 241, 246,
254, 255, 256, 259, 260, 262, 264,
274n20, 299n133
Olson, Barbara and Ted, 256–57
O'Toole, Joe, 36

P

Pauls, Jake, 110–11
Pecoraro, Mike, 76
Peer review, 25–26, 251–53
Pentagon, attack on, 258, 274n20
Physical principles. *See* Laws of nature.
Pileni, Marie-Paule, 286n118
Pilots for 9/11 Truth, 259
Pitts, William, 106, 107, 164, 165, 173
Political Leaders for 9/11 Truth, 259, 260
Polls (about 9/11), xiii, xv, 3–4
Popular Mechanics: on NIST's WTC 7
theory, xvii–xix, 143; on Silverstein's
statement, 119
Porter, Richard, 115, 116
Proe, David, 218–21
Progressive collapse, 148–50, 154, 228–
32, 240–41, 254

Q

Quintiere, James, 251–52, 253

R

Rather, Dan, 121–22, 270
RDX explosives, 126–32, 134, 137–38,
250
Red-gray chips, 62–66, 71, 287n127. *See
also* Nanothermite(s).
Religious Leaders for 9/11 Truth, 260
"Request for Correction," 67–68, 79–81,
288n144
Rice, Condoleezza, 7, 8, 12, 300n143
RJ Lee Report, 40–42, 60–61,
281nn33,34, 282n45
Robertson, Leslie, 36
Rodriguez, William, 81–82, 261, 265,
319nn1,2
Rogers, Kenneth, 78
Rove, Karl, 8
Rudin, Mike, 99–100, 101, 293n42,
296n84
Rumsfeld, Donald, 258
Ruvolo, Philip, 36
Ryan, Kevin: on beam shear studs, 217–
18, 313n23; on "Bush science,"
313n17; on demolition squibs, 34,
35; on Draft Report, 181; on
evidence for energetic nanocomposi-
ties, 57–61; on girder shear studs,
313n19; on NIST advisory meeting,
312n80; on NIST and nanothermites, 302n32; on red-gray chips,
62–65; on steel temperatures, 200–
01; on sulfidation of steel, 49; on
thermal expansion, 217–18, 222–23;
on thermate reaction, 51

S

Saltalamacchia, Anthony, 319n2
Sanchez, José, 82, 319n2
Sarns, Chris, 216, 309nn24,25,29, 313n19
Schneider, Jörg, 122
Scholars for 9/11 Truth, 259
Scholars for 9/11 Truth and Justice, 259
Science: Bush administration's distortion
of, 9–10, 13; restoring its integrity, 9,
13, 54, 260, 275nn35,36, 277n2
Scientific fraud, 13–15; in strict sense,
14–18; in broader sense, 18–26;

committed by NIST, 15, 17, 43, 53, 78, 80, 153–54, 189, 216, 220–22, 237, 239, 245–49, 252, 313n19, 317n91; dry labbing, 16, 317n91; fabrication, 14–17; falsification, 14–18; ignoring (omitting) evidence, 17; plagiarism, 14, 15

Scientific method, 13–26; and extra-scientific considerations, 18–20, 27; and implausible claims, xx, 22–23, 25, 250; and inference to the best explanation, 17; and laws of nature (physics), 24–25; and miracles, 24–25, 251; and most likely hypothesis, xx, 20, 27–31, 125; and peer review, 25–26, 251–53; and straw-man arguments, 22, 29, 72, 125–44, 250; and unprecedented causes, 23, 29, 147–50, 250; as rational empiricism, 17; empirical dimension of, 17–18, 43, 49, 73–74; Whitehead on, 18, 33, 62, 74

Scientific Panel Investigating Nine-Eleven, 259

Scott, Howie, 78

Secret Service, 258

Securacom, 9, 133

Security officer: his rescue, 104–07; his observation of a 7th floor fire (at 10:30 or 12:15), 162–66; interview with, 163, 166, 307n30

Semerjian, Hratch, 139–40, 141

"Seven Is Exploding," 117, 130

Shear studs: for beams, 153, 154; for girders, 153–54, 212–16, 254, 267

Shenon, Philip, 6–8, 274n23

Silverstein, Larry, 118–21, 123, 264

Simulations: visual evidence not "model input" for, 189, 193; of Floor 12 used to model 11th & 13th floor fires, 183, 190. *See also* Fire Dynamics Simulator.

Singh, Indira, 117

Sisson, Richard D., 46, 53

Skeptosis, 51–52, 283–84n78, 302n25

Smith, Guy, 299n133

Smith, Michael, 130–31

Sohmer, Robert, 113

Sol-gel, 58–59, 64

Staelin, Earl, 132–33

Stand-down order, 257

Steel (structural): conductivity of, 200–01, 311n73; its coefficient of linear (thermal) expansion, 219, 314n28; melting point of, 37, 280n22; recovered (from WTC 7), 46–50, 51, 199; sulfidation of, 45–54; temperatures reached by, 152, 197–207, 211–12; vaporized, 47–48

Stein, Ben, 68–69

Steven Jones Group, 44–45. *See also* Jones, Steven.

Straw-man arguments, 22, 29, 72, 125–44, 250

Sulfur, 46, 48, 51, 52, 55, 60, 61, 67, 120; gypsum as possible source of, 48–49, 71–72

Sunder, Shyam, xvii, xviii, xix; and textbook descriptions, 28–29; his interaction with Shane Geiger, 68–70; his "Opening Statement," 273n37; on fire as cause of collapse, 148–49; on fire durations "in any given location," 203–06; on fire temperatures, 310nn46,47, 312n2; on no evidence for explosives, 72; on not interviewing Silverstein, 120–21; on out-of-control fires, 150, 157–58; on question about interior damage, 110–11; on recovered sulfidized steel, 52–53; on red-gray chips, 69, 70–71; on single point of fire ignition on each floor, 175; on solving WTC 7 mystery, xix–xx, 40, 245; on soundness of science behind WTC 7 report, xx, 30–31, 70, 121, 241, 245; on symmetrical appearance of collapse, 229

T

Terrorists: domestic, 55, 255, 259; Muslim (al-Qaeda), xi, 3, 4, 8, 255–56, 257, 258, 259, 270n3

Thermal expansion: as cause of WTC 7's collapse, 24, 148–50, 153–54, 197, 198; differential, 218–21; problems in NIST's theory of, 211–13

Thermal weakening, 197–98, 212

Thermate, 49–50, 51, 54, 61

Thermite(s), 36, 49–50; military forms of, 61; NIST's failure to test for, 66–74. *See also* Nanothermite(s).

"This is an Orange," xiv, 271, 278n2

Thomas, Ian, 218, 221

Tinsley, Nikki, 10

Tompkins, Philip, 230, 241, 316n64

Trimpe, Herb, 55

Tully, Peter, 36

Turner, James M., 140

U

Ucciardo, Frank, 84

Unger, Craig, 275n33

Union of Concerned Scientists, 9, 275nn35,36

UPN 9 News, 84, 100, 102, 130

USGS (US Geological Survey) Report, 42–43, 44–45

US State Department, 120, 300n143

V

Van Auken, Lorie, 120, 121, 205–06

Veterans for 9/11 Truth, 259

Vettori, Robert, 105, 163

Visconti, Nick, 113–14

Von Essen, Commissioner Thomas, 114

W

Wade, Nicholas, 14, 277n4

Walker, Wirt, III, 9, 133

War on terror, xii, 4, 259

Wedge 1 (Pentagon), 258

Whitehead, Alfred North, 18, 33, 62, 74, 277n15

Williams, Forman, 140

Williams, James, 36

Windows: blown-out, 35–36; broken, 126–28

Woodworth, Elizabeth, 309n11, 310n44, 316n78

WPI (Worcester Polytechnic Institute), 46; professors, 46–50, 51, 62, 71, 199; report, 46–47, 50–54, 199

Wright, Decosta, 112, 113

WTC rubble and dust: iron-rich particles in, 41, 42–43, 44, 60, 282n47; molten metal in, 36–39, 62, 66, 245, 280n16, 281n28, 299n133; molybdenum in, 44–45, 48, 58, 60, 246; sulfur and sulfidized steel in, 45–46, 48–49, 50, 52–54, 71, 81, 135–36, 199, 243, 246, 250; unreacted nanothermite in, 62–66; (no) steel recovered from, 46–50, 51, 199

WTC 7: also called Salomon Brothers (and Salomon Smith Barney) building, 115, 163, 306n21; expert testimony that explosives brought it down, 121–22; expressed intentions to bring it down, 117–21; gash down front of, 263–64; how its fires started, 74, 150–51

WTC site (Ground Zero): emissions of volatile organic chemicals at, 55–57, 61; toxic air at, 10; particles suggestive of explosives in air and dust at, 40–45, 60, 62, 66, 254

Wyndham, John, 30, 149

Y

Yli-Karjanmaa, Sami, 224n20

Z

Zachariah, Michael, 139, 141

Zelikow, Philip, 6–8, 274n26

Zogby polls, xiii, xv, 3–4